Letter Writing Among Poets

Letter Writing Among Poets

From William Wordsworth to Elizabeth Bishop

Edited by Jonathan Ellis

EDINBURGH
University Press

Edinburgh University Press Ltd
The Tun – Holyrood Road
12(2f) Jackson's Entry
Edinburgh EH8 8PJ
www.euppublishing.com

Typeset in 10/12pt Goudy Old Style by
Servis Filmsetting Ltd, Stockport, Cheshire,
and printed and bound by CPI Group (UK) Ltd
Croydon, CR0 4YY

A CIP record for this book is available from the British Library

ISBN 978 0 7486 8132 7 (hardback)
ISBN 978 0 7486 8133 4 (webready PDF)
ISBN 978 0 7486 8134 1 (epub)

Contents

Acknowledgements

This book developed out of a lecture series on letter writing that was held in Sheffield in 2010 and 2011. Over one thousand people attended the series which was jointly organised by the University of Sheffield and the city's annual literature festival, Off the Shelf. My thanks first of all, then, to Ingrid Hanson, my event coordinator, who helped run the show with calm efficiency and cheerful intelligence. Maria de Souza and Lesley Webster from Off the Shelf were perfect event partners. I am also grateful to colleagues from both the Faculty of Arts and Humanities and the School of English who were enthusiastic attendees throughout the series. Thanks in particular to Joe Bray, Matthew Campbell, Valerie Cotter, Hamish Mathison, Adam Piette and Angela Wright for helping me spend the entertainment budget so pleasantly. My friends in Catalonia, Jesus Coll and Queralt Suñé of GraficArt, designed a characteristically elegant poster to help promote the series. Moltes gràcies!

The lecture series would never have happened without a generous grant from the British Academy to whom I am extremely grateful. For help in securing research leave and administering the grant, I would like to thank Professor Sue Vice, then Head of the School of English, and Lynda Hodge-Mannion, Faculty Finance Officer.

The talks would not have become a book without the good will and patience of the seven people who initially delivered such inspiring talks and the seven new contributors whose chapters I subsequently commissioned.

At Edinburgh University Press, Jackie Jones was an enthusiastic and model commissioning editor. I have loved talking book covers with project managers Rebecca MacKenzie and Kate Robertson. Cathy Falconer was a meticulous and patient copy-editor. Sincere thanks to Ellsworth Kelly and to the Ingleby Gallery in Edinburgh for allowing me to use such a stunning painting for the cover.

My own thoughts on letter writing have benefited from attending various conferences and workshops over the last few years. I wish in particular to thank Katie Reid and Bethan Stevens, organisers of the *Picture This* conference at the University of Sussex, where I met and exchanged ideas with many epistolary scholars. Editors of several books and journals, in particular Sally Bayley, Tracy Brain, Angela Leighton and Caitríona O'Reilly, have also helped shape my work.

For the last decade I have taught an MA course on twentieth-century letter writing. I'm sure many of our classroom discussions and exchanges have found an afterlife here. My undergraduate students have also endured my elegiac monologues about the death of letter writing in good humour for many years now. Their faith in new forms of correspondence even encouraged me to join Twitter. I hope they, too, will find something helpful here.

Rachel Bower gave generously of her time to read a draft of the introduction at the very last minute. I've attempted to incorporate as many of her insights and suggestions as time allowed.

Last, but not least, thanks as ever to Ana María Sánchez-Arce for making most, if not all, of this happen. This book is dedicated to you.

Cover image is 'City Island' by Ellsworth Kelly. Reprinted by kind permission of the artist.

Excerpts from Lorine Niedecker's poetry from *Collected Works*, ed. Jenny Penberthy. Copyright 2002 by the Regents of the University of California. Reprinted by permission of the University of California Press.

Contributors

Madeleine Callaghan is a Lecturer in Romantic Literature at the University of Sheffield. She is currently finishing a monograph on Byron and Shelley and has published various articles and chapters on Romantic and post-Romantic poetry. She has also co-edited, with Professor Michael O'Neill, a Blackwell Guide to Criticism entitled *Twentieth-Century British and Irish Poetry: Hardy to Mahon* (2011) and been assistant editor for *The Oxford Handbook of Percy Bysshe Shelley* (2012), edited by Michael O'Neill and Anthony Howe.

Matthew Campbell is Professor of Modern Literature at the University of York. He is the author of *Rhythm and Will in Victorian Poetry* (1999) and *Irish Poetry Under the Union, 1801–1924* (2013) and the editor of *The Cambridge Companion to Contemporary Irish Poetry* (2003). He is currently writing a *History of Irish Poetry* for Cambridge University Press.

Jonathan Ellis is Senior Lecturer in American Literature at the University of Sheffield. He is the author of *Art and Memory in the Work of Elizabeth Bishop* (2006) and co-editor (with Angus Cleghorn) of *The Cambridge Companion to Elizabeth Bishop* (2014). He has published numerous articles and essays on twentieth-century poetry.

Anne Fadiman is the author of a work of reportage, *The Spirit Catches You and You Fall Down* (1997), as well as two collections of essays, *Ex Libris* (1998) and *At Large and At Small* (2007). She has been a staff writer at *Life*, editor-at-large of *Civilization* and editor of *The American Scholar*. She is currently working on a short memoir about her father and wine. Fadiman teaches non-fiction at Yale as the Francis Writer-in-Residence.

Hugh Haughton is Professor of English and Related Literature at the University of York. He is co-editor (with Valerie Eliot) of volumes one and two of *The Letters of T. S. Eliot* (2009), and editor of various books, including *The Chatto Book of*

Nonsense Poetry (1988) and *Second World War Poems* (2004). He is also author of *The Poetry of Derek Mahon* (2007). He has published widely on modern poetry and is currently working on a book on poets' letters.

Michael D. Hurley is a Lecturer in English at the University of Cambridge and a Fellow of St Catharine's College. He is the author of *G. K. Chesterton* (2012), co-author (with Michael O'Neill) of *Poetic Form* (2012), and editor of the Penguin Classics edition of *The Complete Father Brown Stories* (2012). Forthcoming books include *A History of Poetics, from Classical Antiquity to the Present* and a co-edited study (with Marcus Waithe) of non-fiction prose styles of the long nineteenth century, *Thinking Through Style*.

Daniel Karlin is Winterstoke Professor of English Literature at the University of Bristol; he has previously held appointments at the University of Sheffield, Boston University and University College London. He is a scholar and editor of nineteenth-century poetry, especially the work of Robert Browning, and has a long-standing interest in poets' letters, having edited a selection of the courtship correspondence of Robert Browning and Elizabeth Barrett. His most recent book, *The Figure of the Singer*, was published by Oxford University Press in 2013.

Hermione Lee is President of Wolfson College, Oxford. Her publications include a study of the novels of Virginia Woolf, a book on Philip Roth, a literary biography of Willa Cather, and many editions and introductions. More recently, she has published *Body Parts* (2005), a collection of essays on life writing, *Biography: A Very Short Introduction* (2009) and *Penelope Fitzgerald: A Life* (2013). She is currently working on a biography of Tom Stoppard.

Angela Leighton has published critical works on nineteenth- and twentieth-century literature, including, most recently, *On Form: Poetry, Aestheticism, and the Legacy of a Word* (2007) and *Voyages over Voices: Critical Essays on Anne Stevenson* (2010). In addition, she has published short stories and poems in many magazines, as well as three volumes of poetry: *A Cold Spell* (2000), *Sea Level* (2007) and *The Messages* (2012). She is currently completing a book on *The Poetics of Sound*, as well as working on a fourth volume of poetry. She is Senior Research Fellow at Trinity College, Cambridge.

Edna Longley is a Professor Emerita at Queen's University Belfast. She is a Member of the Royal Irish Academy and a Fellow of the British Academy. Her publications include *Poetry & Posterity* (2000), *Yeats and Modern Poetry* (2013) and, as editor, *Edward Thomas: The Annotated Collected Poems* (2008). With Peter Mackay and Fran Brearton she has co-edited *Modern Irish and Scottish Poetry* (2011) and with Fran Brearton *Incorrigibly Plural: Louis MacNeice and his Legacy* (2012).

Paul Muldoon is the author of twelve collections of poetry, including *New Weather* (1973), *Quoof* (1983), *Meeting the British* (1987), *Moy Sand and Gravel* (2002) and his most recent book, *One Thousand Things Worth Knowing* (2014). He is Professor at Princeton University and poetry editor of *The New Yorker*. His numerous awards include the T. S. Eliot Prize in 1994 and the Pulitzer Prize in 2003. Between 1999 and 2004 he was Professor of Poetry at Oxford University, where he is an Honorary Fellow of Hertford College.

Siobhan Phillips's essays and poems have appeared in *PMLA*, *Boston Review*, *Twentieth-Century Literature*, *Yale Review*, *Harvard Review* and other journals. She is an assistant professor at Dickinson College and the author of *The Poetics of the Everyday: Creative Repetition in Modern American Verse* (2010). Her current book project is about epistolary intimacy from 1800 to the present.

Thomas Travisano is Professor of English at Hartwick College. He is the author of *Elizabeth Bishop: Her Artistic Development* (1988) and *Midcentury Quartet: Bishop, Lowell, Jarrell, Berryman and the Making of a Postmodern Aesthetic* (1999). He served as principal editor of *Words in Air: The Complete Correspondence Between Elizabeth Bishop and Robert Lowell* (2008), and as co-editor of *Gendered Modernisms: American Women Poets and Their Readers* (1996), *Elizabeth Bishop in the Twenty-First Century: Reading the New Editions* (2011) and the three-volume *New Anthology of American Poetry*. He is the founding president of the Elizabeth Bishop Society and Senior Advisor to the Robert Lowell Society.

Marcus Waithe is a Fellow in English and a University Senior Lecturer at Magdalene College, Cambridge. He is the author of *William Morris's Utopia of Strangers: Victorian Medievalism and the Ideal of Hospitality* (2006). Recent work includes essays on John Ruskin, Thomas Carlyle, William Empson, William Barnes and Geoffrey Hill. With Michael D. Hurley, he is editing a volume of essays entitled *Thinking Through Style*, to be published by Oxford University Press. He is also completing a monograph entitled *The Work of Words: Literature and the Labour of Mind in Britain, 1830–1930*.

Frances Wilson is a biographer and critic. Her publications include *Literary Seductions: Compulsive Writers and Diverted Readers* (1999), *The Courtesan's Revenge: Harriette Wilson, the Woman who Blackmailed the King* (2003) and *The Ballad of Dorothy Wordsworth* (2009). She is currently writing a book about Thomas De Quincey.

Introduction: 'For what is a letter?'

Jonathan Ellis

I

Looking back at the history of letter writing from the perspective of the early twenty-first century, it is striking how often the death of letter writing has been prematurely announced. Yet it shows no sign of happening soon, at least if one counts email, texting and tweeting as letter writing too, a subject that falls outside the reach of this book but is nevertheless addressed by nearly all of its contributors. For a literary genre regularly on its deathbed – obituary notices first begin circulating around the introduction of the Penny Post in 1840 – letter writing has shown a remarkable capacity for survival and reinvention. In the last few years alone, several non-fiction books have been published on the history of letter writing. Editions of letters continue to be published and to sell well. Conferences and workshops on epistolary literature and letter writing remain popular. One of the most frequently visited websites on the internet, *Letters of Note*, is dedicated to the reproduction and transcription of letters, or what it rather quaintly calls 'old-fashioned correspondence' (Usher xv). A new online literary journal, *The Letters Page*, has even been set up, 'which takes correspondence as its theme and the written letter as its primary form' (McGregor).

The aim of this book, however, is not to speculate on the future of letter writing in 'old-fashioned' or digital form, but to reflect on what has already taken place. As Hermione Lee observes in the opening chapter, what follows is 'therefore historical and retrospective, related mainly to the late nineteenth and twentieth century, when people wrote copious letters, but were also increasingly conscious of the possible exposure, during one's life or after it, of the private life, through the publishing of intimate documents'. At the same time, and in the light of various recent scandals such as the Edward Snowden affair, examining the history and nature of letter writing in the past may help us to understand our habits and methods of communication today. It is one of the ironies of modern life that the handwritten letter has probably become the safest way of evading government surveillance.

But what is a letter? And why does this book focus mainly on the correspondence of poets? American poet Mary Ruefle has one of the most eloquent answers to this question in a lecture entitled 'Remarks on Letters':

> For what is a letter, but to speak one's thoughts at a distance? Which is why poems and prayers are letters. The origins of poems, prayers, and letters all have this in common: urgency. They each originate in the pressing need to make a message directed at something unnear, that the absence of the unnear be made to appear present – that the presence of absence be palpably felt – that consciousness create consciousness. (204)

How do we make 'the presence of absence be palpably felt'? This, it seems to me, is the essence and paradox of letter writing. As Janet Gurkin Altman observes in her seminal book on *Epistolarity*: 'the letter straddles the gap between presence and absence; the two persons who "meet" through the letter are neither totally separated nor totally united. The letter lies halfway between the possibility of total communication and the risk of no communication at all' (43). What lies between two people in the course of writing a letter is quite literally the possibility that the letter might not arrive or that in the process of it getting there one of the correspondents might have moved or perhaps even died. Letters attempt to bridge these kinds of gaps in time and space, to straddle the gap between you and me, but, like all material objects, they are susceptible to getting lost and mislaid in the post. An art form of the everyday, they can also, in Emily Dickinson's famous phrase, feel 'like Immortality' (263).

But in what tense do they speak and what do they speak about? For Samuel Richardson, one of the great epistolary novelists, communicating via letter is a form of 'writing, to the moment' (289). Most letters are written in the present tense as a way of appearing in one place when physically elsewhere. Letters bring people closer together without them ever actually touching. They are perhaps the closest literary form to physical flirtation, hence the popularity of letter writing as a means of courtship and seduction. Letters are not just about communicating with the world, however. They can also be a form of self-portrait. 'A true letter', Virginia Woolf once speculated, 'should be as a film of wax pressed close to the graving in the mind' (*Congenial Spirits* 39). Richardson's love of immediacy and Woolf's relish for literary gossip found their preferred outlet in letter writing, but both took time to make the everyday memorable, even momentous. If letter writing is to have a future, either in its traditional form of putting pen to paper or in our more contemporary form of running one's finger over a keyboard or screen, taking one's time remains essential. While the time spent on delivering messages may have speeded up, the time spent on composing them probably needs to slow down.

Time – the contemplation of it, the taking of it, the writing about and in it – is one of the things that letters do consistently well, perhaps better than any other literary genre, as John O'Connell points out in his entertaining if somewhat melodramatically titled *For the Love of Letters: The Joy of Slow Communication* (2012): 'To make the point that, had email existed, writers like Coleridge and Emerson would have used it is, well, pointless. They didn't have email; they couldn't use it. As a result they wrote (and thought, and felt, and existed) differently because they had a different concept of time and space' (169). A great letter, he argues, 'feels like an experiment in slowing down time, or at least in highlighting the lag between clock time and the rate at which we register change. It wants to hold on to and explore the moment because the moment may not . . . end the way anyone wants it to' (67). In email there is no time for time, or if there is, it never feels like it. As Anne Fadiman complains: 'E-mail's greatest strength – speed – is also its Achilles' heel. In effect, it's always December 26. You are not expected to write *Middlemarch*, and therefore you don't' (122). The collected correspondence of writers like Jonathan Swift, Lady Mary Wortley Montagu, Charles Lamb, Jane Carlyle and Ralph Waldo Emerson is certainly on a scale of achievement similar to *Middlemarch*. Indeed, for many women writers like Jane Carlyle, correspondence was the one literary arena in which they were given time to perform, precisely because it was an arena without a public readership, at least not while they were living. Letter writing can sometimes appear a gendered art for this reason.

The great age of Victorian novels like *Middlemarch* is not, incidentally, the great age of letter writing. According to *The Oxford Book of Letters*, edited by Frank and Anita Kermode in 1995:

> The great age of letter-writing was, roughly, 1700–1918. Of course there are many good letters after that – think only of D. H. Lawrence and Virginia Woolf . . . But by the time of the Second World War there were a lot of those telephones about, admittedly less handy than they are now; and the postal service had begun to shrink and slow down. (xxiii)

As is clear from the contents of this book, I find this an unbalanced and unnecessarily severe account of twentieth-century letter writing. Lawrence and Woolf wrote more than their fair share of 'great' letters, not merely 'good' ones. Contributors to this book make the case for other authors, including Edward Thomas, Marianne Moore, Lorine Niedecker, Elizabeth Bishop, Robert Lowell, W. S. Graham, Philip Larkin and Ted Hughes. One could add at least another dozen names to this list, not including writers whose letters have still to be edited, a crucial factor in deciding whether an age is great or not and who among its number actually communicated well in letters.

However one dates the 'great age of letter-writing', there seems little doubt that it is in the past. But is it actually dead? Rebecca Solnit thinks so. In a recent essay in the *London Review of Books*, she connects a change in communication methods to a change in human character. 'In or around June 1995 human character changed,' she states, self-consciously echoing Woolf's famous statement about another shift in character 'on or about December 1910' ('Mr. Bennett and Mrs. Brown' 396). What exactly changed in 1995? What did the world look and feel like before and after this apparent watershed, if indeed it was one? I was twenty years old in 1995. I still wrote and received letters. I had heard of email but didn't know anybody who used it. Mobile phones existed but amongst my friends they were huge ugly things that you kept hidden in a drawer rather than leaving out in the open for everyone to admire. I bought albums, sometimes even singles (remember them?) in a shop, browsed books in a different shop, and wrote all of my essays by hand, activities that in the course of just two decades now sound eccentric, if not down-right old-fashioned. Letters and news were daily or at best twice-daily events, not continual streams of breaking information and recent updates. As Solnit observes wistfully:

> That bygone time had rhythm, and it had room for you to do one thing at a time; it had different parts; mornings included this, and evenings that, and a great many of us had these schedules in common. I would read the paper while listening to the radio, but I wouldn't check my email while updating my status while checking the news sites while talking on the phone . . . Previous technol-ogies have expanded communication. But the last round may be contracting it. The eloquence of letters has turned into the unnuanced sparseness of texts; the intimacy of phone conversations has turned into the missed signals of phone chat. I think of that lost world, the way we lived before these new technolo-gies, as having two poles: solitude and communication. The new chatter puts us somewhere in between, assuaging fears of being alone without risking real connection. It is a shallow between two deep zones, a safe spot between the dangers of contact with ourselves, with others. (32)

Solnit is not the first middle-aged author to lament what she senses is already a 'lost world'. It is no coincidence that most of this mourning occurs in print. Might printed objects like books and newspapers go the way of letters soon? In *Alone Together*, another elegy for an epistolary world that the author concludes has com-pletely vanished, Sherry Turkle describes contemporary existence as essentially lonely. 'The network is seductive,' she admits. 'But if we are always on, we may deny ourselves the rewards of solitude' (3). For Turkle, the language of the network, the status of always being *on*, is synonymous with being a machine. If you are reading this book in a public place, look up at the people around you. How many have some kind of electronic device in their hands or ears? Perhaps you are reading this book on one? Many spend more time interacting with their smart phones than their infi-nitely smarter real-life friends, talking to people they may never have met and may in the case of virtual friends not even exist. Spike Jonze's 2013 film *Her*, in which the central character falls in love with his new operating system, seems to me a fairly accurate representation of contemporary life rather than a depiction of an alterna-tive world. To be connected continuously with everyone is not to be connected to anyone in particular. It is certainly not to be alone or silent. Such habits of being lead to the risk of existing neither here nor there, but lost in a communication vacuum that mistakes immediacy for intimacy, image sharing for presentness, and virtual reality for touch. To be always on is never to be off, to tire oneself out with chattering and leave no time for listening.

A first-year undergraduate student, who was born in or around 1995, recently emailed me the following question: 'If I feel I can get the relevant research from sources purely online, not having to go to the actual library, is it okay to do this?'

The differences between reading books online and in person can be exaggerated. More students can consult an e-book online than can ever borrow a physical copy from a bookshelf. You do not have to worry about inconvenient opening times, misplaced items, other people's irritating marginalia or, most frustrating of all, another reader having borrowed the book before you. But as more and more 'actual' libraries are closed or reduced in scale, with all the opportunities for serendipitous discovery that 'having to go to the actual library' still represents, it is worth carefully considering the gains *and* losses of a shift towards living 'purely online'. One of these losses is letter writing, an exchange of words between writers that does not always make one less lonely than before or more connected, though it can sometimes do both, but does make one pause for thought, if only for a moment. The celebration of such moments, such times, is the subject of this book.

II

The best letter writers have always been adept at making the past sound present, old news fresh, even as newer forms of communication threatened to replace letter writing as the most efficient way of keeping in touch. The nineteenth-century letter writer had the telegraph to contend with, the twentieth-century letter writer the telephone. In our own century, it is difficult to know yet whether inventions such as the BlackBerry and the iPhone are alternatives to what letter writing formerly offered or simply a digital extension of what letters have always done: connect people across time and space. Letter writing has arguably survived in the past not because it is the most immediate or indeed safe means of communication, but because it is one of the most flexible. While letter writing is primarily employed to share news and stimulate news in return, its greatest legacy for literature has been the freedom it offers writers to exchange ideas and thoughts they would not necessarily feel comfortable expressing in public, the freedom moreover simply to practise being a writer. If nothing else, the act of writing and receiving letters is about the discipline of writing and, of equal importance, the significance of engaging with and responding to a reader. As Michael D. Hurley observes in relation to Gerard Manley Hopkins's letters (though he could be speaking about nearly all of the authors addressed in this book), 'dialogue is indeed his letters' life-blood. He asks more from his closest correspondents than that they merely rehearse their own news and views: he invites, and often demands, a meaningful exchange.'

In 1975 Elizabeth Bishop was commissioned to write a review of Sylvia Plath's *Letters Home*. According to Bishop's biographer, Brett C. Millier, the unfinished review 'cost her a good deal of anxiety' (504). Bishop doubted whether it was even possible to review a collection of letters:

> Of course one can't really 'review' letters, or criticise them – at least, not perhaps the way a play, a novel, or poetry can be reviewed and criticised. Letters can only be discussed and then always in terms of the character and life of their writers (not authors). Some letters are better than others; almost

all that eventually get published are, in one way or another, fascinating, to me anyway – but then, so are those that don't get published. (in Ellis 13–14)

Bishop does not dismiss the study of letter writing out of hand. That said, she does question whether letters can be treated in the same way as a play, novel or poem: 'Letters can only be discussed and then always in terms of the character and life of their writers.' Letters, in her view, are thus more factual than fictional. They can be 'discussed' among friends, but one must be careful of scrutinising them too closely. This does not mean that a letter is above criticism, however. Bishop believes 'some letters are better than others' and, by implication, some letter writers more worthy of publication than others.

What might make one letter 'better' than another? Bishop later compares writing letters to 'getting dressed up and going to the symphony concert instead of sitting at home in pajamas and listening to it on the radio: no matter how illiterate, ignorant, or inarticulate, once one takes pen in hand, one has to make an effort; certain formalities are to be observed, unless one was either eccentric or a literary genius' (in Ellis 14). Formality is the key word here. As Hugh Haughton points out in his chapter on poets' letters, 'in every case, the letter is not only a source of information but a *form* of information'. The best letter writers take the form of a letter as seriously as any other art form. Plath's correspondence implicitly fails Bishop's formality test. The draft stalls at the very point her letters are about to be discussed: 'This brings up a delicate, possibly embarrassing question. What about family letters, duty letters, the weekly letter promised to mother from camp, college, or the job in another city?' (in Ellis 14). The 'embarrassing' question, at least as it pertains to Plath's letters home, is never answered by Bishop whose review ends here, a handwritten note in the margin ('S. P. here!') the only sign of more to come. What might she eventually have written? The evidence is not encouraging. In unpublished notes, Bishop protested against women poets who 'stay at home' to write poetry. 'Sylvia Plath avoided this when she wrote about babies, ovens, etc. – but sometimes one extreme is almost as bad as the other' (in Ellis 14). Bishop's characterisation of Plath's poetry in terms of 'babies' and 'ovens' is crude and unfair. Lest we let Bishop have the final word – a recently deceased poet unfairly stereotyped by her older, living rival – it is worth recalling Plath's own journal entry on Bishop from February 1958: 'No reason why I shouldn't surpass at least the facile Isabella Gardner & even the lesbian & fanciful & jeweled Elizabeth Bishop in America' (*Journals* 322). Perhaps it is not surprising neither poet felt able to give the other credit: Bishop, because of her long-standing reluctance to reveal too much of her own life in poetry, Plath, because of her lifelong compulsion to do so. Were both already conscious of their different personas? Bishop the famous eye. Plath the famous I.

In addition to an aesthetic and perhaps even moral prejudice against Plath's poetry, Bishop had a personal reason not to like the majority of her correspondence and to find even the act of writing about it difficult. Plath's letters home were reminders of what Bishop herself never had: a home. In Aurelia Plath's introduction to *Letters Home* she admitted that 'it may seem extraordinary that someone who died when she was only thirty years old left behind 696 letters written to her family between the beginning of her college years in 1950 and her death early in February 1963' (3). As far as we know, Bishop did not write a single letter to her mother, her main carer for the first few years of her life after her father's death when she was just nine months old. Bishop's mother never recovered from this loss. She committed herself to a hospital soon afterwards and last saw her daughter when she was five years old. The very fact that *Letters Home* was edited by Plath's mother must also have stirred painful memories for Bishop. Like all collections of letters, Plath's published correspondence is the written record of more than one person and involves multiple audiences, contexts and readers.

Most of the stereotypes about letter writing revolve around the number two. One person writes a letter; a second person reads it. They then swap roles. There are crossed letters, lost letters, unread and unsent letters, but the idea of two people writing and reading persists. Daily life, disagreement, the vagaries of the postal service and, most obviously, death are just some of the events that intervene to break up this game of exchanging roles, but most of us continue to see letter writing as an identifiable 'I' writing to an identifiable 'you'. This, too, is an activity that is usually thought to be private. Such frameworks are repeatedly questioned in this book. As Hermione Lee cautions: 'It is a mistake to think of a letter as a solitary, independent, free-standing document. It must be seen as part of a relationship that moves through time. And the evidence provided by letters can never quite be trusted.'

The idea of two human beings engaged in a private conversation through letters is a pretty fiction, not an observable fact. Nearly every epistolary friendship is haunted by the presence of other people, whether it be the literal hand of another person sharing in the writing of the letter, the material mark of the postal service or, after this, the less visible traces of the editor who transcribes and selects the letter in a book, right up to our own presence taking up the letter to read again. Frances Wilson's chapter in this book is on precisely this subject, the presence of Dorothy Wordsworth literally looking 'over the shoulder' of her brother William and his wife Mary. The myth of two people, even with letters that are not published, is thus in most cases a reality of more than five or six, from letter writer or letter writers, through the hands of censors, thieves or hopefully, in most cases, postal workers, to recipient or recipients. When thinking about letters, then, one should always think of a number greater than two.

Plath's correspondence with her mother is full of third readers. In a letter dated 7 December 1950, for example, Plath describes to her mother the thrill of reading a letter from her benefactor at Smith, Olive Higgins Prouty. This is how Aurelia transcribes this letter in *Letters Home*:

December 7 1950

Dear Mum,

Your letter and one from Olive Higgins Prouty came in the same mail . . . I was thrilled to see Mrs. Prouty's scratchy, almost illegible hand. Her letter is one I will always keep. She thinks I have 'a gift for creative writing' and wants me to send her some of my poems and drop in to have a cup of tea when I come home on vacation. [*Their meeting inspired an (unpublished) manuscript written*

for – and rejected by – Reader's Digest, *'Tea with Olive Higgins Prouty.'*] She
even said she's having my letter typed up with carbons to send to some of her
alumnae friends. It makes me feel so wonderful that I could even partly express
to her how I felt about Smith, and as Miss Mensel said, it's nice to have a scholarship mean more than a grant of money.

Love, Sivvy (63)

Plath's letter about letter writing appears banal on first reading. The absence of any
kind of epistolary gusto is all the more striking given the subject of the letter, Plath
sharing with her mother the news that Mrs Prouty had recently complemented her
for having 'a gift for creative writing', a gift that has been demonstrated through her
original letter to Mrs Prouty who is now having it typed up. She thus shares news
of her artistic success with her mother while at the same time keeping the actual
content and style of the letter to herself. The same pattern of revelation and secrecy
is obviously repeated later on when Plath was composing *The Bell Jar* and *Ariel*. In
other words, the letter reveals the extent to which Plath was already keeping her
mother at arm's length even as a college freshman. She sends the 'creative' letters
to somebody else.

Aurelia's parenthetical comment about Plath's rejected manuscript has the unfortunate effect of posthumously puncturing her daughter's confidence and optimism.
While she may have impressed Mrs Prouty with her letter, she did not impress
Reader's Digest with her account of the meeting. An editorial comment like this
gives useful information about Plath's writing, but the decision to insert it in the
body of the letter rather than as a foot- or endnote makes Aurelia seem petty and
perhaps even unsupportive. It is as if she is gaining revenge on Plath for not showing
her the letter that Mrs Prouty thought so brilliant.

Letters Home is one of the most notorious examples of how an author's letters can
be mishandled by an editor or editors, but it is not isolated or untypical, as Daniel
Karlin's chapter on Keats's correspondence shows. When authors insert poems in
letters, for example, poems that may not exist in any other form, what should the
editor's response be? Should the poem be reprinted in and as part of the letter, or
can a case be made for its liberation from its letter origins? If the latter, how much
information should the editor share with the reader? Is a note indicating its history
enough? How much editorial work should the editor actually do? Thomas Travisano
gives a very full answer to this question in his chapter which tells the story of his
own editing of the Bishop and Lowell correspondence, a job for which he received
little if any training: 'Like most literary scholars of my era, I never took – indeed
was never offered – an academic course on the reading or editing of a writer's correspondence. At best, a handful of well-known letters might be referenced in an
advanced seminar as ancillary texts to an author's fiction, poems or plays.' As Hugh
Haughton admits, drawing on his experiences of editing T. S. Eliot's correspondence, the editor of an author's letters is particularly visible: 'In the case of a novel
such as *Great Expectations* or of a play like *Waiting for Godot*, an editor is an optional
extra and footnotes a luxury. When it comes to letters, however, the editor acts as
a conduit between the original writer and the reader with the editorial function

rendered visible by the editor's name and a litter of footnotes.' We have to trust the editor and publisher have faithfully represented the original text, an important issue that is particularly acute with regard to letters where so much of the form and meaning is present, as in a poem, in layout, punctuation and spelling, however unorthodox.

This is the subject of my own chapter for this book, on the idea of last letters in the work of Keats, Bishop and Hughes. In his letters to Fanny Brawne, Keats encourages us to think about the physical act of a hand in the process of writing a letter. In doing so, he inspires us 'to imagine the act of letter writers writing and, related to this, the art of letter writing *as* writing. In drawing attention to the hand, we are forced to reconsider that which is mentioned but rarely revealed in most editions of published letters: the paper, the ink, the hand writing.' One can see this most starkly in *The Gorgeous Nothings*, a recent collection of Emily Dickinson's 'envelope writings' which offers a full-colour facsimile edition of the original manuscripts. The Dickinson book shows how much of a letter's meaning inheres in its material form and how poor an approximation transcriptions can often be. In fact, it leads us to question whether we can even talk about these objects as letters or poems at all. As Susan Howe points out in her preface, 'these singular objects balance between poetry and visual art . . . Viewing these "envelopes" as visual objects, while at the same time reading her words for sound and sense, one needs to seize upon luck and accidents – slips on paper slips' (7). The best editions of letters – and *The Gorgeous Nothings* sets a new, possibly unrepeatable standard – reproduce both these aspects of the letter, the words on the page and the page on which they are written.

Letter writers have been aware of the third, usually posthumous reader for centuries. As I have already indicated, he or she can be the letter writer too, but is just as likely to be another reader. Franz Kafka's *Letters to Milena* contains one of the most famous statements on a letter's posthumous life. According to Kafka, letter writing is 'an intercourse with ghosts, and not only with the ghost of the recipient but also one's own ghost which develops between the lines of the letter one is writing and even more so in a series of letters where one letter corroborates the other and can refer to it as a witness. . . . Written kisses don't reach their destination, rather they are drunk on the way by the ghosts' (182–3). Kafka's letter, one of his last to Milena, is at its most basic level troubled by an awareness of mortality. One's own ghost is surely the shadow of one's own death. Above and beyond this very material haunting, Kafka's words also gesture towards a sophisticated theory of letter writing. The person to whom a letter is addressed is ghostly too since he or she is not actually present when the letter is being written. For while the letter addresses somebody in the present as if they were actually there, every letter is in fact read by the recipient in the future. This is further complicated by the fact that the recipient has changed too. Letters are miniature time capsules to be opened not centuries hence, but whenever the letter is ultimately delivered. From the perspective of the writer, the recipient may be dead by the time the letter arrives. The opposite can also be true. We often think of delayed letters or letters from the deceased as oddities, but surely all letters are written by people in the past to people in the future.

This is not how we typically imagine the process of writing and reading letters, although it could be said that letters are often employed by biographers and critics to bring the dead back to life, and that this act of resurrection has something perverse about it. In reading letters, we want to make the ghosts flesh again. We want to see through the epistolary reminders of artistic lives to life once more. This can be a deeply destructive and morbid desire that is at times channelled into amazing creativity. We, too, appear to be acting like a ghost that refuses to live in the present.

Janet Malcolm discusses the allure of letters for the biographer in her book about the Plath industry, *The Silent Woman*:

> Letters prove to us that we once cared. They are the fossils of feeling. This is why biographers prize them so: they are biography's only conduit to unmediated experience. Everything else the biographer touches is stale, hashed over, told and retold, dubious, unauthentic, suspect. Only when he reads a subject's letters does the biographer feel he has come fully into his presence, and only when he quotes from the letters does he share with his readers his sense of life retrieved. (110)

Malcolm's image of letters as 'the fossils of feeling' sounds attractive. It places the biographer-critic in the role of archaeologist, digging back through time to reveal traces of an artist's life. Although she does not see letters *as* feeling – merely 'fossils' – they are clearly closely aligned in her imagination. If everything else 'the biographer touches is stale', letters are presumably authentic, fresh and true. Malcolm employs letters throughout her book as the beguiling and at times rather unpleasant domain of 'real' emotion where people let down their guard about certain feelings, particularly about Plath. But at no stage does she ever question what I would like to term the epistolary fallacy: the idea that letters are autobiography by another name and that there is nothing composed or staged about them. Plath is not unique in this regard. All letter writers put on a show most of the time, regardless of whether they are aware of it or not. All certainly employ conventions and techniques to make something essentially false (language) seem true. None are free of the temptations of fakery and invention. While contributors to this book disagree about how to read or value different forms of epistolary writing, all agree that letters are a performance art: that every letter, however authentic-seeming, is a mix of fact and fiction, self and other, storytelling and wish-fulfilment.

III

According to Hugh Haughton, 'poets' letters are a special case'. In his chapter for this book, he gives various reasons why this might be so, beginning with the tradition of the verse epistle, a form that Madeleine Callaghan praises Shelley for exploiting in both a private letter and a public poem in her chapter in this book: 'The letters communicate with friends, acquaintances and lovers; the poetry seeks to forge connections with an imagined audience. These categories shift and blur, as the letters become addressed to posterity and the poetry speaks intimately to its addressees.' Callaghan's argument about Shelley is surely applicable to other poets too. As Angela Leighton observes in her chapter on W. S. Graham, the line between a letter and a poem is often very thin:

> The letter may be the place where a poem takes shape, where lines of poetry emerge from the prose, where talking to another becomes talking to oneself, and therefore where distinctions break down . . . That the letter involves an address to a named reader, and that it is characterised by time and delay in the writing and sending, are two probably ubiquitous features, but features loosely shared with the lyric poem.

For many epistolary critics, blurring categories and distinctions is the hallmark of literary letter writing. For Margaretta Jolly and Liz Stanley, authors of one of the most thought-provoking essays on 'Letters as/not a genre', 'letters lie on the very borders of what constitutes a genre, for they are continually dissolving and being reinvented in the sheer variety of social relationships they reflect, as well as looking back to the pre-history of writing itself in oral exchange' (97). As Rebecca Earle points out, 'the letter form is a protean, all-inclusive genre, whose very shapelessness is its strength, allowing it to adapt to any expressive requirement' (8). Poets are particularly adept at exploiting the letter form's bordering, edge-like nature and incorporating these discoveries in their poetry. In addition to letters and poems, this book thus also engages with a myriad of hybrid letter-poem forms, from Edward Lear's snail-poems to Ted Hughes's birthday letters, from Keats's poem-in-a-letter to Bishop's package-in-a-story.

The authorship of such hybrid forms is the subject of Paul Muldoon's chapter on the letters of Bishop and Lowell in which he considers 'the extent to which it is appropriate for either the reader or the writer to draw on material from "private" letters in making literature, an issue on which Lowell and Bishop disagreed'. Muldoon's approach to this material is to think about letters 'as the other life that [a poem] might have had' and a poem as 'the other life [letters] might have had'. In other words, he reads Bishop and Lowell as corresponding with each other across all forms of writing, whether in a letter or a poem, unpublished or published. To do so is simultaneously to free the letter from its private origins and to read the poem as a more intimate form of address. His argument certainly encourages us to read both sides of a correspondence and to be careful of assuming too much about either party when we only have one side of the story, as is unfortunately the case with most editions of letters. This issue – who owns the content of a letter, and can either participant in a letter-writing exchange use the other author's words? – is also at the heart of Matthew Campbell's chapter on the automatic writing of George Yeats, and Siobhan Phillips's chapter on Lorine Niedecker's poetry. Campbell describes George's automatic writing for Yeats as a 'gift': 'If George was the mother of the truths which purportedly came to Yeats from an unknown writer, her writing was midwife.' Siobhan Phillips's account of Niedecker's career tells a very different story, of a poet who had 'little immediate company' on the flood-threatened spit of land on which she lived and 'few readers in any location'. For Niedecker, letters were more than a gift she could pass on to important people in her life; they *were* that life. As Phillips states: 'Her house was most important as a space to send and receive mail, and her real "living" lay in the exchanges with far-off others.' This is also the case for Elizabeth Barrett, who attempted to define letter writing as a form of labour, albeit one quite different from more conventional definitions of work in the Victorian period. As Marcus Waithe points out in his chapter, Barrett's letters might be seen as 'a testing ground for unconventional work ethics and excluded modes of produc-tion'. They also challenge the status of letters as secondary to other forms of literary work, like criticism or poetry.

Every contributor in the book addresses the status of letters at some point. For Karlin, the notion 'that poems rank higher in the scale than letters, since letters are at best seen as a sort of hybrid or sub-genre' was 'current in Keats's time and still active in our own'. In a footnote, he expands on this idea: 'It might be thought that Keats has succeeded in challenging this hierarchy; he belongs to a small group of poets (including Emily Dickinson, Gerard Manley Hopkins and Elizabeth Bishop) whose letters can claim equal status with their poetry. But editorial practice suggests that poetry still retains its edge of cultural value.' The aim of this book is not to bring poetry down, as it were, but to make the case for letters, particularly the letters of poets, as deserving of more attention than is currently the case. The reasons why we might read and study poets' letters are various. But we can and should also read them *as* letters. As Hugh Haughton points out: 'The best poet's letters, like Dickinson's or Hopkins's, are as compelling as their poems. . . . In such letters we get something like poetry by other means, as well as lots of detailed commentary on poems, poetics and the intimate worlds of poets.' Haughton's phrase, 'something like poetry', is, for all its inexactness, one of my favourite definitions of letter writing. It acknowledges the closeness of letter writing to poetry and its ambiguous difference. The line between the two may be thin, but it is still there.

I V

Letters do give us biography as well, though, as Hermione Lee cautions, they can be 'dangerous' objects in careless hands. She gives as an example a letter written by Katherine Mansfield (I will not reveal the details of the letter here): 'At least five biographical points of view are required to encompass the letter . . . no paraphrase or commentary can be adequate. The danger of such a letter is that it altogether swamps and overpowers the biographer, who can only gasp, admire and quote.' This book contains at least two chapters that engage with letters from a biographer's perspective, Frances Wilson on the letters between William Wordsworth and his wife Mary, and Anne Fadiman on the letters between Samuel Taylor Coleridge and his son Hartley. Wilson begins her chapter by describing the excitement sur-rounding the discovery of these letters in 1977: 'Wordsworth's twentieth-century readers responded to the content of these letters like a legal team finding evidence to release their client from a life service. The poet had been involved in a miscar-riage of justice: far from being cold and self-absorbed, it transpired that he had sexual feelings for his wife.' Fadiman also reflects on the way in which letters bring the dead back to life. 'Letters', she believes, 'allow us to imagine how things might have gone differently. They dissolve not only the centuries but, perhaps even more important, the knowledge of what the next day would bring. Rather than looking back at our characters' past, we find ourselves worrying about their future.' This is the case even when we know what has happened, as is the reality of reading most collections of letters where the passing of a life and the proximity of the subject's death is literally reflected in the approaching end of the book.

As much as poets' letters are about and for posterity, they are also written in and to the moment. Their momentariness is particularly to the fore when talking about food or drink or holidays. Philip Larkin's letters to his on-off girlfriend, Monica Jones, are some of the best examples of this kind of letter, what Tom Paulin in an oft-cited essay on Bishop's letters calls 'impromptu description' (231). Larkin's letters provide the focus of much of Edna Longley's chapter on what she terms 'epistolary psycho-therapy', the extent to which personal distress 'shapes epistolary relationships; how it gives them a psychological character; whether any therapy actually occurs; whether poems, in the end, do the job better'. My concern here is not so much on Larkin's distress, but on his self-consciousness as a letter writer. Monica Jones appears to have spent much of the fifties and sixties advising Larkin on how to make ration-bought meat edible. Much drinking goes on off-stage as well. The letters also reprint several of Larkin's drawings, many of which depict his various lodgings over the years. A list of Larkin's holiday destinations – Bournemouth, King's Lynn, Pocklington, Sark, York – makes clear how foreign even the idea of foreign travel was in postwar Britain, even for somebody relatively well-off. In such details, one gets a vivid sense of what it must have been like to live and work in 1950s Britain. More than this, one also gets a sense of what it must have been like to be Larkin. There is a famous letter from John Keats to his brother and sister-in-law in America (Hermione Lee also cites from it in her chapter) when he describes the very moment of writing the letter – 'the candles are burnt down and I am using the wax taper – which has a long snuff on it – the fire is at its last click – I am sitting with my back to it with one foot rather askew upon the rug and the other with the heel a little elevated from the carpet' (223) – as an attempt to make present his own life for them. 'Could I see the same thing done of any great Man long since dead it would be a great delight: as to know in what position Shakespeare sat when he began "To be or not to be" – such thing[s] become interesting from distance of time or place' (223). Larkin's letters are full of such moments too, as, for example, when a brown mouse surprises him: 'While writing all that,' he tells Monica on 12 November 1951, 'I noticed a *brown mouse* creep out behind the fireplace & edge along the wainscoting – not very nice! First time I've seen him. He *scuttled* back on realising he wasn't alone. This depresses me rather – Beatrix Potter's all very well in print but . . .' (70).

In later years, as Larkin became more famous and as the prospect of his letters being published grew more real, such Keatsian moments are rarer. He makes jokes about enjoying 'a Larkin afternoon' (437) in the countryside or his latest 'discovery in Larkin studies' (426). Yet even when Larkin is being ironic about his letter-writing skills, he still manages to be both memorable and poignant, as here:

I don't seem to be able to write you the interesting sort of letter I should like to – if I lived in the golden age of English letter writing, and had nothing to do but snuff the candles, draw the curtains, and lodge the kettle on the fire, I'm sure I could do much better. 'Past Turvey's Mill on my walk, dyd see a *Hare*,' etc. A pity we can't live in our imaginations! My kitchen wireless has gone wrong, so I eat my meals in silence – having heard the Archers in the sitting room. All being well, I shall see you next weekend. I don't know whether I shall appear by six – I'll let you know. (381)

As Keats looks back to Shakespeare in his letter from 12 March 1819, so Larkin in this letter, written on 23 November 1967, seems to evoke the very image of Keats in the midst of writing his letter with 'nothing to do but snuff the candles'. Larkin frequently apologised about his letter writing to Monica. 'I'm sorry if I neglect to answer things in your letters,' he wrote on 8 December 1956; 'to some extent I've "always" done it: my parents, & Kingsley [Amis], complained similarly. There may be several reasons – carelessness, forgetfulness perhaps, tho' I *always* write with your *last* letter beside me' (211). In a much later letter, from 26 October 1972, he is still apologising. 'This letter is really weak with fatigue. I would have telephoned, but a letter is more lasting, & I hope to have one from you. You are a brilliant letter writer' (439). Larkin is protesting a little too much here. Even (or perhaps especially) in the letter that proposes not to be 'interesting', one cannot fail to experience all the emotions that great literature depends on, amusement and sadness chief among them. As in the poem 'I Remember, I Remember', when Larkin evokes a golden childhood that he cannot in fact remember, so here he evokes 'a golden age of letter writing' that no longer exists. Yet, in his imagination just as much as in ours, the golden age of letter writing lives again every time we read a letter by Keats, or, I would argue, by Larkin. The image of Larkin, the kitchen wireless 'gone wrong', eating his meals in silence, is an arresting one, and just as memorable in its own way as the image of Keats with his back to the fire and his foot 'askew upon the rug'.

As an aside here, it is worth noting how careful Larkin always was to preserve other people's correspondence. Maeve Brennan, the other woman in Larkin's now-famous romantic triangle, recalls the orderliness of his shelving system: 'He kept his correspondents' letters in shoe boxes, also tied in yearly bundles; most of mine were fastened with silver string or pink ribbon' (145). In the poem 'Maiden Name' Larkin reminisces about his relationship with Winifred Arnott and how their love affair, like her maiden name, is now 'past and gone', but still accessible in 'Packets of letters tied with tartan ribbon' (*Collected Poems* 53). Silver or pink for Maeve. Tartan for Winifred. The librarian in Larkin clearly could not help but colour-code his relationships. Letters allowed him to be intimate with another person, frequently with more than one person, but on his own terms and according to his own time frame. Like the string that bound their love letters, the activity of exchanging letters as opposed to, say, exchanging wedding vows bound him in a sense to somebody else but with ties that he alone could fasten and release. Letters for Larkin were the emotional equivalent of the spatial distance between poet and world immortalised in poems like 'Here' and 'High Windows'. They allowed him to look out and others to look in but only on his say-so.

In 'Here', the poet's speaker moves east from a large town of 'domes and statues, spires and cranes' to a watery land of 'shapes and shingle':

> Here silence stands
> Like heat. Here leaves unnoticed thicken,
> Hidden weeds flower, neglected waters quicken,
> Luminously-peopled air ascends;
> And past the poppies bluish neutral distance
> Ends the land suddenly beyond a beach
> Of shapes and shingle. Here is unfenced existence:
> Facing the sun, untalkative, out of reach. (79–80)

The end-point of the poem, a slippery spit of land out of reach of human touch, does not seem an obvious stand-in for letters, even Larkin's. Letters are the literary form most often associated with conversation and talk, but letter writing represents a very odd form of talk. I talk, you talk. But you might have to wait several days to hear what I am saying, and I will certainly have to wait even more time to hear your response. It is talk not just when I like it but on what I want to talk about. Instead of turning our face to talk to a real person, we choose instead to construct a monologue in words to a person we cannot see or hear. They are literally 'untalkative' and 'out of reach', but so are we. And yet it does not feel that way, which is why we keep returning to letters even when the people who have written them are dead, when letter writing itself is a dying or perhaps even dead form of communication. Here, in a letter, is existence too, or at least something close to it.

WORKS CITED

Altman, Janet Gurkin, *Epistolarity: Approaches to a Form* (Columbus: Ohio State University Press, 1982).

Brennan, Maeve, *The Philip Larkin I Knew* (Manchester: Manchester University Press, 2002).

Dickinson, Emily, *Letters of Emily Dickinson*, ed. Mabel Loomis Todd (New York: Dover Publications, 2003 [1951]).

Earle, Rebecca (ed.), *Letters and Letter-Writing, 1600–1945* (Aldershot: Ashgate, 1999).

Ellis, Jonathan, '"Mailed into space": on Sylvia Plath's letters', in Sally Bayley and Tracy Brain (eds), *Representing Sylvia Plath* (Cambridge: Cambridge University Press, 2011), pp. 13–31.

Fadiman, Anne, 'Mail', *At Large and At Small: Confessions of a Literary Hedonist* (London: Penguin, 2007), pp. 111–25.

Howe, Susan, 'Preface', in *Emily Dickinson: The Gorgeous Nothings*, ed. Marta Werner and Jen Bervin (New York: Christine Burgin/New Directions, 2013), pp. 6–7.

Jolly, Margaretta, and Liz Stanley, 'Letters as/not a genre', *Life Writing* 2.2 (2005): 75–101.

Kafka, Franz, *Letters to Milena*, ed. Willy Haas, trans. Tania and James Stern (London: Vintage, 1999).

Keats, John, *Letters of John Keats*, ed. Robert Gittings (Oxford: Oxford University Press, 1970).

Kermode, Frank, and Anita Kermode (eds), *The Oxford Book of Letters* (Oxford: Oxford University Press, 1995).

Larkin, Philip, *Collected Poems*, ed. Anthony Thwaite (London: Faber and Faber, 2003).

—— *Letters to Monica*, ed. Anthony Thwaite (London: Faber and Faber, 2010).

McGregor, Jon, 'Editorial Note', *The Letters Page*, 30 May 2014, <http://www.theletterspage.ac.uk/letterspage/index.aspx> (last accessed 16 June 2014).

Malcolm, Janet, *The Silent Woman: Sylvia Plath and Ted Hughes* (London: Papermac, 1995).

Millier, Brett C., *Elizabeth Bishop: Life and the Memory of It* (Berkeley: University of California Press, 1993).

O'Connell, John, *For the Love of Letters: The Joy of Slow Communication* (London: Short Books, 2012).

Paulin, Tom, 'Writing to the Moment: Elizabeth Bishop', *Writing to the Moment: Selected Critical Essays 1980–1996* (London: Faber and Faber, 1996), pp. 215–39.

Plath, Sylvia, *Letters Home: Correspondence, 1950–1963*, ed. Aurelia Plath (London: Faber and Faber, 1976).

—— *The Journals of Sylvia Plath: 1950–1962*, ed. Karen V. Kukil (London: Faber and Faber, 2000).

Richardson, Samuel, *Selected Letters of Samuel Richardson*, ed. John Carroll (Oxford: Clarendon Press, 1964).

Ruefle, Mary, 'Remarks on Letters', *Madness, Rack, and Honey: Collected Lectures* (Seattle and New York: Wave Books, 2012), pp. 200–15.

Solnit, Rebecca, 'Diary', *London Review of Books*, 29 August 2013, pp. 32–3.

Turkle, Sherry, *Alone Together* (New York: Basic Books, 2011).

Usher, Shaun (ed.), *Letters of Note: Correspondence Deserving of a Wider Audience* (London: Unbound, 2013).

Woolf, Virginia, *Congenial Spirits: The Selected Letters of Virginia Woolf*, ed. Joanne Hautmann Banks (London: Hogarth Press, 1989).

—— 'Mr. Bennett and Mrs. Brown', in Vassiliki Kolocotroni, Jane Golman and Olga Taxidou (eds), *Modernism: An Anthology of Sources and Documents* (Edinburgh: Edinburgh University Press, 1998), pp. 395–7.

Part I: Contexts and Issues

I Dangerous Letters: A Biographer's Perspective[1]

Hermione Lee

I

Letters are dangerous, seductive, and invaluable for biographers. The familiar gestures of traditional letter writing – 'all my love', or 'thinking of you' – tell us that it is a mistake to think of a letter as a solitary, independent, free-standing document. It must be seen as part of a relationship that moves through time. And the evidence provided by letters can never quite be trusted. Hardly anyone, if closely examined, really means 'all my love'. One of the best expressions of the dangerousness of letters comes in a late sonnet by Tennyson, who very much disliked biography, fame, and the publication of writers' letters, all features of a literary life that were intensifying in his time. Tennyson said, in 1860, 'that the desiring of anecdotes and acquaintances with the lives of great men was treating them like pigs to be ripped open for the public; that he knew he himself should be ripped open like a pig; that he thanked God almighty ... that the world knew nothing of Shakespeare but his writings ... and that there were no letters preserved of Shakespeare' (in Martin 552). This was his warning sonnet about letters:

> Old ghosts whose day was done ere mine began,
> If earth be seen from your conjectured heaven,
> Ye know that History is half-dream – aye even
> The man's life in the letters of the man.
> There lies the letter, but it is not he
> As he retires into himself and is:
> Sender and sent-to go to make up this,
> Their offspring of this union. And on me
> Frown not, old ghosts, if I be one of those
> Who make you utter things you did not say,
> And mould you all awry and mar your worth;
> For whatsoever knows us truly, knows

That none can truly write his single day,
And none can write it for him upon earth. (1342)

Tennyson makes the essential point about the unreliability of letters and their dangerousness as partial evidence: 'There lies the letter, but it is not he / As he retires
into himself and is'.

Biographies of the future will be using letters of a different kind and in a different
way. No one yet knows how far the ephemeral data of emails, texts, blogs and tweets
will be accessible to the life-writers of the next centuries.[2] My thinking in this essay
about letters, autobiography and biography is therefore historical and retrospective,
related mainly to the late nineteenth and twentieth centuries, when people wrote
copious letters, but were also increasingly conscious of the possible exposure, during
one's life or after it, of the private life, through the publishing of intimate documents.

Some biographers working on that period are dubious about using letters at all. At
least one biographer of Virginia Woolf, Lyndall Gordon, thinks, along Tennysonian
lines, that Woolf's letters are a partial and inadequate guide to her inner self, that
they are 'flamboyant performances, at once amusing and irritating', 'written with
the kind of brazen, offhand candour that is not very intimate'. For Gordon, Woolf's
letters were not a serious mode of communication but 'a routine social gesture'
(177). She treats them as dangerous material for the biographer: and so they are. But
performance and social gestures are an essential part of that life-story, as of any life-
story. Yes, letters are performances; but most of us behave differently with different
people, and those differences and contradictions make up who we are.

If you are using a letter in a biography, you must recognise the dangerousness
of enlisting such a performance, and you must have some idea of what the performance entails. It is a mistake simply to use the material of a subject's letters for
factual evidence. You must know something about the context, the content, and
the addressee. You need to access, if you can, the private allusions and references,
which are almost always unexplained in a personal letter. In this respect, the work of
the literary editor and that of the biographer are closely related. Often there is only
one side of the correspondence, and the biographer must try to work out what the
letter is responding to, or what response it is inviting or demanding. In a run of correspondence, you need to be alert to who is initiating the exchange, who is responding, and who is breaking off the sequence of letters. You need to ask why your subject
has chosen to write about an event in a particular way, to a particular person, or in
more than one way to more than one person. Letters, even written on the same day,
may very well lie or contradict each other – especially if the writer, like Virginia
Woolf, has a marked tendency to say one thing to one person and another thing to
another. What a great pleasure it was to see you, and how incapacitated it left me
for normal life afterwards, and how very much we would like to come and visit you
at Garsington, she writes to Ottoline Morrell in May 1917. She didn't seem so much
of a fool as I'd been led to think, though vapid, and I don't see how we can get out of
going to visit her, she writes to Vanessa Bell in the same week (154, 156).

Ever since Samuel Johnson, writing about the difference between biography and autobiography in the 1750s, before the term autobiography had started to be used, said that a person writing about himself was more likely to be truthful than a person writing the life of another, the relationship between biography and autobiography has been important to anyone interested in the narrative of people's lives. Johnson had the optimistic conviction that 'he that speaks of himself has no motive to false-hood or partiality except self-love, by which all have so often been betrayed, that all are on the watch against its artifices'; whereas he that writes the life of another 'is either his friend or his enemy, and wishes either to exalt his praise or aggravate his infamy'. As hardened post-Freudians, we would probably take roughly the opposite view now about the relative truthfulness of biography and autobiography. David Ellis, in his cogent book on *Literary Lives*, argues that because of the 'pervasive influ-ence of the Freudian influence' on the writing of lives, 'subjects' own explanations of their behaviour will usually be regarded with suspicion' (8). The relationship between autobiography and biography is, he suggests, 'often antagonistic. Writing the lives of people who have already written their own is a tricky business' (9).

The question for the biographer of how to use letters is closely linked to the ques-tion of what to do with other autobiographical materials, like diaries and memoirs. What does the biographer do with the subject's own version of themselves? You may want to trust your subject's autobiographical narrative, but you must also bear in mind the possibility of unreliability, disguise, vanity, inauthenticity, reconstruction of the past, and deliberate, or accidental, forgetfulness. Literary autobiographers often shape the story of their own lives through key memories. Some writers channel their memories through a piece of music, or a landscape, or a scene, or the sound of a voice, or a book read early in life: the biographer needs to understand why that particular key unlocks the past. The biographer must ask how the subject has remembered, and shaped, their own life-story, and must read autobiographies, like letters, not just for the information they provide, but for what they do and don't say and for how they choose to say it. Of course literary autobiography can be read just as data of the life; but it is also evidence of what mattered to the subject, and a form of self-dramatisation or disguise.

Some writers, like Henry Green, or Vladimir Nabokov, or J. M. Coetzee, or John McGahern, provide autobiographical narratives so literary, so selected, and so styl-ised that they must be taken, however heartfelt and however close to the facts, as the equivalent of a fiction. One fine, tricky example is Eudora Welty's *One Writer's Beginnings* (1983), a masterpiece of apparent intimacy and self-concealing evasive-ness. It tells the story of her childhood in Jackson, Mississippi, the only child of a mother who was a teacher in West Virginia and a businessman father whose family came from Ohio and who died when she was twenty-two. The memoir tenderly describes her parents as benign and affectionate, and speaks of childhood with poignancy and nostalgic longing. There are very few moments in the narrative which suggest the kind of darkness and trouble in family lives that play so strong a part in Welty's fiction.

Everything is geared, as the memoir's title suggests, to show us someone who was born to shape life into story. But that also implies a high degree of fictionalis-ing within the memoir. Welty's critics and biographers have been suspicious of the celebratory and nostalgic way in which she wrote about her childhood. Carolyn Heilbrun, in *Writing a Woman's Life*, regretted Welty's 'romanticizing' and 'camouflaging' of her past, and read it as a pre-emptive strike against biographers: 'She wishes to keep meddling hands off her life. To her, this is the only proper behaviour for the Mississippi lady she so proudly is' (13–14). Other commentators on the book found it too happy to be credible. Welty's first biographer Ann Waldron tried to counter these suspicions by arguing that Welty's benign presentation of her childhood is a true autobiography in the sense that it shows her capacity for overcoming unhappiness:

> The secret of true happiness is often the ability to recall a childhood as happy, to have worked through all the horrors and terrors and put them behind, and, freed of them, to describe the early years in a family with humour and grace. Eudora makes her childhood look happy, ignoring a difficult mother and a troubled brother, and in doing so she tells us a lot about her own inner strength, her own secure evaluation of herself, and her success at coming to terms with life as it is. (333)

I do not think this biographer pushes hard enough at the concealments of autobiography.

Some writers choose to write their autobiographies explicitly as pre-emptive strikes against the biographers. Doris Lessing, in *Under My Skin*, the first volume of her autobiography, writes warily about the difficulties which go with 'telling the truth' and remembering the past: 'You cannot sit down to write about yourself without rhetorical questions of the most tedious kind demanding attention.' One of these questions is 'Why an autobiography at all?' and her answer is: 'Self defence: biographies are being written.' She comments grimly: 'Writers may protest as much as they like: but our lives do not belong to us' (14). One of the jobs for Lessing's biographer would be to find out why she was so anxious to get in first, and what it was she thought would be misrepresented.

Some literary autobiographers tell lies about themselves blithely, compulsively and outrageously. Muriel Spark said she was writing *Curriculum Vitae* in order to 'put the record straight', in reaction against a 'mythomaniac' version of her life written years before by an ex-friend and fellow Roman Catholic convert, Derek Stanford. She makes a point of insisting that other people have confirmed her accounts of the past and that she has kept a large archive of letters, leading us to believe that her version is going to be the accurate one. But her claim to first-hand accuracy is complicated by the fact that she has already used so much of her life's materials in her novels, and that in her autobiography she omits or plays down or alters some of the most dramatic facts of her life – her disastrous early marriage, her poverty and breakdown in the 1950s. What she wants us to read, she says, is 'a picture of my formation as a creative writer' (11, 14). The critic Bryan Cheyette, in his short study of Spark in 2000, notes that *Curriculum Vitae* 'assumes that there is a simple and unequivocal relationship between her life and work' (4). Spark's own presentation of her life as unproblematically translating into fiction may itself be a form of fiction.

Meanwhile, she mounted a vociferous attack on all other biographical versions of her life as pernicious inaccuracies. This demanding challenge was taken up courageously by her biographer Martin Stannard, who treats Spark's various autobiographical writings as presenting 'different aspect[s] of a personality in conflict' (xxi).

A dangerous and fascinating twentieth-century example of unreliable autobiography is Ford Madox Ford, who has attracted numerous heavyweight biographers (Arthur Mizener, Thomas Moser, Alan Judd, Max Saunders) and who notoriously made himself up in memoir after memoir, reminiscence after reminiscence. Mizener describes this as 'a romantic need . . . to see himself as admirable . . . and to impose on others an improved account of his own life and character'. Mizener thinks this had disastrous results for Ford and did him 'very great harm', and sets out to correct the record, carefully and punitively working through Ford's own versions of his stories (xvi, 316). Alan Judd is more lenient, and devotedly says that Ford creates a 'great rich unreliable tapestry' of his life which 'no biographer could hope to equal' (4–5). Max Saunders constructs a creative, imaginative interplay between Ford's lies and his fiction. Far from 'pointing reprovingly at his inaccuracies, as Mizener relentlessly did', Saunders calls Ford an impressionist, and says: 'Fordian impressionism is an extreme case of memory's transformation of the self' (vi, 70).

Some writers do not set out to lie, but want to create consolidated, dramatically coherent retrospective versions of their lives, so that the themes of their work will emerge from the story they tell of themselves. A mighty and notorious example of this is W. B. Yeats. James Olney, writing on autobiography, uses Yeats as an example in an essay on 'The Ontology of Autobiography'. Olney describes Yeats's autobiographical methods as follows:

> Yeats forgets what passes in time so that he may remember what does not pass in eternity; and misremembering, with a fine disregard, the names, dates and places of a merely individual life, he seeks to embody in the archetypal portraiture and the anecdotal artistry of the *Autobiographies* the very essence of being, purified now of what he in one place calls the 'accident and incoherence' of existence. (260–2)

This presents a considerable challenge for the biographer. Richard Ellmann's biographical writings on Yeats (as Roy Foster puts it) 'followed his subject's example in dealing with his life thematically'. Foster's own two-volume life of Yeats provides a fine example of a biographer wrestling with the persuasive, authoritarian methods of his subject's autobiographies, uncovering their tactics, and reading them as part of the life-story. Foster describes Yeats's autobiographical processes as 'his own heroic self-construction'. He argues that Yeats's *Autobiographies* 'dictate an arrangement for his life, and it is a thematic one' which is 'hard not to follow': indeed most biographical writers on Yeats have done so. 'However,' says Foster, 'we do not, alas, live our lives in themes, but day by day.' His own minutely chronological life of Yeats, he says in starting out, 'attempts to restore the sense of a man involved in life, and in history' (xxvii).

II

Autobiographies are retrospective; letters are written in the heat of the moment. But they may also be tactical dramatisations of a life. As Daniel Karlin, the editor of the Brownings' love letters, has put it: 'A letter *is* an action or gesture, as well as the representation of one.' But, as he goes on to add: 'The story told by the letters is not, it must be emphasized, the raw material of events, but a treatment of those events, a representation – at times, we might even say a fiction' (xii). For biographers, letters are as suspicious-making and tricky to date as autobiographies and memoirs. I give just one example, but an especially dangerous one, a notorious letter written by Katherine Mansfield in 1916.

To read this letter, it is helpful to know that Katherine Mansfield and her lover, later her husband, the literary editor John Middleton Murry, have moved during the war to live near the Lawrences in Cornwall. They have taken two small, very basic cottages next door to each other, in Zennor, a tiny, remote village by the sea near St Ives. Mansfield is already ill with not-yet-diagnosed tuberculosis; her brother has been killed in the war the year before; her relationship with Murry is troubled; he is waiting to hear whether he will be called up for military service. They have known the Lawrences since 1913, and the Lawrences have been married since 1914. The four-way relationship is difficult. Mansfield and Lawrence are rivalrous and in conflict, and she is jealous of his obsession with Murry and his desire to create a 'blood brotherhood' with him, which Murry is resisting. She does not like Frieda Lawrence. In many ways she finds Lawrence ridiculous: 'I suggested to Lawrence that he should call his cottage The Phallus and Frieda thought it was a very good idea,' she writes in another letter at this time. Here, she is writing to Samuel Koteliansky, a Ukrainian Jewish writer and translator, a close friend of D. H. Lawrence, who is also very devoted to her. All these people are in their thirties. Mansfield writes:

I don't know which disgusts one worse – when they are very loving and playing with each other or when they are roaring at each other and he is pulling out Frieda's hair and saying 'I'll cut your bloody throat, you bitch' and Frieda is running up and down the road screaming for 'Jack' to save her!! This is only a half of what literally happened last Friday night. You know, Catalina, Lawrence isn't healthy any more; he has gone a little bit out of his mind. If he is contradicted about *anything* he gets into a frenzy, quite beside himself and it goes on until he is so exhausted he cannot stand and has to go to bed and stay there until he has recovered. And whatever your disagreement is about he says it is because you have gone wrong in your sex and belong to an obscene spirit. These rages occur whenever I see him for more than a casual moment for if ever I say anything that isn't quite 'safe' off he goes! It is like sitting on a railway station with Lawrence's temper like a big black engine puffing and snorting. I can think of nothing, I am blind to everything, waiting for the moment when with a final shriek – off it will go! When he is in a rage with Frieda he says it is she who has done this to him and that she is 'a bug who has fed on my life'. I think that is true. I think he is suffering from quite genuine monomania at present, having endured so much from her. Let me tell you what happened on Friday. I went across to them for tea. Frieda said Shelleys Ode to a Skylark was false. Lawrence said: 'You are showing off; you don't know anything about it.' Then she began. '*Now* I have had enough. Out of my house – you little God Almighty. Ive had enough of you. Are you going to keep your mouth shut or aren't you.' Said Lawrence: 'I'll give you a dab on the cheek to quiet you, you dirty hussy'. Etc. Etc. So I left the house. At dinner time Frieda appeared. 'I have finally done with him. It is all over for ever.' She then went out of the kitchen & began to walk round and round the house in the dark. Suddenly Lawrence appeared and made a kind of horrible blind rush at her and they began to scream and scuffle. He beat her – he beat her to death – her head and face and breast and pulled out her hair. All the while she screamed for Murry to help her. Finally they dashed into the kitchen and round and round the table. I shall never forget how L. looked. He was so white – almost green and he just hit – thumped the big soft woman. Then he fell into one chair and she into another. No one said a word. A silence fell except for Frieda's sobs and sniffs. In a way I almost felt glad that the tension between them was over for ever – and that they had made an end of their 'intimacy'. L. sat staring at the floor, biting his nails. Frieda sobbed. Suddenly, after a long time – about a quarter of an hour – L. looked up and asked Murry a question about French literature. Murry replied. Little by little, the three drew up to the table. Then F. poured herself out some coffee. Then she and L. glided into talk, began to discuss some 'very rich but very good macaroni cheese.' And next day, whipped himself, and far more thoroughly than he had ever beaten Frieda, he was running about taking her up her breakfast to her bed and trimming her a hat.

Am I wrong in not being able to accept these people just as they are – laughing when they laugh and going away from them when they fight? *Tell me.* For I cannot. It seems to me so *degraded* – so horrible to see I cant stand it. And I feel so furiously angry: I *hate* them for it. (263–4)

Even if you knew none of the information provided above, and knew nothing about any of the people involved, you would respond to the brilliant storytelling and the powerful energy of the letter. There is no stopping this description: indeed it is compulsively reiterated. But although it seems to have been written at white-heat, it is also marvellously controlled and expressive. With all its rage and outrage, it has a powerful sense of comedy. It builds up a grotesque scene, relishing every moment, knowing exactly how to master this extreme human material, as a short-story writer knows. It writes the dialogue down as fast and jaggedly as it happened, catching the exact accents and the turns of phrase: 'you little God Almighty', 'I'll give you a dab on the cheek'. It re-enacts the rapid violent incongruous sequences. It picks its words wonderfully as it goes: 'white – almost green . . . hit – thumped'. It has a perfect sense of pace and timing. But it is also extreme, upset and angry, syntactically bordering on loss of control: 'a kind of horrible blind rush', 'round and round . . . round and round', 'He beat her – he beat her to death'.

What is a biographer to do with it? Mansfield's biographers sometimes paraphrase it for the action, using the letter just as data, as Antony Alpers does (205). Or they comment on how Lawrence's violence disturbed and frightened her and affronted her 'rather reserved' nature (Meyers 89); 'Mansfield's love of domestic order and tranquillity was violated by the Lawrences' tempestuous relationship . . . She could bear neither the Lawrences' violent rows nor the marital interaction they were able to establish after a stormy episode' (Smith 101–2). They praise the letter's talent for 'burlesque', or compare it with her stories: 'shows what she could do with her gloves off and no straining for effect'; 'Never has the choreography of a full-blown marital row, with every detail and bit of timing perfectly observed, been so well set out' (Tomalin 148). One biographer, Jeffrey Meyers, laboriously retells the whole letter as an 'operatic' play:

> Act One begins with Lawrence's destruction of Frieda's aesthetic evaluation, leads to her verbal abuse of his assumed omniscience, and ends with his collo-quial threat of punishment and Katherine's exit. Act Two opens with Frieda's absolute judgment . . . which is absolutely unconvincing, and leads to her exit and Lawrence's sudden reappearance as an avenging Fury . . . Act Three reveals a comic reversal of sexual roles, with the defeated male aggressor serving and wooing his lady love. (89–90)

All Mansfield's biographers note that it has the ring of truth: we believe that the events in this letter took place, however much they have been dramatised. If you are Frieda Lawrence or D. H. Lawrence's biographer, though, you might take a different tone with it. Mark Kinkead-Weekes, for instance, draws attention to Murry's weakness in the scene, and to Murry's and Mansfield's inability to understand 'Lawrence's conviction that conflict was part of and necessary for growth' (327). Mansfield's intervention in and manipulation of the friendship between Koteliansky and Lawrence also needs to be considered. At least five biographical points of view are required to encompass this letter. Drama, emotion, comedy, rage, horror, glee: in the face of this performance, no paraphrase or commentary can be adequate. The danger of such a letter is that it altogether swamps and overpowers the biographer, who can only gasp, admire and quote.

III

A different kind of danger arises for biographers when their subject's letters have survived, but cannot be made full use of. The relation between the posthumous archive, its guardians and the biographer is always complex and often perilous.[3] And the accidents, dispersals and obliterations which follow on from any life will fundamentally affect the way that life is turned into narrative. Letters which have come into the public domain long after the life has ended – like Keats's love letters to Fanny Brawne, or the Brownings' 'courtship' letters, or the great Boswell hoard, or Emily Dickinson's fully edited letters – have momentously influenced the telling of the life-story. Letters which have been lost or destroyed (such as Fanny Brawne's to Keats, or most of Edith Wharton's to Henry James, or Cassandra Austen's to her sister Jane) produce dangerous lacunae for the biographer, which it is tempting to fill up with hypotheses and guesswork. How dangerous such lacunae can be is brilliantly illustrated in an anti-biographical story by Edith Wharton, 'The Muse's Tragedy', in which the 'muse' of a famous dead American poet allows his letters to her to be published with suggestive asterisks hinting at a secret passion between them. Later, she admits:

> Those letters I myself prepared for publication; that is to say, I copied them out for the editor, and every now and then I put in a line of asterisks to make it appear that something had been left out. You understand? The asterisks were a sham – *there was nothing to leave out.* (53)

Letters published after the writer's death (as most are, unless you think of Pope or Swift, or Paul Auster and J. M. Coetzee)[4] can overshadow and distort the biography: Philip Larkin's posthumous reputation is a case in point. Where letters do exist, and can be read but cannot be quoted, another danger for the biographer ensues, of simplification and misrepresentation. The American novelist Willa Cather provides a dramatic example of this biographical danger. Willa Cather's selected letters were published in 2013, sixty-six years after her death.[5] In the will she made in 1943, Cather embargoed the publication of her letters – and the dramatisation and adaptation of any of her work 'whether for the purpose of spoken stage presentation or otherwise, motion picture, radio broadcasting, television and rights of mechanical reproduction, whether by means now in existence or which may hereafter be discovered or perfected' (Lee 317). As, in old age, she became more famous and sought-after, and at the same time more alienated from the postwar world, she frequently begged her friends to destroy all her letters, and not to show them to anyone. When the great love of her life, Isabelle McClung, died, in 1938, Cather had all the letters she had written to Isabelle returned to her, and burnt them. She frequently insisted that it was for her work she wanted to be known, not for her life-story, and made strenuous efforts to preserve her privacy. Among early twentieth-century writers, at a time when popular journalism and celebrity culture were on the rise, this was not unusual behaviour. Edith Wharton felt much the same about intrusions into the personal life of the writer, tried hard to get her letters back from her friends, and, after the death of her life's companion, Walter Berry, made away with all the letters to him she could lay hands on. Henry James burnt many of his letters at the bottom of his garden in Rye.

The results of Cather's embargo were, on the whole, unfortunate. Scholars and biographers working on Cather were able to read her letters in libraries and archives, but could not quote them. As a result, her letters were paraphrased over and over again. And paraphrase has done her a long disservice: it is flattening, and often misleading. Her story was told, her secrets were known, but the voice of her letters was not heard. The eventual, long-delayed publication of her letters in 2013, after the death of her last-surviving relative, is leading to a welcome reassessment of her work, her life, and her posthumous reputation.

But for this to have happened, her will has had to be overridden. Surely no justification is needed for this. Sixty-six years after Cather's death, her story and her
secrets are known, her work is securely established in the American canon, her
biography has been written and rewritten. Setting aside her will was the right thing
to do. She is a very great writer, and the more we know about her, the better. To
those who argue that the writer's last commands should be adhered to in perpetuity,
I can only reply that I admire and am grateful to Max Brod and Leonard Woolf for
ignoring the final commands of Kafka and Virginia Woolf that their papers should
be destroyed. And I look forward to a full biography of T. S. Eliot, even though he
forbade it. Writers deserve all the after-lives they can get, if it means they continue
to have readers.

I V

I began this essay with a poet who would have been horrified by such arguments,
and I will end with another, whose letters provide all the justification there can be
for posterity's being able to take possession of a writer's private papers. It was in part
the general dismay at the publication of Keats's love letters in 1878 which provoked
Tennyson's poem 'Old Ghosts'.[6] Now, though, we value Keats's letters precisely for
what Tennyson said the letters of 'old ghosts' could not provide, the vivid presence
of the person 'as he retires into himself and is'. This famous letter of Keats's embodies the paradox of letter writing: that it can be at once a vividly immediate act of
presence and an expression of absence, longing, separation and desire. That is what
makes the letters of 'old ghosts' so seductive and so necessary to biographers: they
make it seem as if the person is there, talking to us; and they remind us that the
person is gone, and cannot be fetched back. Keats's letter, here, enacts, and imagines, exactly what biography wants from letters, an immediate image of the person
who is writing it. Here he is saying goodnight to his brother and sister-in-law, who
were far away in America, and whom he had not seen for nine months. He is writing
from his room in Wentworth Place on 12 March 1819. The letter vividly evokes his
own physical presence while reaching out to its absent recipients.

> . . . the candles are burnt down and I am using the wax taper – which has a long
> snuff on it – the fire is at its last click – I am sitting with my back to it with one
> foot rather askew upon the rug and the other with the heel a little elevated from
> the carpet – I am writing this on the Maid's tragedy which I have read since tea
> with Great pleasure – Besides this volume of Beaumont & Fletcher – there are
> on the tabl[e] two volumes of Chaucer and a new work of Tom Moores call'd
> 'Tom Cribb's memorial to Congress['] – nothing in it – These are trifles – but
> I require nothing so much of you as that you will give me a like description of
> yourselves, however it may be when you are writing to me – Could I see the
> same thing done of any great Man long since dead it would be a great delight:
> as to know in what position Shakespeare sat when he began 'To be or not to
> be' – such thing[s] become interesting from distance of time or place. I hope you

are both now in that sweet sleep which no two beings deserve more [than] you do – I must fancy you so – and please myself in the fancy of speaking a prayer and a blessing over you and your lives – God bless you – I whisper good night in your ears and you will dream of me – (223–4)

Keats, who would be dead, two years later, at the age of twenty-five, on 23 February 1821, here makes himself intensely present to his readers, and to us, whispering his goodnight in our ear. At the same time he seems, even in the act of writing, to see himself in the far distance, an 'old ghost' revisiting us in a dream, a 'great man long since dead'.[7]

NOTES

1. A shorter version of this essay appeared in *Essays in Criticism* 62.4 (October 2012): 461–73.
2. For cogent examples of commentary on this challenge, see Rachel Donadio, 'Literary Letters, Lost in Cyberspace', *New York Times*, 4 September 2005; Chris Fletcher, 'E-manuscripts', *The Author*, Winter 2005; and 'Why the British Library archived 40,000 emails from poet Wendy Cope', Wired.co.uk, 10 May 2011: <http://www.wired.co.uk/news/archive/2011-05/10/british-library-digital-archives> (last accessed 10 June 2014).
3. See Ian Hamilton's *Keepers of the Flame: Literary Estates and the Rise of Biography* (London: Hutchinson, 1992) for a witty and revealing account of such perils.
4. See Paul Auster and J. M. Coetzee, *Here and Now: Letters 2008–2011* (London: Faber and Faber, 2013).
5. *The Selected Letters of Willa Cather*, ed. Andrew Jewell and Janis Stout (New York: Knopf, 2003).
6. For the scandalised reaction to the publication of Keats's letters to Fanny Brawne in 1878, see *The Letters of John Keats*, ed. H. E. Rollins (Cambridge, MA: Harvard University Press, 1958, 1976), pp. 3–8.
7. 'Old Ghosts' was commissioned on 6 January 1877 for the first issue of *Nineteenth Century*, though in the end the issue carried a different poem by Tennyson. It was written originally as a preface to the play *Becket* (begun 1876, printed 1879) and eventually published in Hallam Lord Tennyson's *Alfred Lord Tennyson: A Memoir* (1897: i.xi). There was widespread outrage about the publication of Keats's love letters to Fanny Brawne in 1878. Tennyson had, long before, reacted to the publication of *The Letters and Literary Remains of Keats* by Lord Houghton in 1848, with a sonnet originally called 'To —, After Reading a Life and Letters', though printed in *The Examiner* on 24 March 1849 simply under the title 'Stanzas To —' (and then in *Poems*, 6th edition, 1850). The poem was prefaced by 'Shakespeare's Epitaph', 'Cursed be he that moves my bones', and contained the lines: 'For now the Poet cannot die, / Nor leave his music as of old, / But round him ere he scarce be cold / Begins the scandal and the cry . . . My Shakespeare's curse on clown and knave / Who will not lest his ashes rest!' His son Hallam Tennyson commented: 'My father was indignant that Keats's wild love-letters should have been published; but he said he did not wish the public to think that this poem had been written with any particular reference to [them].' When Keats's letters were sold at auction in 1885 Tennyson wrote a disgusted letter to his old friend Sir Henry Taylor: 'They lately sold at a Public Auction the love-letters of John Keats for more than £500 – the sweat and agony of his heart was worth so much gold. If I could fancy that the dear and noble spirit of you, my old friend, were touched even by the penumbra of such a business, I could only bow my head in shame, and wish that I had never written a line' (Tennyson, *Letters*, vol. 3, ed. Cecil Y. Lang

and Edgar F. Shannon (Oxford: Clarendon Press, 1990), pp. 312–13). Also see *The Poems of Tennyson*, ed. Christopher Ricks, Longman Annotated English Poets series (Harlow: Longman, 1987), vol. 2, p. 297; vol. 3, pp. 17–18. Grateful thanks to Christopher Ricks.

WORKS CITED

Alpers, Antony, *The Life of Katherine Mansfield* (Oxford: Oxford University Press, 1982).

Barrett, Elizabeth, and Robert Browning, *Robert Browning and Elizabeth Barrett: The Courtship Correspondence, 1845–1856*, ed. Daniel Karlin (Oxford: Clarendon Press, 1989).

Cheyette, Bryan, *Muriel Spark* (London: Northcote House, 2000).

Ellis, David, *Literary Lives* (Edinburgh: Edinburgh University Press, 2000).

Foster, R. F., *W. B. Yeats: A Life, I: The Apprentice Mage, 1865–1914* (Princeton: Princeton University Press, 1997).

Gordon, Lyndall, *Virginia Woolf: A Writer's Life* (Oxford: Oxford University Press, 1984).

Heilbrun, Carolyn, *Writing a Woman's Life* (New York: Ballantine Books, 1989).

Johnson, Samuel, *The Idler* 84 (24 November 1759).

Judd, Alan, *Ford Madox Ford* (London: Collins, 1990).

Keats, John, *Letters of John Keats*, ed. Robert Gittings (Oxford: Oxford University Press, 1970).

Kinkead-Weekes, Mark, *D. H. Lawrence: Triumph to Exile 1912–1922* (Cambridge: Cambridge University Press, 1996).

Lee, Hermione, *Willa Cather: A Life Saved Up* (London: Virago, 1989, rev. 2008).

Lessing, Doris, *Under My Skin* (London: HarperCollins, 1994).

Mansfield, Katherine, *The Collected Letters of Katherine Mansfield, 1903–1917*, ed. Vincent O'Sullivan and Margaret Scott (Oxford: Clarendon Press, 1984).

Martin, Robert Bernard, *Tennyson: The Unquiet Heart* (Oxford: Oxford University Press, 1980).

Meyers, Jeffrey, *Katherine Mansfield: A Biography* (London: Hamish Hamilton, 1978).

Mizener, Arthur, *The Saddest Story: A Biography of Ford Madox Ford* (London: Bodley Head, 1972).

Olney, James, 'Some Versions of Memory/Some Versions of Bios: The Ontology of Autobiography', in Olney (ed.), *Autobiography: Essays Theoretical and Practical* (Princeton: Princeton University Press, 1980), pp. 236–67.

Saunders, Max, *Ford Madox Ford: A Dual Life*, vol. 1 (Oxford: Oxford University Press, 1996).

Smith, Angela, *Katherine Mansfield: A Literary Life* (Basingstoke: Palgrave, 2000).

Spark, Muriel, *Curriculum Vitae* (London: Constable, 1992).

Stannard, Martin, *Muriel Spark: The Biography* (London: Weidenfeld & Nicolson, 2009).

Tennyson, Alfred Lord, *The Poems of Tennyson*, ed. Christopher Ricks, Longman Annotated English Poets series (Harlow: Longman, 1969).

Tomalin, Claire, *Katherine Mansfield: A Secret Life* (London: Penguin, 1988).

Waldron, Ann, *Eudora Welty: A Writer's Life* (New York: Doubleday, 1998).

Wharton, Edith, *Edith Wharton: The Collected Short Stories*, ed. R. W. B. Lewis (New York: Scribner's, 1968).

Woolf, Virginia, *The Question of Things Happening, The Letters of Virginia Woolf, 1912–1922*, ed. Nigel Nicholson and Joanne Trautmann Banks (London: Hogarth Press, 1976).

2   Editing Poems in Letters

Daniel Karlin

This chapter is an attempt to think through some of the issues that may arise for editors dealing with poems included in letters, and for editors who have to make sense of their choices. I have had to be selective in my choice of material. First, the poet and the letter writer are the same person; second, the poems are complete; third, they are written or copied within the letter, not sent as an enclosure, whether manuscript or print. These limitations are made for the sake of clarity of focus, not because alternative scenarios are of no editorial interest. To take the first point, Robert Browning's two earliest extant poems, 'The Dance of Death' and 'The First-Born of Egypt', survive only in copies made by Sarah Flower in a letter to her guardian W. J. Fox (Woolford and Karlin 1–4). The context of the letter is interesting, but not textually significant; questions about Sarah Flower's reliability as a copyist, for example, would be the same if the poems existed simply as loose-leaf transcripts. The second point, about the poems being complete, is admittedly a mere convenience; but the third has more substance, because, I shall argue, an author who writes or copies a poem into a letter is doing something different from writing a letter *accompanying* a separate textual entity, whether manuscript or print. Again, the editorial interest of the latter kinds of text is not in question. Poets may send manuscripts, or printed books, to friends or professional correspondents (publishers, editors, reviewers) with significant corrections, revisions and annotations; indeed this is an established category of 'paratext' explored by Gérard Genette.[1] But this procedure is not the same as the one in which the poem is woven into the texture of the letter itself.

A word about methodology. Taking Keats's aphorism to heart ('Nothing ever becomes real till it is experienced'), I begin with a concrete instance of a poem-in-a-letter, and only after a detailed examination of this text, and the different ways in which it has been transmitted, do I discuss in broader terms some of the issues that arise for the theory and practice of literary editing.[2] The particularity of any example may be a hindrance to such general discussion, but it has the advantage of giving readers a real-world problem against which to test their editorial and literary-critical principles.

I A POEM IN A LETTER: THE TEXTUAL TRANSMISSION OF KEATS'S 'WHY DID I LAUGH TONIGHT?'

The reader of Jack Stillinger's rashly titled 'Definitive Edition' of John Keats's poems will come across the following poem on page 323:

Why did I laugh tonight? No voice will tell

    Why did I laugh tonight? No voice will tell:
      No god, no demon of severe response,
    Deigns to reply from heaven or from hell.
      Then to my human heart I turn at once –
5   Heart! Thou and I are here sad and alone;
      Say, wherefore did I laugh? O mortal pain!
    O darkness! darkness! ever must I moan,
      To question heaven and hell and heart in vain!
    Why did I laugh? I know this being's lease –
10   My fancy to its utmost blisses spreads:
    Yet could I on this very midnight cease,
      And the world's gaudy ensigns see in shreds.
    Verse, fame, and beauty are intense indeed,
    But death intenser – death is life's high meed. (Stillinger 1978: 323)[3]

This poem was never published by Keats and first appeared in Milnes's *Life* in 1848. Stillinger's edition has summary textual annotation at the foot of the page and longer notes at the back of the volume. From the footnotes the reader will learn that the text is 'From Keats's letter to George and Georgiana Keats, 14 February–3 March 1819', that the poem was originally untitled ('Heading supplied by editor'), and that the text contains two editorial emendations: the addition of the dash after 'lease' in line 9, and 'death is' in the last line replacing 'Deaths is' in the letter. In the longer note at the back (634) Stillinger gives a more exact dating for the poem: 'before the 19th [of March], when Keats copied the poem in a letter to his brother and sister-in-law'. He also tells us that 'the present text is that of the letter holograph' – an important piece of information, both because many of Keats's letters survive only in the form of transcripts by friends or publishers' scribes, and because it implies (though Stillinger doesn't say so) that the original draft of the poem which Keats copied into his letter is not extant. Stillinger also offers a rationale for his two emendations. I will come to these emendations later in this chapter; first, let us compare Stillinger's text with that of the standard modern edition of Keats's letters, edited by Hyder Edward Rollins for Cambridge University Press in 1958:

    Why did I laugh tonight? No voice will tell:
      No God, no Deamon of severe response
    Deigns to reply from heaven or from Hell. –
      Then to my human heart I turn at once –

Heart! thou and I are here sad and alone;
   Say, wherefore did I laugh? O mortal pain!
O Darkness! Darkness! ever must I moan
   To question Heaven and Hell and Heart in vain!
Why did I laugh? I know this being's lease
   My fancy to its utmost blisses spreads:
Yet could I on this very midnight cease,
   And the world's gaudy ensigns see in shreds.
Verse, fame, and Beauty are intense indeed
But Death intenser – Deaths is Life's high mead.' (Rollins ii, 81)

In his introduction, Rollins states: 'In the texts of all the letters, the spelling, capitalization, and punctuation of the originals are reproduced as exactly as possible' (i, 16). Assuming we trust the editor and the printer, we may take it that what we are looking at is an accurate transcription of Keats's holograph, and it will be immediately obvious that Stillinger's statement that *his* text is that of the holograph needs to be qualified.[4] Stillinger does not reproduce authorial spellings, capitalisation or punctuation in lines 2, 3, 7, 8, 9, 13 and 14 – seventeen changes in all, of which the reader is made aware of two, the others being what editors like to call 'silent' emendations. This is not to imply that Stillinger is behaving in an underhand way. On the contrary, he is more scrupulous than many editors, not just in explaining the textual policy that accounts for the changes he has made, but in providing a complete listing of those changes. However, the reader needs to do some work to get this extra information. The textual policy is outlined in the introduction, under the contentious heading 'Treatment of Accidentals' (16). Stillinger accepts without question the distinction, first propounded by W. W. Greg in his essay 'The Rationale of Copy-Text', between the 'substantives' of a text (basically the words) and the 'accidentals' (punctuation, layout, typography, etc.). Greg himself was aware that the distinction was pragmatic and not absolute – that punctuation, for example, could affect the 'substantive' meaning of a text as much as wording – but he left the door open for editors to treat the two categories with different principles, and Stillinger takes full advantage. On punctuation: 'A great deal of punctuation has been added, especially in poems taken from holographs' (17). On capitalisation: 'Many capitalized nouns and other words have been lowercased, again especially in poems taken from holographs . . . and a few lowercased proper names and personifications have been capitalized' (17). On spellings: 'Misspellings have been corrected, and spellings that were archaic or obsolete in Keats's time have been modernized except where it appears that the old spelling was intended for special effect – humour, atmosphere, or unusual pronunciation' (17). If you want to know how these principles were applied in the case of 'Why did I laugh tonight?' you need to consult Appendix I (708), where Stillinger lists all the changes; and from this list it is possible to reconstruct the unedited holograph text of the poem.

    Whatever you think of Stillinger's general principles, there are some problems with his application of them in this particular text. Take the emendation in line 9

– the addition of the dash after 'lease'. In his longer textual note at the back of the volume, Stillinger remarks:

> The letter holograph's lack of punctuation here should not be considered a substantive matter. While it is possible to construe 9–10 without punctuation ('I know that my fancy spreads this being's lease to its [fancy's] utmost blisses'), Keats rarely wrote such convoluted sentences, and it is much more likely that he was simply using the line ending itself as punctuation. (634)

This statement has to be understood in the light of the general comment in the introduction: 'Keats frequently omitted punctuation at the end of the line, and in some of the copy-text MSS he used almost no punctuation at all' (17). But the last part of that sentence, which is trying to reinforce a particular observation with a larger, vaguer formula, does not in fact apply to 'Why did I laugh tonight?', which has a lot of authorial punctuation, some of it quite expressive (such as the dash after the full stop at the end of line 3, which Stillinger removes, though it is a perfectly normal 'period' feature). We may deduce that Stillinger identified three instances where he thought Keats was 'simply using the line ending itself as punctuation' – lines 2, 9 and 13 – but he does not comment on his addition of commas in lines 2 and 13, presumably because they aren't 'substantive', whereas the change in line 9 is prompted by the need to prevent Keats from appearing to write a 'convoluted sentence'. Without a dash, in other words, readers might misconstrue the syntax. The imposition of meaning here by the editor is licensed by Stillinger's confident assertions about Keats's orthography and literary style.

The treatment of capitalisation and spelling raises similar issues. Again, Stillinger relies on a general observation – 'Keats capitalized ordinary nouns and even adjectives and verbs seemingly at random' (17) – to justify changes in a text where this general observation, even if true, does not apply. There are no capitalised adjectives and verbs in the holograph, but there *is* evidence that Keats was thinking about capitalisation as a 'substantive' practice – in the equivalence of 'God' and 'Deamon' in line 2, for example, or the contrast between the lower-case 'human heart' in line 4 and the upper-case sequence 'Heaven and Hell and Heart' in line 8.[5] Admittedly there is inconsistency in the poem – the lower-case 'heaven' in line 3, and 'fame' in line 13 – but a case could be made for emending in the opposite direction to Stillinger (i.e. capitalising these nouns on the basis that Keats clearly intended to mark out personified or abstract nouns with capitals in this poem). The difference this makes to the texture of the poem becomes palpable – 'substantive', indeed – in the diminution of 'Death' and 'Life' to 'death' and 'life' in the last line. By curtailing the rhetorical flourish of this line, which may not be appealing but is thoroughly Keatsian, Stillinger has exercised his literary judgement just as plainly as in the case of the dash added to line 9.

What of the emendation of 'Deaths is' to 'death is' in the last line? Stillinger explains his decision as follows:

> The present editor takes the letter reading to be a slip of the pen (the final 's' in 'Deaths' anticipating the sound of the next word, 'is'), but Walter H. Evert,

Aesthetic and Myth in the Poetry of Keats (Princeton, 1965), pp. 291–292n., interprets the first word as an intended possessive, 'Death's' (with the inverted sense 'life's high meed is death's,' i.e. is ultimately claimed by death). (634)

Leaving aside the change in capitalisation, the emendation of 'Deaths' to 'death' has been adopted in most editions of Keats's poems (with one significant exception), and it also appears as a silent emendation in some editions of his letters.[6] It is honourable of Stillinger to cite Evert's ingenious reading, and in this instance the point about 'convoluted' syntax would occur to most readers, not as a feature of Keats's writing but as a general feature of English style, where the proximity of two possessives (grinding against each other, as it were) is extremely rare.[7] Here the editor's literary judgement rests on something akin to common ground.

One final point on the emendation of the holograph of this poem. All editions of the poems that I have seen silently remove the speech marks at the end of line 14, and while editors of the letters tend to leave them in, they do so without comment. You can see why editors of the poems might find the speech marks inconvenient, since if Keats intended them to mark the end of an utterance, where does that utterance begin? The 'I' of the poem turns to address his heart in line 5, but there are no speech marks before 'Heart!', and even if there were that speech would end in the following line: '"Heart! Thou and I are here sad and alone; / Say, wherefore did I laugh?"' Perhaps there should be speech marks before 'Verse' in line 13, making the closing couplet of the sonnet into a gnomic utterance like that 'spoken' by the Grecian Urn (which has its own problematic status).[8] The couplet might then be thought of as the answer to the question 'Why did I laugh tonight?' – an answer given by neither Heaven nor Hell, and not even by the poet's own 'heart', but which is arrived at by the process of reflection. Keats reacts against the despair, the dead end of the octave ('To question Heaven and Hell and Heart in vain!'), and finds a way *out* of the impasse in the sestet. Although the structure of the sonnet is 'English' (three quatrains rhyming abab, with closing couplet), its movement of thought is 'Italian' (octave/sestet, with the volta in line 9). Stillinger's emendation of line 9 is especially damaging because it overrides this formal pattern.

So far, the fact that we know this poem because Keats copied it into a letter might seem a merely contingent aspect of its textual history. Wouldn't the debate over its editorial treatment be the same if it existed simply as a loose-leaf MS? But the answer is not so clear-cut. As we shall see, there are different ways of including poems in letters, and in this case Keats copied the text *as he wrote the letter*, so that it belongs integrally to the process of composition of another text. This raises the possibility that his habitual practice as a letter writer influenced his transcription of his own verse – for example, by haste, since we know that Keats wrote rapidly and that the pressure of his emotional state is graphically visible in his handwriting.[9] Whether or not the author behaved differently because he was in 'epistolary mode', editors of the letters certainly have. They are less anxious about clarifying his meaning or 'intention' (a concept to which I will return). Rollins leaves the text of the poem virtually untouched; either he doesn't think that the lack of punctuation at the end of lines is problematic, or he doesn't see it as his business to correct it. He records a stray 'P' at the start of the poem, and gives 'Death' as a variant for 'Deaths' in the last line, not as his own conjecture but as the reading in the then-standard edition of the poems by H. W. Garrod.[10] Gittings prints 'Deaths' without comment; presumably he thinks that most readers will conclude that 'Deaths is Life's high mead' doesn't make sense, and will carry out their own unaided emendations. Readers of printed books in earlier historical periods had to do this as a matter of course; as with the first days of the motor car, to read a book in the sixteenth or seventeenth century was to engage in forward progress interspersed with running repairs. And readers of private correspondence – whether handwritten, or typed on a computer keyboard, or texted on a mobile phone – are still obliged to make sense out of the sender's defective, or idiosyncratic, spelling and grammar. In this sense editors of letters are offering readers a more 'authentic' experience by preserving the look of the holograph; we retain a traditional belief that a writer's 'character' (personality) is embodied in the 'characters' (graphic signs) of their handwriting.[11]

The reader's encounter with this poem will be shaped, therefore, by an editorial judgement as to what kind of experience should be offered. Editors of Keats's poems take 'Why did I laugh tonight?' *as* a poem, placing it alongside others, whether in a chronological sequence or according to any other system of classification. The primary identity of the text, and the editor's primary loyalty, is formal and generic. Editors of the letters, on the other hand, approach the poem as part of a larger entity, and their loyalty is to the *epistolary* genre. This distinction can be clearly seen in what editors have done with Keats's letter to J. H. Reynolds of 25 March 1818, which begins in verse and concludes with prose. Editions of Keats's letters print the whole text, verse and prose, as a letter to this correspondent, using whatever standard heading they employ. In most editions of Keats's poems, by contrast, you will find a *poem* entitled 'To J. H. Reynolds Esq.', though this is not in fact a title but merely a note of the addressee by the lawyer's clerk who copied it and whose transcript is the only extant MS.[12] Although the prose portion of the letter follows 'naturally' and wittily from the last phrase of the verse ('here follows prose', quoting Malvolio as he reads the forged letter in *Twelfth Night*, II, v, 142), it is omitted from the main text, and relegated to the notes.[13] The forced segregation of verse from prose is very striking here; it is as though the poem has to be kept pure from generic contamination, even where verse and prose are in intimate alliance.[14] But this distinction raises issues which go beyond that of the editorial treatment of the text itself. The context of the letter may govern how the poem is read in a wider, interpretive sense. In the case of 'Why did I laugh tonight?' it may be argued that this context is, or ought to be, the primary object of attention. The poem belongs with the letter where it occurs; to detach it from this environment is to create an artificial text, whose 'meaning' has been arbitrarily transformed.

II 'WHY DID I LAUGH TONIGHT?': CONTEXTUAL ISSUES

Keats's mood in the spring of 1819 was volatile. He was still deeply affected by the death of his younger brother Tom the previous December, and furious about the hoax that had been practised on Tom by their friend Charles Wells, who had forged love letters from a pretended admirer of Tom signing herself 'Amena' (Gittings 1971: 355, 440). He was anxious for news of George and Georgiana; the letter begins on 14 February with a question – 'How is it we have not heard from you from the Settlement yet?' – which by the end (3 May) had not yet been answered. His poetic career was in the balance: *Endymion* had failed, and though he was determined not to be crushed by the infamous review in the *Quarterly* which had appeared in September 1818, he knew that he faced a long struggle against the ignorance and prejudice of his critics, if not a shorter one against his own body. In the meantime his domestic and financial circumstances were precarious, and his zest for friendship, his relish for the energy of urban life, alternated with moods of blank lethargy and alienation. His letter to George and Georgiana reflects his restlessness, his abrupt changes of mood and focus, his leaps and bounds and reversals. All Keats's friends worried for him; George and Georgiana were no exception, and Keats knew it. 'Why did I laugh tonight?' is introduced in the letter by way of a response to a particular kind of anxiety that he associated with his older brother and his wife, who, though younger than Keats himself, had through marriage acquired matronly authority:

> I am ever affraid that your anxiety for me will lead you to fear for the violence of my temper continually smothered down: for that reason I did not intend to have sent you the following sonnet – but look over the two last pages and ask yourselves whether I have not that in me which will well bear the buffets of the world. It will be the best comment on my sonnet; it will show you that it was written with no Agony but that of ignorance; with no thirst of anything but knowledge when pushed to the point though the first steps to it were throug[h] my human passions – they went away, and I wrote with my Mind – and perhaps I must confess a little bit of my heart – (Rollins ii, 81)

The poem follows; Keats then adds: 'I went to <bead> bed, and enjoyed an uninterrupted sleep – Sane I went to bed and sane I arose' (82).[15] This passage of the letter comes in a section begun on 17 March (around 'two pages earlier') and begins with a very literal 'buffet': 'Yesterday I got a black eye' (78; from a cricket ball). He took it philosophically: 'we must e{a}t a peck before we die' (78). Immediately, without warning, he changes tack: 'This morning I am in a sort of temper indolent and supremely careless.' This begins a famous passage, one of the set pieces of the letters, which announces the 'Ode on Indolence' and tells us incidentally that Keats has been looking at sculpted Greek vases. Ever the medical man, he attributes this mood to 'my having slumbered till nearly eleven and weakened the animal fibre all over me to a delightful sensation about three degrees on this side of faintness' (78), and the passage ends: 'This is the only happiness; and is a rare instance of advantage in the body overpowering the Mind' (79). At this point the tone changes again; but this time it is because something has happened between the end of one sentence and the beginning of the next, as though Keats were 'writing to the moment' in an epistolary novel:

... overpowering the Mind. I have this moment received a note from Haslam in which he expects the death of his Father who has been for some time in a state of insensibility – his mother he says bears up very well – I shall go to twon tommorrow to see him. This is the world – thus we cannot expect to give way many hours to pleasure – Circumstances are like Clouds continually gathering and bursting – While we are laughing the seed of some trouble is put into <he> the wide arable land of events – while we are laughing it sprouts is grows and suddenly bears a poison fruit which we must pluck – Even so we have leisure to reason on the misfortunes of our friends; our own touch us too nearly for words. (79)[16]

When Keats says that 'we cannot expect to give way many hours to pleasure', it seems clear that he is referring to the kind of pleasure he has just been describing, the pleasure of indolence and reverie, shockingly interrupted by the reminder of mortality and by the bleak clichés with which we confront it ('his mother he says bears up very well'). But the general reflection that follows applies not to this kind of pleasure but to something more hollow, associated with laughter. 'While we are laughing . . . while we are laughing': his mind has changed tack; he is not thinking of the solitary pleasure of contemplation, but of the social pleasure of laughter. 'Why did I laugh tonight?' Such laughter is shared, yet it leaves the speaker of the poem 'sad and alone'. If we look back over the days leading up to 19 March, when Keats copied the poem for George and Georgiana, we can identify a number of social occasions, notably the one which Keats anticipates on 13 March ('We are to have a party this evening – The Davenports from Church row' (76)), and which he describes on 17 March:

On sunday I went to Davenports' were I dined – and had a nap. I cannot bare a day anhilated in that manner – there is a great deal of difference between an easy and an uneasy indolence – An indolent day – fill'd with speculations even of an unpleasant colour – is bearable and even pleasant alone – when one's thoughts cannot find out any th[i]ng better in the world; and experience has told us that locomotion is no change: but to have nothing to do, and to be surrounded with unpleasant human identities; who press upon one just enough to prevent one getting into a lazy position; and not enough to interest or rouse one; is a capital punishment of a capital crime: for is not giving up, through goodnature, one's time to people who have no light and shade a capital crime? Yet what can I do? – they have been very kind and attentive to me. I do not know what I did on monday – nothing – nothing – nothing – I wish this was any thing extraordinary. (77)[17]

I think that 'Why did I laugh tonight?' remembers this evening party with its aftermath of resentment and self-loathing. Enforced participation in vacuous social rituals is accompanied by a helpless sense of obligation ('Yet what can I do? – they have been very kind and attentive to me'), requiring 'the violence of my temperament' to be 'continually smothered down'. It bursts out here, of course: 'an[ni]hilated in

that manner . . . unpleasant human identities; who press upon one . . . capital punishment of a capital crime . . . nothing – nothing – nothing'; but the process Keats
describes leading up to the composition of the poem is not yet complete. '[T]he first
steps to it were through my human passions – they went away, and I wrote with my
Mind – and perhaps I must confess a little bit of my heart.' The *thoughtfulness* which
governs the second part of the sonnet is evident in the long passage which follows
Keats's account of how he received the news of Haslam's imminent bereavement,
which reflects on the impossibility of 'a complete disinterestedness of Mind', on the
need to accept the human reality of that fact, and indeed to accept that if charity
were a universal law of nature, nature itself would implode: 'the Hawk would loose
his Breakfast of Robins and the Robin his of Worms' (79).[18] Men, like animals, prey
on others in order to exist, and their sexual life is no different: 'The Hawk wants a
Mate, so does the Man – look at them both they set about it and procure on[e] in
the same manner' (79). But this is only one view of the matter; Keats remembers a
line from Wordsworth's 'The Old Cumberland Beggar', 'we have all of us one human
heart'; the poet who knows that human beings are predators also knows that 'there
is an ellectric fire in human nature tending to purify – so that among these human
creature[s] there is continually some birth of new heroism' (80).[19] The use of 'continually' answers its earlier use ('Circumstances are like Clouds continually gathering and bursting'), and the 'birth of new heroism' is itself a benign form of fertility,
the reverse of the 'seed' that 'bears a poison fruit'. Human life may not, after all, be
subject to brutal contingency; yet that perspective is itself contingent, provisional:
'I am however young writing at random – straining at particles of light in the midst
of a great darkness – without knowing the bearing of any one assertion of any one
opinion' (80). This 'straining at particles of light in . . . a great darkness' is different
from the 'mortal pain' of 'Why did I laugh tonight?' with its anguished appeal: 'O
Darkness! Darkness! ever must I moan / To question Heaven and Hell and Heart in
vain!' Or rather (as Keats says) it is 'the best comment on my sonnet'; what enables
the poet to 'bear the buffets of the world' is the effort to understand the world, even
if that effort is flawed and misguided. The *attempt* to understand is an action, a form
of struggle, and the energy of that struggle is akin to poetry; the achievement of
understanding itself would be something abstract, poised, passionless, which Keats
identifies with 'philosophy'. He knows that he ought to prefer the latter to the
former, but he is not setting up as a philosopher; instead he steps back (as he often
does) to Milton, not to claim equality but to measure difference, quoting *A Mask*
with a moving blend of assurance and modesty:

> Give me this credit – Do you not think I strive – to know myself? Give me this
> credit – and you will not think that on my own accou[n]t I repeat Milton's lines
>> 'How charming is divine Philosophy
>> Not harsh and crabbed as dull fools suppose
>> But musical as is Apollo's lute' –
> No – no for myself – feeling grateful as I do to have got into a state of mind to
> relish them properly – Nothing ever becomes real till it is experienced – Even
> a Proverb is no proverb to you till your Life has illustrated it – I am ever afraid

that your anxiety for me will lead you to fear for the violence of my temperament continually smothered down . . . (81)[20]

Here, then, we reach the point at which Keats introduces his poem. I would offer the
following as a kind of summary paraphrase of the 'message' he is sending George and
Georgiana: I do not pretend to be a true philosopher, with a balanced and harmoni-
ous view of the world, and the ability to control my own intellectual and emotional
responses; that state is not real to me yet; but I have got to the point where I can
value it over the state I am actually in; this will reassure you that the anguish contained in the poem I am sending you is not despairing (and possibly suicidal); 'Death
is Life's high meed' is the conclusion of a philosopher (even though its very rhetorical excess proves I remain a poet). This cannot claim to be a definitive reading; the
point is that the poem is associated with thoughts and feelings which Keats does not
seek to conceal, but which, on the contrary, he deliberately offers as an interpretative guide. How should editors of the poem respond?

III REFLECTIONS ON THEORY AND PRACTICE

I have featured 'Why did I laugh tonight?' in classes on editorial method at undergraduate and MA level for a number of years. I am grateful to students at Boston
University, the University of Sheffield and the University of Bristol who have all
wrestled with the problem of how to present the poem in editions of Keats's letters,
or poems, or both.[21] The local aspects of this problem – those associated with
Romantic letter writing in general, and Keats's practice in particular – have been
part of this debate, as has the question of whether the text of a poem included in a
letter should be governed by the same editorial principles that apply to the letter, or
whether it has a different status, and, if so, how that difference should be signalled
to the reader. That last phrase, 'the reader', has itself been a major point of contention, since it may be claimed that the reader of Keats's letters needs and expects
something different from a reader of his poems, and that there is in fact a divided
authority in the production of the text itself which demands the application of different editorial principles.

The issue of divided authority goes further if we remember that the original reader
of a letter is its addressee – that unlike most works of art, a letter has no 'public'.
When Emily Dickinson called her poems 'my letter to the World' she was formu-
lating one of her most acute paradoxes, and she herself was a virtuoso exponent
of the art of addressing poems in letters (or in many cases as letters) to particular
correspondents.[22] The question of 'authorial intention' becomes even more vexed
than usual here, as the case of 'Why did I laugh tonight?' makes acutely clear.
Those students who were persuaded that the context of the poem was essential to
its meaning wanted to argue that it should always be presented within that context,
some going so far as to argue that the 'poem' had no separate existence outside the
letter, and that the 'text' we should be editing was a hybrid, whose meaning resided
precisely in the interplay of verse and prose elements. Others pointed out, first, that

Keats had composed the poem with no such intention; second, that even if it now forms part of a hybrid text, this text was created with a particular pair of readers in mind: other readers are not concerned in a personal, private transaction between Keats and his brother and sister-in-law. It is their anxiety he is trying to assuage, not ours. That he makes use of his poem to 'perform' his sanity ('Sane I went to bed and sane I arose') may be an interesting biographical fact, but it gives neither him, as author, nor any subsequent editor a lien on the poem's meaning. Some students then turned the argument on its head: to decontextualise the poem, to read it *outside* the frame of the letter, is to liberate it from its author's attempt to compel us, as proxies for George and Georgiana, to participate in his self-interested demonstration. Not only is it legitimate to include the poem in a volume of poetry by Keats, but it would be better to give only the barest, most neutral indication of its provenance. These students thoroughly approved of Stillinger's method, and only thought he had not gone far enough; they disapproved of annotated editions of the poems (such as Allott or Barnard), which cited some of the letter in the notes, as a form of coercion on their interpretative freedom. Others again pointed out that, pushed to its extreme, this argument wouldn't hold: the decision to decontextualise the poem was as coercive as its opposite. In the end most students took the pragmatic view that an edition of the poems might treat the text differently from an edition of the letters, and that the degree of difference was a matter for editorial judgement which could not be regulated by fixed principles.[23] But students also recognised that the testing of such principles is itself a necessary stimulus to editorial method.

When it came to widening the scope of the debate, two issues stood out. The first related to the taxonomy of 'poems in letters'. 'Why did I laugh tonight?' is an unpublished poem, which we possess because Keats copied it into his letter; but it is not the only poem he copied, and not the only kind of poem. There are versions of poems which were published in his lifetime, either in periodicals or in volume form ('La Belle Dame sans Merci', 'As Hermes once took to his feathers light', 'Ode to Psyche'), and others for which we have several manuscript witnesses: 'To Sleep' ('O soft embalmer of the still midnight'), two sonnets 'On Fame' ('Fame, like a wayward girl, will still be coy' and 'How fever'd is the man who cannot look') and one on the sonnet form itself ('If by dull rhymes our English must be chain'd'). Then there are verses improvised in the course of the letter itself: 'When they were come unto the Faery's Court' and a pseudo-Spenserian skit on Charles Brown ('He is to weet a melancholy Carle'). All these kinds are found in other letters by Keats, both to George and Georgiana and to other correspondents.[24] They are linked by the fact that they are all *in* the letter – that is, they do not *accompany* it – but they do not all have the same motive for being there.[25] The miscellaneous nature of the poems Keats chose to include suggests that authorial intention is a plural and indeed provisional concept. 'Why did I laugh tonight?' serves a particular purpose in his relationship with George and Georgiana, but the motive for including other poems is different, and in some cases obscure: 'La Belle Dame sans Merci', for example, appears abruptly at the start of the portion of the letter written on 21 April, and is followed by a defensively 'humorous' comment, as though Keats regretted exposing himself.[26]

The second major issue, which applies only to some of the poems included in the letter, is that of divided authority. This does not affect the poems that Keats impro-vised in the course of writing – such poems pose editorial challenges of their own, but no other text lies behind or beyond them (assuming they were not subsequently copied and revised by their author). A poem *copied* into a letter, even if it is the only extant witness to the text (as is the case with 'Why did I laugh tonight?'), is open to speculation as to what might have happened in the copying process; as we have seen, such speculation has significantly altered the transmission of the text of this poem. Then there are poems which do exist in more than one version, so that the text of the poem-in-the-letter is in competition, so to speak, with rival texts. In the case of 'As Hermes once took to his feathers light', Stillinger identifies two manu-scripts, and one printed text, which, along with the text in the letter, 'have claims to be the basis for a standard text'. Of these four, only one – the letter text – is Keats's holograph. The others all derive from a manuscript which is not extant. Stillinger prefers one of them – a transcript by Charles Brown – and states candidly that he does so 'arbitrarily' (1978: 636). But such decisions are never truly arbitrary. Behind Stillinger's choice, I think, lies an assumption that the manuscript of a *poem*, even when that manuscript has to be conjecturally reconstructed, trumps the manuscript of a *letter*, even when that manuscript is extant.[27] In turn that assumption belongs to a wider notion, current in Keats's time and still active in our own, that poems rank higher on the scale than letters, since letters are at best seen as a sort of hybrid or sub-genre.[28] But I do not want to fall into the opposite trap; rather I want to suggest that letter and poem constitute different kinds of 'witness', and that the real edito-rial problem is one we make for ourselves by positing a single, and singular, identity for the poem. As with 'Why did I laugh tonight?', the experience of reading 'As Hermes once took to his feathers light' in Keats's letter is different from reading it in a volume of his poems – different enough to make the poem itself different, not just textually but in terms of how it 'signifies'.[29] If we admit this, the question of how to edit the poem changes shape, but it does so in ways that cause difficulties of their own.

Breaking the authority of the single text is an attractive idea. It is often com-bined with the seductive potential of electronic editions: why not create multiple texts, in a virtual 'space' where the reader can browse without restriction and with minimal editorial interference? In the case of Keats's poems, a single platform could offer us the choice of being readers of the letters, or of the poems in chronological sequence, or of the poems in published and unpublished groups; we could puzzle over manuscripts, or look at images of the original printed editions; we could choose plain texts, or ones fully annotated and linked to further scholarly and critical inter-pretation. We need not think of ourselves as bereft of guidance, or of the 'editor' as having shirked his or her responsibility; if we want to be told what to think, we can always click on that option.

We should not, therefore, seek to *resolve* the problem of divided authority, but to *dissolve* it. But the problem won't go away so easily. 'Spatialising' the different versions of a text (so that they are arranged not in a hierarchy but in adjacent compartments) inevitably pluralises both author and reader, and privileges that very fact. It posits the reader's knowledge of a literary work as being, like the work itself, intrinsically mobile, changeable, multifaceted. The more we believe this, the harder it is to acknowledge that it is, after all, only a belief. As an editor I would rather present a text as a singular form, unconstrained by the need to give its other forms equal play. In stating this preference, however (which has been the basis of my own editorial practice over many years), I am conscious of a mental reservation. I do think that the reader who encounters 'Why did I laugh tonight?' in an edition of Keats's poems, as opposed to an edition of his letters, is getting a lesser experience, and that the poem is in some sense a diminished thing in its 'plain' form. This, too, springs from an underlying assumption – one which is not, I suspect, as unusual as 'objective' scholars like to think. The issue of *value* exercises a powerful influence on editorial principle, though this influence is often, like that of an occluded star, detectable only in an argument's eccentric orbit.

NOTES

1. See the section on 'Correspondence' in chapter 14 of Genette's *Paratexts*, 'The Private Epitext'.
2. For Keats's phrase, see below.
3. To be fair to Stillinger, the tag 'definitive' was probably the work of the publisher. It appears on the jacket (and slip-case) but not within the book itself.
4. The issue of trust is not a trivial one. In old-spelling editions where readers do not have access to the original manuscript or printing, there is no way of telling whether a variant spelling is present in the original text, or is in fact the editor's mistranscription or a printer's error. In the case of Keats's letters, editors often resort to general remarks about his 'habitual' orthography, but these may not cover every case; just because Keats often omitted the letter 'r' from words, and was especially prone to write 'you' for 'your' (Rollins i, 17), it doesn't mean that he *invariably* did so. Rollins states that 'errors that resemble those of typewriting, as "firends" and "perpaps", are left unchanged, but are usually commented on' (18), without seeming troubled by the airiness of 'usually'. As far as 'Why did I laugh tonight?' is concerned, Rollins's text is supported by Robert Gittings's edition for Oxford University Press (1970: 231). In 2002 OUP reissued the volume for Oxford World's Classics, in an edition revised by Jon Mee; the poem appears on page 215. Quotations from Gittings are to the original edition.
5. Stillinger does not comment on the emendation of 'Deamon' in line 2 to 'Demon'; this is not one of Keats's habitual spellings – he uses 'demon' earlier in the same letter (Rollins ii, 76) – and it is possible that he had at the back of his mind the term 'daemon', current in poetry of the period and recently used by Leigh Hunt in the preface to *Foliage: Or Poems Original and Translated* (1818): 'taking the Supreme Being for a Daemon'.
6. The exception is Miriam Allott's Longman edition, which has 'But Death's intenser – Death is Life's high meed' (488–9). Allott's copy-text is the letter, but the reading 'Deaths' is not recorded in the notes, whereas the reading 'Death intenser' in Milnes is recorded as a variant; the unwary reader might assume that Milnes is misprinted and that Allott's text is the correct transcription of the holograph. The lack of a note means that Allott offers no rationale for her decision; she probably thought Keats *intended* to write 'But Death's intenser – Death is Life's high meed' but inadvertently transposed 'Deaths' and 'Death' (as well as omitting the apostrophe). 'Deaths' is silently emended to 'Death' in Maurice Buxton Forman's edition of the letters (318).
7. Gerard Manley Hopkins (perhaps not surprisingly) has some deliberate instances, e.g. the

final line of *The Wreck of the Deutschland*: 'Our hearts' charity's hearth's fire, our thoughts' chivalry's throng's Lord'.

8. The quotation marks around the phrase 'Beauty is Truth, Truth Beauty' appear in the first book edition of the poem (*Lamia, Isabella, The Eve of St. Agnes, and Other Poems*, 1820) but do not appear in the only extant MS deriving from Keats's holograph (a transcript by Charles Brown) or in the first printing (*Annals of the Fine Arts* 4 (January 1820): 638–9). See Stillinger 1978: 373 and 653–4, and Stillinger 1974: 245–7. John Barnard, in his Penguin Classics edition of the poems, places the quotation marks around the whole of the last two lines, and has a useful summary of the critical debate (676–7).

9. See Rollins i, 17; also Gittings 1970: xx–xxi.

10. Garrod's edition was first published in 1939. A second edition appeared in 1958, the same year as Rollins's edition of the letters. I comment on Garrod's classification of the poems found in the letter to George and Georgiana below.

11. This principle may be extended – by courtesy, so to speak – to other kinds of text embedded in the letters themselves. For example, Keats copied two extracts from Hazlitt's *A Letter to William Gifford Esq.* (1819) into his letter to George and Georgiana, which are reproduced verbatim in Rollins (ii, 71–3, 74–6). Rollins indicates some of Keats's transcription errors in his footnotes; Gittings (1970: 221–3, 224–6) has only one note pointing out that a repeated phrase is 'due to Keats's hasty copying' (225). I discuss below a significant exception to this rule of respecting the textual integrity of poems within letters, in the case of 'hybrid' editions containing both kinds of text.

12. For the poem's textual history, see Stillinger 1974: 180–1. Stillinger himself, here and in his later edition (1978: 241), properly gives the poem's title as its first line, 'Dear Reynolds, as last night I lay in bed'.

13. All quotations from Shakespeare are from *The Riverside Shakespeare*.

14. A rare exception is John Barnard's treatment of 'O thou whose face hath felt the Winter's wind' (228). This poem occurs in a letter to J. H. Reynolds of 19 February 1818, in which Keats imagines a thrush speaking to him: 'I had no Idea but of the Morning and the Thrush said I was right – seeming to say – / "O thou whose face hath felt the Winter's wind . . ."' (Rollins ii, 233). The whole poem is enclosed in quotation marks, omitted by most editors of the poem who refer to the letter only in a note, if at all; Barnard, however, respects the syntactical joining of prose to verse by prefacing the poem with the portion of the letter I have reproduced above (albeit in square brackets and smaller type), and preserving the quotation marks at the beginning and end, so that it is clear the poem is a dramatic utterance.

15. Note that Keats corrects 'bead' to 'bed' but leaves 'Deamon' in line 2 of the poem.

16. Rollins notes 'twon' for 'town' and 'is grows' for 'it grows', but leaves 'tommorrow' without remark.

17. Rollins notes 'were' for 'where' and 'anhilated' for 'annihilated', but not the lower-case spelling of days of the week, or 'bare' for 'bear'.

18. Compare the vision of ruthless predation in 'Dear Reynolds, as last night I lay in bed': 'the hawk at pounce, / The gentle Robin, like a pard or ounce, / Ravening a worm' (ll. 103–5). In the discussion that follows I have had to be selective; the passage as a whole is too long and complex to deal with here in full. In particular I have omitted Keats's comments on Jesus as a model of pure 'disinterestedness', and I have not dealt fully with his reflections on his own status as an observer of human life, rather than a participant.

19. Keats slightly misquotes the line from Wordsworth, omitting 'of us'.

20. I think the second 'no' in 'No – no for myself' is a slip for 'not', as suggested by Buxton Forman (318). Note also the third occurrence of 'continually', this time associated with a psychological condition; the term 'smothered' leads back to *King Lear*, to the violence of Lear's 'temperament' and his attempts to repress it: 'O how this mother swells up toward my heart! / *Hysterica passio*, down, thou climbing sorrow!' (II, iv, 56–7).

21. Students looked at a variety of editions and only one editorial choice was rejected with near unanimity – that of editors of volumes containing both poems and letters who, when it comes to the poems included in letters, refer the reader to the text printed in the poetry section of the book. Elizabeth Cook, for example, in the Oxford World's Classics volume, prints 'Why did I laugh tonight?' as a separate poem (268–9), and in the letter of 14 February to 3 May 1819 has:

> . . . they went away, and I wrote with my Mind – and perhaps I must confess a little bit of my heart –
> ['*Why did I laugh tonight? No voice will tell' follows*]
> I went to bed, and enjoyed an uninterrupted sleep . . . (465)

Jeffrey N. Cox in the Norton Critical Edition similarly prints the poem separately and inserts a cross-reference in the letter (323, 333). Students did not need prompting to find this practice editorially indefensible.

22. 'This is my letter to the World' is poem no. 519 in the standard modern text (Franklin i, 527–8).

23. For example, how much of the letter should be cited? When Keats tells George and Georgiana to 'look over the two last pages' in order to understand the context of 'Why did I laugh tonight?' (Rollins ii, 81), should that determine what we, as readers, need to see?

24. Altogether Keats composed, or copied, forty poems or extracts from poems into his letters between November 1817 and September 1819; thirty-two are complete poems, eight are extracts; only one ('Old Meg she was a gypsey') is copied twice. Editors who follow any policy other than that of printing the poems in chronological order have to classify them, resulting in some odd decisions: Garrod, for example, places one of the poems which Keats composed impromptu in the letter to George and Georgiana ('When they were come unto the Faery's Court') in a section at the back of the book called 'Trivia', where it is printed in smaller type (563–6); but the Spenserian skit on Charles Brown ('He is to weet a melancholy Carle') is given the dignity of appearing in the main text.

25. At the start of the letter Keats refers to writing 'a little Poem call'd 'St Agnes Eve' – which you shall have as it is when I have finished the blank part of the rest for you' (meaning that he would use up some of the spare paper at the end of the poem MS in writing a letter to them) but there is no indication that this was in fact done (Rollins ii, 58–9).

26. Immediately following the last words of the poem, and referring to the lines 'And there I shut her wild wild eyes / With kisses four', Keats says: 'Why four kisses – you will say – why four because I wish to restrain the headlong impetuosity of my Muse – she would have fain said "score" without hurting the rhyme – but we must temper the Imagination as the Critics say with Judgment' (Rollins ii, 97).

27. Allott and Barnard print the letter text; Cook and Cox use the text published in *The Indicator* (28 June 1820: 304).

28. It might be thought that Keats has succeeded in challenging this hierarchy; he belongs to a small group of poets (including Emily Dickinson, Gerard Manley Hopkins and Elizabeth Bishop) whose letters can claim equal status with their poetry. But editorial practice suggests that poetry still retains its edge of cultural value.

29. These two aspects come together in line 7 where the reader of the letter is given access to the 'moment' of poetry in a way that no annotated edition can supply. The poet's 'idle spright' flees, in his dream, 'Not to pure Ida with its snow <clad> cold skies', while in Stillinger's edition this line is simply 'Not to pure Ida with its snow-cold skies'. In fact Stillinger (inadvertently, I think) does not even record the variant 'snow clad' in his notes.

WORKS CITED

Allott, Miriam (ed.), *The Poems of John Keats*, Longman Annotated English Poets series (Harlow: Longman, 1970).

Barnard, John (ed.), *John Keats: The Complete Poems*, 3rd edn (London: Penguin Classics, 2006 [1977]).

Buxton Forman, Maurice (ed.), *The Letters of John Keats*, 2nd edn (Oxford: Oxford University Press, 1935).

Cook, Elizabeth (ed.), *John Keats: The Major Works*, Oxford World's Classics series (Oxford: Oxford University Press, 2001). Originally published in the Oxford Authors series, 1990.

Cox, Jeffrey N. (ed.), *Keats's Poetry and Prose*, Norton Critical Editions series (New York: W. W. Norton, 2009).

Franklin, R. W. (ed.), *The Poems of Emily Dickinson*, 3 vols (Cambridge, MA: Harvard University Press, 1998).

Garrod, H. W. (ed.), *The Poetical Works of John Keats* (Oxford: Oxford University Press, 1939).

Genette, Gérard, *Paratexts: Thresholds of Interpretation* (Cambridge: Cambridge University Press, 1997). Originally *Seuils*, 1987.

Gittings, Robert, *John Keats* (Harmondsworth: Pelican Books, 1971).

—— (ed.), *Letters of John Keats: A New Selection* (Oxford: Oxford University Press, 1970).

Greg, W. W., 'The Rationale of Copy-Text', *Studies in Bibliography* 3 (1950–1): 19–36; reprinted in *Collected Papers*, ed. J. C. Maxwell (Oxford: Oxford University Press, 1966).

Milnes, Richard Monckton (later Lord Houghton), *Life, Letters, and Literary Remains, of John Keats*, 2 vols (London: Edward Moxon, 1848).

Rollins, Hyder Edward (ed.), *The Letters of John Keats 1814–1821*, 2 vols (Cambridge: Cambridge University Press, 2011 [1958]).

Shakespeare, William, *The Riverside Shakespeare*, 2nd edn (Boston: Houghton Mifflin, 1997).

Stillinger, Jack (ed.), *The Poems of John Keats* (London: Heinemann, 1978).

—— (ed.), *The Texts of Keats's Poems* (Cambridge, MA: Harvard University Press, 1974).

Woolford, John, and Daniel Karlin (eds), *The Poems of Browning, Volume 1: 1826–1840* (Harlow: Longman, 1991).

3 Editing Twentieth-Century Letters: The Road to *Words in Air*

Thomas Travisano

On Monday, 26 June 2006 my wife Elsa, my two children and I set out in a heavily laden Honda Odyssey from our home in Oneonta, New York, and drove northeast through a torrential downpour on a two-day journey to Great Village, Nova Scotia. Our two cats, Sarah and Hilary, remained behind at home. My family was accompanying me on a pilgrimage to the site of the poet Elizabeth Bishop's most beloved childhood home, which provided the locale for such luminous poems as 'First Death in Nova Scotia', 'Sestina' and 'The Moose', and such equally luminous stories and memoirs as 'Primer Class', 'Gwendolyn' and 'In the Village'. On the morning of our departure – after a frantic excavation of my attic produced a shipping box large and strong enough to hold it – I had posted to my publisher, Farrar, Straus and Giroux, a typescript of 328,000 words. The typescript consumed more than two reams of paper – 1,085 pages – and the act of printing these pages on a high-speed laser-jet had consumed most of the previous day. Into the shipping box I also slipped a Microsoft Word version of the text that took up just a modest fraction of a single compact disc. The box that went into the mail on that rainy June morning was the product of more than seven years of labour – the labour required to transcribe, date, order and annotate a body of more than 450 illegibly handwritten or insouciantly typed and dated letters that had been committed to paper between 1947 and 1977 by two renowned American poets who were also devoted friends. In printed form, these 450 letters and their notes and apparatus would fill nearly 900 pages and would appear between covers in 2008 as *Words in Air: The Complete Correspondence Between Elizabeth Bishop and Robert Lowell*.

On 27 June, the day after those typescript pages had been boxed and mailed, our minivan crossed the United States border into Canada under bright sun and soaring cobalt-blue skies. We passed through the province of New Brunswick, entered Nova Scotia, and had nearly reached Great Village when, to our surprise, we received an urgent call from our cat-sitter, Kim, back in Oneonta. Kim gave us news that we would find confirmed in the local papers when we returned. The pounding downpour we left behind in Oneonta had continued unabated, and our small city, nestled along the Susquehanna River, had experienced major flooding when the river overflowed its banks. Parts of Main Street were under more than a foot of water and the streets of several nearby villages in the Catskill Mountains to the south were still more deeply awash. Kim, living just a few doors down from Main Street, asked permission (promptly granted) to relocate herself and her four singularly fleecy and copiously shedding cats from her low-lying apartment to our family home a few blocks away. Ours was a tall, wood-framed structure on a fieldstone foundation – 'safe as houses' – that stood more securely on higher ground. In this ark, Kim and an enlarged menagerie of felines would ride out the storm until the floodwaters finally receded.

A day after our call from home, when our Honda Odyssey had arrived in Great Village, and the family had had the chance to settle into Bishop's former home (then serving as an informal writers retreat), I visited a vital local gathering place, the Masstown Market – my nearest node of internet access – and received a far more welcome item of instant twenty-first-century electronic communication. Annie Wedekind, Assistant Editor at FSG, announced – in an email date-stamped 5:00 pm on 28 June – the receipt of the manuscript of *Words in Air*: 'The ship has arrived safely to port, and what a majestic giant she is. I can't wait to dive in (to mix metaphors).' Though much editorial work would lie ahead, the road to *Words in Air* was nearing its end. Yet the trek down that road was anything but linear or clearly marked. The road to *Words in Air* was a journey that lasted more than three decades, and it began with the letters of Ezra Pound.

Like most literary scholars of my era, I never took – indeed was never offered – an academic course on the reading or editing of a writer's correspondence. At best, a handful of well-known letters might be referenced in an advanced seminar as ancillary texts to an author's fiction, poems or plays. When Bishop offered at Harvard in fall 1971 a course on 'Just *letters* – as an art form or something' (*One Art* 544), she was very much ahead of her time. So my understanding and appreciation of letters as a literary genre evolved only gradually, led on unsystematically by curiosity, need or chance. The validity and importance of correspondence as a literary genre in its own right dawned on me only a little at a time, and the nuts and bolts of how to assemble and edit a mass of casually composed missives into a printed volume accessible to the common or uncommon reader was something I had to pick up more or less on the fly.

The first glimmers of what would turn out to be my lifelong engagement with literary letters (and letters *as* literature) began in 1972, the opening semester of my final undergraduate year at Haverford College. I was transitioning from an obsessive T. S. Eliot phase into the early stages of a mania for the life and work of Ezra Pound. I was particularly drawn to Pound's brashness and his insistence that literature in general and poetry in particular could really matter. In these undergraduate days I found all but the most widely anthologised *Cantos* tough going. I was excited about Pound's criticism, his early Imagist and epigrammatic lyrics, his remarkable translations from Latin, Greek, Chinese and Old English sources, and in particular the intricate ironies, multi-layered cross-references and subtle cultural critiques found in *Hugh Selwyn Mauberley* and *Homage to Sextus Propertius*.

Along with Pound's poetry and criticism, I found myself devouring *The Letters of*

Ezra Pound: 1907–1941 (New Directions, 1950). These letters provided not only an unbuttoned look at Pound's extraordinary personality and singular mode of expression, but an insider's guide to the making of modernism as a literary movement in the words of its chief impresario. Thus, when Harriet Monroe, editor of *Poetry*, was hesitating yet again over Pound's insistence that she publish Eliot's 'Love Song of J. Alfred Prufrock', he wrote to her on 31 January 1915 from Coleman's Hatch, where he was serving as Yeats's private secretary:

'Mr. Prufrock' does not 'go off at the end.' It is a portrait of failure, or of a character which fails, and it would be false art to make it end on a note of triumph. . . . A portrait satire on futility can't end by turning that quintessence of futility, Mr. P. into a reformed character breathing fire and ozone. (50–1)

Editor D. D. Paige commented aptly that the tone of Pound's critical and epistolary style, 'with its coruscations, its ellipses, its dogmatisms, its gay carnival air, its unwillingness to enjoy the safety gravity offers . . . and its championing of fresh writers', offered a 'tremendous lure' (xviii) both to Pound's fellow correspondents and to a reader of his letters such as myself. This volume revealed at least two things to me: 1) that letters could themselves offer compelling examples of literary style, and 2) that letters could provide an insider's look into the operations of literary networks and the making of literary history.

Not surprisingly, the best portion of Pound's *Letters* derives from his heroic early period: the dozen years from 1912 to 1924 when Pound was operating out of London or Paris and talent-scouting for *Poetry*, *The Little Review* and other publications, while working to engineer, on a shoestring, a great period in literature and the arts. The volume is full of letters such as this introductory solicitation to Amy Lowell, whom he then knew solely on the basis of her work:

Dear Miss Lowell:
I'd like to use your 'In a Garden' in a brief anthology *Des Imagists* that I am contemplating – unless you've something you think more appropriate.

The letter concludes, charmingly, with the benediction 'The Gods Attend You' (24). And there are wry comments such as this from Pound to James Joyce in 1920:

News item or rather phrase of conversation from ex-govt. official: 'The censorship was very much troubled by it (*Ulysses*) during the war. Thought it was all code.' (154)

Even as Pound scanned the scene assiduously for promising writers, he made clear in his correspondence how well he understood the importance of funding for an artistic movement that would be unlikely to pay for itself, at least in the short run. Thus, in an era before the proliferation of academic teaching posts and foundation grants, Pound wrote to that Maecenas of modernism John Quinn: 'Thanks, apologies and congratulations. If there were more like you we should get on with our

renaissance.' And Pound added in the same letter: 'A great age of painting, a renaissance in the arts, comes when there are a few patrons who back their own flair and
buy from unrecognized men' (54).

Yet vivid as they are, Pound's letters do not present a complete picture of the
man. As his editor Paige notes, 'He very rarely writes gossip or sends news of himself'
(xix), an absence that Paige recognised while making a selection among 'thousands
of pages of letters'. Yet, if Pound's correspondence is short on introspection or
personal revelation, it is very long on personality. It is impossible to miss Pound's
voice or his bristling, wittily expressed array of convictions. Another facet of Paige's
volume that might be said to leave out the whole man is that it goes very lightly
indeed into Pound's increasingly extreme politics. One finds only four direct references in *The Letters* to Mussolini, and none after 1936. Significantly, the volume –
published in 1950, at a time when Bishop was often visiting Pound at St Elizabeths
Hospital during her tenure as Poetry Consultant to the Library of Congress – reaches
its close in March 1941, several months before the United States entered World
War II, and it contains just a single letter from that year. Certainly the compelling
energy of the volume had steadily waned following Pound's fateful move from Paris
to Rapallo, Italy, in the winter of 1925. Moreover, the brilliant array of correspondents he addressed in his London and Paris years had by then been replaced by a
decidedly less intriguing crowd.

Bishop's 'Visits to St. Elizabeths / [1950]' (*Poems* 131–3), published in 1957, is
modelled on the nursery rhyme 'This is the House that Jack Built', and Bishop finds
that within this 'house of Bedlam', Pound – 'the poet, the man' – is many things at
once. He is 'tragic', 'talkative', 'honored', 'old [and] brave', 'cranky', 'cruel', 'busy',
'tedious' and, finally, 'wretched'. Lowell relished Bishop's poem, noting in a letter
that 'I've read it aloud to people several times' (*Words in Air* 203). As a college
senior I had not yet read Bishop's 'Visits' – nor, indeed, anything else by Bishop. But
I found the heroic, funny and irreverent early Pound so compelling that – spurred
by his death on 1 November 1972 – I felt prompted to take part in my own unlikely
exchange of letters.

After reading Pound's obituary in the *New York Times*, I left a handwritten note
with the secretary of Haverford College's president suggesting that the college flag
be flown at half-mast in Pound's honour. I don't think I had any great expectations
for the success of my missive, nor even that it might receive any sort of reply. So I
was surprised to find in my campus mailbox the next day a signed answer on presi-
dential letterhead from John R. Coleman – a busy man, not merely as Haverford's
president, but also as a labour economist, as Chairman of the Board of the Federal
Reserve Bank of Philadelphia, and as the soon-to-be author of the remarkable *Blue-
Collar Journal: A College President's Sabbatical* (Lippincott, 1974). Still, Coleman
found the time to send a letter regretfully declining my eccentric request and pointing out that such public gestures of mourning could not be undertaken lightly. He
himself had recently lost a dear friend and highly regarded colleague, yet as the
institution's president he could not give way to an impulse to include the entire
college in his sorrow.

Following my graduation from Haverford, I enrolled as a PhD candidate at the University of Virginia. It was here, in the spring of 1975, that I first encountered the work of Elizabeth Bishop and Robert Lowell in a graduate course on Contemporary American Poetry offered by poet and scholar Alan Williamson, the recent author of *Pity the Monsters: The Political Vision of Robert Lowell* (Yale, 1974). My classmates and I read every other poet on the syllabus from A. Poulin's anthology *Contemporary American Poetry*, which, like many anthologies of the day, omitted Bishop. Fortunately, however (for me, at least), we explored Bishop and Lowell in more depth, reading them from Bishop's *The Complete Poems* (FSG, 1969), Lowell's *Life Studies* and *For The Union Dead* (combined as a Noonday paperback) and Lowell's recently published *History* (FSG, 1973) – still in hardcover. Both poets were then still very much alive, and I quickly fell under their spell. Each volume contained examples of epistolary poems. These included Bishop's 'Letter to N.Y.' and 'Invitation to Miss Marianne Moore' and a large number of unrhymed sonnets in Lowell's *History* inspired by letters sent to him, including 'For Elizabeth Bishop 3. Letter with Poems for Letter with Poems' – an adaptation of a 27 February 1970 missive from Bishop to Lowell. What I could not know at the time was that behind these poetic volumes with their epistolary fragments stood nearly three decades of correspondence between the two poets, including detailed discussions of many of the poems that I had just been studying. Nor could I know that Bishop and Lowell had recently weathered a heated epistolary debate over Lowell's incorporation of letters from his estranged wife Elizabeth Hardwick in *The Dolphin*, another volume published in 1973.

By 1977 I had determined to write a doctoral thesis on Bishop, which would prove to be one of the earliest dissertations on Bishop and the first to consider her entire career. When I learned in the fall of 1978 – shortly before meeting Bishop at a reading at the University of Virginia – that Marianne Moore's papers were now available at the Rosenbach Museum and Library in Philadelphia, I determined to go there and read the letters. I mentioned this planned visit to 'Miss Bishop' in a letter dated 9 September 1978, and soon thereafter I spent three days at the Rosenbach reading Bishop's letters to Moore. In the afternoon of my third and final day, Patricia C. Willis of the Rosenbach came to me in a state of mild alarm and told me that Bishop had called her to bar access to the reading of these letters to Moore. Willis (later the distinguished curator of the Yale Collection of American Literature at the Beinecke Rare Book & Manuscript Library) told me very kindly that she would let me finish my day's work – she would not send me home. This allowed me to read all of Bishop's letters to Moore through 1940. But future access to the letters was definitely blocked. I have always wondered if it was not my naïve announcement to Bishop that I was on my way to read her letters to Moore which inspired that restrictive phone call to the Rosenbach. In any case, I found the material I most needed, because it was in her earliest letters to Moore, when the elder poet was serving actively as Bishop's mentor, that Bishop would reveal crucial aspects of her development as an artist, insights that I desperately needed as I worked to clarify my understanding of that development. Following her famous 1940 contretemps over 'Roosters', their correspondence would remain cordial but Bishop would never again send Moore a poem for her commentary and approval or discuss with Moore her evolving aesthetic principles.

In my 9 September letter to Bishop I had added that,

> I would also like to see the letters between you and Robert Lowell in the Houghton Library at Harvard, which Prof. [Irvin] Ehrenpreis tells me requires your permission, and the consent of Elizabeth Hardwick. I wonder if you would mind agreeing to let me see these letters, which, I suspect, will help me immeasurably in tracing your more recent thinking on poetry. (VC 117.24)

Based on the restriction Bishop soon placed on the reading of her letters to Moore, I never brought up again my request to study her letters to Lowell, although as fate would have it I did, of course, have the opportunity to return to those letters in the years following Bishop death in October 1979. My own letters to Bishop, including one I sent on 6 February 1979 after I had enjoyed the chance to meet her following her reading at the University of Virginia, turned up again only recently among a group of papers acquired from the estate of Bishop's partner Alice Methfessel by the Vassar College Libraries Special Collections, which serves as the major repository of Bishop's papers. I confess that it is somewhat startling to encounter my younger self in these early letters, in which I not only ask this great poet for access to her private correspondence but pose an array of questions about her influences and artistic theories that might have taken her weeks to answer – and that she had the great good sense to dodge.

The director of my dissertation on Elizabeth Bishop was J. C. Levenson, the Edgar Allan Poe Professor of English (now Emeritus) at the University of Virginia. Levenson, a noted expert on modern poetry and a devotee of Bishop's work, is nonetheless principally known as perhaps the world's leading scholar of Henry Adams. The confluence of my work on Bishop and Professor Levenson's work on Adams meant that – again as fate would have it – the irregular course of my engagement with literary letters took a favourable turn in the summer of 1979, when I fell into a job as a graduate research assistant working on the massive three-volume *Letters of Henry Adams: 1858–1892*, of which Levenson was the principal editor. This undertaking was supported by the Massachusetts Historical Society and by major grants from the National Endowment for the Humanities and other sources. As such, it was carried out on a nearly industrial scale. During a succession of summers, Levenson was joined at Virginia's Alderman Library for work on the letters by a phalanx of professional colleagues, including Ernest Samuels (the Pulitzer-winning biographer of Adams), as well as Charles Vandersee, Viola Hopkins Winner and Jayne Newcomer Samuels. The first three volumes of the Adams *Letters*, the ones on which I briefly worked, were published to great acclaim by Harvard University Press in 1982. The final three volumes, *The Letters of Henry Adams: 1892–1918*, appeared in 1988. My own role on the project was not only transient – lasting merely one summer – but exceedingly humble, involving either proofreading the text of the letters in a cellar room in Alderman alongside one of the co-editors, or – more rarely and much more fun – scouting around the upper floors of the Library in search of annotations to Adams's copiously allusive epistles. What I could not have known at the time was that through this brief and wholly unplanned exposure to the methodology of editing letters, I was able to pick up a sense of how a substantial body of correspondence might be turned into a book – the key elements of this process being teamwork and a judicious division of labour.

Despite the fact that Professor Levenson was overseeing the editing of an important body of correspondence on a very substantial scale, he never to my knowledge offered a course on the reading or the editing of letters. Editing an author's letters might occupy a senior scholar for years, or even decades, but the assumption during my era of graduate study was that literary instruction would involve engagement with the 'real' or 'primary' texts in the canonical genres, that is, with fiction, poetry or plays. Thus, the sole formal class I took from Levenson was a seminar on Wallace Stevens, Williams Carlos Williams and (of course) Ezra Pound.

My dissertation, 'Elizabeth Bishop: Introspective Traveler', was accepted in the summer of 1981, and in the fall of 1982 I took a teaching post at Hartwick College, a small, student-centred liberal arts college in rural Oneonta, New York. Despite the fact that teaching rather than scholarship was the decided focus of my institution, I persisted through to the publication of my thesis as *Elizabeth Bishop: Her Artistic Development* in 1988. By then, a significant body of Bishop's papers had become available at the Vassar College Libraries, her letters to Lowell at the Houghton Library and to Moore at the Rosenbach Museum were now accessible, and I was able to incorporate citations from several of her letters to both Moore and Lowell into my book.

In 1989, a more substantial exploration of this literary trio appeared in David Kalstone's *Becoming a Poet: Elizabeth Bishop with Marianne Moore and Robert Lowell*, which had been edited to completion after Kalstone's death by Robert Hemenway and published by Farrar, Straus and Giroux. Even before the publication of Kalstone's groundbreaking work, my own thinking had turned toward the need for a group study combining Bishop and Lowell with two of their most important contemporaries and peers, Randall Jarrell and John Berryman. I wanted to understand how this circle had developed – just under the radar – as an important and cohesive literary quartet and how a shared aesthetic had developed, sometimes with the support of but often in opposition to an array of powerful literary mentors. For a book such as this, letters would be crucial, and I needed to study not only the correspondence these four poets exchanged amongst themselves but also their epistolary exchanges with a range of mentors and contemporaries.

Thus I found myself visiting archives all over the landscape and reading letters to and from elder poets and teachers such as Moore, Pound, Eliot, R. P. Blackmur, Cleanth Brooks, John Crowe Ransom, George Santayana, Allan Tate, Mark Van Doren and William Carlos Williams, along with many others. Much of this correspondence remains unpublished. I also studied epistolary exchanges with contemporaries such as Flannery O'Connor, Theodore Roethke, Delmore Schwartz and Peter Taylor. Also swimming into my ken along the way were such important published volumes as *Randall Jarrell's Letters* (1982), *We Dream of Honor: John Berryman's Letters to His Mother* (1988) and Elizabeth Bishop's *One Art: Letters* (1994). I still have on my office shelves bulky black three-ring binders full of holograph letters that sport labels such as 'Berryman, Jarrell and Lowell to Blackmur, Tate and Southern Review' and 'JOHN BERRYMAN: Diaries, Correspondence, MS.; Lowell to Berryman, 1953–1970'.

The immediate result of all of this epistolary trawling was the critical study *Midcentury Quartet: Bishop, Lowell, Jarrell, Berryman and the Making of a Postmodern Aesthetic* (Virginia, 1999). However, what struck me most in the course of my research into this volume was the sheer size, importance and literary quality of the letters between Elizabeth Bishop and Robert Lowell. I yearned to share this correspondence with the world, and when Frank Bidart, a protégé of both poets and the literary executor or co-executor of each estate, visited Hartwick's campus in 1998 and heard about my plan, he urged me to send a proposal to publish their letters to Farrar, Straus and Giroux's Editor-in-Chief and President, Jonathan Galassi. The proposal was promptly accepted, and I set to work immediately. Since Hartwick College has no graduate students, I looked to smart, highly motivated undergraduates for my research assistants – preferably sophomores, since they would then have time to learn their craft before graduation. Their work was funded by modest grants from the college. These undergraduates proved more than equal to their assigned tasks, which began with providing a rough transcription of each poet's letters, ultimately totalling, as mentioned, more than 300,000 words. Bishop and Lowell acknowledged to one another their notably illegible handwriting. So I decided to create a pool of Lowell transcription specialists and a pool of Bishop transcription specialists. Each pool could then develop real experience and expertise in dealing with their author's singularly awful holograph style. These dedicated and increasingly skilful amanuenses helped me to puzzle out many seemingly indecipherable passages.

For a long time I kept my photocopies of the letters separate – Lowell in one set of files and Bishop in another – to simplify the process of transcription. But the real excitement came when I began to put the letters together. Each correspondent was inconsistent when it came to dating. Sometimes a full date would be spelled out, but in other letters the year would be missing. Worse yet, a letter might be headed with nothing more specific than 'Thursday' or 'Sunday'. Still, through a patient sifting of cross-references and internal evidence, it became possible to accurately sequence (or so I believe) each and every one of the letters in relation to the others, although it was not always possible to assign an exact date to a given letter. What then emerged before my very eyes was a remarkable dialogue and a remarkable story. It seemed to me that such a dialogue and such a story demanded from me, as the volume's principal editor, an emphasis on narrative. This meant, as 'A Note on the Text and Annotation' explains, that the text must be 'at once complete, faithful, and highly readable' (*Words in Air* xxix). It also meant that the annotations would be brief, functional and placed on the same page as the letters in question. The aim of the annotations would be to provide information that 'the poets themselves do not explain in the narrative' but that was mutually understood between them as the epistolary exchange went forward.

During the transcription, editorial and annotation process that preceded my June 2006 delivery of the typescript of the letters, I had worked primarily with undergraduates at Hartwick College. But in the two years that led to the book's publication in 2008, work on the volume went forward with a professional team that included Galassi, Wedekind and Saskia Hamilton, an accomplished poet and the highly skilled editor of *The Letters of Robert Lowell* (FSG, 2005).

Not only did my personal road to *Words in Air* begin with Ezra Pound, but Pound wrote himself – literally – into the text of the volume not merely in the form of frequent anecdotes, jokes and allusions shared between Bishop and Lowell, but in the form of Pound's own writings. A 25 February 1948 letter from Lowell to Bishop was handwritten on the verso of a typed letter from Pound to Lowell. Lowell mentions in his letter to Bishop that he has just received a letter of praise and shrewd appreciation from George Santayana and adds, 'It was all rather indescribably moving to me' (*Words in Air* 28). But what about Pound's own demanding missive that had been peremptorily dispatched from St Elizabeths (and which is reproduced here exactly as written)?

> to Jarrel / Tate / Spender / ?
> discuss: Brooks Adams.Frobenius, Gesell, essential Loeb /
>   Ford, W. L. to Tate.
> Barry Domville 'Admiral to Cabin Boy'
> Has Tate anything of Devlin's / or has L?
> what any one else know of him.
>
> Tate's question re / Marianne /
> O.K. but see what others think / IN ANY CASE NEVER
> more than ONE wumman at a time.
> Tate's re /   some prof /
>   ?? usual time lag or not? (*Words in Air* 28)

Lowell explains to Bishop: 'What's on the inside of this page Ezra wants sent to 12 writers, me, Randall, Allen, Williams, Cummings, Wyndham Lewis, Auden, Spender – I forget the rest – "action within 24 hours" whatever that means.' My youthful image of a heroic and humorous Pound skilfully promoting the arts wilts rather badly in the face of Pound's eccentric but (for that period) characteristic onslaught on Lowell.

On the other hand, Pound comes off rather better – at least to my mind – in a verse tribute to *Life Studies* that he sent to Lowell upon reading the poems in manuscript. Lowell cites the entire poem in a 3 December 1957 letter to Bishop:

> 'Mr Lowell of Boston
>   No light Baby-Austin
> but when the garbage froze   or
> the vast accumulation of residues
> caused exacerbation,
>   a bulldozer
> was wanted for deep excavation . . .

whether I can corrugate
castigate or elevate this nonsense
into somethink worthy the occasion
      REEMains to be sawn
rough, hew them as we will.' (*Words in Air* 239)

Lowell comments, 'This does seem unusually clear for Ezra. But, whose nonsense? His or mine? I'm not sure if enthusiastic flattery is meant or fierce abuse.' Perhaps Lowell is simply being modest when he disclaims understanding, but my own reading takes the poem as enthusiastic flattery or, better yet, as well-considered praise. As I read it, Pound praises the verse vehicle of *Life Studies* as no mere mini-car, but as a literary force much like a bulldozer, carving its way through frozen garbage and the 'accumulation of residues' and engaging in a 'deep excavation' of conservative Boston's social habit and error. It was a similar mode of understanding that brought Pound to appreciate in an earlier age the work of Eliot (who reflected too, in 'Prufrock', on conservative Boston) and Joyce (who reflected in *Dubliners*, *Portrait* and *Ulysses* on Ireland). Perhaps Pound's sense of literary and cultural values, and his sometimes self-deprecatory sense of humour, had not entirely deserted him.

Yet in one way the correspondence between Bishop and Lowell radically differs from the letters of Pound. While Pound 'very rarely writes gossip or sends news of himself', Bishop's and Lowell's letters offer, as I put it in my introduction, 'a smorgasbord of literary gossip' (*Words in Air* x). And their letters offer as well an ongoing, intimate and deeply moving personal exchange. I am grateful to Pound for starting me on my journey into the world of literary letters, and eternally grateful to Bishop and Lowell for composing and ultimately sharing with the world their own unique and extraordinary body of letters.

WORKS CITED

Bishop, Elizabeth, *One Art: Letters*, ed. Robert Giroux (New York: Farrar, Straus and Giroux, 1994).
—— *Poems* (New York: Farrar, Straus and Giroux, 2011).
—— and Robert Lowell, *Words in Air: The Complete Correspondence Between Elizabeth Bishop and Robert Lowell*, ed. Thomas Travisano with Saskia Hamilton (New York: Farrar, Straus and Giroux, 2008).
Pound, Ezra, *The Letters of Ezra Pound: 1907–1941*, ed. D. D. Paige (New York: New Directions, 1950).
Travisano, Thomas, letter to Elizabeth Bishop, Vassar College Libraries Special Collections, folder 117.24, 9 September 1978.
Wedekind, Annie, 'One other thing . . .', email message to the author, 28 June 2008.

4 Just Letters: Corresponding Poets

Hugh Haughton

I

Letters are mobile texts. By their very mobility, however, they tend to slip between genres. They generally fall by the wayside in the institutional study of literature, which is primarily organised in terms of the established genres of fiction, poetry and drama, or viewed thematically as criticism, travel literature, history and biography. The inherently 'literary' nature of letters is recognised when they figure as epistolary poems, which have been with us since the time of Horace, and in epistolary novels, which have been with us since the time of Richardson and Laclos. When they have not been 'turned into' literary texts like these, however, letters themselves get short shrift. Their fate is to be treated as supplementary texts, hovering uneasily in the borderland between a 'document' and a 'work'. Technically, however, as Jonathan Allison has pointed out in a letter in the *London Review of Books*, letters are actually 'primary' texts, though their status is usually thought of as a rather 'secondary' form of primary text, and they are rarely treated as a genre in their own right.[1] Falling between 'text' and 'document', between 'primary' and 'secondary' text, letters occupy a fluid space between a writer's literary *oeuvre* and its non-literary hinterland, between the work of art and biography.

Perhaps partly because the tradition of the verse letter winds its way from Horace's *Epistulae* to Ted Hughes's *Birthday Letters* and beyond, poets' letters are a special case. Writing of Marianne Moore, Richard Howard observed that 'a poet's letters constitute a crucial dimension of the poet' (62).[2] Howard is a poet who has proved himself a master of the epistolary poem in his virtuosic Browning-esque book *Two-Part Inventions* (1974) and his remark opens up the two-part nature of poetic correspondence. It also prompts us to enquire into that 'crucial dimension' by looking at the light poets' letters throw on their poems and reflecting on what I want to call the poetics of the letter itself. My thoughts about this grow naturally out of my experience of editing the first two volumes of T. S. Eliot's *Letters*, but they also serve as a prelude to a study of modern poets' letters and epistolary poetics more generally that I am currently undertaking.

The porous borderline between poems and letters confronts us immediately when we see the faintly pencilled letter written by Emily Dickinson to Helen Hunt Jackson in 1879, which segues almost instantly into a poem:

> Dear friend, To the Oriole you suggested I add a Humming Bird and hope they are not untrue –
> A Route of Evanescence
> With a revolving Wheel
> A Resonance of Emerald
> A Rush of Cochineal
> And every Blossom on the Bush
> Adjusts it's tumbled Head –
> The Mail from Tunis, probably –
> An easy Morning's Ride – (Johnson ii, 639)[3]

This is an example of a letter that becomes a poem, or a poem sent in and as part of a letter. Which is it? The poem is a riddle, but its status is riddling too. As the inscription records, the tiny missive is a portrait not of a multi-coloured wheeled vehicle but of a tiny mobile bird, 'a Humming Bird', and Dickinson says it was written at the suggestion of Helen Jackson as an accompaniment to her earlier poem about the Oriole ('One of the ones that Midas touched'), which Jackson said she knew 'by heart' (Franklin 558–9). It's not what we call an epistolary poem, but the poem and letter are written in response to her correspondent. It also, as it happens, includes the unexpected image of the whirring bird in flight as 'The Mail from Tunis', a postal vehicle which foregrounds the relation between poetry and correspondence. The Mail embodies 'A Route of Evanescence', 'Resonance' and a rush of colour, causing each blossom that receives it (like readers) to adjust its 'tumbled Head'. In this respect, the text is the very image of a poem – though the squashed lines and small page complicate the margins – as well as being an actual letter.

Dickinson chose not to publish her poems in her lifetime, preferring to circulate them in manuscript letters to friends or collect them in 'fair copy' form in home-bound fascicles. This has left her editors and readers in a unique position, generating fraught critical and editorial discussions about the proper ways to reproduce and publish her texts while respecting her distinctive forms of composition and practices of dissemination. In Dickinson's case the line between the poem and the letter is a tantalisingly thin one, making the two forms structurally intertwined. Both form part of a personal network in which letters, poems and objects are exchanged.

If Dickinson is a special case of a poet's use of letters to circulate poems, this also foregrounds many of the reasons which make the correspondence of poets such a fertile 'dimension' of their work. While it is common for poets to exchange poems with friends and other poets, as Dickinson does, it is rare for other artists to do the same with their work. Novels, paintings, plays and string-quartets don't generally get exchanged in letters as poems are. This gives poets' practice a unique status as a first form of quasi-publication (or circulation) as well as providing an opportunity for an exchange of readings of the poem by poet and correspondents, generating both authorial self-commentary and detailed critical responses by fellow poets – as between Hopkins and Bridges, Robert Frost and Edward Thomas, Elizabeth Bishop and Robert Lowell or Marianne Moore. Reading such two-part inventions and being privy to the exchange of poems and criticism between writers gets the reader closer to both the moment of writing and the moment of first textual release, the poet's voice and its echo in the ears of its first readers.

When we get a letter, we speak of 'hearing' from someone, as if the letter were a projection of the writer's voice. The notion of a poet's 'voice' is uniquely intertwined with the history of poetry, and reading poets' letters offers us a unique opportunity of hearing the writers' voices outside their poetic texts. This is partly a question of biography, but it also opens up the tissue of relations between 'poem' and 'world', 'voice' and 'vision', the personal text and cultural work, as well as poet and audience.

Any poem is both marginal and central, potentially an act of cultural resistance and a new focus, an act of recentring. Letters offer ways of thinking about the relation between the poem as a marginal instance of writing, circulating among a few people, and the poem as a representative act in relation to a larger audience (real and/or notional), particular coteries and networks of friends and family, as well as the cultural centre. Emily Dickinson said 'My Business is Circumference' (Johnson i, 412), but in a letter to Benjamin Bailey of 13 March 1818, John Keats worries equally eloquently about the notion of 'the centre':

> Aye this may be carried – but what am I talking of – it is an old maxim of mine and of course must be well known that every point of thought is the centre of an intellectual world – the two uppermost thoughts in a Man's mind are the two poles of his World he revolves on them and everything is southward or northward to him through their means – We take but three steps from feathers to iron. Now my dear fellow I must once for all tell you I have not one Idea of the truth of any of my speculations – I shall never be a Reasoner because I care not to be in the right . . . So you must not stare if in any future letter I endeavour to prove that Apollo as he had a cat gut string lute to his lyre used a cat's paw as a Pecten . . . My Brother Tom desires to be remember'd to you – he has just this moment had a spitting of blood poor fellow. Remember me to Greig and Whitehe[a]d – (73–4)

The words come immediately after a sonnet, 'Four seasons fill the Measure of the Year', which Keats encloses (or writes out) in the letter (as Dickinson did with 'Humming Bird'). The words measure the peculiar kinds of truth poems foster (Dickinson's 'not untrue'). For Keats what is crucial is the way a poem can make any 'point of thought' (as on a circumference) 'the centre of an intellectual world'. Following the sonnet about the symbolism of the seasons, this makes a perfect case for the peculiar centrality of poetry as well as its relationship to the incidental and to other people. After making this arresting claim, Keats runs on to mock himself and Apollo while recording his brother Tom spitting blood, a symptom of the tuberculosis that killed him. The letter not only gives us Keats's idea of a poem becoming 'the centre of an intellectual world' but also provides a concrete measure of his social world (including his brother Tom, Greig, Whitehead and the recipient Benjamin Bailey) in which that thought, like the sonnet, germinated. The letter itself moves between the 'poles of his world' as Keats uses it to transfer the poem from his world into his friend Bailey's, and it is every bit as compelling poetically as the great verse letter to J. H. Reynolds of twelve days later, which speaks of things 'all disjointed come from North and south' and gives us comparable epistolary insights into the disjointedness and joined-up-ness of Keats's world (79–82).

Keats's claim that 'every point of thought is the centre of an intellectual world' offers a model for writing and reading poems, while situating the texts in transit in the space of correspondence. Writing to Marianne Moore on 27 March 1953, Wallace Stevens said that 'The web of friendship is the most delicate thing in the world – and the most precious' (771).[4] One of the things that letters do is reveal poems and letters as comparable juggling acts in a web of friendship (and enmities), revealing them as texts that respond to their occasions and their addressees, weaving centrifugal and miscellaneous experience into centripetal textual form. In this chapter I want to pursue this line of thought by juggling with a series of letters and poems written by late nineteenth-century and modernist poets for whom the epistolary impulse was closely aligned with the poetic, including Emily Dickinson, Edward Lear, Robert Frost, T. S. Eliot and Marianne Moore.

The great American poet Elizabeth Bishop wrote a poem called 'Letter to N.Y.' to her friend Louise Crane, a letter in 'meter' with the 'meter' of a taxi flaring like 'a moral owl' within it (*Poems, Prose, and Letters* 61). However, Bishop was generally more interested in letters as such rather than writing letter-poems, and it is one of her great gifts as a poet to be able to mimic within her poetry the intimate, joking, conversational tone of her letters. In 1951 she said that Dickinson's letters have 'structure and strength', describing this as 'the sketchiness of the water-spider, tenaciously holding to its upstream position by means of the faintest ripples, while making one aware of the current of death and the darkness below' (690). Later, writing in 1971 from Ouro Preto, she told her friends the pianists Arthur Gold and Robert Fitzdale she was preparing a series of seminars at Harvard on 'Letters': 'Just *letters* – as an art form or something. I'm hoping to select a nicely incongruous assortment of people – Mrs. Carlyle, Chekhov, my Aunt Grace, Keats, a letter found in the street, etc. etc. But I need some ideas from you both – just on the subject of letters, the dying "form of communication"' (*One Art* 544). Bishop's letter, with its commitment to 'Just *letters*' and sense of the 'nicely incongruous' as she moves from the literary world of Carlyle and Keats to a 'letter found in the street', tells us a lot about the talkative, circumstantially grounded art of poems like 'The Moose' and 'In the Waiting Room' – as well as her sense of the kinship between the art she was interested in and ordinary letter writing.

If for Bishop in 1971 letters were a 'dying "form of communication"' (the inverted commas catching her distrust of what was already a cliché), in the twenty-first century they are on their deathbed. With email, text-messaging, Twitter and all the multiplying forms of digital communication, letters seem a thing of the past. What used to be called 'mail' we now call 'snail mail', the mail coach having been replaced by rail mail, and air mail now dissolved into the ether as email (though we don't talk of eletters). The sheer speed of digital and internet communication has changed the time signature of correspondence, making the present a poignant juncture to look back on 'Just *letters*' as 'an art form or something', as Bishop did in 1971. As Wallace Stevens said, 'the imagination is always at the end of an era', and now seems a good time to look back on the culture of correspondence, as well as the strange correspondence between poems and letters.

In a letter-poem entitled 'Resistance Days', dated January 2001, the Irish poet Derek Mahon, writing from Paris, opens with a characteristic sense of obsolescence:

> This sort of snail-mail that can take a week
> best suits my method, pre-*informatique*,
> I write this from the S. Louis, rm. 14 –
> or type it, rather, on the old machine,
> a portable, that I take when I migrate
> in 'the run-up to Christmas.' Here I sit
> amid the hubbub of the rue de Seine
> while a fly snores at a window-pane.
> Old existentialists, old beats, old punks
> sat here of old; some dedicated drunks
> still sing in the marketplace, and out the back
> there's an old guy who knew Jack Kerouac. (248)

Mahon once praised Swift as an 'eminently situational' poet, and he writes as one himself, as this poem simulating a letter insists. It is a report from the 'here and now' of his hotel on the Rue de Seine, dated and placed, but written with an acute sense of the there and then of 'old existentialists' and 'old beats'. The text foregrounds the materiality of the poem (and letter) as *writing*, as well as the extraneous material he is writing about. It's not only an instance of obsolete 'snail-mail' but typewritten and in every sense 'pre-*informatique*'. This demonstrates the poet's acute cultural time-sense as well as built-in sense of obsolescence while insisting on what Seamus Heaney calls 'the place of writing', as letters tend to do. Mahon goes on:

> I inhale the fashions of the sexy city,
> its streets streaming with electricity

The fluid letter-poem, with its casual, throwaway rhyming couplets, is an attempt to tap into those 'streaming' streets and capture not only the 'electricity' of the city, but (through that illuminating rhyme) the word 'city' lit up within 'electricity'. Mahon likes to quote Raymond Chandler's axiom 'No art without the resistance of the medium', and the rhymes of 'Resistance Days' give the letter something to resist and resist with, aligning it to earlier poems like 'The Yaddo Letter' and 'The Hudson Letter', in which the poet tried to break out of closed forms and develop a more flexible, exposed and prose-like response to New York in the mid 1990s. Mimicking letters here is a challenge to expanding the tonal, formal and rhetorical universe of verse, setting up a more ambiguous, circumstantially inflected sense of the boundary as well as continuum between prose and verse. This is what letter-poems do from one direction, and poets' actual letters from the other.

II

Thinking of 'snail mail' brings to mind two pictorial letters from the great Victorian nonsense poet and illustrator Edward Lear, who was as idiosyncratic a letter writer as his American contemporary Emily Dickinson.

The first of these is a brilliant epitome of snail mail. The text of this note to Evelyn Baring of 19 February 1864 winds itself around the shell of a snail that bears not only the words but the bearded features of its author (Noakes 194). Lear was a traveller, topographical painter and travel writer and this letter is both a traveller's text and a travelling one. Snails may be slow but they travel, and this bearded and bespectacled snail bears not only the name of its addressee – someone actually called Baring – but a portrait of the letter writer as middle-aged snail. As stamps bear the head of the monarch, the letter bears the head of its author. This comic self-portrait in letter form tells us something about the form of the letter, about its materiality, its mimetic relationship to its author, and its essential mobility (however slow).

Lear was an often dazzling letter writer, and his correspondence shimmers with the playfulness that went into his verse. 'Letters are the only solace of my life at

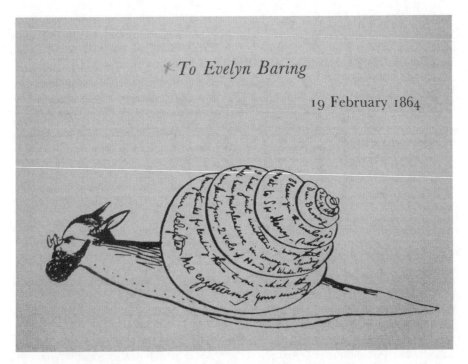

Figure 4.1. Edward Lear's illustrated letter to Evelyn Baring, 19 February 1864.

present, except sardines and omelettes,' he told Lady Wyatt in December 1870, while in 1861 he said his letters 'would be quite as fit to read 100 years hence as any body else's naughty biography' (Noakes 226). Another letter to Marianne North of June 1871 includes a series of images illustrating his reception of one of her letters (230–2). They show him finding it 'insufficiently stamped', then executing 'a rapid Stampede to the Post Office', delivering 'an extampary and affecting discourse', and concluding with a triumphant image, in which 'Mr Lear stamps and dances for joy on securing Miss North's letter'. Each illustration includes a different kind of 'stamp' and the sequence dramatises a complex dance of relationships that is both ritualised and 'extampary', a word that suggests both 'extempore', officially franked, and bearing the author's energetic personal stamp. It turns the receiving of the letter into a tour de force of writing and illustrates the crucial interdependence in all correspondence of writing and receiving, posting and reading. Like Keats and Dickinson, Lear often enclosed poems with his letters, circulating them among friends prior to publication. Indeed his letters, with their blend of nonsensical play, travel writing and biography, are the best guide to the world of the Dong with the Luminous Nose, the Pobble who has no toes and his other nonsensical protagonists. Lear wrote a poem entitled 'How pleasant to know Mr. Lear!', and the letters give his readers a pleasurable sense of the displaced poet within his far-flung social worlds, transforming our sense of his dancing, unhappy and 'extampary' poems.

Unlike 'How pleasant to know Mr. Lear!', the late poem 'My Agèd Uncle Arly' doesn't purport to be autobiographical. Nonetheless it is quoted in a letter of 4 June 1884 to Lear's friend Lord Carlingford with the following introduction:

> Having a notion that you have a little more leisure while you are at Balmoral (as I see by the papers you are about to be) . . . I shall send you a few lines just to let you know how your aged friend goes on
>
>   O my agèd Uncle Arly!
>   Sitting on a heap of Barley
> Through the silent hours of night!
>   On his nose there sate a cricket;
>   In his hat a railway ticket –
> But his shoes were far too tight!
> Too! Too!
>   far too tight! (Strachey 212)

As John Byrom has pointed out, the name 'UncLE ARly' includes (albeit 'unclearly') the letters of the author's name, 'Lear', but this letter explicitly equates the author and his avuncular protagonist as well as relating the tight shoes to the letter writer's feet (the letter also includes a drawing of a swollen-footed Lear hobbling on ski-like crutches). In March 1886, Lear sent a copy of the completed poem to Ruskin, prefaced by an allusion to Gray's 'Elegy', 'E'en in our ashes' (echoing 'E'en in our ashes live their wonted fires'), and saying he esteems it 'a thing to be thankful for that I remain as great a fool as ever I was'. Two days later, sending it to the wife of a doctor, he describes it as 'the last Nonsense poem I shall write', calling it 'stuff begun years ago for Lady E Baring'. According to his editor Vivien Noakes (who doesn't quote the letter to Carlingford), on 5 March he made twelve copies to send to friends, as well as referring to 'another poem about the same ingividgual', recorded as an 'Incomplete MSS – found in the brain of Mr Edward Lear on dissection of the same – in a post-mortem examination' (Noakes 546).[5] Such letters confirm the live role of the epistolary audience in the composition and distribution of his nonsense poems, whose primary audience was a network of friends. However, they also anticipate our post-mortem sense of this most 'ingividgual' of artists and poets, as he reframes the poem autobiographically for different correspondents.

Taken together, Lear's images – with letters like these – remind us that every letter is part and parcel (rather like a parcel) of a larger social network, a textual response that is designed to provoke a response. In any exchange of letters the writer is always a reader and the reader a writer, and I want to suggest this is true in a different sense of poems, which are also never private and always circulate within a larger system of exchange which gives them meaning in their own time, and then after the death of the author in 'post-mortem examination'. James Wright wrote in a letter to Donald Hall that 'friendship is everything. It may not be entirely why we write our poems. But it is certainly why we have the courage to give those poems to each other' (455). Manuscripts aren't found in any brain, of course, but the manuscripts of letters like Lear's are taken up into Derrida's archive where they will inevitably be read in relation to the mind of the dead author and his friends, forming a crucial archival embodiment of his mental and corporeal life.

III

In a letter of December 1852 to Susan Gilbert (Dickinson), Emily Dickinson wrote 'Ere this intelligence reaches you, I shall probably be a snail' (Johnson i, 216). In another of 1869 (between Lear's to Baring and North) she wrote: 'A Letter always feels to me like immortality because it is the mind alone without corporeal friend. Indebted in our talk to attitude and accent, there seems a spectral power in thought that walks alone' (Johnson ii, 460). Dickinson's letters exhibit her 'spectral power' as a writer who walked alone, or at least wrote in a profoundly 'ingividgual' way. Nonetheless her letter to her friend and sponsor T. W. Higginson, like all letters, implies the existence of corporeal friends, a solitude rehearsed in the imagined presence of another person, as well as 'attitude and accent', and Higginson was to play a crucial role in the eventual posthumous publication of her poems and creation of her reputation. Many of Dickinson's poems, while unpublished in her lifetime, circulated in letters, and it was in her letters to Higginson and others that Dickinson talked publicly about her art, her religious ideas and her cryptic selfhood, and crossed the threshold of her self-imposed enclosure within her 'Father's ground'. The letters situate her riddling poems in a Puritan New England network of family and friends, which gives her particular lyrics not only 'corporeal' presence but a local habitation and a name. The famously reclusive Dickinson disliked photography, avoiding daguerreotypes, but in one of her earliest letters to Higginson of July 1862 she penned a brief self-portrait: 'I had no portrait, now, but am small, like the Wren, and my Hair is bold, like the Chestnut Bur – and my eyes, like the Sherry in the Glass, that the Guest leaves – Would this do as well?' (Johnson ii, 267). There is at least one portrait of Dickinson, but the subsequent correspondence with Higginson offers an unrivalled document of her encrypted self-fashioning.

Dickinson wrote another characteristically cryptic poem, which, though in no sense a letter-poem like Bishop's 'Letter to N.Y.' or Mahon's 'Resistance Days', identifies her poem with a letter:

> This is my letter to the World
> That never wrote to Me –
> The simple News that Nature told –
> With tender Majesty
>
> Her Message is committed
> To Hands I cannot see –
> For love of Her – Sweet – countrymen –
> Judge tenderly – of Me (Franklin 235)

Dickinson's 'news' is never simple, but the poem equates itself with a 'letter to the World'. If the idea of 'the World' writing to anyone, even a poet, is absurd, the idea of the poem as a letter to the world captures something about the curious ontological status of poetry and its peculiar relationship to both writing and audience. What would it be for the world to write to her? How could it write to anyone? However absurd, the idea suggests the poem is akin to a letter but written to the world itself rather than to a friend. This embodies a very special form of correspondence but also a very distinctive paradigm of lyric. 'World' here might mean something like 'Society' or 'The Literary World' rather than the planet, but Dickinson's poem plays on the relationship between them. This poem letter passes on nature's 'Message' but not 'the World's', and is committed not to 'the World' as such but to 'Hands I cannot see' (the hands of anonymous 'countrymen'). Like a letter, the poem depends on response, on being 'judged', and its author aspires to being judged 'tenderly' at the hands of her 'countrymen'. Dickinson's actual letters embody a parallel universe to the poems, while anchoring their metaphysical universe, as letters do, in her time and place.

The earlier letter attributed 'immortality' to letters, while another poem insists 'A letter is a joy of earth – / It is denied the gods' (Franklin 604). In that sense, a letter is a 'joy of earth' which *feels like* 'immortality' even though steeped in mortality while the poem is a 'letter to the world' entrusted to 'hands I cannot see'. Another poem takes an even more haunted view of letters, when it refers to God, the presumed author of the biblical writing on the wall, as 'Balthazzar's Correspondent' (558). It was in her correspondence with Higginson that Dickinson introduced herself to 'the world' as well as offering some of her most haunting statements about poetics, such as her remark in 1876 that 'Nature is a Haunted House – but Art – a House that tries to be haunted' (Johnson ii, 554).

The nineteenth century was invested in biography as no earlier period, and the notion of the 'Life and Letters' of artists, like politicians, painters and historians, became an important literary institution. As the case of Emily Dickinson dramatises vividly, we always need to read the story of poets' letters in terms of the history of their publication, and how they are editorially mediated to us. There was something of a wave of epistolary publication after the death of the Romantic poets, as indeed after the deaths of Gray, Cowper and Burns before them, with the publication of Monkton Milnes's *Life and Letters of Keats* in 1848 providing an important watershed (or letter-shed). There was an even more significant one, however, at the close of the biographically inflected nineteenth century in the wake of the death of Victorian poets. The death of the poets was kept from their poems in Auden's sense but it gave birth to their correspondence, and this significantly changed the ways their life and work would be read, contributing to the self-conscious nature of modern poets' letters.

After Baudelaire's death, Arthur Symons said that 'to understand' what we can of Baudelaire we must read every text and document and 'above all, the letters', which had been first published in 1906 (Symons 141). In most instances, of course, the initial publication of correspondence in England and elsewhere was overseen and controlled by the writers' literary executors in the family, and was thus subject to rigorous selection and censorship. The most high-profile example was the 1895 two-volume edition of Matthew Arnold's letters edited by G. W. E. Russell. Ian Hamilton observes that this consisted only of 'the letters which the Arnold family considered suitable, or partly suitable, for publication. Hundreds of others, we can reliably surmise, were burned.' This meant, he said, that 'Mrs Arnold was able to make sure that the 1895 *Letters* raised no eye-brows, and especially not her own' (*The Trouble with Money* 182–3). It was not until *The Letters of Matthew Arnold to Arthur Hugh Clough*, which drew on earlier, non-censored and non-familial letters, appeared in 1932 that, as Hamilton says, 'the cold fish was shown to have been edgy and excitable, affected and verbose' (184).

Raising eyebrows is not the main function of letters, but the capacity to surprise and to reveal unexpected dimensions of the writer is. The custodians of correspondence, however, nearly always close members of the family or appointed by them, are often the very last people to be able to estimate the public significance of a writer's correspondence, as Hamilton documents in *The Keepers of the Flame: Literary Estates and the Rise of Biography* (1992).

The 1890s, the decade of the Wilde trial and *The Yellow Book*, was a famously scandalous decade, but the keepers of the flame of the great Victorians were mainly keen to prevent any scandal emerging from the publication of poets' letters. This meant many were consigned to the flames, and selective and tailored versions were published. Nevertheless, the decade was a watershed in the history of poetic correspondence. Mrs Sutherland Orr's *Life and Letters of Robert Browning* appeared in 1891, while Emily Dickinson's *Letters* was published in 1894, edited by Mabel Loomis Todd, Austin Dickinson's mistress. During the same decade, other family members oversaw the publication of letters of their poetic relatives. In 1897 Hallam Tennyson published his two-volume *Alfred Lord Tennyson: A*

Memoir, composed during the five years since his father's death, and built around what Christopher Ricks calls 'his amassing, cutting, and (on occasion) shielding, towards the classic Victorian form, a life and letters' (*Oxford Dictionary of National Biography*). Others include *Letters of Matthew Arnold, 1848–1888* in two volumes (1895); *Letters of Elizabeth Barrett Browning*, in two volumes, edited by Frederic G. Kenyon in 1897; *Letters of Robert Browning and Elizabeth Barrett Barrett 1845–1846* in two volumes (edited by their son) in 1899; and Dante Gabriel Rossetti's *Letters to his Family* (edited by his brother W. M. Rossetti). This meant that during the closing decade of the century the correspondence of most of the major poets of the time emerged into the light of day. This extended their *oeuvre* significantly to embrace formal and informal letters as well as published poems, complicating and animating the relationship between the two. This epidemic of epistolarity changed the ways poetry would be read, and the ways poets would write letters and poems.

The Brownings' posthumously published courtship correspondence became probably the most enduring monument of the role of poets' letters in their lives. They reveal they fell in love with each other by reading each other's 'sphinxine' verse and letters, a love affair with both poetry and each other carried out in letters. Elizabeth Barrett wrote that she 'had done most of her talking by post, of late years' (Barrett and Browning 10), and the letters that passed between her and Robert Browning combine epistolary romance, biography and dramatised poetics in duet form. Asking him whether he knows Tennyson, Barrett jokes that 'anybody is qualified, according to everybody, for giving opinions about poetry. It is not so in chymistry and mathematics' (21). 'Self-consciousness' is one of the things they have in common, and their correspondence not only brims with self-informed 'opinions about poetry' of every kind, but plays out a self-conscious dramatisation of poetry and poetics in action. In one of her letters Barrett wrote that 'I am inclined to think that we want new forms . . . as well as thoughts – the old gods are dethroned' (36). In one of Browning's he said his poems give '*no* knowledge of me', and that 'these scenes and song-scraps *are* such mere and very escapes of my inner power, which lives in me like the light in those crazy Mediterranean phares I have watched at sea – wherein the light is ever revolving in a dark gallery bright and alive, and only after a weary interval leaps out, for a moment, from the one narrow chink' (15). Reading the letter, we catch a reflection of that light, and experience the rhythm of Browning wrestling to embody it in a prose that is as sinuously mobile as his verse. Their correspondence, while responsive to the conventions of the letter, also represents one of the 'new forms' Barrett aspired to.

Early on she asked whether Browning knew 'Tennyson with a face to face knowledge', and in fact it was Tennyson, one of the many recipients of a posthumous 'Life and Letters', who wrote the most powerful poetic tribute to the 'face to face knowledge' provided by the after-life of letters. Though in one of his letters he wrote that he would 'as soon kill a pig as write a letter' (Bevis 235), *In Memoriam* describes the galvanic effect of Tennyson's reading of the correspondence of his dead friend Arthur Hallam. Reading 'the noble letters of the dead' – 'those fallen leaves which kept their green' – he is once more 'touched' by his dead friend:

And strangely on the silence broke
   The silent-speaking words, and strange
   Was love's dumb cry defying change
To test his worth; and strangely spoke

The faith, the vigour, bold to dwell
   On doubts that drive the coward back,
   And keen through wordy snares to track
Suggestion to her inmost cell.

So word by word, and line by line,
   The dead man touched me from the past,
   And all at once it seemed at last
The living soul was flashed on mine,

And mine in this was wound . . . (Tennyson 946–7)

Hallam's letters are 'fallen leaves' that paradoxically 'kept their green', surviving their moment and their apparently ephemeral status. This tribute in poem 95 of *In Memoriam* to 'The noble letters of the dead' is a reflex of Victorian biographical piety, but Tennyson, with his paradoxical compounding of *pietas* and perversity, transforms it into an indirect defence of poetry and its 'silent-speaking words'. Observing the way Hallam's texts trace 'Suggestion to her inmost cell', he suggestively celebrates his dead friend's letters as if they were poems (or poems aspiring to be such letters):

So word by word, and line by line,
   The dead man touched me from the past,
   And all at once it seemed at last
The living soul was flashed on mine

'Word by word, and line by line' refers to the text of the letters but inevitably, occurring word by word in a line of verse, offers itself to the reader as a model of poetry, giving a mesmeric account of the stanza about reading that we are actually reading. With characteristically honest doubt, Tennyson notes that it only *seemed* as if 'The living soul was flashed on mine', but the flashing lines acknowledge the uncanny force of the posthumous revelation of a 'living soul' in the surviving letters. The word 'line' and the mirroring in the line of 'word by word' and 'line by line' set up a reverberation between letters and poems that goes far beyond any conventional biographical *pietas*. Like Victorian 'Lives and Letters', this gives us a new insight into the poetic after-life of the letter.

IV

The best poet's letters, like Dickinson's or Hopkins's, are as compelling as their poems. Eliot thought Keats's greatness was 'manifested more clearly in his letters than his poems' (*The Use of Poetry* 100), and, following the great wave of Victorian correspondence, the letters of twentieth-century poets like Rilke, Marianne Moore, Robert Frost, Hart Crane, Elizabeth Bishop, George Oppen, Robert Lowell, Philip Larkin and Ted Hughes have become crucially intertwined with their *oeuvres*. In such letters we get something like poetry by other means, as well as lots of detailed commentary on poems, poetics and the intimate worlds of poets. There are some poets whose letters are especially valuable for crucial statements about poetry and belief that offer cues, clues and keys to reading not found elsewhere. This is the case with Keats, whose letters about 'negative capability', the poet having 'no identity', Wordsworth's 'Egotistical Sublime' and the counter-Miltonic claim that 'English should be kept up' have entered the bloodstream of subsequent poetry criticism (Keats 43, 157, 326). This is also true of Gerard Manley Hopkins, Rimbaud (in the 'Lettre d'un voyant') and Rilke (in the *Letters to a Young Poet* and *Letters on Cezanne*), as well as the Scottish poet W. S. Graham and the American Objectivist George Oppen. Like Keats, Robert Frost thought 'English must be kept up' (though in his case American English), and like those great exponents of mannerist vernacularism the Brownings, Dickinson and Hopkins, he became a dazzling instance of the letter writer as creator of an epistolary poetics. We can see this in the series of letters elaborating his idea of 'the sound of sentences' written before and after the publication of *North of Boston* (1913). His letter to John Bartlett of 4 July 1913, for example, provides an essential insight into his idea of the primacy of *hearing* in reading, and of *speech* in verse:

> The Bungs, Beaks, Bucks, Fourth-of-July, 1913.
> . . . I alone of English writers have consciously set myself to make music out of what I may call the sound of sense. Now it is possible to have sense without the sound of sense (as in so much prose . . . that makes very dull reading) and the sound of sense without sense (as in Alice in Wonderland which is anything but dull reading). The best place to get the abstract sound of sense is from voices behind a door that cuts off the words. . . . The sound of sense, then. You get that. It is the abstract vitality of our speech. It is pure sound – pure form. One who concerns himself with it more than the subject is an artist. But remember we are only talking of the raw material of poetry . . . if one is to be a poet he must learn to get cadences by skillfully breaking the sounds of sense with all their irregularity of accent across the regular beat of the metre. (Frost 664)

In a case like this, hearing from the poet helps us hear poems like 'The Oven Bird' which celebrates a bird that knows 'in singing not to sing' (116). Frost says, with notable effrontery: 'I alone of English writers have consciously set myself to make music out of what I may call the sound of sense.' The letter is addressed from

'The Bungs, Beaks, Bucks, Fourth-of-July, 1913' (which a later letter gives as 'The Bungalow, Beaconsfield, Bucks'), and the play on 'the sound' of the names establishes an atmosphere of jokiness and word-play in which the English places are rejigged as five-letter words in a display of American musical fireworks for the fourth of July. The nonsensical-sounding address is integral to the claims it makes about the sound of sense. It is part of the same performance, and, with Frost, performance and form go hand in hand, whether in poetry or in letters. To get the real flavour of Frost's poetics, we have to savour and weigh the letter in the way it invites us to read poems, as well, of course, to feel the drama of its being developed in England in dialogue with Edward Thomas and with the American correspondents (like John Bartlett) he wanted to help create the taste by which his poetry was to be enjoyed.

If the interest of Frost's letters, like those of other poets like Hopkins and Keats, depends in large measure on their epistolary poetics, other poets' letters might be thought of as more important as biographical or literary documents, documenting the writer's engagement with print culture, and acting as portraits of the artist in his or her world. This is true of the letters of Yeats, Louis MacNeice, John Betjeman, Philip Larkin, Anne Sexton, Allen Ginsberg and Sylvia Plath, to name a few. Others again are primarily of interest because of the evidence they provide about the history of authorship, the annals of publishing, the history of the book, or intellectual history. But where such letters may usually be read in documentary terms, they also offer a poetics of the letter itself, a literary performance which can be compared to a poem.

All poets' letters offer material of these different, overlapping kinds, and any generous selection or comprehensive edition will probably offer examples of all. Stevens's letters, for example, are full of replies to questions about his poems and mini-lectures on his ideas about poetry. Nevertheless he told Ronald Latimer in 1935 that 'I don't want anything that I say in these letters to be regarded as anything more than a bit of letter-writing' (302). For poetry readers, some bits of letter writing throw light on poems or poetics – like Hopkins's sketches of 'inscape' and 'instress'. Others document a writer's engagement with the institutions of print culture mediated through other writers, editors and publishers. Others again provide mirrors of their writer, whether indirectly like Stevens, talking about his interest in art, exotic objects and politics, or directly, reporting on the writer's intimate biography – like Coleridge's epistolary account of childhood memoirs in the late 1790s, Bishop's autobiographical reports from Brazil, Marianne Moore's 'Sojourn in the Whale' letters about the New York art scene, or Larkin's recently published *Letters to Monica*. Each kind of letter can directly affect our readings of poems. For historians of culture, on the other hand, along with experts on the history of the book, editors of texts, and commentators on modernism, letters are primarily cultural documents. For biographers and biographically inclined readers, they are primarily cultural documents. There is an overlap as well as differences between these reading constituencies, and in every case, the letter is not only a source of information but a *form* of information, a literary performance with a bearing on poetry.

I became aware of this during the process of transcribing, sorting and annotating the multifarious material which went into *The Letters of T. S. Eliot*, a process that was not always what Emily Dickinson called 'a joy of earth'. Poets' letters show that, though poets may sometimes wander lonely as a cloud, they don't live among them. They are crucially and creatively dependent on friends, in particular other poets, as well as society more generally. Letters remind us that even the best-wrought lyric urn is a social construct; it depends on the life of *crowds* quite as much as *clouds*. 'Life without poetry is, in effect, life without a sanction,' wrote Stevens to Latimer in 1935, adding: 'There is no more secret about this sort of thing than there is, say, to the stock exchange' (299). If Eliot, working at Lloyd's Bank in London, and Stevens, working for the Hartford Accident and Indemnity Company, seem more obviously caught up in economic culture than many other poets, they remind us that all letters form part of a larger system of exchange. Poets' letters remind us that poems too are always part of an exchange, born out of the economic conditions of the time and dialogue with writers from the past and present.

Letters can distract us from art, however, tempting readers and critics to slide too easily from poetry into biography. W. H. Auden forbade posthumous publication of his own correspondence, and in a review of Oscar Wilde's *Letters* in 1963, he penned a ferocious critique of literary correspondence in general:

> When we were young, most of us were taught that it is dishonourable to read other people's letters without their consent, and I do not think we should ever, even if we grow up to be literary scholars, forget this early lesson. The mere fact that a man is famous and dead does not entitle us to read, still less to publish, his private correspondence. We have to ask ourselves two questions – firstly, 'Would he mind?' and, secondly, 'Are the contents of such historical importance as to justify publication even if he would?' (*Forewords and Afterwords* 302)

Contrasting writers to politicians, statesmen and generals, about whom we are 'entitled to know anything about their lives that sheds light upon their public acts', Auden says 'the average productive poet or novelist or dramatist is too busy, too self-centred, to spend much time and trouble over his correspondence'. The only exception was 'love letters', but 'since knowledge of an artist's private life never throws any significant light upon his work, there is no justification for intruding on his privacy'. Keats's letters to Fanny Brawne or Beethoven's to his nephew should either never have been published or, 'like psychological case histories, published anonymously'.

Observed strictly, Auden's mischievous and dogmatic essay would consign most editions of letters and most biographies of writers to the dustbin. Nevertheless, Auden wrote a brilliant essay discussing Byron's *Don Juan*, in which he argued that 'from the beginning, his letters seem authentic but . . . very little of his poetry', whereas 'the more closely his poetic *persona* came to resemble the epistolary *persona* of his letters to his male friends . . . the more authentic his poetry seems' (*The Dyer's Hand* 401). Auden wrote his own poetic 'Letter to Lord Byron', a brilliant imitation of the Byronic letter in verse form, which offers not only the best self-portrait of Auden but a satirical portrait of the 1930s *Zeitgeist*, revelling in the kind of prosaic, contingent detail that gave momentum to Byron's letters. Auden followed it a few years later with his brilliant wartime long poem *New Year's Letter* (1940), and such works did much to relaunch the verse letter as a modern form. It is an irony that the publisher of both these books was T. S. Eliot, another poet who expressed notable ambivalence about the publication of his letters.

Eliot dramatised his mixed feelings on this score in *The Elder Statesman*, where Lord Claverton is confronted by a woman who has copies of his love letters, and mention is made of their saleability, existence in photocopies and archives, and possible uses in court as evidence of scandals and indiscretions in his youth. The play demonstrates the poet's self-consciousness about the materiality of letters, their different kinds of value, and their uses in biography, blackmail and court. In her introduction to *The Letters of T. S. Eliot* (1988), Valerie Eliot documents her husband's initial determination to prevent posthumous publication of his letters and reluctant agreement that they could only be published if she edited them (*Volume 1* xvii). Contrary to Auden's claim that poets are 'too self-centred, to spend much time and trouble over his correspondence', the scale of Eliot's suggests he spent a high proportion of his life doing precisely that, in this respect more like a politician or general than an archetypal poet.

Two texts illustrate Eliot's ferocious ambivalence. The first is in a letter of May 1930 to his brother Henry:

> And I am glad to have the letters to make ashes of. I should never have wanted to read them again, with all the folly and selfishness; and I dont want anyone else ever to read them and possibly print them; and if I could destroy every letter I have ever written in my life I would do so before I die. I should like to leave as little biography as possible. So that's done and done with.

A little earlier his mother had said she had all his letters from his schooldays, Harvard and his Prufrockian year in Paris – so this letter documents the ferocity of the younger Eliot's anxiety about letters, biography and their uses, and explains the huge absences in the first volume, which effectively begins when he is in London in 1914. In a 1917 review about Turgenev, Eliot called the expatriate Russian 'a perfect example of transplantation' but said 'a writer's art must be racial . . . it must be based on the accumulated sensations of the first twenty-one years'.[6] In burning the correspondence from his first American years Eliot ensured that the evidence of his own accumulated racial sensations was lost for ever (as all published correspondences document often invisible records of comparable defining absences).

Against this, Eliot wrote in *The Use of Poetry* that Keats's 'greatness' was 'manifested more clearly in his Letters than in his poems', calling them 'the most important ever written by any English poet' (100). In 1933 he also delivered a lecture at Harvard on English poets as letter writers, where he said: 'The desire to write a letter, to put down what you don't want anybody else to see but the person you are writing to, but which you do not want to be destroyed, but perhaps hope may be preserved for complete strangers to read, is ineradicable' (*Letters, Volume 1* vi). Business letters and *jeux d'esprit*, letters to family and fellow writers, postcards and *cris de coeur* all bear testimony to this fundamental 'desire to write a letter', explaining the many kinds of letter Eliot spent so much of his many-sided life writing.

From hapless Francophile Prufrock to Pope of Russell Square, from penniless expatriate Harvard PhD student to Nobel laureate, Eliot's letters chart the rise and rise of one of the most influential writers of his time. They show him in very different incarnations as poet, critic, philosopher and expatriate American, as well as churchman, friend, editor, Christian, husband, patient and nurse, as well as a clown ('almost, at times, the Fool'). In 1914 he told Conrad Aiken letters should be 'indiscretions', since otherwise they are 'simply official bulletins' (*Letters, Volume 1* 82). As time went on, however, more and more of his correspondence took the form of official bulletins, documenting his role in the literary culture of his time as editor of *The Criterion* and publisher at Faber and Faber, as well as a poet and social and literary commentator in constant demand for lectures and articles. His huge correspondence speaks to all the reading constituencies mentioned earlier. Though as a poet dedicated to 'impersonality' Eliot insisted that 'the more perfect the artist, the more completely separate in him will be the man who suffers and the mind which creates' (*Selected Essays* 18), questions about the relation between his life and work are inescapable. The letters give us a unique insight into the world and voice the poems issue from. They also invite us to puzzle over the relationship between Eliot's own intellectual investments and his enigmatic multi-vocal poems.

Letters, as Emily Dickinson suggests, have a peculiar relationship to both mortality and immortality. While poems are generally published during their author's lifetime – though not in the case of Dickinson's – letters generally appear posthumously mediated via an editor. Editions of letters are documents of *authorship* but, though usually *authorised*, are not *authored*. Working as co-editor of the letters of Eliot, an author deeply ambivalent about letters, made me acutely conscious of this. In the case of a novel such as *Great Expectations* or a play like *Waiting for Godot*, an editor is an optional extra and footnotes a luxury. When it comes to letters, however, the editor acts as a conduit between the original writer and the reader with the editorial function rendered visible by the editor's name and a litter of footnotes. The editor of Eliot's letters has to confront a huge archive of correspondence of all kinds, some tidily catalogued in Faber archives, some held in libraries, and many stored by his widow in her flat in Kensington. In the face of this vast archive, you have to decide how much of the huge amount of material should be published, what is of 'historical importance' and what 'private', and how the latter relates to the former. More importantly, the flat housed the huge incoming correspondence from Eliot's family, friends and fellow writers – including Woolf, Joyce, Wyndham Lewis, Ezra Pound and most of the major intellectuals of the day. This gave an unparalleled view of his letters as part of a huge interconnected system of exchange, while foregrounding the technical problem of how to register that exchange through annotation without over-burdening the book.

In 1935 Eliot wrote a preface to the *Selected Poems* of Marianne Moore, a poet with a fascination for prose and letters who, through her editorship of *The Dial*, was, like Eliot, one of the most influential writers of her time. Indeed, William Carlos Williams likened her to a 'rafter holding up the superstructure' of what he called 'our uncompleted building', a 'caryatid' (Williams 146). Unlike Eliot, however, the caryatid-like Moore was incapable of writing a dull letter. When Richard Aldington praised the absence of Americanisms in Eliot's work, he wrote back that:

> If I can write English prose – and I imagine that there are more Americanisms in my prose than you wish to see – it is due to two causes: an intensive study of two years of the prose of Bradley, and an inherited disposition to rhetoric, from innumerable ancestors who occupied themselves with the church, the law, or politics! On the other hand, this gives my prose, I am aware, a rather rheumatic pomposity – I am conscious of this stiffness, but I do not trust myself elsewhere (*Letters, Volume 2* 506).

The letter tells us a lot about his epistolary as well as critical style. This did not prevent him relishing Moore's ludic baroque manner, and, having published the *Selected Letters* of Ezra Pound and Joyce, he said in July 1959 that 'One of the books which obviously must in the fullness of time be published . . . will be *The Letters* of Marianne Moore' (cited in Moore ix). Moore's *Selected Letters* reveal her to be a figure comparable to Eliot, writing from the heart of the New York art scene in correspondence with and as commentator on the major writers of her time. She has a lecture entitled 'Idiosyncracy and Technique' and her letters, like her poems and essays, are triumphs of idiosyncracy and technique, packed with literary judgements and observations about innumerable natural and cultural worlds.

Moore's poem 'England' speaks idiosyncratically and technically about culture and letters. Having initially spoken of England 'with its baby rivers and little towns, each with its abbey or cathedral', she goes on to invoke 'Italy with its equal / shores', 'France, "the chrystal of the nocturnal butterfly"' and 'the East with its snails', before moving on to the poem's real ground, her native America:

> the wild man's land; grass-less, links-less, language-less
>   country – in which letters are written
>   not in Spanish, not in Greek, not in Latin, not in short-
>   hand
> but in plain American which cats and dogs can read! The
>   letter 'a' in psalm and calm, when
> pronounced with the sound of 'a' in candle, is very
>   noticeable but
>
> why should continents of misapprehension have to be ac-
>   counted for by the
> fact? (Schulze 99–100)

After having apprehended several continents as well as 'continents of misapprehension', Moore speaks here of letters in two distinct but interdependent senses. We initially assume 'letters' means correspondence, but she goes on to speak of the pronunciation of 'the letter "a"' and we realise the term here covers correspondence, literature ('the profession of letters') and literal letters on the page, while relating all these to speech, and making us see and hear the importance of how letters are pronounced. In other words, the poem makes us think both of script – written letters – and speech – how letters (in every sense) *sound*. She is hearing letters – as well as situating them in a cultural context, affirming in her less than plain style 'plain American which cats and dogs can read'. Her celebration of the vernacular is comparable to Frost's of the 'sentence sound', but no language is so plain 'cats and dogs' can read it, and the last clause undermines the idea of straight communication it seems to be affirming, reinforcing Moore's simultaneous commitment to democracy and refusal to dumb down to her audience.

Moore's verse here almost gives the illusion of being chopped-up prose, like a letter itself. The jagged left-hand margin is hard at work to keep the prose feel while also disrupting it. In a letter about *The Waste Land* she told Yvor Winters that 'for the litterateur, prose is a step beyond poetry . . . and then there is another poetry that is a step beyond that' (Moore 192). Moore's virtuosic correspondence offers the best point of entry into the eclectic, concrete and concerted universe of her poems, offering a sense of both the intimate audience of her friends and the larger intellectual and cultural world she inhabited. As an illustration we could take a poem that mirrors an earlier letter of hers and takes as its subject an object that Louise Crane had enclosed in a letter to Moore. On receiving it, Moore wrote on 1 March 1937:

> Dear Miss Crane,
>   . . . A nautilus has always seemed to be something supernatural. The more I look at it the less I can credit it, – this large yet weightless thing, with a glaze like ivory on the entrance and even on the sides. How curious the sudden change of direction in the corrugations, and the transparent oyster white dullness of the 'paper'. The wings are so symmetrical I should not know any part had been broken if you had not said so.
>   The clipping you enclose [a clipping from *Town and Country* which lists celebrities as 'intellectuals or bohemians' and lists Moore as the former] makes me need a house by no means transparent. (Moore 381)

Seven months later Moore sent Crane a poem entitled 'The Paper Nautilus' as 'a weak expression of a powerful incentive', saying 'always thinking of the shell as Louise's nautilus, it would be morbid to suppress them'. It is sent as a 'Valentine' and begins:

> For authorities whose hopes
> are shaped by mercenaries?
>   Writers entrapped by
>   teatime fame and by
> commuters' comforts? Not for these
>   the paper nautilus
>   constructs her thin glass shell. (Schulman 238)

The poem keeps the context of the original letter, relating the particularised account of the marine creature (with its 'dull / white outside' and 'close- / laid Ionic chiton folds') to the world of 'teatime' celebrities invoked by the clipping enclosed with it. It is a characteristic celebration of an animal life that also acknowledges Crane's gift while embodying her own defensive biographical and aesthetic strategy as 'the watchful maker of it'. The poem incarnates and dramatises the abiding fascination with morphology that links her investment in animals and poems. Her prose letter has been wholly reconfigured as a recognisably stanzaic poem, but its origins, like Dickinson's 'Humming Bird', lie in a letter, and in the exchange represented by letters between women. We are invited to recognise the creative force of gender in the assertion that 'the paper nautilus / constructs *her* thin glass shell' and dwell upon the affinity between the 'paper' used to construct shell, letter and poem.

Moore's correspondence represents a very different version of literary authority from that of her friends, the mandarin Eliot and maverick Ezra Pound. Eliot, Pound and Moore were all editors and impresarios of modernism and their correspondence documents and performs their role in shaping other people's texts, magazines, books and lives. Like their poems, their letters are above all literary performances, performances which cast light on their *oeuvres* in prose and verse but also on the institutions of modernism. Though they are far away from the relatively marginal literary milieus of Hopkins and Emily Dickinson, their letters are equally crucial in revealing the ways poems circulate among groups of correspondents before and after publication, as *The Waste Land* circulated between Pound and Eliot. There is no better measure of the different ways in which Eliot, Pound and Moore performed their divergent notions of literary authority than their very different correspondences.

V

One thing all poets' letters document is the fact that poets need other people (other poets in particular) to write to. There are no 'single' poets, however singular (like Moore) or solitary (like Emily Dickinson). Without exception poets need a 'web of friendship', a group of friends and editors with which to share poems, exchange gossip, swap shop-talk and be competitive. This was as true in the era of Byron, Coleridge, Keats and Elizabeth Barrett as in that of Frost, Eliot, Pound and Moore, or later Bishop and Lowell, while in the very recent past Ted Hughes called letter writing 'excellent training for conversation with the world', a claim ferociously embodied in his *Selected Letters*. Friendship and competition are the threads that bind these correspondences together and establish the conditions of modern lyric within the smaller sphere of personal correspondence, creating a crucial bridgehead to the larger public sphere (and 'world').

Emily Dickinson spoke of a poem as a 'letter to the world', and poets' letters are not only an important 'dimension' of their work, as Richard Howard argued, but essential instruments for gauging the ways their poetry (and that of others) addresses and engages with the world. This brings us back to where we started, the Dickinson text that is both a letter and a poem, and which gives permanent form to a 'Route of Evanescence' that comes to us like 'mail'.

NOTES

1. In a letter to the editor, Jonathan Allison wrote: 'I would quibble with Nick Laird's claim in his review of the *Letters of Louis MacNeice* that the letters "remain mostly secondary texts" in that they "help explain the life not the work" (*LRB*, 3 March). Strictly speaking, an author's letters are primary, not secondary texts, but even loosely speaking I can't agree that the letters are of secondary importance.' *London Review of Books*, 17 March 2011.
2. Introducing *The Letters of Wallace Stevens*, Howard called poets' letters 'that indispensable genre' (Stevens vii).
3. The poem is in Franklin 559.
4. See also Robin G. Schulze, *The Web of Friendship: Marianne Moore and Wallace Stevens* (Ann Arbor: University of Michigan Press, 1996).
5. Noakes doesn't include the letter to Carlingford in the *Selected Letters* or refer to it in her edition of the verse.
6. 'Turgenev', *The Egoist* 4.11 (December 1917): 167.

WORKS CITED

Auden, W. H., *The Dyer's Hand* (London: Faber and Faber, 1963).
—— *Forewords and Afterwords* (New York: Vintage, 1974).
Barrett, Elizabeth, and Robert Browning, *Robert Browning and Elizabeth Barrett: The Courtship Correspondence*, ed. Daniel Karlin (Oxford: Oxford University Press, 1990).
Bevis, Matthew, 'Tennyson's Humour', in Robert Douglas-Fairhurst and Seamus Perry (eds), *Tennyson Among the Poets: Bicentenary Essays* (Oxford: Oxford University Press, 2009), pp. 231–58.
Bishop, Elizabeth, *One Art: The Selected Letters of Elizabeth Bishop*, ed. Robert Giroux (London: Chatto & Windus, 1994).
—— *Poems, Prose, and Letters*, ed. Lloyd Schwartz and Robert Giroux (New York: Library of America, 2008).
Eliot, T. S., *The Letters of T. S. Eliot, Volume 1: 1898–1922*, ed. Valerie Eliot and Hugh Haughton (London: Faber and Faber, 2009).
—— *The Letters of T. S. Eliot, Volume 2: 1923–1925*, ed. Valerie Eliot and Hugh Haughton (London: Faber and Faber, 2009).
—— *Selected Essays* (London: Faber and Faber, 1932).
—— 'Turgenev', *The Egoist* 4.11 (December 1917): 167.
—— *The Use of Poetry and the Use of Criticism* (London: Faber and Faber, 1933).
Franklin, R. W. (ed.), *The Poems of Emily Dickinson: Reading Edition* (Cambridge, MA: Harvard University Press, 2003).
Frost, Robert, *Collected Poems, Prose and Plays*, ed. Richard Poirier and Mark Richardson (New York: Library of America, 1995).
Hamilton, Ian, *The Keepers of the Flame: Literary Estates and the Rise of Biography* (London: Pimlico, 1992).
—— *The Trouble with Money and Other Essays* (London: Bloomsbury, 1998).
Heaney, Seamus, *The Place of Writing* (Atlanta: Scholars Press, 1989).

Howard, Richard, *Paper Trail: Selected Prose, 1965–2003* (New York: Farrar, Straus and Giroux, 2004).

Hughes, Ted, *The Selected Letters of Ted Hughes*, ed. Christopher Reid (London: Faber and Faber, 2009).

Johnson, Thomas H. (ed.), *The Letters of Emily Dickinson*, 3 vols (Cambridge: Belknap Press, 1958).

Keats, John, *Letters of John Keats: A Selection*, ed. Robert Gittings (Oxford: Oxford University Press, 1975).

Lear, Edward, *Complete Verse and Other Nonsense*, ed. Vivien Noakes (London: Penguin, 2006).

Mahon, Derek, *New Collected Poems* (Loughcrew: Gallery Press, 2011).

Moore, Marianne, *The Selected Letters of Marianne Moore*, ed. Bonnie Costello, Celeste Goodridge and Cristanne Miller (London: Faber and Faber, 1998).

Noakes, Vivien (ed.), *Selected Letters of Edward Lear* (Oxford: Oxford University Press, 1988).

Ricks, Christopher, 'Tennyson, Alfred', *Oxford Dictionary of National Biography*, <http://dx.doi.org/10.1093/ref:odnb/27137> (last accessed 7 July 2014).

Schulman, Grace (ed.), *The Poems of Marianne Moore* (London: Faber and Faber, 2003).

Schulze, Robin G. (ed.), *Becoming Marianne Moore: The Early Poems 1907–1924* (Berkeley: University of California Press, 2002).

Strachey, Constance (ed.), *Letters of Edward Lear* (London: T. Fisher Unwin, 1909).

Stevens, Wallace, *Letters of Wallace Stevens*, ed. Holly Stevens (Berkeley: University of California Press, 1966).

Symons, Arthur, *The Symbolist Movement in Literature* (New York: Dutton, 1919).

Tennyson, Alfred Lord, *The Poems of Tennyson*, ed. Christopher Ricks (London: Longman, 1969).

Williams, William Carlos, *Autobiography* (New York: New Directions, 1951).

Wright, James, *A Wild Perfection: The Selected Letters of James Wright*, ed. Anne Wright and Sandra Rose Maley (New York: Farrar, Straus and Giroux, 2005).

Part II: Romantic and Victorian Letter Writing

5   Wordsworth's Sweating Pages: The Love Letters of William and Mary Wordsworth

Frances Wilson

I

In 1977, a previously unknown exchange of thirty-one letters between William and Mary Wordsworth was sold by Sotheby's. Written when the couple had been married for a decade, they describe sexual longing and what Wordsworth called 'the lively gushing thought employing spirit stirring passion of love', which was 'very rare' in 'married life . . . even among good people' (*Love Letters* 59). The correspondence was occasioned by two unusual periods of separation which coincided, importantly, with the absence of Wordsworth's sister Dorothy, who lived with the family and would find such expressions 'obnoxious'. Without Dorothy to look over their shoulders, husband and wife at last 'avail[ed]' themselves 'of the opportunity' to reveal the depth of their attachment (59). 'Fail not to write to me without reserve,' Wordsworth implored in the first of his 'heart-feeding' letters, as Mary called them, written when he was visiting his patron in Leicestershire on 22 July 1810. 'Never have I been able to receive such a letter from you, let me not be disappointed, but give me your heart that I may kiss the words a thousand times!' (42). Their letters, Wordsworth told Mary, would be 'entrusted to [her] keeping' and 'deposited side by side' as a 'bequest' for whichever one of them should survive the other (60). So diligent was Mary in the performance of her task that they remained hidden for one hundred and fifty years, until a stamp-dealer from Carlisle found them in a salvage sack he had bought for a fiver.

'O My William!' Mary replied from Grasmere on 1 August:

> It is not in my power to tell thee how I have been affected by this dearest of all letters – it was so unexpected – so new a thing to see the breathing of thy inmost heart upon paper that I was quite overpowered, and now that I sit down to answer thee in the loneliness and depth of that love which unites us and which cannot be felt but by ourselves, I am so agitated and my eyes are so bed-immed that I scarcely know how to proceed . . . (46)

Unexpected indeed. The man who made his letters, so he told Thomas Moore, 'as bad & dull as possible' to guard against the 'horror' of their being '*preserved*' (1909), who explained to Charles Lamb that he had an 'almost insurmountable aversion from letter writing', revealed that he could 'write on' to his wife 'to the end of time' (48). Wordsworth could write on to his critics to the end of time as well: when his comments about the 1800 edition of *Lyrical Ballads* did not please the poet, Lamb described in a letter to Thomas Manning how 'The Post did not sleep a moment. I received almost instantaneously a long letter of four sweating pages from my Reluctant Letter-Writer' (231).

'How happy I was to learn', Wordsworth told Mary in his second letter, that 'thy delight in reading had if possible been more exquisite than mine in writing'; 'My love and dearest darling,' he says on another occasion, 'am not I good in writing thee such frequent and long Letters, Let me praise myself' (178). Nor would those who knew the author have thought credible this 'breathing of [his] inmost heart': Wordsworth was described by Shelley in 'Peter Bell the Third' as a 'solemn and unsexual man', and by Coleridge (for whom in the poem 'The Pains of Sleep' 'To be beloved is all I need, / And whom I love, I love indeed') as 'by nature incapable of being in Love' (*Collected Letters* 305). For Thomas De Quincey, 'the most interesting circumstance in [Wordsworth's] marriage, the one which perplexed us exceedingly, was the very possibility that it should ever have been brought to bear . . . [Wordsworth] never could . . . in any emphatic sense, have been a lover' (130). The sexlessness of Wordsworth's persona permeates his poems as well: G. Wilson Knight, in *The Starlit Dome*, described *The Prelude* as 'peculiarly non-sexual' (23), while for Lionel Trilling, Wordsworth 'carries the element of quietude to the point of the denial of sexuality' (135). While he filled his poetry with wise children, brave mothers, stoical animals and ancient solitaries, there is, as Camille Paglia put it, the 'radical exclusion of one human type: the adult male of active virility . . . a stone in the road arouses more fellow-feeling in Wordsworth than does a masculine man' (304).

Wordsworth's twentieth-century readers responded to the content of these letters like a legal team finding the evidence to release their client from a life-sentence. The poet had been involved in a miscarriage of justice: far from being cold and self-absorbed, it transpired that he had sexual feelings for his wife, the woman he variously described as 'a phantom', an 'apparition', a 'spirit' and a 'dancing shape'. It was finally possible, Jonathan Wordsworth announced in the *London Review of Books*, to imagine what Wordsworth would 'look like in bed'. It was at least possible to imagine what he looked like in bed reading Mary's letters:

> I came in last night wet and read both the Letters in bed. Thine was the tenderest and fondest of all I have received from thee, and my longing to have thee in my arms was so great, and the feeling of my heart so delicious, that my whole frame was over powered with Love & longing. Well was it for me that I was stretched upon my bed, for I think I could scarcely have stood upon my feet for excess of happiness and depth of affection. (*Love Letters* 210)

It was also finally possible to imagine Mary in bed, albeit in a state of exhaustion from looking after five children under seven years old: 'I have never gone to bed this week without being wearied-out from head to foot,' she tells William. Carrying her newborn son around Grasmere Vale, Mary is mistaken for a pauper; she has 'become', so she tells Wordsworth, 'like nobody in my looks and appearance', but to us she has become at last like somebody. The formally ghostly figure is fleshed out into a forty-year-old woman with greying hair and missing teeth, struggling to put on weight in order to seem more comely to her husband.

The subject of these letters is not only love. They are filled with gossip, local description, the 'vexed' problem of Coleridge, shared concerns about the children, and news – Wordsworth was visiting the House of Commons in May 1812 when the prime minister, Spencer Perceval, was murdered in the lobby ('O William that murderer was perhaps with thee in the members gallery last week,' wrote Mary). Their perennial topic, however, is bodies: their own and those of other people. Mary writes about the children's worms ('no more raspberries'), the partial paralysis of their two-year-old daughter Catharine following a stroke ('I have tied Catharine's left Arm down to make her use her right . . . I think the confinement causes her to move more straight'), the baby she puts to her breast in order to read her husband's letters undisturbed ('Cath[arine] is terribly jealous of him'). Wordsworth describes his eye infection ('really it has made no progress these ten days'), his digestion ('my stomach failed a fortnight since from too much talking'), his piles ('my old enemy'), his bowels (a 'great quantity of thin mucous . . . is involuntarily discharged'), the bowels of Daniel Stuart (who has 'had a discharge of blood and slime which brought him to the edge of the grave') and Sara Hutchinson (who became ill on a walk because she was 'unable to attend leisurely to a call of nature'), likewise the appearances of his friends' wives (Mrs Montagu is 'utterly odious to me', Humphry Davy's bride is 'full of affectation, never letting her features alone'), the enormous breasts of a woman he encounters ('two great hay cocks'), his dining companions in London (Mr Price is 'destroying' himself 'by gluttony', Miss Price is 'a deformed Creature', General Fitzpatrick has 'a complexion as yellow as a frog', Lady Crewes is a 'fat unwieldy woman'), and the miraculous improvement in Dorothy's well-being: 'Her throat and neck are quite filled up; and if it were not for her teeth she would really look quite young. I never saw a more rapid and striking improvement in the health and appearance of anyone' (Love Letters 35). While Wordsworth is 'giddy at the thought of seeing thee once more', Mary 'trembles' at 'the joints' at the prospect of their reunion.

Mary Wordsworth may, as Thomas De Quincey said, have been a woman of 'few words' – 'she could only say "God Bless You"' (De Quincey 129) – but her letters, written in spare moments of busy days, are long and conversational, filled with the delicate phrases we would expect from the hand that contributed the finest lines to Wordsworth's daffodil poem, 'They flash upon the inward eye, / Which is the bliss of solitude'. Wordsworth clearly depended on Mary's gentle mockery: 'You often laugh at me about duty,' he writes of his impending visit to her sister, Sara Hutchinson, 'and this is a pure march of duty' (Love Letters 36). Patient, poised and pitch-perfect, it is Mary's narrative perspective that sets the tone of their family life: 'Whining

Thomas', she writes of their three-year-old son, 'has grown more ravenous after string than ever, he now *sneaks* upstairs into our drawers and be it tape stays laces or anything in the likeness of string he has no mercy upon it' (54).

While we see Mary in the present tense of her day-to-day life, Wordsworth is as inaccessible in this exchange as he ever was. It is curious that the man who wrote so much about his own interior should remain unknowable to his readers: despite the considerable trace he left, the workings of Wordsworth's private world have always seemed mysterious. Even when we can see him most clearly – in De Quincey's accounts of Wordsworth's 'serviceable' legs ('it was really a pity . . . that he had not another pair for evening dress parties'), his cutting the pages of a new book with a buttery knife and beating down the rent of Allan Bank ('he was . . . a somewhat hard pursuer of what he thought fair advantages') – Wordsworth does not seem quite there (135). What Wordsworth's letters to Mary confirm is that he faded out in solitude. Despite his fetishising of the isolated artist, he was incapable of being alone: 'I cannot bear it,' he tells her (*Love Letters* 38). A natural collaborator, Wordsworth depended on others – be it Dorothy, Coleridge or Mary – for his completion. 'I am every moment seized with a longing', he writes to his wife, 'that you might see the objects which interest me as I pass along, and not having you at my side my pleasure is so imperfect that after a short look had rather not see the objects at all' (59). This is not sentiment but an expression of high anxiety: without the presence of someone he loves, Wordsworth is only half there.

How has the discovery of this correspondence changed the biographical portrait of Wordsworth's marriage? His happiness with Mary was, after all, never in doubt; his household was known as 'the family of love' and Wordsworth's readers unite in bemoaning the dulling effect of domestic harmony on his later work. Added to which it has been possible to imagine what he 'looked like in bed' since 1916, when Wordsworth's relationship with the French Royalist Annette Vallon – a secret contained in the family circle – was revealed. Shelley's 'solemn and unsexual man' has long been unmasked as an 'adult male of active virility': Annette Vallon conceived her daughter, Caroline, within weeks of meeting Wordsworth, and Mary also became pregnant instantly, her first child appearing eight months after the wedding. It was not because they confirmed Wordsworth's feelings for his wife that these letters were greeted with such excitement, but because they dispelled – or so it was hoped – the rumour that he had feelings for his sister.

In her introduction to *The Love Letters of William and Mary Wordsworth*, Beth Darlington hopes that we will now hear no more of the thesis forwarded by F. W. Bateson in *Wordsworth: A Reinterpretation*, that Wordsworth's marriage was 'a desperate remedy' to cure himself of his passion for Dorothy (156–7). 'More than any biographical documents known hitherto,' Darlington writes, 'these new letters show us, without distortion, who William and Mary Wordsworth were and what sort of love bound them so compellingly together as man and wife' (20). Pamela Woof, in her edition of Dorothy Wordsworth's *Grasmere and Alfoxden Journals*, concedes that the '"incest theory" proposed in the mid fifties by F. W. Bateson, has waned somewhat since the discovery in 1977 of passionate love letters between Wordsworth and his wife' (xxvii).

'Incest theory' aside, the 'sort of love' that 'bound' Wordsworth and Mary 'so compellingly together' was not as straightforward as Darlington and Woof suggest. Because Wordsworth was 'passionate' about Mary it does not mean that he was not also passionate about Dorothy – the two women did not erase one another. After all, we know that Wordsworth's love for Dorothy, as his daughter Dora later said, was 'of no common nature'; fifty years after his marriage, Wordsworth wrote that without the presence of his sister in his life, 'the Phasis of my Moon would be robbed of light to a degree that I have not courage to think of'. Far from normalising the frequently 'misconstrued' Wordsworth ménage, as Darlington puts it (22), this exchange undermines the view of the relationship between Wordsworth, his wife and his sister as one in which, as Mary E. Burton put it in *The Letters of Mary Wordsworth 1800–1855*, they 'live[d] together in perfect harmony until they die[d]', with Dorothy happily accepting her new position in her brother's life. Dorothy is the only person who would have been surprised by these letters, and it is from Dorothy that they were kept a secret.

II

The letters fall into two batches. The first seven were exchanged in July and August 1810, when William and Dorothy left Mary and the children in Grasmere in order to visit Wordsworth's patron, Sir George Beaumont, at his Leicestershire home of Coleorton Hall. Dorothy then went on alone to see Thomas and Catherine Clarkson at their new home in Bury St Edmunds while Wordsworth journeyed to the Welsh borders to see Mary's sister Sara Hutchinson, who was keeping house for her brother on his farm at Hindwell. The relationship between Wordsworth and Coleridge was currently under strain, and in October that year it would break down. Three years earlier, Coleorton had been the stage of a confrontation between the two poets when Coleridge imagined with horrific clarity what Wordsworth looked like in bed. A guest of the Wordsworths, who were currently living on the Coleorton estate, Coleridge had suffered an agony of jealousy over his suspicion that Wordsworth was teaching Sara to 'withdraw herself from my emotions'. He later described what he saw, or thought he saw, in the bedroom as a 'horrid phantasm' of Wordsworth with Sara, her 'beautiful breasts uncovered'. 'O agony!' Coleridge had written in his notebook, 'O the vision of that Saturday morning – of the Bed – O cruel! Is he not beloved, adored by two' – referring to Sara and Mary – '& two such Beings' (96).

Revisiting Coleorton in July 1810, Wordsworth was now warding off the jealousy of another of the beings by whom he was beloved and adored. 'D[orothy] is gone to Church,' his first letter to Mary begins, 'and I seize with eagerness the opportunity to write to my dearest love.' His letter ends with him asking Mary to send a reply which will wait for him at Hindwell. Her letter, he instructs, is to be

for myself and of which I need only read parts to the rest of the family – I know that S[ara Hutchinson] will take no offense at this for my soul demands such letters, they seem to unite me to you person & spirit body and soul, in the privacy of sacred retirement, spite of the distance that separates us . . . But I must turn from these . . . thoughts to things external, and more fit to be trusted to this frail paper. (*Love Letters* 39)

Mary's reply was duly waiting. She had wept with 'happiness' on receiving Wordsworth's letter, which had given her 'a new feeling', she wrote, 'for it is the first letter of love that has been exclusively my own'. With characteristic elegance, Mary described her happiness with William as the 'unconsciousness that I had my *all in all* about me – *that* feeling which I have never wanted since the solitary night did not separate us' (49). She circles around the problem of maintaining the fiction that Dorothy plays an equal role in the marriage; the length of Mary's letters to Dorothy must be seen to be the same as those she writes to William: 'as I can but write her a short letter, when you write to her you do not give her to understand that you have received a longer one – this would make her uneasy' (53). An unmarried person, Wordsworth explained to Mary, could not 'feel' the 'loneliness' of physical separation; even Sara Hutchinson, the recipient of Coleridge's adoration, would not understand 'how I have longed to be with you' (36). In order to 'awaken' Sara 'to a sense of th[e] longing' he was suffering during his sojourn at Hindwell, Wordsworth would give her one of Mary's less passionate letters to read. The most ardent letter he 'kept to [him]self and only read [Sara] such parts as related to matter of fact. The general strain of it was too sacred and too intensely connubial for any eye but my own' (88). Similarly, Mary would write to Wordsworth of 'the blessed bond that binds husband and wife so much closer than the bond of Brotherhood – however dear and affectionate a family of Brothers [&] Sisters may love each other' (82).

Wordsworth's second letter was another 'gift from the whole undivided heart for your whole and sole possession'. He recalls their first parting as lovers when Mary left their home of Racedown in Dorset in 1797 after a seven-month visit, and imagines what might have happened had they then thrown caution to the wind:

> You would have walked on Northwards with me at your side, till unable to part from each other we might have come in sight of those hills which skirt the road for so many miles, and thus continuing our journey . . . I fancied that we should have seen so deeply into each others hearts, and been so fondly locked in each others arms, that we should have braved the worst and parted no more. (62)

Dorothy's account of Mary's stay at Racedown, described at the time to her friend Jane Pollard, was of a gang of three. Together, Dorothy, William and Mary were 'as happy as human beings can be; that is, when William is at home'. When he is away, 'you cannot imagine how dull we feel and what a vacuum his loss [occasions]' (*Early Years* 181). Her awareness that a bond was developing from which she was excluded is revealed in the first letter Dorothy sent Mary after her departure, in which she describes the momentous day when Coleridge leapt over the gate behind their house, jumped the stream and bounded into their lives: 'You had a great loss in not seeing Coleridge. He is a wonderful man. His conversation teems with soul, mind, and spirit. Then he is so benevolent, so good tempered and cheerful, and, like William, interests himself so much about every little trifle' (188). Rather than telling Mary how much she is missed, Dorothy lets her know that she has been replaced by a more compatible companion for William. As for herself, left alone with Coleridge, Dorothy implies that she would never 'feel dull'.

Initiating a private correspondence with Mary, Wordsworth was taking a tremendous risk. Writing and reading were shared in the Wordsworth household, where love letters were addressed to everyone. 'I will not say, how dearly I love you all,' Coleridge had written in 1807, 'as perhaps it is a misfortune, that so enormous is the difference between my Love of you & of others, that it seems as if I loved nothing & nobody else.' In one letter to Mary, Wordsworth makes a 'blunder', realising that the 'tender and overflowing expressions of Love which were meant for no eyes but thine' had been penned 'by mistake' on a frank addressed to 'Miss W—'. He 'crossed and re-crossed the Frank and part of it I fear will still be legible; at all events the very attempt to hide will give offense – I have not blotted the sheet so that it is impossible to make out the obnoxious expressions' (Love Letters 157). The letters that could be shown to Sara Hutchinson to teach her the difference between sibling and married love would represent for Dorothy a form of primal scene. The Wordsworths clearly conducted their marriage as though it were an illicit affair: stealing kisses, whispering in the dark, hiding billets-doux.

Following the death of their mother, Dorothy, aged six, had been separated from her father and brothers and raised by an aunt in Halifax. She did not meet William again until her adolescence, after which her fantasy of adult life became one of living in a self-contained and self-sufficient trinity with her brother and a like-minded companion. Virginia Woolf described it as consisting of 'William and Nature and Dorothy', but the third party was initially to be Annette Vallon, then Dorothy's childhood friend Jane Pollard, after which it was temporarily realised in Coleridge. The continuation of Dorothy's place in the trinity with Mary Hutchinson was confirmed by Wordsworth on the morning of his wedding when, as Dorothy recorded it in her journal, they exchanged vows of their own: 'I gave him the wedding ring – with how deep a blessing! I took it from my forefinger where I had worn it the whole of the night before – he slipped it again onto my finger and blessed me fervently' (Grasmere Journals 126). The later heavy 'crossing and recrossing' of these lines to make them illegible – possibly by Dorothy but more probably by William – suggests that Mary was to be kept ignorant of what Woolf called his 'strange love' for Dorothy just as Dorothy was to be kept ignorant of William's 'obnoxious' love for Mary. The letters to Mary were a secret from his sister, and Dorothy's journal entries were kept a secret from his wife.

Dorothy's Grasmere Journals, a love letter to her brother on the eve of his wedding, provide the context in which Wordsworth's love letters to Mary should be read. It is as if the language of longing was one that Dorothy and William had learned together, much as his poems were born of walks, thoughts, visions and talks shared to such a degree that, as Virginia Woolf put it with perfect acuity, 'they hardly knew which felt, which spoke, which saw the daffodils or the sleeping city; only Dorothy stored the mood in prose, and later William came and bathed in it and made it into poetry.' In her opening entry on 14 May 1800 Dorothy records her misery at the departure of William and their brother John, who has been staying with them in Dove Cottage throughout the year: 'Wm and John set off into Yorkshire after dinner at ½ past 2 o'clock – cold pork in their pockets . . . My heart was so full that I could hardly speak to W when I gave him a farewell kiss' (1). The purpose of William's journey – to visit Mary and cement their ties – is not mentioned, and the presence of John, part of their current domestic trinity, is also elided. Throughout the journal, Dorothy describes her life as consisting of only William and herself. If the presence of John is necessary in order that he be excluded, the exclusion of Dorothy is necessary to create the tension of Wordsworth's and Mary's letters. Dorothy's journal was begun in William's absence, and William's first letter to Mary begins at the point of Dorothy's absence; William opens with the name 'Dorothy', just as Dorothy's journal opens with the name 'William'. Similarly, the longing Wordsworth expresses for Mary to complete his perceptions – 'I am never instructed, never delighted, never touchd by a tender feeling but my heart turns instinctively to you. I never see a flower that pleases me but I wish for you . . .' – repeats the sense of William as the continuation of herself which Dorothy describes throughout her journals (see Wilson for an extension of this thesis).

The Wordsworth circle was composed of ever shifting triangles, and there were other trinities apart from that of Mary, Dorothy and William. Mary told William that his was 'the first letter of love that has been *exclusively my own*' (my emphasis), but it was not the first letter of love that she had received. During the years when William's future was seen to lie with Annette Vallon, who was raising their daughter in France while the war continued to prevent traffic between the two countries, it seems that his brother John had harboured hopes that he and Mary might one day marry. Between 1800 and 1802 John sent 'Dearest Mary' seventeen letters, on one occasion writing twice in an evening just for the 'pleasure of talking to you a little again'. After hearing the news of her engagement, he had attached to the end of a letter being written to Mary by Dorothy one of his own: 'I have been reading your letter over and over again My Dearest Mary till tears have come into my eyes and I know not how to express myself . . . But whatever fate Befal me I shall love thee to the last and bear thy memory to the grave.' This was the last letter that John would write to her before his death at sea in 1805. Wordsworth's feelings for Mary Hutchinson were kept from the painfully shy John, while John's feelings, we imagine, were kept from his powerful older brother.

III

The next twenty-five letters were exchanged between 23 April and 10 June 1812, when Wordsworth was in London and Mary was taking a tour of the Wye with two of her children, leaving the others at home in the care of Dorothy. Their subject continues to be love, but this time the meaning of the word is examined in relation to Coleridge rather than Dorothy. The interest of the exchange no longer lies in the story Wordsworth and Mary tell Dorothy about their relationship, but in the story Wordsworth tells Mary about his relationship with Coleridge.

When Wordsworth and Coleridge met in 1797, Coleridge had been the contented husband and father while Wordsworth was 'unhappy, dissatisfied, full of craving', as Coleridge put it in his notebooks (118). Fourteen years later and Wordsworth was enjoying the love of a wife and young children while Coleridge 'whirled about without a center – as in a nightmair – no gravity – a vortex without a center' (119). In 1810, heavily dependent on opium and desperately in love with Sara Hutchinson, Coleridge had moved in with the Wordsworths at Allan Bank. The experience of having him as part of their household was described in a letter from Dorothy to Catherine Clarkson:

> [Coleridge's] whole time and thoughts, (except when he is reading, and he reads a great deal), are employed in deceiving himself, and seeking to deceive others. He will tell me that he has been writing . . . when I *know* he has not written a single line. This Habit pervades all his words and actions, and you feel perpetually new hollowness and emptiness. I am loth to say this, and burn this letter, I entreat you . . . He lies in bed, always till after 12 o'clock, sometimes much later, and never walks out – Even the finest spring day does not tempt him to seek the fresh air; and this beautiful valley seems a blank to him. He never leaves his own parlour except at dinner and tea, and sometimes supper, and then he always seems impatient to get back to his solitude – he goes the moment his food is swallowed. Sometimes he does not speak a word, and when he does talk it is always very much and upon subjects as far aloof from himself and his friends as possible. (*Middle Years* 399)

In October of that year Coleridge accepted the invitation of Basil Montagu, a mutual friend who was passing through the Lakes, to travel with him to London where he could consult a doctor and recover his health. Prior to their departure Wordsworth had privately warned Montagu about what he was taking on, a conversation which Montagu then tactlessly repeated to Coleridge, including the statements that he – Coleridge – had been an 'absolute nuisance' and that Montagu had been 'commissioned' to say that Wordsworth had 'no hope' of him. Montagu's remarks resulted in the worst crisis of Coleridge's life, which he expressed in terms of love: 'Not *Loved* . . . How perceptibly has [Wordsworth's] love for poor C[oleridge] lessened since he procured other enthusiastic admirers! – As long as C . . . was the *sole* Admirer and Lover, *so long* he was loved. – But poor C. *loved*, truly loved!' (*Notebooks* 118).

The tables had turned once again: five years earlier, when Coleridge had returned from Malta, it had been Wordsworth who was mourning the love of his friend in the opening stanza of 'A Complaint':

> There is a change – and I am poor;
> Your love hath been, nor long ago,
> A fountain at my fond heart's door,
> Whose only business was to flow;
> And flow it did; not taking heed
> Of its own bounty, or my need.

The 'fever of thought & longing & affection & desire' that Wordsworth now described feeling towards Mary must be seen in relation to the chill wind blowing in the direction of Coleridge, whose great subjects were precisely the fever of thought and longing and affection and desire. 'The events of last year,' Coleridge wrote in his notebooks, 'and emphatically of the last month, forced me to perceive – No one on earth has ever LOVED me' (229).

The purpose of Wordsworth's journey to London was to settle, rather late in the day, the 'ugly affair of Coleridge'. 'Coleridge called here yesterday at 4 o'clock,' he tells Mary on 29 April. '– I find he has wished to tell his story to the B[eaumonts] with plentiful abuse of me to which they would not listen. This is scandalous conduct on his part, and most ungrateful.' 'I hope you will shortly get the unpleasant business of C's off your mind,' Mary replies sympathetically (*Love Letters* 110). 'Let me first speak of C[oleridge]'s affair,' Wordsworth writes on 2 May. 'I have seen a Letter in which without naming me, though clearly meaning no other Person he calls me his bitterest Calumniator, describes the agony he has suffered in consequence of the behaviour of one (meaning the same person) who had been in his heart of hearts . . . This conduct is insufferable and I am determined to put an end to it' (122). Discussing Coleridge with Charles Lamb brings on a bout of Wordsworth's famous 'indigestion': 'I do not know that I ever was more rouzed in my life; and I feel the effects in my stomach at this moment' (124). Coleridge's attempts to support himself and his family by a course of public lectures are described as 'a most odious way of picking up money, and scattering about his own and his friend's thoughts', and Wordsworth imagines, with evident pleasure, that they will not 'bring him much profit. He has a world of bitter enemies, and is deplorably unpopular . . . you cannot form a notion to what degree Coleridge is disliked or despised' (125). According to Lady Beaumont, Wordsworth gloats, Coleridge 'will let no one talk but himself' (110) and he nurses the flattering suggestion of Henry Crabb Robinson, 'not a little interesting', that 'there was in Coleridge's mind a lurking literary jealousy of me. I totally rejected that supposition . . . Robinson is a very clever man' (136).

Her husband's lengthy letters provide Mary with no report of the 'half-reconciliation' – as Coleridge called it – of the friendship (*Notebooks* 125), no record of the exchanges – verbal and otherwise – between the two poets, no sympathy towards Coleridge's wounded state, no account of Wordsworth's own distress – apart from the condition of his stomach – at the whole affair. Mary is simply told that 'the business between C[oleridge] and me is settled by a letter', following which Wordsworth bursts into song: 'O my Mary, what a heavenly thing is pure & ever growing love: such do I feel for thee, and D[orothy] and S[ara] and all our dear family' (*Love Letters* 146). Coleridge's exclusion from any circle or triangle is confirmed, and Wordsworth's letters now refer once more to Dorothy as part of his union with Mary. Recalling the early days of their marriage, he reminds Mary that 'Then thou hadst only me & D – to think of'; later he describes himself as 'a Husband, and a Father, and a Brother, the blessedest of men' (201). And it is to Dorothy rather than to his wife that he sends a copy of the freezing statement he presents to Coleridge, in which Wordsworth 'solemnly denied' having 'commissioned M[ontagu] to say to C that I had no hopes of him'. 'I have not heard the particulars of what passed between C and you on your reconciliation,' Mary writes on 8 June; 'in the darkness which I am in – the case seems to me seeming to rest upon the word of one and the word of the other – I should be at a loss to fix upon which of the two I ought to depend' (249).

Today we are concerned less with the differing accounts of what passed between Montagu and Coleridge than with lining up in support of one or other of the poets. The partisanship which bedevils readers of Wordsworth and Coleridge inevitably comes into force when we respond to these letters, particularly if we have an edition of Coleridge's *Notebooks* to hand: 'Horrid Thought! It seems as if I alone of all men had *Love!* As if it were a sense, a faculty to which there was no corresponding Object!' (*Notebooks* 119). The Wordsworth we see here is the man described by Coleridge as being incapable of love, and by Southey as being obsessed with his good name: 'the one thing to which W would sacrifice all others is his own reputation, concerning which his anxiety is perfectly childish – like a woman of her own beauty' (448–9). Wordsworth's granite pride and unbending desire for self-preservation stand in marked contrast to Coleridge's heroic misery: whose side we take in their argument depends on whether we are supporters of cool rationality or of fervour, but any sympathy we might strive to feel for Wordsworth is hampered by his emotional inaccessibility. Coleridge blazes from his notebooks with astonishing vivacity; he is in the room with us, his lips parted, his eyes flashing, his despair in full force like a river bursting its banks, while Wordsworth remains time-locked, a stiff figure in a black coat confiding one thing to Mary, another thing to Sara Hutchinson and something else to Dorothy while all three women, as Coleridge bitterly put it, do 'his very eating and drinking for him'.

Romanticists know that it is not possible to love both men equally, and Wordsworth knew this as well: it is his awareness of Coleridge as the more sympathetic presence that motivates him to reiterate to Mary his wretched friend's unpopularity. Wordsworth expresses to his wife not his own indifference to Coleridge but his desire that she should feel indifferently towards him, that she should take her husband's side rather than that of the loveable man for whom – as Mary knew all too well – loving and being loved were of such importance. Before his marriage, Wordsworth had himself been excluded from a trinity which consisted of Coleridge and Mary and Sara Hutchinson: in 'A Daydream', Coleridge described a tender evening at the Hutchinsons' Yorkshire farmhouse, Gallow Hill, being cossetted by Mary and Sara. The scene remained indelible: 'in one quiet room we three are still together':

Thine eyelash on my cheek doth play –
'Tis Mary's hand upon my brow!
But let me check this tender lay,
Which none may hear but she and thou!
Like the still hive at quiet midnight humming,
Murmur it to yourselves, ye two beloved women!

Coleridge's memory recalls the line in his notebook where, following the account of seeing Wordsworth and Sara Hutchinson together on the bed, he bemoans his friend's luck in being 'beloved, adored by two – & two such Beings!'

Mary's letters duly make no reference to Coleridge other than as an irritant to her husband's health and time and, on 23 May, she consolidates her unity with Wordsworth by referring to a different recollection of Gallow Hill:

> I *do* not regret that this separation has been, for it is worth no small sacrifice to be thus assured, that instead of weakening, our union has strengthened those yearnings towards each other which I used to so strongly feel at Gallow Hill – & in which you sympathized with me at the time – that these feelings are mutual now, I have the fullest proof, from thy letters and the power of absence over my whole frame. (*Love Letters* 183)

Now visiting the landscape around Tintern Abbey, Mary is reliving lines written by Wordsworth rather than by Coleridge. 'With a beating heart did I greet the Wye – O Sylvan Wye thou Wanderer through the woods!' she writes to her husband on 29 May (193). 'Lines Composed a Few Miles above Tintern Abbey' meditates on the difference between the mature man Wordsworth saw himself as being in 1798, when the poem was composed, and the idealist he was five years earlier in 1793 when he last walked along the Wye. It is a poem about change and return which evolves into a hymn to Dorothy: 'my dear, dear Sister'. In the period between his first and second visits to the abbey Wordsworth had fallen in love with Annette Vallon, discovered the poet in himself, and formed an alliance with Dorothy and Coleridge. 'I paced this tract once alone on foot,' he now writes to Mary on 7 June, 'and great part of it in the same way with Dorothy and C[oleridge].'

Seeing Tintern Abbey for the first time in 1812, Mary, who has replaced Annette, represents a proxy Wordsworth but also a duplicate Dorothy. It is Dorothy with whom she identifies, describing to her husband her toothache: 'I was quite frightful to look at – indeed I was the exact pattern of D[orothy] at Coleorton when she had her new tooth put in' (193). In London, inhabiting what he called in 'Tintern Abbey' 'lonely rooms, and mid the din / Of towns and cities', Wordsworth revisits his poem about revisiting and replaces Dorothy with Mary, telling his wife that the 'very evening' he received her letter,

> I had been reading at Lamb's the Tintern Abbey, and repeated 100 times to myself the passage O Sylvan Wye thou Wanderer through the woods, thinking of past times, & Dorothy, dear Dorothy, and you my Darling . . . oh that I could have been with you. I long to be with you, I feel nightly and daily, waking & asleep the necessity of my not prolonging our separation. (227)

Wordsworth's canonical reference to '*the* Tintern Abbey' (my emphasis) reveals the status the poem held in his household: Mary's pilgrimage to the scene of its composition is that of a tourist to a national monument, and like many a sightseer she does not know quite what to look at: 'Oh with what a fervent heart did I greet the river Wye for thy sake & for its own loveliness,' Mary tells Wordsworth, realising only later that it was the River Dee she was greeting (103).

His finest tribute to Mary was written as Wordsworth imagined her 'by the waters and under the shade of the Wye'. In this letter, the twenty-seventh in the batch of thirty-one, he recalls 'over again my past self and thy past self also . . . from the hour of our first walks at Penrith till our last parting at Chester, and till thy wanderings upon Wye'. He is back in the terrain of 'Tintern Abbey', and not trusting himself 'to this senseless & visible sheet of paper' he asks Mary instead to 'find the evidence of what is passing within me in *thy* heart, in thy mind, in thy steps as they touch the green grass, in thy limbs as they are stretched on the soft earth'. 'The green grass' and 'the soft earth', the rolling cadence of his words recall the lines in 'Tintern Abbey' where Wordsworth describes his love for 'the round ocean, and the living air, / And the blue sky . . . and of all that we behold from this green earth'. The 'exhortation' which follows, in which Wordsworth asks Mary to find his heart in

> thy own involuntary sighs & ejaculations, in the trembling of thy hands, in the tottering of thy knees, in the blessings which thy lips pronounce, find it in thy lips themselves, & such kisses as I often give to the empty air, and in the aching of thy bosom . . .

echoes his exhortation to Dorothy in which he asks that 'the mountain mists be free, / To blow against thee'. The crescendo of Wordsworth's letter, in which he imagines himself and Mary together on the Wye, 'under the shade of the green trees, by the rippling of the waters' (*Love Letters* 229–30), leans on the lines in 'Tintern Abbey' in which Wordsworth commissioned Dorothy to always remember 'That on the banks of this delightful stream, / We stood together'. Nor must Dorothy ever forget that

> after many wanderings, many years
> Of absence, these steep woods and lofty cliffs,
> And this green pastoral landscape, were to me
> More dear, both for themselves and for thy sake.

On 3 June 1812, however, Wordsworth tells Mary that

> You cannot think how much dearer the Wye is to me since you have seen it; I loved it deeply before on most tender remembrances & considerations but now that you have seen it also & know it, & we [now?] can talk of it together what a sanctity will it attain in my mind, and of all my Poems the one [in] which I speak of it will be the most beloved by me. (241)

Dorothy would have found this particular passage from her brother to Mary the most 'obnoxious' of them all.

The passage of letters between Wales, London and Grasmere was so slow that Mary and Wordsworth remained unaware that on 4 June their daughter, Catharine, being cared for by Dorothy, had suddenly died. Six months later, 'Whining Thomas', lover of string, died also. The lives of the Wordsworths now changed, the circle closed more tightly, Mary fell into a depression and the happiest years of the marriage were over. The letters now marked the difference between the idealistic couple William and Mary once were and the mature couple they had become. Returning to their exchange, Mary inscribed 'Two days before Catharine died!' beneath the date of the letter she had sent to William on 2 June, and 'Our Child has been 4 days dead!' on the final letter she sent her husband, on 8 June.

The correspondence was then buried at the back of a drawer, 'as a bequest for the survivor of us'. But its role for Mary had been described already by Wordsworth, in the lines he addressed to Dorothy in 'Tintern Abbey':

> If solitude, or fear, or pain, or grief,
> Should be thy portion, with what healing thoughts
> Of tender joy wilt thou remember me,
> And these my exhortations

WORKS CITED

Bateson, F. W., Wordsworth: A Reinterpretation (London: Longman, 1956).

Coleridge, Samuel Taylor, Coleridge's Notebooks: A Selection, ed. Seamus Perry (Oxford: Oxford University Press, 2002).

—— Collected Letters of Samuel Taylor Coleridge, vol. 3, ed. Earl Leslie Griggs (Oxford: Clarendon Press, 1956–71).

De Quincey, Thomas, William Wordsworth, Recollections of the Lakes and the Lake Poets, ed. David Wright (Harmondsworth: Penguin, 1970).

Knight, G. Wilson, The Starlit Dome: Studies in the Poetry of Vision (Oxford: Oxford University Press, 1941).

Lamb, Charles, Works of Charles and Mary Lamb, VI–VII Letters, ed. E. V. Lucas (London: Methuen, 1905).

Moore, Thomas, The Journal of Thomas Moore, 1836–1842, vol. 5, ed. Wilfred S. Dowden (Delaware: University of Delaware Press, 1988).

Paglia, Camille, Sexual Personae: Art and Decadence from Nefertiti to Emily Dickinson (Harmondsworth: Penguin, 1990).

Southey, Robert, New Letters of Robert Southey, ed. Kenneth Curry (New York: Columbia University Press, 1965).

Trilling, Lionel, The Opposing Self: Nine Essays in Criticism (New York: Viking, 1959).

Wilson, Frances, The Ballad of Dorothy Wordsworth (London: Faber and Faber, 2008).

Woolf, Virginia, 'Four Figures: IV. Dorothy Wordsworth', The Common Reader, Second Series (London: Hogarth Press, 1935), pp. 164–72.

Wordsworth, Dorothy, The Grasmere and Alfoxden Journals of Dorothy Wordsworth, ed. Pamela Woof (Oxford: Oxford University Press, 2002).

—— and William Wordsworth, The Letters of William and Dorothy Wordsworth, The Early Years, 1787–1805, ed. Ernest De Selincourt (Oxford: Clarendon Press, 1967).

—— The Letters of William and Dorothy Wordsworth, The Middle Years, 1806–1811, ed. Ernest De Selincourt (Oxford: Clarendon Press, 1969).

Wordsworth, Jonathan, 'Wordsworth in Love', London Review of Books, 15 October 1981, pp. 9–10.

Wordsworth, William, and Mary Wordsworth, The Love Letters of William and Mary Wordsworth, ed. Beth Darlington (London: Chatto & Windus, 1982).

6   The Oakling and the Oak: The Tragedy of the Coleridges

Anne Fadiman

I

From Samuel Taylor Coleridge to Thomas Poole
24 September, 1796

My dear, very dear Poole
. . . Mrs Coleridge was delivered on Monday, September 19th, 1796, half past
two in the Morning, of a SON. . . . When I first saw the Child, I did not feel
that thrill & overflowing of affection which I expected – I looked on it with a
melancholy gaze – my mind was intensely contemplative & my heart only sad.
– But when two hours after, I saw it at the bosom of it's Mother; on her arm;
and her eye tearful & watching it's little features, then I was thrilled & melted,
& gave it the Kiss of a FATHER. . . .
   It's name is DAVID HARTLEY COLERIDGE. (*Collected Letters* 1, 235–6)

Samuel Taylor Coleridge, the new father, was twenty-three years old. It was five
years after he went up to Jesus College, Cambridge, as a classical scholar of dazzling
promise; three years after he drank, whored, neglected his studies, ran up debts,
considered shooting himself, accepted a bounty of six and a half guineas to join the
15th Regiment of Light Dragoons, covered his buttocks with saddle sores, repeatedly fell off his horse, was discharged, and returned to Cambridge; two years after he
dropped out; one year after he met William Wordsworth; one year after he married
Sara Fricker; six months after he published his first book of poems.
   That passage from Coleridge's letter to his friend Tom Poole, a local tannery
owner with progressive and literary inclinations, sounds, if not insanely besotted,
at least like the handiwork of a potentially devoted husband and father. But if you
were to read the entire letter, you might notice that Hartley's birth isn't mentioned
until the middle of the second paragraph. You might notice that in the third paragraph, Coleridge remarks casually, 'Mrs Coleridge was taken ill suddenly – & before
the Nurse or the Surgeon arrived, delivered herself.' Sara gave birth in their Bristol

cottage with no midwife in attendance – and no husband either. Coleridge was away in Birmingham. Hartley arrived a month prematurely, so you can't entirely blame his father for not being there; on the other hand, you could hardly call the absence auspicious. You might also take issue with Coleridge's breezy claim that his wife had had 'a wonderfully favorable time'. If my husband were a hundred miles away while I delivered my first child entirely alone in drafty lodgings, the words 'wonderfully favorable' might not spring to mind. And I might sigh if his signal contribution to the occasion were three sonnets, the last of which, written after seeing his son for the first time, reflected, as he put it, on 'All I had been, and all my child might be!' ('Sonnet: To a Friend Who Asked, How I Felt When the Nurse First Presented My Infant To Me' 4).

Hartley Coleridge began life with limitless promise – 'all my child might be' – and ended it universally viewed as a failure. He is remembered not for his poems or his essays, though he wrote some fine ones, but for two things and two things only: he was the son of Samuel Taylor Coleridge, and he was a disappointment. He has been called a misfit, a dreamer, a sinner, a castaway, a wayward child, a hobgoblin, a flibbertigibbet, a waif, a weird, a pariah, a prodigal, a picturesque ruin, a sensitive plant, an exquisite machine with insufficient steam, the oddest of God's creatures and, most frequently – by his father, his mother, his brother and his sister; by William Wordsworth, Dorothy Wordsworth and Thomas Carlyle; and by countless others over the years – 'Poor Hartley'.

I will not call him Poor Hartley. Relieved of the adjective that has followed him around like a cringing cur for nearly two centuries, he will be, simply, Hartley. (Although the 'David' referred to in his father's letter – an homage to David Hartley, the eighteenth-century metaphysical philosopher – faded away before baptism, Hartley was still stuck with one great man for his first name and another for his last.) And that raises the question of what I should call his father, he of the abscessed buttocks and the great poems. 'Coleridge' not only grants him sole proprietorship of a last name that belongs just as rightfully to his son but also makes the father sound like an adult and the son – forever – like a child. For the sake of parity, I should call him 'Samuel'. However, he detested that name, which he considered 'the worst combination of which vowels and consonants are susceptible' (CL 2, 1,126). He signed his poems with a variety of pseudonyms, from Aphilos to Zagri. His most celebrated alias was Silas Tomkyn Comberbache, the name under which he enlisted in the Dragoons and with whom he shared a set of initials: S.T.C. Since that is how he liked to refer to himself, sometimes in Greek, I will call our ill-starred pair Hartley and S.T.C. – with the rueful realisation that, as always, Hartley gets the short end of the stick.

In an untitled sonnet, Hartley once wrote, 'The world were welcome to forget my name, / Could I bequeath a few remembered words' ('Could I but harmonise . . .' 9–10). He was doomed to the opposite fate. No one remembers his words, but no one forgets his name – or at least half of it. And thus, even though it has been said that only Milton and Wordsworth wrote better sonnets (his father certainly didn't – the sonnet was his weakest form); even though an anthology of *The World's Best Essays* published in 1900 allotted more space and more praise to Hartley than

to S.T.C.; even though Hartley was funnier than his father, by far – nonetheless, he
has been as thoroughly eclipsed as an asteroid passing behind Jupiter. It is therefore
not surprising that eleven lines of doggerel on the Greek alphabet which S.T.C.
wrote for his son were auctioned a few years ago (along with a lock of S.T.C.'s hair)
for £4,250, whereas a signed Hartley poem went for £40; or that S.T.C. has inspired
enough books to panel a library, whereas Hartley has been the subject of only one
since 1931; or that in the fourteen-volume *Cambridge History of English Literature*,
S.T.C. gets a twenty-three-page chapter all to himself, in which his 'genius' is mentioned eleven times, whereas Hartley is allotted less than a page and a half – one
thirty-ninth of a chapter called 'Lesser Poets'.

II

From Samuel Taylor Coleridge to John Thelwall
13 November, 1796

My dear Thelwall
I ought indeed to have written to you and have felt no little pain from having
omitted it. But the Post will not wait while I am writing apologies. . . . My Wife
& little one (his name David Hartley) are marvellously well – Give my love
to your's –
     Write immediately. (CL 1, 253–4)

Today, when speed trumps style and everyone's correspondence looks alike, homoge-
nised by uniform fonts on the large screens of our computers or the tiny screens of our
telephones, it is hard to conceive how central the letter was at the time S.T.C. wrote
those lines to the left-wing reformer John Thelwall. 'The Post will not wait' was no
metaphor: a carriage drawn by four horses – painted in a livery of black and scarlet,
with the Royal Coat of Arms on the doors and the stars of the four principal orders
of knighthood on the upper panels – was about to leave for London, carrying a load
of mail-bags, a timepiece that kept it on a strict schedule, a bugle that announced its
arrival, and a small arsenal (pistol, blunderbuss, cutlasses) to repel robbers. The letter
would be enclosed not in a gummed envelope but in a wrapper, or merely folded and
sealed with wax. As soon as Thelwall saw the address, he would immediately recognise the sender by his handwriting, penned with a quill – the primary wing-feather
of a goose, with plume still attached, that had been sharpened with a pen-knife and
dipped in an inkwell. (S.T.C. and Hartley both wrote swift, slanting cursive whose
illegibility has bedevilled two centuries of scholars. Both wrote confidently, with few
blots or cross-outs. Hartley's lines often tilted upwards to the right.)
     Until 1839, five years after S.T.C.'s death, the recipient paid the postage, based on
the distance travelled and the number of sheets. The postal clerk held the letter in
front of a candle in order to count the pages. Recipients were likely to be annoyed if
a correspondent had large handwriting, favoured wide margins, or wrote dull letters
(hardly a danger with either Coleridge). Chronically strapped for cash, S.T.C. was

famous for approaching MPs, who had the privilege of free postal franking, and badgering them into signing his mail so he could read it without getting charged.

When a biographer recounts a life, the fact that he knows its outcome is encoded into every sentence. But when S.T.C. and Hartley wrote letters, or when others wrote letters about them, they had no idea how things would turn out. Excerpts from letters form the scaffold on which I have hung the story of this sad relationship because they allow us to imagine how things might have gone differently. They dissolve not only the centuries but, perhaps even more important, the knowledge of what the next day would bring. Rather than looking back at our characters' past, we find ourselves worrying about their future.

III

From Samuel Taylor Coleridge to Humphry Davy
25 July, 1800

My dear Davy
. . . Hartley is a spirit that dances on an aspin leaf – the air, which yonder sallow-faced & yawning Tourist is breathing, is to my Babe a perpetual Nitrous Oxyde. Never was more joyous creature born . . . (CL 1, 612).

Hartley was not quite four when his father wrote those ecstatic lines. Their recipient, the chemist Humphry Davy, supervised a laboratory that investigated the medical properties of gases, hence the reference to nitrous oxide, which Davy had christened 'laughing gas' and experimentally administered to his friend the previous year. S.T.C. enjoyed it thoroughly.

If air intoxicated Hartley, Hartley intoxicated S.T.C. – and had since that first embrace, two hours after the father first laid eyes on the son. S.T.C. confided to a friend that he composed poetry with a nappy pinned to his knee, warming by the fire, and that when Hartley laughed, he was so overcome with fondness that he wept. By the time Hartley was seven, it is no exaggeration to say he had inspired some of the greatest poems ever written in English. There is 'Frost at Midnight', in which S.T.C. looks at the 'Dear Babe, that sleepest cradled by my side' (44) and hopes that as a man he will

> wander like a breeze
> By lakes and sandy shores, beneath the crags
> Of ancient mountain, and beneath the clouds . . . (54–6)

There is the conclusion to Part II of 'Christabel', in which Hartley is the 'little child, a limber elf, / Singing, dancing to itself' (656–7). And there is 'The Nightingale', in which S.T.C. comforts Hartley by carrying him outside to the orchard:

> He beheld the moon, and, hushed at once,
> Suspends his sobs, and laughs most silently,

While his fair eyes, that swam with undropped tears,
Did glitter in the yellow moon-beam! (102–5)

After the Coleridges moved to the Lake District in 1800, Hartley became a frequent visitor at the home of William Wordsworth, who was soon smitten himself. In
'To H. C., Six Years Old', he calls Hartley a 'faery voyager' (5) and a 'blessed vision'
(11); in 'Ode: Intimations of Immortality from Recollections of Early Childhood', a
'six years' Darling of a pigmy size' (86).

A penumbra of impossible expectation began to settle around Hartley's head.
Like S.T.C.'s letter to Humphry Davy, these poems describe him as more spirit
than mortal, a child who did not walk so much as levitate. Furthermore, the 'faery
voyager' was generally agreed to be a prodigy. Charles Lamb called him 'the small
philosopher' (Lamb 45). Mrs Basil Montagu, a family friend, marvelled at the con-
tinent of Ejuxria, an imaginary land that Hartley equipped with its own senate,
legal system and language (which he claimed to have translated). But some of the
encomia had ominous undertones. Hartley's uncle, the poet Robert Southey, wrote,
'I have a feeling that such an intellect can never reach maturity – the springs are of
too exquisite workmanship to last long' (*Collected Letters of Robert Southey* no. 840).
S.T.C. observed, 'He is a very extraordinary creature, & if he live, will I doubt not
prove a great Genius' (*CL* 1, 650).

'*If he live*'? What must it feel like to be a child simultaneously acclaimed as a
genius and acknowledged by his own father to hang by a thread?

Jean-Paul Sartre counted himself lucky that he was an infant when his father
died. He wrote in *The Words*, 'Had my father lived, he would have lain on me at
full length and would have crushed me' (19). Those are harsh words. But it's true
that parents can be crushing – particularly fathers, particularly with eldest sons. The
diciest role of all may be that of the son of a famous writer who, like Hartley, hopes
to be a writer himself. An 1833 review of the only book of poetry Hartley published
in his lifetime praised the verse for embodying 'no trivial inheritance of his father's
genius', but also quoted the old saying that 'the oakling withers beneath the shadow
of the oak' (Review of *Poems* 517, 521).

There are exceptions, of course. Some oaklings of well-known literary oaks have
flourished – among them Auberon Waugh, Anthony West, Martin Amis, Rosanna
Warren, Andre Dubus, Christopher Buckley and Alexandra Styron. I have long
been interested in what makes some oaklings thrive and others wither because, in
a minor way, I'm an oakling myself. My father was a critic and essayist. My mother
was the only woman war correspondent in China during the Second World War.
The upside of this print-smudged parentage was that I was raised in a home with six
thousand books, plenty of literary conversation, and empirical evidence that writing
was something you could actually do for a living. The downside was that I knew that
no matter what I did, my parents would already have done it better. Throughout my
life I have been asked, 'Was Clifton Fadiman your father?' Even now, in my fifties,
I am defined by daughterhood. Well-meaning readers still tell me that I have inher-
ited some of my parents' talent.

In a poem he sent Hartley as a gift, the diarist Barclay Fox addressed him as 'Scion of Genius! on whose favoured head / His wondrous mantle fell' (Fox 39). This, of course, was to be taken as a compliment. It never would have occurred to Fox that Hartley might have preferred to wear a mantle of his own making.

IV

From Samuel Taylor Coleridge to Hartley Coleridge
3 April, 1807

My dear Boy
    In all human beings good and bad Qualities are not only found together, side by side as it were; but they actually tend to produce each other – at least, they must be considered as twins of a common parent, and the amiable propensities too often sustain and foster their unhandsome sisters. (For the old Romans personified Virtues and Vices, both as Women.) (CL 3, 9–11)

When S.T.C. wrote these words, Hartley was ten. They were planning to visit relatives in Ottery, and S.T.C. was moved to proffer some advice on deportment. After speeding through his son's Virtues, including kindness and imagination, he took a protracted epistolary tour of his Vices, from Hartley's 'labyrinth of day-dreams' to his 'habits of procrastination' to his offences as a 'young FILTH-PAW' who fingered food at the table and thereby made people with weak stomachs turn sick. 'Among the lesser faults,' added S.T.C., 'I beg you to endeavor to remember, not to stand between the half opened door, either while you are speaking or spoken to. But come in – or go out – & always speak & listen with the door shut. – Likewise, not to speak so loud, or abruptly – and never to interrupt your elders while they are speaking – and not to talk at all during Meals.' In order to ensure that the letter's contents were fully absorbed, S.T.C. recommended that Hartley reread it 'every two or three days'.
    Much had happened, little of it happy, since S.T.C. calmed Hartley's tears by carrying him to the orchard and showing him the moon. He had become estranged from his wife, a woman whom their friend Richard Reynell described as 'sensible, affable, and good-natured – thrifty and industrious, and always neat and prettily dressed' (Rawnsley 74). Maybe so, but Sara was no intellectual, and her husband's want of steadiness, both emotional and financial, had turned her into a nag. 'If my wife loved me, and I my wife, half as well as we both love our children, I should be the happiest man alive,' S.T.C. wrote. 'But this is not – will not be' (CL 2, 775).
    When Hartley was two, S.T.C. decamped for ten months to Germany. Upon his return, he fell in miserable, unrequited love with the sister of the woman who was to marry William Wordsworth. When Hartley was seven, S.T.C. left for two and a half years in Malta and never returned to his family, which by then included another son, Derwent, and a daughter, Sara. It fell to Hartley's dull but morally irreproachable Uncle Southey to house, feed, and play surrogate father to the Coleridge children. From that point on, S.T.C. and Hartley spent only short, confusing stretches together. As Charles Lamb put it, S.T.C. 'ought not to have a wife or children; he

should have a sort of *diocesan* care of the world, no parish duty' (Holmes, *Darker Reflections*, 537).

By the time Hartley was ten, he was a dreamy boy who misplaced his books and slates; who was so bad at sports that he was said to have two left hands; who bit his arm in paroxysms of self-directed rage; who refused to continue reading once Robinson Crusoe left his island. 'He is afraid of receiving pain to such a degree that, if any person begins to read a newspaper,' wrote Southey, 'he will leave the room, lest there should be anything shocking in it' (1887: 174). Hartley was undeniably a peculiar child. However, in S.T.C.'s hectoring letter I hear a guilt-ridden absentee father claiming to enumerate his son's flaws but in fact enumerating his own. S.T.C. was a procrastinator, constantly promising that he was about to finish poems and essays he hadn't started. S.T.C. was a day-dreamer, prone to bumping into people, missing coaches, and failing to recognise that the image in a mirror was himself. S.T.C. talked too much. He once grabbed the button of Charles Lamb's coat and wouldn't stop talking. Lamb took out his pen-knife and cut off the button.

I showed what I think of as 'the filth-paw letter' to a friend of mine, Janna Malamud Smith, who happens to be an oakling herself – the daughter of Bernard Malamud, as well as a writer and a psychologist at Harvard Medical School. Janna responded, 'I imagine the boy felt vividly the sense that what was being called fondness for him was really something else – something critical, likely stemming from parental shame. In psychotherapy we are very interested in the way people unconsciously project qualities they find unbearable in themselves onto intimates' (Smith).

In an early poem, S.T.C. wrote of Hartley, 'Ah lovely Babe! in thee myself I scan' ('To an Infant', *Poetical Works* 91). Indeed he did. In Hartley, he scanned his own disorganisation, his own irresponsibility, his own lack of follow-through. And so did the rest of his circle. Dorothy Wordsworth noted, 'Hartley is as odd as ever, and in the weak points of his character resembles his father very much' (Wordsworth et al. 19).

Reading their letters, I often forget who's writing, since both so often begin with excuses for not having written sooner – in S.T.C.'s case, because of toothache, headache, insomnia, gout, cough, boils, inflamed eyes, swollen testicles and 'raging epistolophobia' (*CL* 3, 436); in Hartley's, because he lost the letter to which he was replying; because he had taken ill after wearing excessively thin breeches in bad weather; because of, as he charmingly put it, 'a stupifying head-achey cold, which sticks to me like a poor and homeless relation, in spite of the broadest hints to depart' (*Letters of Hartley Coleridge* 35).

Was Hartley a born procrastinator? Or did he grow into one because his father kept telling him he was?

v

From Hartley Coleridge to William Wordsworth
16 May, 1815

My dear Sir

Being now tolerably established a Collegian, feeling my gown rather less burthensome, and myself less strange, I hasten to perform my promise of scribblelation, and to become my own historian. (*Letters of Hartley Coleridge* 11)

When he wrote these lines from Merton College, Oxford, Hartley was eighteen and as absent-minded as ever: the letter was written to Wordsworth but mailed to Lamb. Southey described his nephew at this age as 'very short' – he was just over five foot – 'with remarkably strong features, some of the thickest and blackest eyebrows you ever saw, and a beard which a Turk might envy'. Also, 'awkward by nature', though possessed of an intellect that 'will soon overcome all disadvantages that his exterior may incur, if he do but *keep the course*' (Griggs 1929: 62–3).

The course in question was Oxford, and he managed to keep it, immersing himself in Pindar and Aristotle and dazzling his friends with his conversation. A fellow student later recalled:

His extraordinary powers as a converser (or rather a declaimer) procured for him numerous invitations to what are called at Oxford 'wine-parties'. . . . He would hold forth by the hour (for no one wished to interrupt him) on whatever subject might have been started – either of literature, politics, or religion – with an originality of thought, a force of illustration, and a facility and beauty of expression, which I question if any man then living, except his father, could have surpassed. ('Hartley Coleridge' 1851: 278)

Hartley might have fared even better had those gatherings been tea parties, not wine parties. He was drinking seriously, a habit he dated to the spring of 1816, when he failed to win Oxford's Newdigate Prize for English verse. The loss made him feel, as he put it, that 'all my aims and hopes would prove frustrate and abortive' (D. Coleridge 1851: lxxxix). He turned to alcohol for consolation and, for the rest of his life, was unable to turn away.

That same year, Hartley's father was moving in the opposite direction by attempting to shake his addiction to laudanum (opium dissolved in alcohol, a commonly used painkiller). S.T.C. had started taking opium more than two decades earlier in order to calm his sleep, among other reasons. It eventually provoked nightmares in which he was clawed by monstrous talons, infected with shameful diseases, and buried alive – although, in a more innocent phase, it also provoked the sensuous vision of Xanadu memorialised in 'Kubla Khan' in 1797. 'Kubla Khan' was not published until 1816, the year that S.T.C. placed himself in a kind of private rehab, under the care of a benevolent Highgate doctor named James Gillman, to whom Hartley teasingly referred as 'Doctissimus'. Dr Gillman dispensed S.T.C.'s laudanum, of which he had previously consumed up to a quart a day, in regulated doses. S.T.C. planned to stay for a month. He stayed for eighteen years.

In 1819, at the age of twenty-two, Hartley received a second-class degree in Literae Humaniores. He had prepared for his examination during a summer of furious study at Southey's house in Keswick, devoting himself so completely to his books that he did not even take meals with his family, though he occasionally appeared for tea attired in a loose toga and slippers. Two months later, he was elected with high distinction as a Probationer Fellow at Oriel College. In his old school in the Lake District, the boys huzza'd and the headmaster proclaimed a holiday. When he heard the news, S.T.C. overflowed with what he termed 'Fatherly Pride' (*CL* 4, 937) and invited Hartley to Highgate to celebrate his glorious future.

That future was short-lived. Within a year, Hartley lost his fellowship at Oriel. The provost and fellows of the college decided unanimously that he was 'not fit to be received permanently into the Society'. Hartley had failed to attend chapel regularly and associated with 'bad company', a term redolent of bums and barmaids but that in fact referred to undergraduates from colleges other than Oriel. Most serious, wrote the provost, 'he was often guilty of intemperance and came home in a state in which it was not safe to trust him with a candle' (*Letters of Hartley Coleridge* 301). On one occasion, the Dean found him in the gutter.

To make matters worse, Hartley failed to dress for dinner, did not always bother to shave, and stank of tobacco. In short, he was simply not what the Oriel Common Room – a circle of pious, formal, stuffy men – had in mind. It was as if all of S.T.C.'s fears about Hartley's deportment with his relatives in Ottery had been realised in a distorted and magnified form.

The news hit S.T.C., as he wrote to a friend, like 'a peal of thunder from a cloudless sky' (*Letters of Hartley Coleridge* 33). He screamed in his sleep and wept so profusely that when he awoke, his pillow was wet with tears. He attempted to intercede – with the best of intentions, but in ways guaranteed to make Hartley feel even more impotent than he already did. He wrote a 1,617-word letter to the provost and fellows of Oriel that Hartley was to copy, sign and send. He also wrote five drafts of a letter he planned to send to the provost himself, in one of which, with spectacular irrelevance, he quoted fifteen lines from 'Frost at Midnight' and four from Wordsworth's 'To H. C., Six Years Old'. In a frenzy of denial and ena-bling that will be familiar to the family of any alcoholic, he attempted to draw a Jesuitical line between intemperance (in which he admitted Hartley occasion-ally indulged) and the *habit* of intemperance (of which he claimed Hartley was innocent).

When I recently mentioned Hartley Coleridge to an English professor at Yale, she said, 'Ah yes, Hartley! Didn't he lose his fellowship at Oriel?' I thought how strange it was that people who know little else about Hartley have somehow heard of what S.T.C.'s friend Harriet Martineau called 'the great catastrophe, the ruinous blow' (Martineau 551).

I would like to interject a small reality check. In the academic sphere, Hartley did better than his father, who dropped out of Cambridge. He did better than Wordsworth, who took his degree from Cambridge 'without distinction'. He did better than Southey, who dropped out of Oxford. And he did better than Byron, who dropped out of Cambridge, and Shelley, who was expelled from Oxford. Hartley *graduated* – with a second! Nearly two hundred years after the fact, why do we continue to associate him with the loss of a job for which he was unsuited and that he probably would not have enjoyed? Might the memory of this episode be less adhesive – and might Hartley have been more resilient – had his father viewed it as a disappointment rather than an apocalypse?

VI

From Samuel Taylor Coleridge to Thomas Allsop
8 October, 1822

My dearest Allsop
. . . It was reserved for the interval between six o'clock and 12 on THAT SATURDAY Evening to bring a Suffering which, do what I will, I cannot help thinking of & being affrightened by, as a terror of itself, a self-subsisting separate Something. (CL 5, 251)

Two years had passed since Hartley left Oriel. He had come to London to try his hand as a writer and failed to make ends meet, though he wrote a good deal of poetry and contributed some witty essays to London Magazine. S.T.C.'s response to his efforts must have made him writhe: 'You have made the experiment of trying – to maintain yourself by writing for the Press – and the result – I do not know, what conclusion *you* have drawn from it – has been such, as makes *me* shrink, and sink away inwardly, from the thought of a second trial' (CL 5, 243).

On 'THAT SATURDAY', less than two weeks after S.T.C.'s rebuke, father and son rushed to London from Highgate together to run some urgent errands. Both were exhausted, having spent many days and nights at the sickbed of Hartley's brother, Derwent, then a hardworking but undistinguished Cambridge undergraduate, who lay ill with typhus. As soon as they arrived in London, Hartley asked S.T.C. for money to repay a debt. S.T.C. gave it to him, and they agreed to meet again at 6:00 pm at a shop on York Street. As Hartley vanished into the crowd, his father was overcome by an awful presentiment. He described it thus to his young friend Thomas Allsop:

When he had passed a few steps – [I called] Hartley! – Six! O my God! think of the *agony*, the *sore agony*, of every moment after six! – And tho' he was not three yards from me, I only saw the color of his Face thro' my Tears! (CL 5, 251)

S.T.C., who was all too familiar with Hartley's tendency to flee or hide rather than face criticism, somehow knew his son would not return. He waited for him on York Street, alone, until midnight.

In most families the squall would eventually have blown over. The son would have repaid the debt; the father would have accepted his apology. Not the Coleridges. Hartley and his father never saw each other again.

Both continued to profess their love, mostly in letters to friends, since after a year or two they stopped writing to one another. Hartley moved back to the Lake

District, within walking distance of Wordsworth and Southey but more than 250 miles from his father. Money was tight, and travel by mail coach was arduous. The journey from London to Penrith, the coach stop closest to Hartley's home, would have taken over thirty hours. Under the circumstances, it would have been easy to let a year pass. And then another. And, eventually, twelve. Hartley, immobilised by shame, and S.T.C., immobilised by his failure as a father, both did what they did best – procrastinated, until it was too late.

A year before his father's death, Hartley published a collection of poetry to mostly excellent reviews. It opened with a sonnet dedicated 'TO S. T. COLERIDGE', crediting his 'Father, and Bard revered!' for both his poetic art, 'Whate'er it be', and his love of nature, 'Which, mixt with passions of my sadder years, / Compose this book' (1–13).

In one of his late poems, the 'Bard revered' wrote of Hartley: 'For still there lives within my secret heart / The magic image of the magic Child' ('The Pang More Sharp Than All' 36–7). S.T.C. died in 1834, at the age of sixty-one. When Hartley heard the news, he wrote an anguished letter to his brother, regretting that he had not been at his father's side to hear his last words and pray with him before his death. 'I can only hope that no painful thought of me adulterated the final out gushing of his spirit,' he wrote. 'I never forgot him – no, Derwent, I have forgot myself – too often – but I never forgot my father' (*Letters of Hartley Coleridge* 162–3).

S.T.C.'s will contained a codicil providing funds to cover 'board, lodging, and raiment' for 'my dear son Hartley' (Griggs 1929: 138–9): a godsend, since Hartley never made a steady living. Although he had worked for a while as a schoolmaster, he feared his students and, years after he stopped teaching, continued to have nightmares about 'big boys . . . hooting, pelting, spitting at me, stopping my ways, setting all sorts of hideous scornful faces at me' (*Letters of Hartley Coleridge* 128). He wrote an unfinished series of biographies of worthy men of Yorkshire and Lancashire. He also failed to finish what his brother called 'an Essay on his father's life and genius' (D. Coleridge 1851: 363) that was to introduce a new edition of S.T.C.'s *Biographia Literaria*. It is hard to imagine an assignment more certain to induce paralysis.

Hartley never married. He could not support a wife, and, in any case, he assumed no woman could be attracted to a man as 'ill-omen'd and unsightly as Wordsworth's melancholy thorn on the bleak hill-top' (*Letters of Hartley Coleridge* 99). He told a friend he wanted to found an Ugly Club, of which he would serve as chairman. During the last twelve years of his life, he lived with a farmer and his wife at Nab Cottage, a solitary slate-roofed house that clung to the north bank of Rydal Water. Above his mantel hung the cocked hat, feather and sword that Silas Tomkyn Comberbache had brought back from the Dragoons: a reminder, perhaps, that his father had had his share of failure too.

Even after his hair turned white, many people still treated Hartley like a child, a role to which his father had accustomed him, according to Derwent, through 'an affection, which never ceased to regard its object as in some sort an infant still' (D. Coleridge 1851: xxiii). Hartley colluded in his own infantilisation by wearing a boyish blue jacket, calling himself a 'poor elf' ('Lines – ' 11) and remarking, in one of his sonnets, that 'still I am a child, though I be old' ('Long time a child, and still a child, when years . . .' 13). A visitor to Nab Cottage remarked, 'He reminded you of a spy-glass shut up, and you wanted to take hold of him and pull him out into a man of goodly proportions and average stature' (Hillard 161). Had Hartley been taller, he might have found it easier to feel like an adult. In his essay 'Brief Observations upon Brevity', he wrote, 'I am brief myself; brief in stature, brief in discourse, short of memory and money, and far short of my wishes' (H. Coleridge [1851] 2009: 25).

He still walked as if levitating. One friend said he needed stones in his pockets to keep his feet on the ground. When he was out for a stroll he would sometimes hatch an idea for a sonnet, run into the nearest farmhouse, borrow paper, and dash it off in ten minutes, beating time with his foot and shouting when he came up with a particularly good line.

At intervals he disappeared on benders, spending a month or more away from Nab Cottage, drinking in alehouses and sleeping in barns and ditches – hardly the sort of wandering like a breeze that S.T.C. had in mind when he wrote 'Frost at Midnight'. The local farmers were glad to take him in. They far preferred him to Wordsworth, who was formal and solemn; 'Li'le Hartley', as they called him, always had 'a bit of a smile' (Hartman 138–9).

His drinking worsened. He sometimes had to be dragged home. Unlike his father, he had no Doctissimus to help him deal with his addiction, and even if he had, as Wordsworth observed, 'he would not stay in any house where he was to be watched and controuled' (Wordsworth et al. 612).

VII

From Derwent Coleridge to Hartley Coleridge
28 September, 1846

My dear Brother,
    Ill news fly fast. I have heard that you have set fire to your bed curtains, and cannot doubt that such an occurrence (under the circumstances) must be attended, and may possibly be followed, with a good deal that is disagreeable to your feelings, if not otherwise detrimental to your comfort. (D. Coleridge letter)

The provost of Oriel had been right: it was not safe to trust Hartley with a candle. He was, of course, drunk when the fire started. Derwent's response was agonised but unsympathetic, the lament of a kind man who, after years of forbearance, had finally lost his patience. Nowhere did he say, 'Hartley – thank God you didn't die!' Instead, he reminded Hartley to repay the cost of the bed curtains. He instructed Hartley to summon his moral strength and drink only water. He said he could not see Hartley because 'my health would immediately give way under the misery which it w^d occasion me'. He bade his brother farewell.

But two years later, when Hartley, at the age of fifty-two, stumbled home drunk on a cold winter night and caught bronchitis, Mrs Wordsworth summoned Derwent, and he made the long journey from London to Nab Cottage to be with his brother when he died. Hartley was surrounded by friends. Like his father, he loved babies, and on his deathbed, he asked to hold a neighbour's infant daughter in his arms.

Wordsworth, who buried Hartley next to his own family in the Grasmere churchyard, and joined him there the following year, told Hartley's cousin that 'Derwent took away all his Books and papers, and will probably write a Memoir of Him. . . . Hartley used to write a great deal, but rarely, I suppose, finished any thing' (Wordsworth et al. 886).

Hartley turned out to have finished more than Wordsworth – or anyone else – could have imagined. Year after year, with little hope of publication or, in the case of most of his prose, of even a single reader, he had worked long into the night, writing by candlelight with a quill pen (often broken). Derwent went through every page of Hartley's notebooks and made fair copies for the printer. He even copied out his brother's marginalia. Including the work Hartley had published in ephemeral journals during his London phase, there was enough for two volumes of essays and notes, and two volumes of poetry, most of it new – more than a thousand pages in all. The poems were introduced by a 194-page memoir in which Derwent described Hartley as 'acute and sagacious, often under the disguise of paradox; playful and tender, with a predominance of the fancy over the imagination, yet capable of the deepest pathos; clear, rapid, and brilliant' (D. Coleridge 1851: xx). And thus we owe most of what we know about Hartley Coleridge to his less picturesque but in many ways more fortunate brother, a happily married clergyman who had been named for a river rather than for an eminent philosopher; who had never been called a genius; who had not been the subject of immortal poems; who, as the younger son, had been at least partially shielded from the great oak's shadow.

WORKS CITED AND CONSULTED

Bate, Walter Jackson, *Coleridge*, Masters of World Literature series (New York: Macmillan, 1968).

Bates, Alan (ed.), *Directory of Stage Coach Services 1836* (Newton Abbot: David & Charles, 1969).

Bok, Sissela, 'Reassessing Sartre', *Harvard Review of Philosophy* 1.1 (1991): 48–58.

Booth, Martin, *Opium: A History* (New York: Thomas Dunne, 1996).

Bostetter, Edward E., 'Coleridge's Manuscript Essay *On the Passions*', *Journal of the History of Ideas* 31.1 (1970): 99–108.

Brewer, David J. (ed.), *The World's Best Essays from the Earliest Period to the Present Time*, vol. 3 (St Louis: Ferd. P. Kaiser, 1900).

Browne, Christopher, *Getting the Message: The Story of the British Post Office* (Stroud: Alan Sutton, 1993).

Campbell, James Dykes, *Samuel Taylor Coleridge: A Narrative of the Events of His Life* (London: Macmillan, 1896).

Carlyle, Thomas, letter to Thomas Story Spedding, 19 October 1847, *The Carlyle Letters Online*, <http://carlyleletters.dukejournals.org> (last accessed 7 July 2014).

Christie's, Auction records for Printed Books sale, South Kensington, London, 20 November 1998, <http://www.christies.com/salelanding/index.aspx?intSaleID=8624> (last accessed 7 July 2014).

Coleridge, Derwent, letter to Hartley Coleridge, 28 September 1846, Coleridge Collection, Harry Ransom Center, University of Texas at Austin.

—— *Memoir of Hartley Coleridge by His Brother*, in Hartley Coleridge, *Poems*, vol. 1 (London: Edward Moxon, 1851).

Coleridge, Hartley, *Bricks Without Mortar: The Selected Poems of Hartley Coleridge*, ed. Lisa Gee (London: Picador, 2000).

—— *Essays and Marginalia* (Memphis: General Books LLC, 2009).

—— *Letters of Hartley Coleridge*, ed. Grace Evelyn Griggs and Earl Leslie Griggs (London: Oxford University Press, 1941).

—— *New Poems Including a Selection from His Published Poetry*, ed. Earl Leslie Griggs (London: Oxford University Press, 1942).

—— *Poems*, vol. 1 (Leeds: F. E. Bingley, Corn-Exchange, 1833).

Coleridge, Samuel Taylor, *Biographia Literaria*, Everyman's Library 11 (London: J. M. Dent & Sons, 1949).

—— *The Complete Poems*, ed. William Keach (London: Penguin, 2004).

—— *Letters of Samuel Taylor Coleridge*, ed. Ernest Hartley Coleridge, 2 vols (Boston: Houghton Mifflin, 1895).

—— *The Poetical Works of Samuel Taylor Coleridge: Including Poems and Versions of Poems Now Published for the First Time*, ed. Ernest Hartley Coleridge (Oxford: Oxford University Press, 1912).

—— *Selected Poems of Samuel Taylor Coleridge*, ed. Richard Holmes (London: Penguin, 2003).

—— *Selected Poetry and Prose of Coleridge*, ed. Donald A. Stauffer (New York: Modern Library, 1951).

—— and Hartley Coleridge, *The Collected Letters of Samuel Taylor Coleridge*, electronic edition, 6 vols of Samuel Taylor Coleridge letters, plus Early Family Letters and Letters of Hartley Coleridge, Intelex Past Masters, <http://www.nlx.com/collections/33> (last accessed 7 July 2014).

Coleridge, Sara, *Memoir and Letters of Sara Coleridge* (New York: Harper & Brothers, 1874).

Fox, Caroline, *Memories of Old Friends: Being Extracts from the Journals and Letters of Caroline Fox*, ed. Horace N. Pym (London: Smith, Elder & Co., 1883).

Fry, Paul H., 'Honorable Toil? Coleridge and Wordsworth in Retirement', *Yale Review* 98.2 (2010): 77–91.

Griggs, Earl Leslie, 'Coleridge and His Son', *Studies in Philology* 27.4 (1930): 635–47.

—— *Hartley Coleridge: His Life and Work* (London: University of London Press, 1929).

Hainton, Raymonde, 'Derwent Coleridge: The Romantic Child', *Coleridge Bulletin Online* new series 8 (1996), <http://www.friendsofcoleridge.com/MembersOnly/hainton_derwent.html> (last accessed 7 July 2014).

—— and Godfrey Hainton, *The Unknown Coleridge: The Life and Times of Derwent Coleridge 1800–1883* (London: Janus, 1996).

'Hartley Coleridge', *The Literary World* 20 (1879): 322.

'Hartley Coleridge', *New Monthly Magazine and Humorist* 92 (1851): 276–85.

Hartman, Herbert, *Hartley Coleridge: Poet's Son and Poet* (London: Oxford University Press, 1931).

Hillard, George S., 'Hartley Coleridge', *Littell's Living Age* 21 (1849): 161–2.

Holmes, Richard, *Coleridge: Early Visions, 1772–1804* (New York: Pantheon Books, 1989).

—— *Coleridge: Darker Reflections, 1804–1834* (New York: Pantheon Books, 1998).

J. W. H., 'Hartley Coleridge. His Father's Love, His Wayward Life, and Some of the Verse He Wrote', *New York Times*, 18 September 1897.

Jamison, Kay Redfield, *Touched with Fire: Manic-Depressive Illness and the Artistic Temperament* (New York: Free Press Paperbacks, 1993).

Jay, Mike, 'The Fruitful Matrix of Ghosts: The Psychic Investigations of Samuel Taylor Coleridge', *Times Literary Supplement*, 5 May 2006, p. 14.

Jury, Louise, 'Coleridge's descendants sell papers that reveal family's views on a maverick poet', *The Independent*, 21 August 2006.

Keanie, Andrew, *Hartley Coleridge: A Reassessment of His Life and Work* (New York: Palgrave Macmillan, 2008).

Lamb, Charles, *The Letters of Charles Lamb: With a Sketch of His Life*, ed. Thomas Noon Talfourd, vol. 1 (London: Moxon, 1837).

'Literary Quakers', *Knickerbocker* 39 (1852): 514–18.

Martineau, Harriet, 'Lights of the English Lake District', *Atlantic Monthly* 7 (1861): 541–58.

Millea, Alice, e-mail to Anne Fadiman, 22 August 2011.

Paris, John Ayrton, *The Life of Sir Humphry Davy* (London: Henry Colburn and Richard Bentley, 1831).

Plotz, Judith, 'The *Annus Mirabilis* and the Lost Boy: Hartley's Case', *Studies in Romanticism* 33.2 (1994): 181–200.

—— 'Childhood Lost, Childhood Regained: Hartley Coleridge's Fable of Defeat', *Children's Literature* 14 (1986): 143–8.

—— *Romanticism and the Vocation of Childhood* (New York: Palgrave, 2001).

Pryor, Felix (ed.), *The Faber Book of Letters: Letters Written in the English Language 1578–1939* (London: Faber and Faber, 1988).

Rawnsley, H. D., *Literary Associations of the English Lakes*, vol. 1 (Glasgow: James MacLehose and Sons, 1894).

Review of *Letters of Samuel Taylor Coleridge*, ed. Ernest Hartley Coleridge, *Atlantic Monthly* 76 (1895): 397–413.

Review of *Poems*, by Hartley Coleridge, *The Quarterly Review* 49 (1833): 517–21.

Review of *Poems by Hartley Coleridge with a Memoir of His Life*, by Derwent Coleridge, *Littell's Living Age* 29 (1851): 235–8.

Robinson, Roger, 'Hartley Coleridge', lecture, Kilve Court, 7 September 1996, <http://www.friendsofcoleridge.com/membersonly/Robinson_Hartley_Col.html> (last accessed 7 July 2014).

—— 'STC's grandson compares Derwent with Hartley and Sara', *Coleridge Bulletin Online* new series 2 (1993), <http://www.friendsofcoleridge.com/MembersOnly/robinsonderwent.html> (last accessed 7 July 2014).

Sartre, Jean-Paul, *The Words: The Autobiography of Jean-Paul Sartre* (New York: George Braziller, 1964).

Sisman, Adam, *The Friendship: Wordsworth and Coleridge* (New York: Viking, 2006).

Smith, Janna Malamud, e-mail to Anne Fadiman, 22 March 2011.

Sotheby's, Auction records for English Literature, History, Children's Books and Illustrations sale, London, 13 December 2007.

Southey, Robert, *The Collected Letters of Robert Southey*, electronic edition, ed. Lynda Pratt, Tim Fulford and Ian Packer, Romantic Circles, University of Maryland, <http://www.rc.umd.edu/editions/southey_letters> (last accessed 7 July 2014).

—— *Robert Southey: The Story of His Life Written in His Letters*, ed. John Dennis (Boston: D. Lothrop, 1887).

Stephens, Fran Carlock, *The Hartley Coleridge Letters: A Calendar and Index* (Austin: Humanities Research Center of the University of Texas, 1978).

Taylor, Anya, *Bacchus in Romantic England: Writers and Drink, 1780–1830* (London: Macmillan, 1999).

Tirebuck, William, 'Introduction', *The Poetical Works of Bowles, Lamb and Hartley Coleridge* (London: Walter Scott, 1887), pp. vii–xxii.

Towle, Eleanor H., *A Poet's Children, Hartley and Sara Coleridge* (London: Methuen, 1912).

Ward, A. W., et al. (eds), *The Cambridge History of English and American Literature*, 18 vols (New York: G. P. Putnam's Sons, 1907–21).

Wordsworth, William, et al., *Letters of the Wordsworth Family from 1787 to 1855*, vol. 3, ed. William Knight (Boston: Ginn & Company, 1907).

—— and Samuel Taylor Coleridge, *Lyrical Ballads with a Few Other Poems*, Poetry First Editions series (London: Penguin, 1999).

Yarnall, Ellis, *Wordsworth and the Coleridges with Other Memories Literary and Political* (New York: Macmillan, 1899).

Youngquist, Paul, 'Rehabilitating Coleridge: Poetry, Philosophy, Excess', *ELH* 66.4 (1999): 885–909.

7 'Any thing human or earthly': Shelley's Letters and Poetry

Madeleine Callaghan

Shelley's letters have seldom received sustained critical exploration. Yet earlier discussions of the letters have yielded fascinating ideas as to Shelley's epistolary practice. Enno Ruge's argument that 'the literary principle for his self-fashioning [in the letters]' is 'not predominantly poetical, but derived from the sentimental epistolary novel of the eighteenth century' (112) points up the literary qualities that underpin Shelley's self-presentation in the letters. However, this chapter will shift the terms of his discussion to show that there is a comparable mode of self-fashioning across the letters and the poetry. Stephen Greenblatt's seminal study defines self-fashioning in these terms: 'it invariably crosses the boundaries between the creation of literary characters, the shaping of one's own identity, the experience of being molded by forces outside one's control, the attempt to fashion other selves' (3). This sense of self-fashioning's possibilities and its limitations seems anticipated by Shelley as he sought to write poetry that concealed and revealed the self and its relationship with others. Shelley's sense of the problem of self permeates his writing, as he lamented to Leigh Hunt in 1819: '*self*, that burr that will stick to one. I can't get it off yet.'[1] But Shelley seeks to connect self to other in the letters and the poetry, aiming to effect 'a going out of our own nature' (*A Defence of Poetry* 682).[2] The letters communicate with friends, acquaintances and lovers; the poetry seeks to forge connections with an imagined audience. These categories shift and blur, as the letters become addressed to posterity and the poetry speaks intimately to its address-ees. As Ruge suggests: 'With a larger, perhaps posthumous readership in mind, Shelley may have given some of his letters a more literary form and so designed them to outlast the immediate communicative situation' (112). The balance between communicating with friends and creating texts of abiding literary value comes to the fore in the relationship between some of Shelley's letters and the poetry addressed to his intimate acquaintances. The *Letter to Maria Gisborne* and the prose letter to John and Maria Gisborne bring the relationship of these two intimate forms to the fore.

As Timothy Webb writes with reference to Keats's letters, 'a major preliminary obstacle to a full recognition of Keats's achievement has been created by our slow-ness in evolving a poetics of the letter' ('Cutting Figures' 146–7). The same might easily be said of Shelley. Where the letters of Shelley's contemporaries Keats and Byron are applauded in critical circles, Shelley is frequently neglected in a consideration of the poet as letter writer. Shelley's letters, despite their abundant scope, such as his under-appreciated travelogue-style letters to Thomas Love Peacock, his movingly intimate early letters to Mary Shelley, and his self-controlled missives to Byron, do not show Shelley deliberately developing, as Keats does, images of poetic creation, or, like Byron, engaging in amusing gossip about his peers. Shelley's letters are kaleidoscopic, taking in every element of the poet's life in such a way that it becomes challenging to define the letters in any single way. This problem of definition can make the reading experience a challenge for anyone seeking to find 'Shelley'. In part, the difficulty of reading Shelley's letters as revelatory of a clearly defined self is anticipated and even created by Shelley himself. Daisy Hay notes the impossibility of any such critical enterprise: 'Shelley is particularly engaged with the illusory nature of the epistolary self, and . . . as a result, he is both obscured and revealed by his correspondence' (208). This problem of the self is theorised by Charles Taylor, who shows that 'to study persons is to study beings who only exist in, or are partly constituted by, a certain language' (35). Shelley's acute awareness of this power of language to fashion and refashion the self recurs throughout his letters and his poetry. The *Letter to Maria Gisborne* and the prose letter to John and Maria Gisborne reveal the limits of self-presentation in both genres even as the connections between the verse epistle and the prose letters suggest the complex yet rich relationship between poetry and prose.

Focusing on the *Letter to Maria Gisborne*, dated 1 July 1820, and Shelley's letter to John and Maria Gisborne, dated 30 June 1820, amongst others, this chapter will discuss the continuities between the letters and the poetry.[3] The boundary between the poetry and the letters is fluid, and, owing to Shelley's attempt to connect with specific readers in both genres, I will treat the *Letter to Maria Gisborne* as a letter in poetic form. Writing a poem that focuses on communicating with a clearly defined audience, even complementing the contents of the letter written the day before to the same recipients, Shelley deliberately sought to access the verse epistle's balanced and urbane formal qualities. Though it was largely out of fashion after the Augustan age, Lisa Vargo defines the verse epistle in the Romantic period as 'balancing a backward look at tradition with a desire to communicate contemporary concerns about sociability, political perspectives, gender roles, and poetic self-definition' (1,465). Where Shelley comes to seem unique is how carefully he articulates these concerns by running them through the self. The editors of the Longman edition note the parallels between the poem and Leigh Hunt's verse epistles in *Foliage* and John Keats's epistles and sonnets to named friends (432). Shelley had anticipated the *Letter to Maria Gisborne*, first published by Mary Shelley in her *Posthumous Poems* (1824), being circulated amongst his friends in London. The poem, though apparently addressed to Maria Gisborne, had a wider implied audience than the prose letter. In the Romantic period, the verse epistle, though often a means to address the nation through a specific addressee (Vargo 1,468), could be rather more private as well. Shelley capitalises on the movement between public and private utterance, shifting between larger political statement and intimate memory, just as he would in the prose letter.

The *Letter to Maria Gisborne* stands in close relation to Shelley's letter to John and Maria Gisborne, but the prose letter is, as we might expect, a more private piece of correspondence than the verse epistle. The addressees of the prose letter and the verse epistle were close friends who had a long-standing connection with Mary's father, William Godwin. Maria Gisborne had been a friend of William Godwin; he had also proposed marriage after the death of her first husband, but was declined. Maria instead married John Gisborne, a merchant, in 1800, and moved with him and her son Henry Reveley (from her first marriage) to Rome in 1801. Mary and Shelley, with a letter of introduction from Godwin, met the Gisbornes on 9 May 1818, and their friendship blossomed, with Maria acting as a creative spur for Shelley. She drew his attention to the history of the Cenci family (which inspired his play *The Cenci*) and taught Shelley Spanish by supervising his reading of Pedro Calderón de la Barca. At this juncture of their friendship, Shelley had invested heavily in Henry Reveley's project to construct a steamboat, and felt great personal interest in the project. This interest was to be one of the few moments of enjoyment in an otherwise difficult time in his life (see *Longman* 428–31 for a full account of the personal context of the poem). Shelley's personal life was in turmoil. He was under attack from William Godwin, whom he refers to as 'the only sincere enemy I have in the world', even as he retained respect for Godwin's intellect (*Letters* ii, 202). At the same time, he was also anxious about Elena Adelaide Shelley, the mysterious 'poor Neapolitan' (*Letters* ii, 206) who may or may not have been his daughter. The Gisbornes were the only people in whom Shelley confided the existence of the child. According to James Bieri, 'establishing Elena Adelaide's parentage is one of the great bafflements Shelley left for his biographers' (106). There is certainly no decisive proof for any hypothesis regarding her origins. The child's health was only one concern of many; Shelley also suffered from the problems surrounding his relationship with Mary Shelley, and his fears over his creative disappointments. These delicate personal circumstances make the letter clearly intended merely for private consumption; there could be no question of the Gisbornes sharing the intimate details in the prose letter. Yet the letter never descends into mawkish self-pity. Here, as in the *Letter*, Shelley keeps a clear sense of his audience, and weaves into his writing several different ideas, thoughts and emotional effects. If the prose letter was for the eyes of the Gisbornes alone, the verse epistle keeps in mind the public implied by the form. The *Letter to Maria Gisborne*, unlike the prose letter, offers a more public facing yet carefully intimate space for Shelley to express his circumstances to his coterie of London friends.

The *Letter to Maria Gisborne* displays the complexity of the relationship between the prose letters and the poetry. Opening with buoyant poise, the *Letter* generates allusion after allusion to create a self-portrait of an urbanely independent poet. The self-portrait that opens the poem clashes with the flagging self-assurance described in the prose letter of 30 June 1820 where Shelley shares his anxieties with the Gisbornes. Such openness underlines the level of intimacy between himself and the Gisbornes. Practical problems of the day dictate the beginning of the prose letter, whereas the *Letter*'s aesthetic polish allows the poet to refine rather than represent 'any thing human or earthly' (*Letters* ii, 363), which Shelley, only half-ironically, instructed his reader not to search out in his writing. In the *Letter* Shelley celebrates the independence of the poet who writes for his 'magic circle' ('To Jane: The Recollection' 44) rather than contend for laurels:

> The spider spreads her webs, whether she be
> In poet's tower, cellar or barn or tree;
> The silkworm in the dark green mulberry leaves
> His winding sheet and cradle ever weaves;
> So I, a thing whom moralists call worm,
> Sit spinning still round this decaying form,
> From the fine threads of verse and subtle thought –
> No net of words in garish colours wrought
> To catch the idle buzzers of the day –
> But a soft cell, where when that fades away,
> Memory may clothe in wings my living name
> And feed it with the asphodels of fame,
> Which in those hearts which most remember me
> Grow, making love an immortality.[4] (*Letter to Maria Gisborne* 1–14)

Shelley immediately draws attention to its status as 'a poem in rhyming couplets, a form which belongs to the distinct, if flexible, category of "verse-letter" or "verse-epistle"' (Webb, 'Scratching at the Door', 120). Whereas the prose letter attempts to connect on a practical and emotional level with its readers, here Shelley privileges the aesthetic and literary potential of poetry. Shelley's allusions bear witness to the immortality of the poets whom he quotes and suggest his own aspirations: 'I *will* live beyond this life' (*Letters* i, 214). Shelley begins with an expansive gesture where the spider 'spreads her webs', which, as Leader and O'Neill argue, 'reverses Swift's derogatory view' of the poet.[5] Shelley's spider and silkworm, whose precursors inhabit the works of poets from Mark Akenside to Edward Young, keep allusions in play, positive and negative, only to insist on the personal quality of his own work. Poetry, as *A Defence* argues, has an immortality of its own,[6] as its silken threads preserve the 'decaying form' of the man. The 'soft cell' of poetry that surrounds him will preserve his name in memory, keeping it alive though he has perished. Though love is described as 'an immortality', Shelley makes both love and poetry immortal, anticipating his sense in *A Defence* that 'the great secret of morals is love; or a going out of our nature, and an identification of ourselves with the beautiful which exists in thought, action, or person, not our own . . . The great instrument of moral good is the imagination . . . Poetry enlarges the circumference of the imagination' (*Major Works* 682). *A Defence of Poetry* is preoccupied with love as a means of escaping the limitations of selfhood, just as poetry enlarges the imagination and thereby affects an analogous process. Love and poetry, united in *A Defence* through their moral effects, are, in the *Letter*, made creative of one another. The final two lines of the quoted poetry show Shelley finding creative solace in the idea of his poetry fuelling his memory, a memory which will live on through the love of others. Likewise, his love is made immortal by its enshrinement in poetry. Here, love and poetry become symbiotic, a symbiosis incarnated in the epistolary form, a form addressed from one self to other selves.

The rhymes, though adhering closely to the heroic couplet form expected of the verse epistle, gain strength through their inevitability in the final four quoted lines. John Creaser explains: 'Rhyme consequently turns attention to the medium, and, through its usual position at the line-turn, to what most distinguishes verse from prose' (438). Shelley's rhymes of 'name' with 'fame' and 'me' with 'immortality' gain in pathos owing to the intimate relationship between the poet and the intended reader. The friends who would read the poem would be aware of the unsigned review (by J. T. Coleridge in the *Quarterly Review*) – in effect, a public poison letter – which, without stooping to calling him such a name, had reduced Shelley's character to 'worm' (Barcus 124–35). But Shelley keeps such despondency beneath the surface.[7] The 'asphodels of fame', which have an obvious correspondence with Shelley's painful awareness of his lack of fame and domestic peace in the letter, become smoothly conditional. But the pivotal 'may' of 'Memory may clothe in wings my living name' betrays his insecurity about finding an audience. This insecurity comes to the fore in the prose letter of 30 June 1820 as Shelley directly faces the fear he only alludes to in the poem, namely the problem of reputation.

> What remains to me? Domestic peace and fame? You will laugh when you hear me talk of the latter; indeed it is only a shadow. The seeking of a sympathy with the unborn and the unknown is a feeble mode of allaying the love within us; and even that is beyond the grasp of so weak an aspirant as I. Domestic peace I might have – I may have – if I see you, I shall have – but have not, for Mary suffers dreadfully from the state of Godwin's circumstances. (*Letters* ii, 206–7)

Searching for consolation, Shelley singles out domestic peace and fame as possible emollients for his bitter losses, yet he is forced to confront his lack of renown in England, and the distance between Shelley and Mary owing, in part, to Paulo Foggi's attempt to blackmail them (Bieri 252). As in his later *A Defence of Poetry*, Shelley moves to conjuring a sympathetic audience among 'the unborn and the unknown'. However, where *A Defence* evinces a fragile faith in the idea of posterity rescuing the reputation of a poet unpraised in his own lifetime,[8] in his letter to the Gisbornes, Shelley arrests his hopes, calling such sympathy merely a 'feeble mode of allaying the love within us'. Shelley leaves the dark implication hanging in the air that such a 'feeble mode' may be the only one hope available to the poet, but it is a hope that cannot be fulfilled. The *Letter* is illuminated by the prose letter, as Shelley's hopes, fears and rich literary lineage are present throughout both. Although the reader does not require the prose letter to appreciate the *Letter*, the relationship between the two texts allows the reader of both a subtly inflected reading of the poem.

The concerns that preoccupy the poetry surface in Shelley's prose letters in different modes, forms and expressions. The sense of isolation that surfaces in the prose letter of 30 June 1820 is, for example, a prominent feature of the *Letter to Maria Gisborne*. In his poem Shelley can plumb the depths of his isolation rather than moving politely to a more genial topic as he must in his prose letter. In the prose letter, Shelley attempts to mitigate any potential social awkwardness that may arise from Mary's plea for financial aid for her father. When he explains the situation, Shelley takes care to point out why he alludes to Mary's prose letter, adding an extra instruction to the Gisbornes that they should 'not pay the money into Godwin's hands' (*Letters* ii, 206). Such a condition allows Shelley a practical reason to write to them after Mary's letter, a reason that goes beyond an attempt to ensure that their friendship will survive a rejection of their request. Shelley expresses his sense of humiliation at having to throw himself upon their charity while making clear that this is not the first shameful occasion suffered by the poet: 'How little did I believe that I could have been party in making a demand of this kind on you. The reflection is full of bitterness, as most of the draughts are which life presents to me' (*Letters* ii, 206). To close the first paragraph with such a reflection leaves a deliberate gulf between this paragraph and the next,[9] where the space between the two allows the Gisbornes to reflect on Shelley's difficulties. The silence is both tactful and tactical, inviting without demanding recognition of the troubles through which the beleaguered poet is passing and has passed.

Where the letter must perform this instrumental task, the poem allows Shelley to explore his feelings around such isolating and depressing circumstances. Despite his knowledge and consent that the poem would be shared with a wider audience, the illusion of private communion allows Shelley the space to write a poem fascinated by the presence and absence of intimate friends. Where the prose letter was intended for the eyes of John and Maria Gisborne, and potential posthumous readers, the *Letter* itself would be shared amongst the wider coterie of London friends, a group where individuals come to be referred to by name in the poem. Here, as elsewhere, Shelley makes sound mirror sense as his couplets emphasise the strain of separation:

> You are not here . . . the quaint witch Memory sees
> In vacant chairs your absent images,
> And points where once you sat, and now should be
> But are not – I demand if ever we
> Shall meet as then we met – and she replies,
> Veiling in awe her second-sighted eyes;
> 'I know the past alone – but summon home
> My sister Hope, – she speaks of all to come.'
> But I, an old diviner, who knew well
> Every false verse of that sweet oracle,
> Turned to the sad enchantress once again, (*Letter to Maria Gisborne* 132–42)

The opening four words, with their steady weighted monosyllables, reveal a distance that words cannot fully cross. The prose letter does not confront this isolation, attempting instead to tempt its readers into a visit. Shelley makes his punctuation mirror the possibilities of its attainment. His sentence construction, 'I might have – I may have – if I see you, I shall have – but have not' (*Letters* ii, 207), performs an arpeggio of conditions, moving through the tenses from the potential at the beginning, to the central request, 'if I see you, I shall have', and back to the flat 'but have not'. Shelley leaves no doubt that the only way that his state can be remedied is by the appearance of the Gisbornes, but his word-play and immediate turn back to more descriptive family news allows him to avoid placing the Gisbornes under pressure, despite his longing for their company.

In the *Letter*, no such *politesse* is required. By attempting to impose presence onto absence, Shelley's 'quaint witch Memory' torments, yet leavens the pain of separation. The rhyme of 'be' and 'we' sets up the ideal situation in a full rhyme, but the rhyme of 'home' and 'come', with its appearance as eye rhyme contrasting with its status as half-rhyme, subtly points up the impossible conditions of Shelley's desire for their return. Hope, so often coupled with despair in Shelley's imagination,[10] is refused, along with her 'fake verse', in favour of 'the sad enchantress' Memory. Rather than imaginatively uniting with Maria Gisborne as he does in his letters to Leigh Hunt,[11] Shelley recreates their shared memories, reminiscences subsiding into a philosophical reflection on 'The jarring and inexplicable frame / Of this wrong world' (159–60). Shelley affirms the poet's ability to recollect the past, preserving it in crystalline poetic form:

> Why should not we rouse with the spirit's blast
> Out of the forest of the pathless past
> These recollected pleasures? (*Letter to Maria Gisborne* 190–2)

The insistence on memory's capacity to 'rouse' the soul is an effort by Shelley to defend his strain to preserve, if only in imaginative form, his relationships, and thereby himself, from the creeping 'despondency' that shadowed the prose letter. Memory, though imperfect, offers a buffer from the alienating circumstances of life. Like Wordsworth, Shelley promotes memory as vital to poetic achievement: 'Poetry is the spontaneous overflow of powerful feelings: it takes its origin from emotion recollected in tranquillity' (Wordsworth 611). Yet the question in the *Letter* seems far less affirmative than Wordsworth's prose statement. The patchwork of memories, both memories of a personal nature and remembered literary allusions, form the poem, making memory central to the poet's achievement. But memory itself does not earn the poet's entire faith. The *Letter* seems to test rather than assume the possibilities of memory.

Shelley's *Letter* embodies the witty 'familiar style' (*Letters* ii, 108) he himself valued in correspondence. As in Mary Shelley's letter to Maria Gisborne of 18 June 1820, where she playfully writes 'Where am I? Guess! In a little room before a deal table looking out on a poderè – Whose voice is that? Henry, does not your heart beat? By heaven, 'tis Miss Appolonia Ricci – Nay here we are we have taken possession – What do you say?' (i, 146), Shelley's sportive lines reveal an easy intimacy with his correspondent. As Donald Davie observes of Shelley's choice of addressee: 'She [Maria Gisborne] is not a peg to hang a poem on, but a person who shares with him certain interests and certain friends and a certain sense of humour' (141). This connection would be appreciated by the coterie who read the poem while Shelley lived, but by the time of Mary Shelley's *Posthumous Poems* in 1824, this personal context became less important as Maria's memory faded. In spite of

Shelley's close relationship with his addressee, she is not the only audience that he entertains. By focusing his attention on a specific coterie of readers, particularly one so significant for Shelley's intellectual development, Shelley could manoeuvre himself perfectly into writing a verse epistle which manages to satisfy the required eloquence of the 'verse' element alongside the need for urbanity suggested by the 'epistle'. Reminiscent of Shelley's request in a prose letter of 26 May 1820 that Henry 'write me an adamantine letter, flowing not like the words of Sophocles with honey, but molten brass & iron, & bristling with wheels & teeth?' (*Letters* ii, 203), Shelley's poem assumes a similar timbre where the indefatigable energy seems 'bristling' with engineering and scientific metaphors. There is a sense of renewed self-confidence in the *Letter*, as Shelley repeatedly styles himself as a creator unfettered by any extraneous demands:

And here like some weird Archimage sit I,
Plotting dark spells and devilish enginery,
The self-impelling steam-wheels of the mind
Which pump up oaths from clergymen, and grind
The gentle spirit of our meek reviews (*Letter to Maria Gisborne* 106–10)

Humorously adopting the role of Archimago of Spenser's *Fairie Queene* and the Archimage of Thomson's *The Castle of Indolence*, Shelley sketches a portrait of himself as the dangerous magician capable of dark enchantment.[12] As Ford notes, '[t]he "gentle spirit of our meek reviews" is sufficiently ironic, but the irony is not bitter. And the pumped-up oaths from clergymen are like one of Shelley's youthful experiments in the laboratory' (14). Despite William Keach's argument that the lines 'sound like deliberate self-parody to a reader that recalls some of the images of imaginative freedom in *Prometheus Unbound*' (113), the levity and wit of the passage belie any notion of it as simply self-parody. The reference to the 'self-impelling steam-wheels of the mind' reflects Shelley's very real enthusiasm for the work in which he and Henry were engaged. He writes with childlike enthusiasm to John and Maria Gisborne to beg: 'Tell us of the Steamboat! This Steamboat is a Sort of Asymptote which seems ever to approach & never to arrive. But courage!' (*Letters* ii, 179). The comic quality of the lines mitigates any sense that Shelley is peeved by the boat's failure to materialise. The eagerness of the quotation from the prose letter does not remain simply personal in the poem. The 'self-impelling' quality of the 'steam-wheels of the mind' suggests the poet's steely self-will, a will that drives the poetry forward.

The image of a will-driven poetry seems to contradict Shelley's assertion in *A Defence of Poetry* that 'poetry is not like reasoning, a power to be exerted according to the determination of the will. A man cannot say, "I will compose poetry"' (*Major Works* 696). Yet Shelley does not depart too far from the ideals articulated in his later prose poem. The enchanting quality of poetry, despite Shelley's mischievous reference to the poet 'Plotting dark spells', reminds us that 'poetry thus makes immortal all that is best and most beautiful in the world; it arrests the vanishing apparitions which haunt the interlunations of life, and veiling them or in language or in form sends them forth among mankind' (A Defence of Poetry, Major Works 698). The quasi-magical power of poetry is asserted rather than undercut by the mechanical imagery. The will-driven element that Shelley brings out seems a celebration of poetry's power to assert itself as the words seem self-generated by the 'steam-wheels of the mind'. The mind and poetry itself blur as 'the mind which feeds this verse / Peopling the lone universe' (Lines Written among the Euganean Hills 318–19) becomes the poem itself even as it remains separate from it. These lines, despite their levity, create an arena in which Shelley can say, with Prometheus, 'Yet am I king over myself' (Prometheus Unbound I, 492) in the face of the Furies of his personal life.

Shelley's longing for community suffuses many of his letters, and his disappointment when plans failed to harden into actions proved a major source of pain. Writing to Horace Smith in 1821, Shelley does not attempt to suppress his sadness at a cancelled visit: 'I cannot express the pain and disappointment with which I learn the change in your plans, no less the afflicting cause of it. Florence will no longer have any attractions for me this winter, and I shall contentedly sit down in this humdrum Pisa, and refer to hope and to chance the pleasure I had expected from your society this winter' (Letters ii, 348). Memory cannot assist; a major part of the disappointment consists of having no salving recollections to which to cling. Hope, as in the Letter, appears more cruel than kind. Where in the prose letter to the Gisbornes, Shelley had requested their presence as a balm for his domestic strife, in the Letter, poetry and the power of language allow Shelley to come as close to presence as possible. Though he cannot be there, he images forth their mutual friends to bask in the glow of the company he craved. Despite his antipathy to London, which is depicted as a devouring and monstrous sea, Shelley cannot bring himself to disown entirely a city which houses his dearest friends and intimate enemies. Shelley begins with Godwin:

> You will see
> That which was Godwin, – greater none than he
> Though fallen – and fallen on evil times – to stand
> Among the spirits of our age and land,
> Before the dread tribunal of to come (Letter to Maria Gisborne 196–200)

Shelley loads the description of Godwin with Miltonic allusions, from 'dread tribunal' (Paradise Lost III, 326) to 'though fall'n on evil days, / On evil days though fall'n' (Paradise Lost VII, 25–6),[13] his high language insisting on Godwin's genius despite his wrongs. This urge to offer a just monument to Godwin is a theme of Shelley's letters to the Gisbornes, as he appeals particularly to Maria for her opinion based on her previous acquaintance with his father-in-law. As previously noted, Godwin is referred to on 26 May 1820 as 'the only sincere enemy I have in the world' (Letters ii, 202) as Shelley distinguishes between Godwin's mind and his character, even pausing to praise 'the moral resources of his character' (Letters ii, 203). Where Shelley's letter does not use allusions to bolster its praise, here Shelley returns once again to Milton, alchemising the dross of personal opinion into the gold of achieved poetic eloquence. This principle continues through-out Shelley's miniatures of his friends. Passing through a series of tributes and characterisations, the poem seems to bask in the warmth of its imagined com-munity. Shelley's sketches convey intimacy with and esteem for those whom he mentions. Including Samuel Taylor Coleridge, Leigh Hunt, Thomas Love Peacock and Horace Smith, Shelley conversationally runs through a series of quasi-introductions:

> You will see Hunt – one of those happy souls
> Which are the salt of the earth, and without whom
> This world would smell like what it is – a tomb;
> Who is, what others seem – his room no doubt
> Is still adorned with many a cast from Shout,
> With graceful flowers tastefully placed about;
> And coronals of bay from ribbons hung,
> And brighter wreaths in neat disorder flung,
> The gifts of the most learn'd among some dozens
> Of female friends, sisters-in-law, and cousins. (*Letter to Maria Gisborne* 209–18)

Hunt, now 'salt of the earth', is pictured in the context of the society Shelley missed, among his stylish accoutrements and his various women. Mischievously, Shelley paints him almost in the mode in which he himself was often described and thereby condemned: surrounded by significant women with whom he may or may not be having a sexual relationship. Hunt is abstracted from his political and public role as chief provocateur of the Tory government and instead becomes the centre of a hub of social exchange. Shelley often wrote to Hunt to encourage him in his political analyses of the repressive state of England, such as on 23 December 1819: 'What a state England is in! But you will never write politics. I don't wonder; but I wish then that you would write a paper in the *Examiner* on the actual state of the country, and what, under all the circumstances of the conflicting passions and interests of men, we are to expect – but what, as things are, there is reason to believe will come – and send it me for my information' (*Letters* ii, 166). Alienated from England, Shelley clung to any scraps of news, and saw Hunt as a major player in the British political world. As in *Adonais*, where Hunt is transformed into a mute and almost feminised figure, Shelley chooses to abstract Hunt from his public role, picturing him in a domestic and thereby intimate sphere.

Following this affectionate portrait, Peacock receives a sideswipe as Shelley alludes to his silence following Peacock's marriage:

> have you not heard
> When a man marries, dies, or turns Hindoo,
> His best friends hear no more of him? – but you
> Will see him, and will like him too, I hope,
> With the milk-white Snowdonian antelope
> Matched with this cameleopard – His fine wit

Makes such a wound, the knife is lost in it.
A strain too learnèd for a shallow age,
Too wise for selfish bigots; – let his page,
Which charms the chosen spirits of the time,
Fold itself up for the serener clime
Of years to come, and find its recompense
In that just expectation. – (*Letter to Maria Gisborne* 235–47)

Shelley had mourned that Peacock, with his post in India and new wife, had 'something better to do than read scrawls' (*Letters* ii, 362), but Shelley's reproach seems less malicious than amused and amusing. Despite the potential aggressiveness of this style of communication, Shelley seems more inclined to encourage his friends to restore contact than attempt to embarrass or pressure them into bending to his will as his urbanity sparkles with wit rather than anger. The mock question exacts a smile from its audience rather than appearing as a genuine condemnation of Peacock's callousness as Shelley finishes his introductions with aplomb. George Saintsbury points out the aptness of Shelley's description: 'not only is Peacock peculiarly liable to the charge of being too clever, but he uses his cleverness in a way peculiarly bewildering to those who like to have "This is a horse" writ large under the presentation of the animal' (240). There seems no censure in Shelley's description; though Peacock's wit is compared to a knife, this seems more suggestive of his sharp insights rather than his intellectual violence in view of the 'selfish bigots' who follow the comparison. Suggestive of his own hopes of posthumous appreciation, Shelley affirms that Peacock will receive his literary due in the future with 'just expectation', as the apparently private joke ('With the milk-white Snowdonian antelope / Matched with this cameleopard') bears witness to their continued intimacy. As Timothy Webb notes, the line 'Now Italy or London, which you will!' (289) acquires 'extra resonance' if aimed at Hunt as well as the Gisbornes ('Scratching at the Door' 126), yet Shelley includes Peacock and Smith, both of whom had also received firm invitations to visit the Shelleys. Longing to be reunited with his friends, 'Oh! that Hunt, Hogg, Peacock and Smith were there, / With everything belonging to them fair! –' (294–5), Shelley's verse epistle unites with his prose letters in their shared yearning for desired society.

London comes to represent the heart of Shelley's friendships, but this is not Shelley's final position. The state of England, which preoccupies Shelley in the prose letter when he carefully changes the subject after his admission of despondency, reappears in the *Letter to Maria Gisborne* as Shelley will not segregate the political from the personal. Stephen Greenblatt points out the importance of the self-fashioning writer dramatising 'the point of encounter between an authority and an alien' (9), but Shelley estranges this encounter by imagining the perspective of his friend. Pressing Maria for news of England, Shelley extols the importance of her behaving as 'water does a sponge' (255). It seems Shelley longs to soak up her experiences in the same manner. Demanding 'What see you?' (257), Shelley makes clear that he will not be satisfied with a merely picturesque description of the city by night:

But what see you beside? – a shabby stand
Of hackney-coaches – a brick house or wall
Fencing some lordly court, white with the scrawl
Of our unhappy politics; or worse –
A wretched woman reeling by, whose curse
Mixed with the watchman's, partner of her trade,
You must accept in place of serenade – (*Letter to Maria Gisborne* 265–71)

Playing ventriloquist, Shelley begins to direct Maria to write the kind of letter he would like to receive in a gesture of confidence in Maria's writing skill and the intimacy between the two friends. Yet when in the prose letter Shelley shifts to brisk political questioning, the shift seems as if Shelley wants to change the subject after an admission of his 'struggle with despondency': 'Well, what think you of public affairs in England? How can the English endure the mountains of cant which are cast upon them about this vulgar cook-maid they call a Queen?' (*Letters* ii, 207). In the poem, Shelley insists on receiving an unvarnished picture of the wrongs of London even when his words actually go on to sketch the degradation about which he longs to hear. Visually precise, Shelley moves from the 'scrawl / Of our unhappy politics' to a description of a prostitute that manages to avoid condemnation or disdain in favour of empathetic horror increased by his sharing of the political burden with 'our' rather than 'your' politics. The prostitute, sketched in the poem as a 'wretched woman', seems shadowed by the Queen's own possible indiscretions. Shelley wrote to Peacock on 12 July 1820 of his amazement that the English public should hail her as a heroine when 'she has, as I firmly believe, amused herself in a manner rather indecorous with any Courier or Baron' (*Letters* ii, 213). Shelley suggests in the *Letter* what he states in the prose letter: 'It is really time for the English to wean themselves from this nonsense, for really their situation is too momentous to justify them in attending to Punch and his Wife . . . And Peers and Peeresses to stalk along the streets in ermine! It is really time to give over this mummery. Whilst "that two-handed engine", &c.' (*Letters* ii, 207). The horrifying gap between the 'lordly courts' and the desperate spectacle of the prostitute and the watchman subtly insists that this 'nonsense' must be dealt with by the people. The shared political emphasis of both the prose letter and the verse epistle shows Shelley as ensuring that the principles of the man remain the same as those of the poet, if differently expressed.[14] Despite the prose letter and the *Letter* being products of diverse genres, their shared preoccupations reveal their complex connection. Shelley takes poetic advantage of the biographical circumstances and personal beliefs which, already recalibrated for his addressees, are transformed in his poem into a deliberate aesthetic creation.

A poetic form of power allows Shelley to affirm his hopes for the future, where his friends will reassemble in Italy, following his fears of becoming overtaken entirely by despair: 'Next winter you must pass with me; I'll have / My house by that time turned into a grave / Of dead despondence and low-thoughted care' (*Letter to Maria Gisborne* 292–4). Shelley alludes to Milton's *Comus* with 'low-thoughted care' to rescue the lines from offering merely personal revelation (*Major Works* 787).

Recovering his equilibrium, Shelley makes detailed plans, from their reading to their meals, to lure his friends to Italy:

> We will have books, Spanish, Italian, Greek;
> And ask one week to make another week
> As like his father, as I'm unlike mine,
> Which is not his fault, as you may divine. (*Letter to Maria Gisborne* 296–9)

Keeping witty intimacy present in the lines, Shelley matches pain with humour as he laughingly alludes to his schism from his father without succumbing to misery and doubt. Earlier in his life, Shelley had written emotionally charged letters to his father: 'Think not that I am an insect whom injuries destroy – had I money enough I would meet you in London, & hollow in your ears Bysshe, Bysshe, Bysshe – aye Bysshe till you're deaf' (*Letters* i, 149), but here, Shelley retains an urbane wit that matches the polish of the rest of the poem. Such mobility allows the *Letter to Maria Gisborne*, like the prose letter to the Gisbornes of 30 June 1820, a shimmering quality where it dances through various states, moods and ideas, despite its dealings with 'despondency' (*Letters* ii, 207). This quality sparks Timothy Webb's insight that 'Shelley's poem introduces many of the themes which haunt his more "serious" texts but, within the framework of this verse-epistle, they are suspended and held in place (though not forgotten) by the processes of genial translation and the restraining conventions of the verse-epistle' ('Scratching at the Door' 134). Rather than adhering to generic demands, Shelley chooses to move between various states, just as his prose letter does, as the poet refuses to simplify his emotional range.[15] The movement between revelation and restraint keeps the poetry in motion just as in the prose letters. Closing with another Miltonic allusion to 'fresh woods and pastures new' (*Lycidas* 193 and *Letter to Maria Gisborne* 323), Shelley manages to create a tension between the affirmation of *Lycidas*'s closing line and his own more uncertain path. Such uncertainty becomes aesthetically productive for Shelley as he deliberately works with and against '*self*, that burr that will stick to one. I can't get it off yet' (*Letters* i, 109). This lament becomes central to the creative process in *Letter to Maria Gisborne* as Shelley structures his verse epistle around the preoccupations that fired the prose letter. As Michael O'Neill states: 'Such a point [the poetry's self-awareness] is often explored by Shelley's poetry; too deftly self-aware for biographical readings to seem more than ploddingly literal-minded, the poems are themselves intrigued by the links and gaps between man and poet' (138). This experimentation with the idea of the 'I', in the prose letter to the Gisbornes and in the *Letter to Maria Gisborne*, represents Shelley's sophisticated epistolary practice, where the letter becomes far more than mere ore to be mined by biographical criticism just as the poem becomes far more than simply a verse version of a private letter. Both the prose letter and the *Letter to Maria Gisborne* bring Shelley's concerns and confidence into startling poetic life.

NOTES

1. Percy Bysshe Shelley, *Letters of Percy Bysshe Shelley*, ed. F. L. Jones, 2 vols (Oxford: Clarendon Press, 1964), i, 109. All quotations from Shelley's letters will be taken from this edition.
2. Percy Bysshe Shelley, *A Defence of Poetry*, in *Percy Bysshe Shelley: The Major Works*, ed., intro. and notes Zachary Leader and Michael O'Neill, Oxford World's Classics series (Oxford: Oxford University Press, 2003), p. 682. All quotations from the poetry and prose of Shelley (except for the *Letter to Maria Gisborne*) will be taken from this edition.
3. As the editors of *The Poems of Shelley* point out, the dating is fraught as Mary's dates do not agree: 'Mary's date is "Leghorn, July 1, 1820" in 1824 but "Leghorn – June 1820" beneath her transcription of the poem now in the Huntington Library.' The *Letter to Maria Gisborne* and letter 575 may have been enclosed in Mary's 7 July letter. Percy Bysshe Shelley, *The Poems of Shelley, Volume 3: 1819–1820*, ed. Jack Donovan, Cian Duffy, Kelvin Everest and Michael Rossington (London: Longman, 2011), p. 425n. Hereafter *Longman*.
4. Percy Bysshe Shelley, *Letter to Maria Gisborne*, in *Longman* 433–6. All quotations from the *Letter to Maria Gisborne* will be from this edition.
5. 'Notes to the *Letter to Maria Gisborne*', *Major Works*, 784.
6. See, for example, 'All high poetry is infinite; it is as the first acorn which contained all oaks potentially' (*A Defence, Major Works*, 693).
7. The question regarding the intended readers of the *Letter* is explored by Timothy Webb, who concludes that 'inter-reading' was expected, and that Shelley would be aware that the Gisborne family and various friends (Hunt, in particular) would read the poem ('Scratching at the Door' 126).
8. 'Even in modern times, no living poet ever arrived at the fullness of his fame; the jury which sits in judgement upon a poet, belonging as he does to all time, must be composed of his peers: it must be impanelled by Time from the selectest of the wise of many generations' (Shelley, *A Defence of Poetry, Major Works*, 680).
9. The original letter is, according to F. L. Jones, untraced: 'A MS. copy in Mary Shelley's hand is in Lord Abinger's Library' (*Letters* ii, 208).
10. See, for example, *Alastor* 639, or *Hellas* 39. For the complete range of Shelley's use of 'hope', see *A Lexical Concordance to the Poetical Works of Percy Bysshe Shelley*, compiled and arranged by F. S. Ellis (London: Bernard Quadrich, 1892; repr. Johnson Reprint Company, 1967), pp. 335–6.
11. Daisy Hay makes this point: 'Both understood the importance of expressing their concern and affection for the other, but it was Hunt who established a model of epistolary theatricality which allowed them to bridge the distance between them imaginatively' (213).
12. See *Longman* 445n; the editors also point out that Shelley had been described as 'a sort of good stupid Archimago' in a review of *Laon and Cythna/The Revolt of Islam* in the *Quarterly Review* 21 (April 1819): 467.
13. John Milton, *Paradise Lost*, in *John Milton: The Complete Poems*, ed. John Leonard (London: Penguin, 1998), p. 179 and p. 269. All quotations from Milton's poetry will be taken from this edition.
14. The poem is by no means an attempt to render in poetry the issues that had dogged Shelley in his letter. Shelley emphatically underscored this element of his theory of poetry, writing: 'nothing can be equally well expressed in prose that is not tedious and supererogatory in verse.' Shelley, 'Preface to *Prometheus Unbound*', *Major Works*, 232.
15. Ann Thompson makes the point that Shelley understands but alters the genre: 'Shelley was clearly aware of the literary tradition of the verse epistle but he avoids its public, didactic dimension' (147).

WORKS CITED

Barcus, James (ed.), *Shelley: The Critical Heritage* (London: Routledge & Kegan Paul, 1975).

Bieri, James, *Percy Bysshe Shelley: A Biography: Exile of Unfulfilled Renown, 1816–1822* (Newark, DE: University of Delaware Press, 2005).

Creaser, John, 'Rhymes, Rhyme, and Rhyming', *Essays in Criticism* 62.4 (2012): 438–60.

Davie, Donald, 'Shelley's Urbanity', *Purity of Diction in English Verse* (London: Routledge & Kegan Paul, 1967), pp. 133–59.

Ellis, F. S. (arr. and comp.), *A Lexical Concordance to the Poetical Works of Percy Bysshe Shelley* (London: Bernard Quadrich, 1892; repr. Johnson Reprint Company, 1967).

Ford, Newell F., 'The Wit in Shelley's Poetry', *Studies in English Literature, 1500–1900* 1.4 (1961): 1–22.

Greenblatt, Stephen, *Renaissance Self-Fashioning: From More to Shakespeare* (Chicago: University of Chicago Press, 1980).

Hay, Daisy, 'Shelley's Letters', in Michael O'Neill and Tony Howe (eds), *The Oxford Handbook of Percy Bysshe Shelley* (Oxford: Oxford University Press, 2012), pp. 208–22.

Keach, William, *Shelley's Style* (New York: Methuen, 1984).

Milton, John, *John Milton: The Complete Poems*, ed. John Leonard (London: Penguin, 1998).

O'Neill, Michael, *Romanticism and the Self-Conscious Poem* (Oxford: Clarendon Press, 1997).

Ruge, Enno, '"Is the entire correspondence a fiction?": Shelley's Letters and the Eighteenth-Century Epistolary Novel', in Werner Huber and Marie-Luise Egbert (eds), *Alternative Romanticisms* (Essen: Studien zur Englischen Romantik 15, 2003), pp. 111–21.

Saintsbury, George, *Essays in English Literature, 1780–1860* (London: Dent, 1895).

Shelley, Mary Wollstonecraft, *The Letters of Mary Wollstonecraft Shelley*, ed. Betty T. Bennett, 3 vols (Baltimore: Johns Hopkins University Press, 1980–8).

Shelley, Percy Bysshe, *Letters of Percy Bysshe Shelley*, ed. F. L. Jones, 2 vols (Oxford: Clarendon Press, 1964).

—— *Percy Bysshe Shelley: The Major Works*, ed., intro. and notes Zachary Leader and Michael O'Neill, Oxford World's Classics series (Oxford: Oxford University Press, 2003).

—— *The Poems of Shelley, Volume 3: 1819–1820*, ed. Jack Donovan, Cian Duffy, Kelvin Everest and Michael Rossington (London: Longman, 2011).

Taylor, Charles, *Sources of the Self: The Making of Modern Identity* (Cambridge: Cambridge University Press, 1989).

Thompson, Ann, 'Shelley's "Letter to Maria Gisborne": Tact and Clutter', in Miriam Allott (ed.), *Essays on Shelley* (Liverpool: Liverpool University Press, 1982), pp. 144–59.

Vargo, Lisa, 'The Verse Epistle', in Frederick Burwick, Nancy Moore Goslee and Diane Long Hoeveler (eds), *The Encyclopedia of Romantic Literature*, vol. 3 (Malden, MA: Blackwell, 2012), pp. 1,465–9.

Webb, Timothy, '"Cutting Figures": Rhetorical Strategies in Keats's *Letters*', in Michael O'Neill (ed.), *Keats: Bicentenary Readings* (Edinburgh: Edinburgh University Press, 1997), pp. 144–69.

—— 'Scratching at the Door of Absence: Writing and Reading "Letter to Maria Gisborne"', in Alan M. Weinberg and Timothy Webb (eds), *The Unfamiliar Shelley*, The Nineteenth Century series (Farnham: Ashgate, 2009), pp. 119–36.

Wordsworth, William, *William Wordsworth: The Major Works*, ed. Stephen Gill, Oxford World's Classics series (Oxford: Oxford University Press, 2011).

8 'Another sort of writing'? Invalidism and Poetic Labour in the Letters of Elizabeth Barrett

Marcus Waithe

Writing to his father one morning at the beginning of his literary career, Thomas Carlyle remarked that 'I was just sitting down to my work . . . when your letter a few minutes ago was handed in to me' (*Carlyle Letters Online* 2 April 1823). His next sentence attempts a complicated differentiation: 'I lay aside my author-craft, and willingly betake me to another sort of writing.' Carlyle's later testimony suggests that he laboured under some awkwardness in writing these words. In *Reminiscences* (1881; 1887), he celebrated the dignity of his father's work as a stonemason, while anxiously confessing the paternal view of poetry and lettered eloquence as 'idle tattle' ('James Carlyle' 6). Read in this light, the compound word 'author-craft' defends the working credentials of his adopted vocation as an essayist. By analogy with the stonemason's trade, it declares his calling an honourable path, demanding of skill and application. Letter writing is conceived as a different function, in that it entails a suspension of professional duty. Yet as a reverend communication, addressed to the head of the family, Carlyle's words cannot afford to be entirely secondary. The transition marked by 'lay aside' is softened by the blithe neutrality of 'another sort' and generic continuity is affirmed by the word 'writing'. We are left wondering whether the distinction between literature and letters can hold. Carlyle implies that correspondence is at best supplemental; but the common instrument and common method – the same stylus, the same search for adequate words – suggest that 'work' must be a quality of both, or neither.

This question of the appropriate measure, or quantum, of epistolary labour is especially pertinent to the case of Elizabeth Barrett, whose letters are the subject of this chapter. Barrett's adherence to the Carlylean Gospel of Work (*Past and Present* 201; Houghton 242–63; Briggs 124–47) coincided with a life lived to an unusual extent through the surrogate offices of correspondence.[1] Growing up amid the seclusion of rural Herefordshire, and often confined to the house by illness, she took to letter writing as a way of developing intellectual friendships. Her first such exchange was pursued in the early 1830s with the blind scholar Hugh Boyd. That early experience was replicated in letters to the eminent classicist Uvedale Price and, most enduringly, in writing between 1836 and 1854 to the poet and dramatist Mary Russell Mitford. Barrett's letters to Mitford ran in parallel with the body of correspondence that will be my focus: the 573 letters of clandestine 'courtship correspondence' exchanged with her fellow poet Robert Browning between January 1845 and the fateful day in September 1846 when the pair eloped to Italy to escape the influence of Barrett's possessive father.

In common with previous exchanges, the letters sent to Browning have the quality of an intellectual calendar, serving as a report on reading and poetic experience. They are nevertheless unusual. Daniel Karlin has observed that they represent 'one of the longest, fullest, most self-contained correspondences in English literary history' (xi). That interest is magnified by their coinciding with Barrett's most exclusive period of social retirement, so as to enact, over a relatively short span of time, an unusually productive tension between physical and intellectual presence. Barrett had not been permitted to meet Boyd for almost a year after their first letter (Berridge 20), and similarly it required months of intense exchange before she plucked up the courage to meet Browning, on 20 May 1845. Their correspondence also occurred at a time when both parties were more than usually mindful of their reputation as poets. Barrett was basking in the critical success of her *Poems* (1844), but still a decade away from the crowning achievement of *Aurora Leigh* (1856). Browning, by contrast, was relatively unknown, and nursing the wounds of criticism aimed at his *Sordello* (1840) (Litzinger and Smalley 5). Still, he had been experiencing a measured revival of fortunes with the positive reception of *Bells and Pomegranates* (1841–6) (Litzinger and Smalley 6–7), and though he would not experience public renown until the publication of *The Ring and the Book* (1868–9), Barrett's position as a 'devout admirer & student' of his works offered hope of better things to come (*BL.* To RB. 11 January 1845 8).

While many Victorian writers kept up a voluminous correspondence, Barrett's years of illness meant that she especially relied on letters to make her social and professional contribution. To that extent, letters functioned as a primary action, rather than a temporary substitute for real presence. Acceptance of this reality warred with her consciousness that they were a product of her life as an invalid, and thus in some way intimate with incapacity. Recalling the language of imprisonment employed in Harriet Martineau's *Life in the Sick-Room* (1844) (69), she admitted that her habit of 'talking by post' brought to mind 'people shut up in dungeons [who] take up with scrawling mottoes [sic] on the walls' (*BL.* To RB. 3 February 1845 1). She also confessed to 'a profound conviction that where a poet has been shut from most of the outward aspects of life, he is at a lamentable disadvantage' (*BL.* To RB. [17 April 1845] 3). The manuscript of this letter reveals an interpolation of the word 'outward' whose effect is to buttress the idea of exclusion, while retaining competence over the 'inward' world. In what follows, I will address the relationship between Barrett's letters and her invalidism, and then as triangulated between invalidism, letters and poetry.

Through letter writing, Barrett explored and negotiated the conflict between her ill-health and Carlyle's injunction that all should 'work'. Carlyle had begun to articulate his vision of man as a 'tool using animal' in the satirical pages of *Sartor*

Resartus (1833–4), but it was in *Chartism* (1839) and *Past and Present* (1843) that it emerged as his chief tenet, such that the 'condition of England' (*Past and Present* 1) was seen as blighted by a 'self-cancelling Dothingism and *Laissez-faire*' (*Chartism* 167). Though there were warnings in these works of what lay ahead, it was not until the publication of *Latter-day Pamphlets* (1850) that his rhetoric hardened to the point of alienating his admirers, as sympathy for the work-starved became an assault on groups thought guilty of a 'lazy refusal of work' (27).

That Barrett found nothing in her own circumstances to disqualify her esteem for the Sage of Chelsea is in various ways revealing. In a letter to Mary Russell Mitford, she effusively observed that she was 'an adorer of Carlyle' (27–8 March 1842, Raymond and Sullivan i, 378). Writing to Browning, she referred to 'the great teacher of the age, Carlyle, who is also yours & mine' (*BL* 27 February 1845 2). She must have sensed that Browning would take pleasure in her praise of Carlyle, as the two men were already friends. But any affectionate bias ran first and foremost in the other direction: as Rosemary Ashton observes, it was Carlyle's modest praise of Browning's poetry that 'predisposed her to like and admire him [Browning]' (225).

Barrett did not actually make Carlyle's acquaintance until after her marriage, when the couple made a visit home from Florence in July 1851. Her having read him many years before she met him accounts for an occasional boldness in privileging the written text over the spoken position of the man. Writing to Browning on 17 February 1845, she asks, 'And does Mr. Carlyle tell you that he has forbidden all "singing" to this perverse and froward generation, which should work and not sing?' (*BL* 17 February 1845 12). Her rebuttal finds its stress in a denial of the opposition between 'work' and song, yet goes further: 'And have you told Mr. Carlyle that song is work, and also the condition of work?' (*BL* 17 February 1845 12). Radical as it sounds, Barrett's query draws its force from concurrent insistence on uncritical devotion, and from the echo of Carlylean rhythm in her own words. She notes that 'I am a devout sitter at his feet – and it is an effort to me to think him wrong in anything' (*BL* 17 February 1845 12). Resistance entails the unsettling of this faith, combined with an uneasy or 'ruffled' feeling, induced by the thought of Carlyle 'putting away, even for a season, the poetry of the world' (*BL* 17 February 1845 13). Thus Carlyle is found to be in the 'wrong' not because his creed promotes an intrinsic disregard for poetry, but because he has not adhered consistently to the letter of his own doctrines.

Carlyle would later praise the 'active poets' who are 'incessantly toiling to achieve' (*Latter-day Pamphlets* 261). While this was largely a reiteration of Barrett's own determination to equate 'work' and 'song', it is clear that in pledging allegiance as his 'disciple' (*BL* 17 February 1845 13), she would need to find ways of reconfiguring the stress on able-bodiedness, to encompass a broader view of the 'active'. Epistolary exchange played a crucial part in this process. In one respect, letters served as a repository for all idle faculties excluded from the poetic. They acquired from this a sacrificial function, as writing literally 'thrown away', or 'given up' to social discourse. At the same time, they could offer hope of something more enduring. In what follows, I will show how Barrett's letters eluded secondary status, and became a testing ground for unconventional work ethics and excluded modes of production.

Biographers have tended to divide Barrett's ill-health into two phases, the first of which was precipitated by a fall from her pony at the age of fifteen (Berridge 18). The second turning point was marked by her brother's death at sea off Torquay, in July 1840. It delivered a nervous shock that precipitated her final resolution to 'seclude myself' (Berridge 150) at the prospect of leaving Herefordshire for London. Barbara Dennis ascribes this later period of ill-health, which began in Barrett's early thirties, to 'a form of tuberculosis' (43), a verdict that leans heavily on George Pickering's medical assessment that she 'suffered from a chronic lung affliction' (260). The limitation of retrospective diagnosis is that it de-emphasises the vagueness of the malaise, a crucially self-reinforcing attribute that ensured the capacity of invalidism to signify at the level of perception and identity. Maria Frawley rightly observes that an avoidance of medical details among invalids reflected a 'cultural mentality', or '"sick role"', that was 'scripted in various ways by society and inflected by other dimensions of identity' (3–4).

In her letters to Browning, Barrett would alternate between downplaying her condition as a temporary impediment and urging it as a non-negotiable fact about herself. The latter tendency is apparent in her efforts at self-mythologisation. She looks in on herself as one 'leading a life of such seclusion' (BL [10 November 1845] 1). Coy references to Mariana in the moated grange (BL 6 June 1845 8) take turns with the figure of a hibernating dormouse (BL 11 January 1845 6). Less playfully, she reflects on the time-decaying action of a life lived in 'Books and dreams' (BL 20 March 1845 3), and the distant prospect of 'the outward world' aligned not only with winter, but with all that lies beyond 'the threshold of one room' (BL 20 March 1845 3). Amidst these complaints, and in the spirit of Martineau's closing chapter on 'Some Gains and Sweets of Invalidism' (147–60), we glimpse the seductions of an identity whose limits correspond to the physical compass of a bedchamber.

Discussing the depiction of a female literary gathering in Fraser's Magazine, Linda Peterson notes a surprising willingness to 'acknowledge women writers and editors as active participants in the London literary scene' (2). Her analysis depends on recognising the power of connections between status, involvement and social visibility (19). Barrett transgresses these connections simply by being bedridden, and as such obliges us to consider an alternative basis for public status and reputation. The essay devoted to her in Richard Hengist Horne's A New Spirit of the Age (1844) indicates the form this could take. The author conjures a sense of mystery with the information that she is 'Confined entirely to her own apartment, and almost hermetically sealed' (134), indeed 'scarcely seen'. This denial of visual evidence extends to the pointed omission of an author-portrait to accompany the several others included, and even playful speculation as to 'the very existence of the lady in question' (135). Thus Barrett's invalidism emerges less as a secondary characteristic than as a primary authorial quality.[2]

These formations of authorship and identity were neither stable nor necessarily comfortable. Allusions to Barrett's invisibility, and the dubious proof of her existence, tally with her self-description as a 'disembodied spirit' (BL [10 November

1845] 1); but they are complicated by the additional irony that she was a contributor to Horne's volume, a fact that lends these speculations the quality of a discourteous erasure operating under the cover of an in-joke. The essay's emphasis on withdrawal also colludes with perceptions of the unphysical, and therefore unlaboured, nature of composition. Habits of seclusion are one thing, but when the element of production recedes from view, they may hint at resignation, even avoidance.

Similar concerns are broached in modern studies. Pickering regards Barrett's invalidism as a pattern of life left over from a 'previous organic illness' (261), though by attributing this persistence to 'the fears of her doctors' he stops short of the personal scrutiny favoured by more recent commentators. Dennis broaches the same question when discussing Barrett's refusal to make new acquaintances after the move to Wimpole Street, and her discouragement of visitors 'to the point of refusing their advances with lies' (45). Berridge takes such suppositions the furthest, interpreting illness as a 'cover', a means of controlling one's daily fate that converts passive affliction into subtle control, 'a common enough loophole for frustrated and intelligent Victorian women' (18). It is not necessary to endorse this cultural interpretation of illness to detect a similar spirit in Barrett's playful equivocations about a meeting in the spring: 'A little later comes my spring,' she wrote to Browning on 27 February 1845 (BL 1). Her deferrals play the double-game of insisting on the proper season for a meeting while altering the terms of seasonality. She even ventures a backhanded acknowledgement of such stratagems: 'I observe that you distrust me, and that perhaps you penetrate my morbidity' (BL 20 March 1845 1). Equally, Barrett observes a malleability in sickness when chastising Browning for not taking sufficient care of his health: 'for you let people make you ill,' she writes, 'and do it yourself upon occasion' (BL 10 March 1846 5).

This emphasis on control tallies with the possibility that invalidism might partly be self-directed, a consoling demonstration of the mind's ability to regulate the body. In all these aspects, it trades a model of absolutely depleted capacity for one of deflected and diverted energy. Yet the patient cannot allow such marginal agency to be apprehended by friends and family: a need to control impressions reflects the problematic relation between invalidism as a 'cultural mentality' (Frawley 3) and the contemporary work ethic. This does not mean that the two tendencies were in polar opposition. The discourses of retirement and work had in fact a common source. Evangelicalism, as Frawley notes, 'ratified affliction as God-Given' (33), so that anxieties about the performance of work were not excluded from states of affliction. The result was a double bind that made convalescence a peculiarly conflicted predicament (39). Barrett's emphasis on mental labour partially secured the coherence of her position, by taking visible performance out of the equation. The essay about her in A New Spirit of the Age acknowledges this possibility. Insofar as it dwells on Barrett's 'indefatigable "work" by thought, by book, by the pen' (135), it opens the possibility that an invalid might yet be thought a 'worker'.

This recourse to mental 'labour' is complicated by the parallels drawn with physical process. In an early letter to her mother, Barrett recalls a promise to employ 'any mental exertion' that might be required to 'shake off bodily torture' (Kelley and Hudson 128). The effort meets with mixed results: 'I HAVE exerted all my energy,' she explains, 'all my locomotive intellect, all the muscular power of mind, and I HAVE found that in some degree bodily anguish may be repressed from APPEARING, yet it has failed to be overcome.' Two tendencies emerge from this anxious report, the first of which concerns the limited effect of 'mental exertion' on any corresponding physical outcome. The point of resistance in this case is her bodily self, and the lesson derived one of enduring separateness. The mind can 'repress', but not 'overcome', the stubborn anguish of her frame. At the same time, the passage represents an early example of her insistent application of bodily metaphors in the description of mental process: this 'exertion' requires 'locomotive' and 'muscular' power. Evaluative and linguistic deference to the action of the limbs wards off the charge of malingering, but potentially concedes too much ground, leaving her vulnerable to a definition of work that excludes all but the physical. Despite consistent allusion to the possibility of mental labour, she proves susceptible to the culture's privileging of demonstrable action. '[I]f I could "rake & hoe",' she laments, '.. or even pick up weeds along the walk, .. which is the work of the most helpless children' (BL [9 December 1845] 4).[3] She thereby identifies with a subject even less capable than the 'minors' among whom her other intellectual hero, Ralph Waldo Emerson, dismissively grouped the invalid, in his essay on 'Self-Reliance' (1841) (Raymond and Sullivan iii, 18; Emerson 162). When 'much head-work of my own' is reported (BL [8 August 1845] 3), and combined with other kinds of reading and writing, she guiltily confesses that 'bodily exercise is different', that the effort of projection entailed by correspondence has made her 'inclined to be idle' (BL [8 August 1845] 3), by which she means physically so. While the letter to her mother indicates prior sources for this tendency, the unintentional irony in her self-description as a 'devout sitter at his [Carlyle's] feet' (BL 17 February 1845 12) signals the framing of the problem as one of intellectual 'influence' encountering stubbornly physical limits.

Carlyle associated 'work' with a rhetoric of mobilisation, according to which monied 'idleness' corresponded to sedentary habits. The roots of this emphasis can be traced to the same bourgeois Protestant assumptions that informed the category of 'able-bodiedness' enshrined in the New Poor Law of 1834 (Frawley 43). The attention to movement also builds subtly on the peripatetic or excursive element in Romantic literature and philosophy (Helsinger 138–9; Wallace 52–3). Barrett's periodic complaint that she felt poetically disabled by not witnessing the world of nature as a physical beholder owes much to this tradition, as does Martineau's chapter on 'Nature to the Invalid', where a window view ensures the 'mind has had an airing' (69). The connection between these two strands of post-Romantic moral consciousness – love of nature, and the excursive element – is illuminated by the example of Ruskin, who connected the railway's despoliation of landscape to an annihilation of the old travelling effort by which tourists earned their reward of a beautiful view (The Stones of Venice 3–4).

Barrett's dependence on morphine suggests a further point of connection to Romantic tradition, though in this respect she understood motion as the problem, and opium as a solution. Complaints of 'palpitation' (BL 4 February 1846 3) effectively ruled out exercise as a remedy, despite Browning's best efforts to encourage walking outside. Palpitation diverted the energy of life away from 'giving move-ment to the body', leaving it 'imprisoned undiminished within it, & beating and fluttering impotently to get out, at all the doors & windows' (*BL* 4 February 1846 3). By employing morphine to tranquillise this 'restlessness' (*BL* 4 February 1846 3), Barrett effected less a dissipated alternative to healthy movement than a release from a parallel world of agonised trembling. The association with imagination and contemplation figured by Thomas De Quincey was in this way avoided. There are no sublime journeys through hallucinated spectacle to report, and few deliberate connections to poetry. The obvious exception occurs at the close of this concerted explanation of her dependency: as if resorting to the last piece of justification avail-able to her, she enigmatically suggests to Browning, in a hand so slanting that it might be about to fall off the page, that 'the lotus-eaters are blessed beyond the opium-eaters; & the best of lotuses are such thoughts as I know' (*BL* [4 February 1846] 4). It is a parallel, nevertheless, that insists on discontinuity between the Homeric fable and her own 'amreeta draught' or 'elixir' (*BL* [4 February 1846] 4), whose stilling effect acts not against Odyssean adventure, but against the senseless movement of one already awkwardly reclined.

While the seclusion of her sick chamber was readily aligned by observers with capacities of invention, Barrett herself understood this retreat as an evasive action, the recourse of 'one who could have forgotten the plague, listening to Boccaccio's stories' (*BL* [20 March 1845] 7). Her wish to avoid an 'unbecoming' spectacle of 'infirmity' (*BL* [15 May 1845] 2), and an attendant concern to ward off any associa-tion between sickness and poetry, placed her letters in the awkward position of a buffer. They became the guardian of many qualities determinedly excluded from the poetic, and a crucial arena in which she negotiated the conflict between her accept-ance of Carlyle's injunction that all should 'work' and the daily reality of physical confinement. Letters could be written in bed, of course, with movement largely restricted to the wrist. They functioned in this way not only as the symptomatic context for a stationary predicament, but as the means by which it was structured and perpetuated. Apparently relishing the idea of a disembodied reach, Barrett observed to Browning that 'I write in fact almost as you pay visits, . . . & one has to "make conversation" in turn, of course' (*BL* [1 May 1845] 4). The emphasis here is on a social action, notwithstanding the cloistered predicament of the author. She would have letters governed by the same expectations, and the same scope for reply and debate, as polite intercourse. Even as her 'almost' signals that this can't quite be so, she expresses a will for things to be different, affording a momentary glimpse of the epistolary form becoming at once more intimate, reciprocal and remote.

Letters also represent an escape from the pedestrian life on the very literal level that they entail one's words being conveyed by paid emissary. In the hopeful early days of their correspondence, the written word was conceived less as a substitute than as a full-blown alternative, its declaratory power overcoming all effects of labour and distance. As Browning playfully boasted, the disproportion between effort and outcome could be absurd, and in a way alchemical: 'Three scratches with a pen, even with this pen, – and you have the green little Syrenusæ where I have sate and heard the quails sing' (*BL* [15 April 1845] 4). The exoticism of far-off location is magically resolved into the singularity of the writer's fixed yet imaginative station. In the manner of Emerson's provocation that 'the wise man stays at home' ('Self-Reliance' 180), and Arthur Hugh Clough's later one in *Amours de Voyage* (1849), Browning concludes that 'all you gain by travel is the discovery that you have gained nothing, and have done rightly in trusting to your innate ideas' (*BL* [15 April 1845] 4). These reassurances eventually conflict with the 'argument' he must adopt as a suitor who wishes to remove his beloved from the parental home. Travel becomes less an effort 'to prove limitation' (Clough 94) than a bid to overcome it. Browning's flattering consolations give way accordingly to thoughts of an Italian journey that will realise Elizabeth's yearnings for 'another atmosphere' (*BL* 3 February 1845 13).

The physical comfort of letter writing conduces also to emotional comfort. Replying to Browning's first approach, Barrett ventures the thought that his entering the 'crypt' (*BL* [10 January 1845] 4) of her surroundings at any earlier stage might put him off forever. First suggesting infection, and then death by boredom, she eventually settles on the urge for flight as a worst-case scenario: 'you might have . . . *wished* yourself "a thousand miles off",' she imagines, 'which would have been worse than travelling them' (*BL* 11 January 1845 5). Written communication occurs at a 'safe distance' without incurring such risks of disappointed spectacle. Its ebbs and flows were not only predictable with the post, but susceptible to regulation and control. Love 'on the page' could be purified of the physical, and its development carefully regulated, at least until the beloved became a lover in turn, and found herself writing that 'it is certainly not my turn to write, though I am writing' (*BL* [18–19 December 1845] 3). Here, a sense of epistolary decorum, and perhaps ambition for a more reciprocal outlet, run up against the form's unilateralism and univocalism. These qualities are signalled by the present participle in 'I am writing', which makes the present speak beyond itself without losing its identity. Something of this power is allowed by the so-called 'posting rule' introduced to English contract law by *Adams v Lindsell* in 1818 (Treitel 24–30). The rule accords the recipient of an offer power to accept and thereby form a contract at the point of posting, such that a fictional meeting of minds occurs 'in course of post'. Disregarding the practical agency of the postal service for purposes of contract formation invests the sender with an enhanced efficacy. In this way, it shadows by inexact analogy the informal acts of courtship correspondence. The effect of the acceptance is to bind the offeror, in this case Browning, thereby preventing him from making offers to third parties. If instead Browning is regarded as the offeree, then similarly the comfort comes from knowing that a meeting of minds may already have occurred, and that no additional note will cross disastrously.

The necessary gap between utterance and reciprocation is susceptible to similar analysis. With a letter, there is always room for a reply, or indeed a delay of the kind Barrett repeatedly introduced with her quibbles about the progress of the spring. This, too, is a source of comfort, though one that consoles with a measure of self-delusion once the anxiety that a reply has been misdirected or intercepted is overtaken by the thought that it will soon be sent, albeit belatedly. While the rationale in *Adams v Lindsell* aimed at enforcing a resolution through the mechanism of a legal fiction, a pair of lovers will readily take refuge in the practical gaps between expression and delivery. At its most extreme, this nineteenth-century concern with the potency of letters emerges in the United States' 'dead letter office', mentioned in Herman Melville's 'Bartleby the Scrivenor' (107), where offers are kept 'alive' in perpetuity. Though an offer is ordinarily deemed to have been destroyed by the death of the offeror, this repository conjures the idea that some vestige of life has been preserved, because in order to facilitate the passage of a surrogate will, the senders transferred their privilege of living presence to the post. Browning is interested, similarly, in the idea that letters might have a life of their own. He refers to 'the distance so palpably between the most audacious step *there*, and the next .. which is no where, seeing it is not in the letter' (*BL* [6–7 January 1846] 1). His words cast letter writing as a kind of 'going', though one whose status is confined to the motion of a single 'step'. As such, it offers no scope for secondary action or 'irrevocable words' (*BL* [6–7 January 1846] 1) that can trump the finality of the primary missive.

The sense in which letters might travel in miraculous ways attracts a measure of approval in Carlyle's *Past and Present* (1843). Musing on the historical window afforded by a medieval manuscript – in this case, *The Chronicle of Jocelin* (c. 1173–1202) – Carlyle writes that 'The most extinct fossil species of Men or Monks can do, and does, this miracle, – thanks to the Letters of the Alphabet' (44). Difficulties arise when the 'fossil species' in question is a living poet, so that the startling animation of written letters heightens an unfortunate contrast with the 'embalmed' state of their originator. Something of this impression is communicated by Dante Gabriel Rossetti's report of a meeting with the Brownings in 1851, in which he remarked of 'Mrs. B' that 'She looks quite worn out with illness, & speaks in the tone of an invalid' (Fredeman 181). By this 'tone' he implies not only the speech characteristics of a recognisable human 'type', but the more unstable notion that the animation and presence of speech are tinctured in some way with their deathly opposite. Carlyle could gasp in awe at the power of the dead 'voice' to communicate through lettered remnants, but he also meant to formulate a political theory of speech. In particular, he hoped that a new class of public orator, or 'Speaking Man' (*Past and Present* 243), would resume his powers and 'point', and clear away the dissipated governing class. This version of the hero was aligned with 'The Speaking Function' (243), through which he envisaged 'Truth coming to us with a living voice, nay in a living shape, and as a concrete practical exemplar' (243).

Barrett's invisible hand was responsible for the essay on Carlyle that Horne included in *A New Spirit of the Age*. In it, she applied to Carlyle an adapted version of Buffon's adage that 'Le style est l'homme meme' (9): 'of him,' she writes, 'it is pre-eminently true, that the speech is the man!'[4] But she also insists that he 'proceeds, like a poet', employing the term here – as in her letters on the subject to Browning – in a broadened, spiritual sense, in the hope of exonerating Carlyle's tendency to cast disfavour on poetry itself. Notwithstanding this loosened usage, the word 'poet' installs a written premise for such 'speech', thereby helping Barrett towards a constructive processing of Carlyle's unnerving advice that she should 'use "speech" rather than "song"' (1 September 1844, Raymond and Sullivan ii, 441). The audible suggestiveness of 'song' in its conventional denotation as written poetry also helps Barrett put the case that poetry should concede no inferiority to speech, since it possesses cognate powers. A similar effect is apparent in her writing to Mary Russell Mitford that Carlyle '*writes thoughts*' (Raymond and Sullivan i, 386). With these examples in mind, it is tempting to interpret the 'tone' that Rossetti detected in 'Mrs. B's' voice as a subtle denial on her part of the assumed connection between speech and signs of life. By demoting present utterance, Barrett's letters muster a subtle resistance to Carlyle's emphasis on the oratorical.

The reverse side of this downgrading of speech is apparent in Barrett's simultaneous claim for the presence, 'life' and labour of her letters. In *The Printed Voice of Victorian Poetry* (1989), Eric Griffiths took issue with Jacques Derrida's theory of writing, in particular the claim that 'writing' represents a threat to Western culture's nervous 'praise of living speech' (Derrida 141). The title of that work recasts a resonant phrase from Browning's *The Ring and the Book* (1868-9): ''Twas the so-styled Fisc began, / Pleaded (and since he only spoke in print / The printed voice of him lives now as then)' (Book 1, 165-7). In like manner, Barrett refuses to see writing as a surly upstart railing against supplemental status, and insists on the possibility of life on the page. Since her letters share qualities with human speech, there is no need for a defensive position, nor even much sense of 'printed' limitation. Not merely a substitute for audible presence, her letters propose an available and genuinely voiced alternative. The principle recalls Isaac Disraeli's formulation that 'We converse with the absent by Letters, and with ourselves by Diaries' (206). But while Barrett's letters 'converse', they do not betoken an absence of 'ourselves'. Responding to Browning's allusion to a previously missed opportunity of 'really seeing' her (*BL* [10 January 1845] 3), she remarks on the compensation of having 'learnt to know your voice' as a correspondent (*BL* 11 January 1845 6). Words, according to these accounts, approach the Coleridgean status of 'living Things' (*Collected Letters* 625-6), and they even transmit the presence of living subjects. Looking back on their early exchanges, Barrett assures Browning that his 'were <u>vital</u> letters' (*BL* 19 February 1846 1). In this way, they were trustworthy carriers of identity, but more than that: 'I felt your letters to be <u>you</u> from the very first' (*BL* 19 February 1846 1).

By May 1845, Browning was complaining that 'it is high time you <u>saw</u> me, for I have clearly written myself <u>out</u>!' (*BL* [16 May 1845] 4). Instead of projecting presence, he regards the epistolary routine as a substitution that threatens to waste or abolish the body. The following year, Barrett was still defending the social primacy of the form: 'It is a way of meeting, .. this meeting in letters' (*BL* [24 March 1846] 2). Her notion of 'talking upon paper' as a 'social pleasure' comparable to any other hints at a more developed and more challenging conception of the voice in letters. But here she must acknowledge the desiccated oddity of the 'talking' (*BL* 3 February 1845 1), and even its subversive possibilities. Barrett's consciousness of this emerges more playfully in a reference to the work of archaeological detection she was obliged to apply to this social intercourse with a man she had not yet met: '<u>You</u> are to be made out by the comparative anatomy system,' she writes to Browning. 'You have thrown out fragments of <u>os [bone].. sublime</u> .. indicative of soul-mammothism – and you live to develop your nature, .. <u>if</u> you live' (*BL* 17 February 1845 5). 'Soul-mammothism' may be Carlylean phraseology, and even a replication of the way the reader in *Past and Present* is invited to 'peep' into the past, as if 'a deep-buried

Mastodon . . . were to *speak* from amid its rock-swathings' (43). But its humour endows written words with a perverse or denatured vitality that potentially marginalises, or makes unnecessary, the 'speaking voice' Carlyle himself privileges. And where that voice does break through into the discourse of the letters, its vitality is disembodied or supernatural: '[T]hese are the days of mesmerism & clairvoyance,' she teases, in claiming what seems impossible knowledge of Browning's 'skulls & spiders' (*BL* 27 February 1845 7).

Just as Barrett imputes qualities of voice and vitality to the (un)dead letter, so she associates the form with unconventional modes of production. Indeed, the 'work' performed by letters turns out to be conditioned by the same invalidism that precluded submission to the Gospel of Work. Resistance to the idea of bedridden work, and indeed the likelihood of Carlyle's disapproval, gives rise to a perversity that signifies the awkward condition, and eventually the power, of Barrett's approach. Most obviously, letters document activity, in a manner similar to a diary, and the narratives they contain impose form on passing time. They are also material artefacts in their own right, proofs of effort in a manual script. This testimonial function applies not only individually, but to the accumulated weight of correspondence, and the possibility of posthumous publication, as Barrett herself indicates on suggesting that Mitford's correspondence might one day appear in 'folio shape' (*BL* 3 February 1845 3). In the same letter, she speaks of signing and sealing her 'contract' as Browning's 'articled' correspondent (*BL* 3 February 1845 5). She also invokes the finalities of communication by post, as discussed above in relation to *Adams v Lindsell*. But the contract she devises contains terms that stress the essentially unfinished nature of epistolary work, or at least her desire permanently to enshrine the principle of impermanence: the agreement entails 'taking no thought for your sentences (nor for mine), nor for your blots (nor for mine), nor for your blunt speaking (nor for mine), nor for your badd speling (nor for mine)' (*BL* 3 February 1845 4). We are reminded of all the ways in which letters stop short of presentable work. According to this view of the materiality of letters, they represent a form of 'production', but one raw or unrefined. At the same time, we are conscious of the artfulness involved in disclaiming effort and precision, and of the eye to posterity of a published poet writing to a fellow poet.

These stipulations show Barrett's concern to characterise her letters as an effusive mode. They also insist on pleasure, warding off the spectre of duty by banning 'reference to the conventionalities of "ladies & gentlemen"' (*BL* 3 February 1845 4) and upbraiding Browning for his occasional failure to exhibit an unlimited appetite for correspondence (*BL* [27 January 1845] 4). While this insistence on enjoying oneself might detract from the emphasis on activity over idleness, its opposite purpose is clarified by Barrett's enlarged and enlarging understanding of poetic labour. Denying its appeal as a mere substitute, she insists that 'I seem to live while I write – it is life, for me' (*BL* 20 March 1845 5). There is a hint of 'making do' in the tagged 'for me', but she confidently adds that 'one lives in composition surely .. not always .. but when the wheel goes round & the procession is uninterrupted' (*BL* 20 March 1845 5). Hovering between work and distraction, distance and presence, letters share many of the qualities that trouble the status of poetry, and in that respect they stand in as a symbolic equivalent for it, performing a critical task that relies precisely on that dubious status.

Letters also possess the straightforward social utility, or stable addressee, that poetry lacks. Here defending her experience of having 'lived all my chief joys' 'in poetry & in poetry alone' (*BL* 20 March 1845 4), Barrett approaches a conception of the sufficiency and even the advantages of a vicarious form. Her subject is poetry, but the medium in which she expresses her thoughts is a letter. While the genius of poetry enlivens correspondence as a form that must do without speech, the social purpose of the letters rubs off on the poetry. And when the letters report on the work of poetry, they become in themselves a form of production, as literary criticism. In this role, they declare and fulfil ends that go far beyond the immediate object of communication. An ancillary consequence of this reading is that it challenges the unhealthy primacy that Angela Leighton sees critics giving to the courtship correspondence as the arena in which Barrett appears 'as the heroine of a love story' (4), rather than as a poet. The connections between literary writing and this mode of loving by letter upset that dichotomy.

Though I have stressed the status of these letters as testaments, this was by no means a straightforward function. More often than not, they bore witness to illness, rather than to conventional production. Even love's labours were caught in this web. Browning's complaints of a headache, and Barrett's evident pleasure in returning sympathy and concern (*BL* [24 November 1845] 3), indicate the extent to which such reports became a currency to be traded. One might say that they were perversely generative in this respect, subjecting supposedly fixed ailments to a form of rhetorical inflation determined by the communicative aims of courtship. Indeed, the idea of an elusive able-bodiedness begins to seem a function of the invalidism to which it stands opposed. Carlyle's various ailments, ranging from chronic dyspepsia to the meta-affliction of hypochondria, can be understood in this light. His poor health offers an explanation for his increasing valuation of the man of action, even as he became less capable of action himself, and in later life was embroiled in the multi-volume quagmire of *Frederick the Great* (1858–65). Similarly, Barrett's high estimation of certain active pleasures – whether 'experience', 'nature' or simply walking in the open air – were a symptom of the invalidism, of the 'signal disadvantages' (*BL* 20 March 1845 4), that ruled them out. Her idealisation of untrammelled physical prowess only makes sense, this is to suggest, in the context of a dialectic between incapacity and action. In these conditions, able-bodiedness operated less as a fact than as a personal and social virtue.

What Barrett called her 'Carlyleship' (Raymond and Sullivan i, 422) seems less at odds with her personal circumstances when viewed in the light of the connections between invalidism and physical work. No doubt her long-standing concern with the faculty of 'mind' (*An Essay on Mind*) and her insistent defence of 'invisible' labour were strategies better suited to her circumstances, and to her life as a poet. But the apologetic passage quoted from Carlyle's letter to his father has offered a basis for thinking about the interrelation of letters and literature as 'idle' forms, and notably the awkward resemblance between epistolary distraction and literary vocation. While the young Carlyle sought to head off such difficulties by consigning correspondence to a different category of writing, Barrett's letters were the means by which she articulated and partially resolved her predicament as an invalid 'worker'. This meant reconceiving what possibilities of 'life' and 'voice' were available in written correspondence, and indeed what unconventional forms of productivity it might evoke.

Letters were records of daily effort, collectable eventually in a volume or corpus; but they also served as external markers of literary production, reporting the progress of particular poems or essays. Similarly, the work of literary criticism performed by these epistles was combined with a labour of love, with flirtation in short, which should never be 'laboured' in the sense of earnest or dogged. This facility points to the power of the letters to do their own work, and to stand in for other works, even as they disclaim the status of work for themselves. For these reasons, letters can operate as a comforting, and sometimes experimental, proxy for the more personally fraught medium of poetic and literary production. They evoke the condition of a writing whose work dare not speak its name, and in their con-fidence of witness and audience remedy the absence of testament that plagues all 'invisible' labours in a culture that struggles to place its confidence in works of the mind.

NOTES

1. This chapter refers mainly to the period before Elizabeth Barrett became Elizabeth Barrett Browning by marriage, and so the former usage is preferred.
2. Frawley relates the association between authorship and invalidism to such Victorian publishing ventures as *The Invalid's Own Book, The Solace of an Invalid, An Invalid's Day, Literary Gleanings by an Invalid* and *The Idle Hours of an Invalid* (11–12).
3. I have preserved Barrett's and Browning's usage in their letters of a double point ellipsis (..). Here, as elsewhere in the book, a triple point ellipsis (. . .) signifies my own omission.
4. This essay was later republished as 'Contributions Toward an Essay on Carlyle' (*The Complete Works of Elizabeth Barrett Browning*, vol. 6, pp. 312–21).

WORKS CITED

Adams v Lindsell [1818], 1 B & Ald (Barnewell & Aldersons Reports), 681.

Ashton, Rosemary, *Thomas and Jane Carlyle: Portrait of a Marriage* (London: Chatto & Windus, 2002).

Barrett, Elizabeth, 'Contributions Toward an Essay on Carlyle', *The Complete Works of Elizabeth Barrett Browning*, vol. 6, ed. Charlotte Porter and Helen A. Clarke (New York: Thomas Y. Crowell & Co., 1900), pp. 312–21.

—— *An Essay on Mind, with Other Poems* (Edinburgh: James Duncan, 1826).

Berridge, Elizabeth, *The Barretts at Hope End: The Early Diary of Elizabeth Barrett Browning* (London: John Murray, 1974).

Briggs, Asa, 'Samuel Smiles and the Gospel of Labour', *Victorian People: A Reassessment of Persons and Themes 1851–67* (Harmondsworth: Penguin Books, 1971), pp. 124–47.

The Browning Letters [BL], Wellesley Special Collections and Armstrong Browning Library,

Baylor University Digital Collections, <http://digitalcollections.baylor.edu/cdm/landingpage/ collection/ab-letters> (last accessed 7 July 2014).

Browning, Robert, *The Ring and the Book: The Poetical Works of Robert Browning*, vol. 7, ed. Stefan Hawlin and T. A. J. Burnett (Oxford: Clarendon Press, 1998).

Buffon, Georges Louis Leclerc, 'Discour sur le style', *Oeuvres complètes de Buffon: Matière générales*, vol. 1 (Douai: 1822), pp. 1–10.

The Carlyle Letters Online, ed. Brent. E. Kinser, Duke University Press, <http://carlyleletters. dukejournals.org> (last accessed 7 July 2014).

Carlyle, Thomas, *Chartism: The Centenary Edition of the Works of Thomas Carlyle*, vol. 4, ed. H. D. Traill (London: Chapman & Hall, 1899).

—— 'James Carlyle', in Ian Campbell and K. J. Fielding (eds), *Reminiscences* (Glasgow: Kennedy & Boyd, 2009), pp. 1–33.

—— *Latter-day Pamphlets: The Centenary Edition of the Works of Thomas Carlyle*, vol. 26, ed. H. D. Traill (London: Chapman & Hall, 1898).

—— *Past and Present: The Centenary Edition of the Works of Thomas Carlyle*, vol. 10, ed. H. D. Traill (London: Chapman & Hall, 1897).

Clough, Arthur Hugh, *Amours de Voyage*, *The Poems of Arthur Hugh Clough*, ed. F. L. Mulhauser, 2nd edn (Oxford: Clarendon Press, 1974), pp. 94–133.

Coleridge, Samuel Taylor, *Collected Letters of Samuel Taylor Coleridge*, vol. 1, ed. Earl Leslie Griggs (Oxford: Clarendon Press, 1956).

Dennis, Barbara, *Elizabeth Barrett Browning: The Hope End Years* (Bridgend: Seren Books/Poetry Wales Press, 1996).

De Quincey, Thomas, *The Confessions of an English Opium-Eater* (Oxford: Oxford University Press, 1998).

Derrida, Jacques, *Of Grammatology*, trans. Gayatri Chakravorty Spivak (Baltimore: Johns Hopkins University Press, 1976).

Disraeli, Isaac, *Curiosities of Literature*, vol. 2 (London: Routledge, Warne & Routledge, 1863).

Emerson, Ralph Waldo, 'Self-Reliance', in David Mikics (ed.), *The Annotated Emerson* (Cambridge, MA: Belknap Press of Harvard University Press, 2012), pp. 160–85.

Frawley, Maria H., *Invalidism and Identity in Nineteenth-Century Britain* (Chicago: Chicago University Press, 2004).

Fredeman, William E. (ed.), *The Correspondence of Dante Gabriel Rossetti*, vol. 1 (Cambridge: D. S. Brewer, 2002).

Griffiths, Eric, *The Printed Voice of Victorian Poetry* (Oxford: Clarendon Press, 1989).

Helsinger, Elizabeth K., *Ruskin and the Art of the Beholder* (Cambridge, MA: Harvard University Press, 1982).

Horne, R. H. (ed.), *A New Spirit of the Age* (London: H. Frowde, 1844).

Houghton, Walter, *The Victorian Frame of Mind, 1830–1870* (New Haven: Yale University Press, 1957).

Karlin, Daniel (ed.), *Robert Browning and Elizabeth Barrett: The Courtship Correspondence 1845– 1846* (Oxford: Clarendon Press, 1989).

Kelley, Philip, and Ronald Hudson (eds), *The Brownings' Correspondence*, vol. 1 (Winfield, KS: Wedgestone Press, 1984).

Leighton, Angela, *Elizabeth Barrett Browning* (Bloomington: Indiana University Press, 1986).

Litzinger, Boyd, and Donald Smalley, *Robert Browning: The Critical Heritage* (London: Routledge, 1995).

Martineau, Harriet, *Life in the Sick-Room: Essays by an Invalid* (Peterborough, ON: Broadview Press, 2003).

Melville, Herman, 'Bartleby', *The Piazza Tales* (New York: Sampson Low, Son & Co., 1856), pp. 32–108.

Peterson, Linda H., *Becoming a Woman of Letters: Myths of Authorship and Facts of the Victorian Market* (Princeton: Princeton University Press, 2009).

Pickering, George, *Creative Malady: Illness in the Lives and Minds of Charles Darwin, Florence Nightingale, Mary Baker Eddy, Sigmund Freud, Marcel Proust, Elizabeth Barrett Browning* (London: George Allen & Unwin, 1974).

Raymond, Meredith B., and Mary Rose Sullivan (eds), *The Letters of Elizabeth Barrett Browning to Mary Russell Mitford 1836–1854*, 3 vols (Winfield, KS: Wedgestone Press, 1983).

Ruskin, John, *The Stones of Venice: The Library Edition of the Works of John Ruskin*, vol. 10, ed. E. T. Cook and Alexander Wedderburn (London: George Allen, 1904).

Treitel, G. H., *The Law of Contract*, 11th edn (London: Sweet & Maxwell, 2003).

Wallace, Anne D., *Walking, Literature, and English Culture* (Oxford: Clarendon Press, 1993).

9 Passion and Playfulness in the Letters of Gerard Manley Hopkins

Michael D. Hurley

Hopkins felt things very deeply, that much is clear from his poems. A bird's flight moves him to 'ecstacy!'.[1] A starlit night inspires such joy that he cannot explain, only repeatedly exclaim, his over-spilling pleasure: 'Look at the stars! look, look up at the skies!' (128–9). Even common garden weeds – their everyday 'wildness and wet' – stir him to rhapsody (130; 153). He also writes of 'Frightful, sheer, no-man-fathomed' despair (167). But whether he is recording epiphanic delight or its terrible obverse, his verses share the same white-hot intensity. And it is not so much the themes of his poems as their vital expression which determines this intensity: they dramatise a struggle, they perform the experiences they describe. Rhythmically, his verse is calculatedly 'abrupt' and 'stress',[2] and it is for this reason he thought his innovative metre, 'sprung rhythm', could be employed to 'good effect' in 'passionate passages' (CII 705). A similar strategy of jolt and tension operates linguistically, where unexpected if not incommensurate elements are yoked together, either in the juxtaposition of word and phrase, or by collapsing anomalous elements into compound coinages. Syntax collaborates in this heightening too, as sense units strain against line endings, and easy fluency is otherwise suspended in favour of a kind of stuttering sincerity.

Hopkins's letters confess the same passionate and polarised sensibility his poems seek to instantiate, but in a way that complicates as well as elaborates our understanding of that sensibility. His missives of joy extend from youthful superlatives about being 'almost too happy' (CI 36) – splashing about on the Cherwell, for instance, he calls 'the summit of human happiness' (CI 30) – to more mature but no less tempered expressions of euphoria, such as attends his conversion to Roman Catholicism ('the happiness it has been the means of bringing me I cd. not have conceived' (CI 98)). Contrastingly, the letters also record his 'nervous weakness' (CII 676), 'a distress of mind difficult both to understand and to explain', which threatened 'mind or body or both' (CII 950); a 'disease' of 'melancholy' that, in later life, became 'more distributed, constant, and crippling'; a state of paralysis 'much like madness' (CII 731). The letters thus complement what we know of Hopkins through his poems. They provide circumstantial and psychological contexts for the fervour that animates his verse, as they tell us about his compositional habits, the rationale for his prosodical experiments, his literary and aesthetic tastes. But the letters also reveal a side to Hopkins's personality that is absent from his verse, a side to him that is indeed at odds with the ardency of his entire poetic enterprise: they reveal a richly silly sense of humour.

Although Hopkins did very occasionally dabble in light verse – notably, his wittily over-engineered 'Trio of Triolets' and his newly found comic verse 'Consule Jones' – the vast majority of his poetic composition, and all of it he thought worth anything, was straight-faced stuff. No sniggering, warns Robert Bridges in his editor's preface to the notes for the first edition of Hopkins's poems in 1918; 'this poet is always serious' (Bridges 97). Exasperation, even distaste, may be appropriate reactions; but not laughter. The eccentricities of his poems are not whimsical. If the reader cannot in the end condone his stylistic extravagances – 'the peculiar scheme of prosody invented and developed by the author', 'errors of what may be called taste', 'Oddity and Obscurity' (Bridges 95, 96, 97) – the reader must at least hold off smirking at them. Bridges's schoolmasterly steer is consistent with Hopkins's own explicit and uncompromising investment in artistic seriousness: 'Want of earnest I take to be the deepest fault a work of art can have' (CII 724); 'without earnestness there is nothing sound and beautiful in character' (CII 530). He is indeed never so hard on his contemporaries as when they seemingly exhibit this fault of 'trying style on' (CII 782).

It is correspondingly surprising, then, to find that Hopkins's letters do court absurdity for its own sake, and that they revel in the humorous possibilities of 'trying style on'. Having recently moved to Ireland, he writes to his sister in cod Irish: 'Im intoriely ashamed o meself. Sure its a wonder I could lave your iligant corspondance so long onanswered' (CII 701). On going up to Oxford, he assumes the persona of Arthur Flash de Weyunhoe and addresses his father with mock formality: 'I write with mingled feelings of gratification and expectation to inform you of my successes, pleasures, and monetary circumstances at college' (CI 51). To his friend Alexander Baillie, for no reason at all, he opens his communication in pseudo philosophy:

Dear Baillie,
                    Yes. You are a Fool.

I can shew it syllogistically, by an Epimenidiculum or paradoxling. For you will allow that he who lies is a fool in the long run, and that he who lies without any object to gain thereby is immediately and directly a fool. Now you are not a fool. But you say you are a fool. Therefore you lie. Syllogistically then.

MAJOR PREMISS
He who lies without an object to gain is a fool.

MINOR PREMISS
You have lied without an object to gain.

CONCLUSION.
Therefore you are a fool.

Epimeniddicularly proved . . . (CI 41)

Along with tomfoolish ventriloquy, Hopkins also had a taste for practical joking. The following episode he shares with his mother is a nice example of how he makes an incident that amused him all the more amusing for his reader, through his parenthetical commentary:

> Sir Gore Ouseley came up the other day to give the last of a course of lectures on organ-music (illustrated) at the Sheldonian Theatre. The organ is new; the organist said to be a genius: he cries (like Du Maurier's man) over his own playing. The audience, which was large and brilliant, included Miss Lloyd in a black bonnet and yellow ribbons. Sir Gore (ghastly as this is, what else can you say? – his name in a book of Mallock's would become Sir Bloodclot Reekswell) wanted us to agree with him that such and such an example was in a better style than such and such another, livelier, one, but we were naughty and would not; the more griggish the piece the more we clapped it. (CI 330–1)

Hopkins is well paired here with the music he calls 'griggish'. That adjective – meaning extravagantly lively, full of frolic and jest – is of his invention (the OED offers only two citations, both from Hopkins: the one given here and another describing how the holidays have put him in a 'griggish mood' (CII 558)).

As a gloss on his particular and pervasive brand of exuberant mischief, 'griggish' is certainly more expressive than 'naughty'. But his humour is not always so innocently freewheeling. It can also turn wittily waspish:

> I was asked to my friends at Howth to meet Aubrey de Vere. However he was called away to London and when I came he was gone. I was disappointed, till it was mentioned that he did not think Dryden a poet. Then, I thought and perhaps said, I have not missed much. And yet you share this opinion or something like it with him. Such are the loutish falls and hideous vagaries of the human mind. (CII 947)

In this baiting note to Bridges, Hopkins overreaches for comic effect ('and perhaps said' is very good, as is 'loutish falls'). But he is not merely being funny. As other letters confirm, he felt strongly about Dryden's importance as an exemplar of manliness in poetic style (as against the 'unmanly and enervating luxury' exemplified by Keats (CII 930)). While Hopkins has, therefore, a happy capacity for clowning to no other end than to amuse himself and his correspondents, his humour may also, as here, have a definite target. In presenting Hopkins as a poet who is 'always serious', Bridges offers the concomitant, 'this poet has always something to say' (Bridges 97). But the later condition does not necessarily require the former. It is important not to confuse terms. For Hopkins, being serious is not the opposite of silliness, it is the opposite of insincerity: 'seriousness' is 'not gravity but the being in earnest with your subject – reality' (CII 782).

The genre of nonsense poetry, which flourished in Hopkins's lifetime, teases instructively at this distinction. In the masterly hands of Edward Lear in particular (whose limericks Hopkins enthusiastically recommended to his mother (CI 224)), the sense is not so much abandoned as it is embarrassed; silliness shades into satire. Hopkins's verse happens to share many of the stylistic features of nonsense writing,[3] and earnest wit, albeit of a rather different kind, finds pungent expression in his verses too. For all his punning and wrenched rhyming, his rhythmical lurching and portmanteau coining, his subject – his 'reality' – is always explicit. His verbal and prosodic play is conducted with keen instrumental purpose. By the same token, Hopkins has much to say in his letters, even – or especially – when he is at his most waggish. Here is another example:

> Swinburne has a new volume out, which is reviewed in its usual own style: 'The rush and the rampage, the pause and the pullup of these lustrous and lumpophorous lines'. It is all now a 'self-drawing web'; a perpetual functioning of genius without truth, feeling, or any adequate matter to be at function on. There is some heavydom, in long waterlogged lines (he has no real understanding of rhythm, and though he sometimes hits brilliantly at other times he misses badly) about the *Armada*, that pitfall of the patriotic muse; and *rot* about babies, a blethery bathos into which Hugo and he from opposite coasts have long driven Channel-tunnels. I am afraid I am going too far with the poor fellow. Enough now, but his babies make a Herodian of me. (CII 990)

The parodic review, the metaphor of 'waterlogged' lines priming the subject of the *Armada*; the alliterative pratfall clatter of 'pitfall of the patriotic muse' and 'blethery bathos' about babies; and the idea of Hopkins the Herodian: it is all funny, and yet none of it is frivolous. His lampoon of Swinburne as the stylist without substance is not undermined by his self-caricature as the fulminating fool. We are invited to smile at Swinburne, and at Hopkins too, but we are in no doubt that a substantial point is being made. The mordancy of such passages hints at a darker and more conflicted side to Hopkins's impassioned personality. 'It is possible even to be very sad and very happy at once and the same time,' he explained to his father in a postscript to a difficult letter written in the immediate wake of his decision to convert to Catholicism (CI 117). He demonstrates that capacity for double-vision in a range of contexts. Where his poems typically distil pure emotional states, his correspondence is frequently marked by tonal texture, if not tension. Humour has an important role to play in establishing that mixed tone. Perhaps the most arresting effects of Hopkins's humour are not, however, where it allows him to accommodate mixed tones. It is where he uses humour to unbalance and destabilise the tone. Biographers have speculated on whether Hopkins was suffering from what is now called bi-polar disorder, and even more than the poems, the letters provide credible evidence for that diagnosis ('You are certainly wrong about Hyde being overdrawn,' he advises

Bridges, 'my Hyde is worse' (CII 826)). But the letters also confound the neat thematic divisions between ecstasy and agony that the poems invite. For his most passionate outpourings are, in his letters, rarely given the polarised treatment they receive in the poems.

It is the most unexpected and extraordinary thing. Even when he is at his lowest, when he cannot possibly pretend to be happy, he nonetheless manages to be funny. Where poetic composition is hospitable to sheer emotional release, letters demand a more reflexive propriety. 'Do not again address me with that alphabet of initials, please,' he requests in a postscript to Bridges (CI 164); and ten years later, in another postscript, presumably after Bridges had lapsed since last time: 'Usen't you to call me by my Christian name? I believe you did. Well if you did I like it better' (CI 260). This may seem like a small thing, but it suggests Hopkins's commitment to the letter as an intimately personal form of communication (he is also very sensitive to handwriting, his own and other people's), such that he checks the flow of his feelings with an awareness that he is not, or at least not primarily, writing for himself; he is writing *to* someone. His ironic asides, witticisms and consciously bathetic moments are intended to amuse his readers, but also to reassure them that he has not lapsed into solipsism, and forgotten them.

The emotional intensity that finds such creative profit in his poems is not so much inhibited in his letters as it is sporadically punctured; the mood is spiked. Sometimes the effect is worked by juxtaposition, as in this deadpan afterthought:

> My gas does flicker but I have ceased to care for it or to notice it. My neighbour has got a new burner, lucky for him: it does not perceptibly lessen my light. On the other hand he has lost eight teeth. (CI 248)

Other times, a light-hearted sentiment is woven into a heavy-hearted confession:

> I like my pupils and do not wholly dislike the work, but I fall into or continue in a heavy weary state of body and mind in which my go is gone (the elegance of that phrase! as Thackeray says, it makes one think what vast sums must have been spent on my education!), I make no way with what I read, and seem but half a man. (CII 563)

Here is a similar example of light woven into dark, where the fact that it is addressed to Bridges, himself a physician, sharpens both the comedy and the confession:

> I must write something, though not so much as I have to say. The long delay was due to work, worry, and languishment of body and mind – which must be and will be; and indeed to diagnose my own case (for every man by forty is his own physician or a fool, they say; and yet again he who is his own physician has a fool for his patient – a form of epigram, by the bye, which, if you examine it, has a bad flaw), well then to judge of my case, I think that my fits of sadness, though they do not affect my judgement, resemble madness. Change is the only relief, and that I seldom get. (CII 734)

On other occasions, it is the dark that is woven into the light:

> This morning I gave in what I believe is the last batch of examination-work for
> this autumn (and if all were seen, fallen leaves of my poor life between all the
> leaves of it), and but for that want I might prance on ivory this very afternoon.
> (CII 968)

Such examples of Hopkins's wit, the silly and the sardonic, expose the inadequacy
of his popular reputation for austerity.

Given Bridges's early and influential promotion of him as being 'always serious', it
is especially ironic, and moving, to find in the very last letter written by Hopkins to
Bridges – after a correspondence lasting some twenty-six years – that Hopkins is the
one defending himself for always joking:

> Dearest Bridges, – I am ill to-day, but no matter for that as my spirits are good.
> And I want you too to 'buck up', as we used to say at school, about those jokes
> over which you write in so dungeonous a spirit. I have it now down in my
> tablets that a man may joke and joke and be offensive; I have had several warn-
> ings lately leading me to make the entry, tho' goodness knows the joke that
> gave most offence was harmless enough and even kind. You I treated to the
> same sort of irony as I do myself; but it is true it makes all the world of difference
> whose hand administers. (CII 989–90)

It is tempting to conclude that Bridges exclusively promoted Hopkins's seriousness –
as the editor of his verse following the poet's death, but also in destroying the letters
where Hopkins's purportedly offensive jokes appear – because Bridges lacked any
sense of humour himself. But Bridges must be given credit for preserving and publishing Hopkins's verses, which might well have been lost otherwise. Bridges wanted
the best for them; he wished Hopkins to be taken as a writer of substance, and so
presented him as such. 1918 was in some ways a more propitious time to publish
Hopkins's innovative poetry than the late Victorian period in which he lived. But
an early twentieth-century readership carried its own powerful prejudices too, as
Bridges would have been well aware. Even a critic such as Donald Davie, who cham-
pioned Hopkins as 'the greatest Victorian poet', entertains his superlative judgement within a strictly comparative context: 'it is only fair to remind the reader that
the Victorian age produced little great poetry in any case' (160). Likewise, though
William Empson accords Hopkins's poems a privileged position in his influential
Seven Types of Ambiguity, he cannot resist the reactionary habit of his period that
sought to dismiss nineteenth-century poets en masse, as purveyors of 'pure sound',
empty 'atmospheres' and 'imposed excitement' (20–1).

If Bridges went too far, then, in advocating Hopkins's passion – such that he
obscured Hopkins's playfulness – he may be forgiven for helping to get Hopkins's
voice heard at all. It should be remembered as well that Bridges helped shape
Hopkins's voice not only after his death, but also while he was alive. Bridges is the
recipient of by far the greatest number of Hopkins's letters still extant, and it is clear

from this correspondence how much Hopkins valued the opportunity to share and test his literary interests. In some ways, curiously, the balance of authority between the men seems to rest with the unpublished, part-time poet-priest over the future poet laureate: from Hopkins's designation of Bridges as a man destined to take a second-class degree at Oxford (CI 164), to his impatience with Bridges's constant and anxious desire for approbation ('You seem to want to be told over again that you have genius and are a poet and your verses beautiful' (CI 374)), to his contra-distinctive confidence in his own verse style. But in spite of Hopkins's fierce intellectual self-reliance, Bridges's opinion as a reader and critic mattered enormously to him. 'There is a point with me in matters of any size when I must absolutely have encouragement as much as crops rain; afterwards I am independent,' he explained to Bridges (CII 736), who is addressed as the primary source of that much-needed encouragement.

Encouragement came in the form of sceptical critique as well as cheering support, and Hopkins does not by any means agree with all of his friend's views. On one occasion they fell out of contact for eighteen months, after a dispute over religion, and possibly politics. When it comes to strictly literary matters, too, he expresses more frustration at Bridges's misreading and dispraise than at anyone else's. 'And don't *you* say *my* lines don't scan,' he writes in a postscript to one rangy dispatch (CI 268). The emphasis – *you* – indicates 'you who should know better', but also perhaps 'you of all people', given the extended criticisms Hopkins makes of Bridges's own verse in this letter. Many of Hopkins's exchanges with Bridges are poised equivocally in this way, somewhere between condescension and compliment, deference and disappointment. 'You so misunderstand my words . . . that I am surprised, and not only surprised but put out. For amongst other things I am made to appear a downright fool' (CI 327); 'What you now say shews me that you must have fallen into some unaccountable misunderstanding' (CI 354); and so on. Such observations simultaneously affirm Hopkins's faith in Bridges's critical acumen and also his belief that any faults of incomprehension lie with Bridges the reader rather than Hopkins the writer: he is 'surprised'; it is 'unaccountable'. However exasperated Hopkins may become at his friend's apparent misreadings, though, he is never impervious to them. While he was an undergraduate he honoured his friend Alexander Baillie as his 'sole congenial thinker in art', and hoped that he might approve of his endeavours – for 'if you do not, who will . . .?' (CI 43). After Oxford, Bridges succeeds Baillie in this role:

> I laughed outright and often, but very sardonically, to think you and the Canon [Dixon] could not construe my last sonnet; that he had to write to you for a crib. It is plain I must go farther on this road: if you and he cannot understand me who will? (CII 918)

Although Hopkins admired Dixon's poetry (and he wrote a number of important letters of literary criticism to him, as he did to Baillie and others too), when it comes to Hopkins's desire to be rightly read as a poet, Bridges is the pre-eminent figure. 'I cannot think of altering anything,' he declares at Bridges's derogation of *The Wreck of the Deutschland*. But then he immediately qualifies his cussedness with a rationale both revealing and affecting: 'Why Shd. I? I do not write for the public. You are my public and I hope to convert you' (CI 282). Not influence, or persuade: *convert*. The word could hardly be more loaded for Hopkins, and it is worth pausing over; but the context for his writing the poem in the first place, and his sending it to Bridges, is also pressingly relevant.

On first taking up his vocation as a priest, Hopkins had given up his previous vocation as a poet, burning all his youthful poems, his 'Slaughter of the Innocents' (House and Storey 165). This purgation by fire was largely symbolic – he had in fact saved corrected copies of his most valued compositions, which he sent on to Bridges – but the gesture sealed a self-imposed poetic silence that would last for almost seven years. Whatever the objective merits of the *Deutschland*, then, for Hopkins it carried enormous personal significance for being his first substantial poem since his renunciation of versifying, and his first in sprung rhythm ('I had long had haunting my ear the echo of a new rhythm which now I realized on paper' (CI 317)). The poem was, in the end, rejected by the Jesuit journal *The Month*, as it was largely derided by the few Jesuits with whom he shared it: Cyprian Splaine judged it 'unreadable', and Clement Barraud 'could hardly understand one word of it'.[4] By the time Hopkins came to send Bridges the *Deutschland*, therefore, he was surely eager for praise, even if he was braced for disappointment. 'You will see that my rhythms go farther than yours do in the way of irregularity' (CI 267), he warns in a letter sent more than four months before he eventually posted the *Deutschland*.

Bridges hated the poem. Worse, he offered no 'serviceable criticisms', simply protesting against his 'whole policy and proceedings' (CI 282). Hopkins responds at first with magnanimity, turning a joke at his expense into a commendation of his joker: 'Your parody reassures me about your understanding the metre.' But then he changes tack: 'Only remark, as you say there is no conceivable licence I shd. not be able to justify, that with all my licences, or rather laws, I am stricter than you and I might say than anybody I know' (CI 280). It is an outlandish claim, but one at least in part substantiated by several further paragraphs of verse theorising. Hopkins's discussions in poetics are extremely wide-ranging. They are also deliciously wry. The grammatical switching of 'my licences, or rather laws' is characteristic: it is not Hopkins correcting himself mid-sentence; he is swiping at Bridges, who mistakes for 'licences' prosodic 'laws' he has failed to perceive. (Other letters confirm this: 'Bridges treats it [i.e. sprung rhythm] in theory and practice as something informal and variable without any limit but ear and taste, but this is not how I look at it' (CI 413); Bridges's own attempts in the metre are described by Hopkins as 'mitigated sprung rhythm' (CI 344).)

Hopkins rounds off his discussion in the same vein of insouciant sarcasm: 'You ask may you call it "presumptious jugglery". No, but only for this reason, that *presumptious* is not English' (CI 282). The letter does not quite leave off literary criticism here, on this whiff of self-amused pettifogging. In a final few paragraphs, Hopkins switches one last time. It is here that the 'I cannot think of altering anything', 'I hope to convert you' provocation appears, which is immediately followed by one of the most tender supplications to be found in any of his letters: 'You say you would not for any money read my poem again. Nevertheless I beg you will. Besides money, you know, there is love' (CI 282).

It is hard to imagine a more poignant appeal, one that asks for critical dispassion, without favour; one that refuses to change, but hopes to 'convert': a plea for rereading that invokes love as its warrant. Yet Bridges was intractable. 'I must tell you I am sorry you never read the Deutschland again,' Hopkins admits a couple of letters later, in which he also encloses a new poem, 'The Loss of the Eurydice', and asks for 'no bilgewater about it' (CI 295). Clearly not a man to be put off easily, Hopkins can tolerate disagreement, and in a specific sense thrives on the dialectical spur. Dialogue is indeed his letters' life-blood. He asks more from his closest correspondents than that they merely rehearse their own news and views: he invites, and often demands, a meaningful exchange.

A colon thus continues the 'bilgewater' comment, softening the provocation into a promise: 'I will tell you what that is and till then excuse the term.' He subsequently expounds at length on how the 'Eurydice' might best be read, and the *Deutschland* better reread; and he would, in other letters, provide many more lessons on verse theory in general and how it applied to the reading of his verses in particular. It was not until almost thirty years after Hopkins's death, with the publication of Bridges's 1918 edition of his poems, that his verse received a wide audience and popular acclaim. It has taken rather longer for him to be recognised as 'a literary theorist of first importance' (Wimsatt 150). This sentiment is, even today, unlikely to be accepted by all critics; and it should be noted that the particular quotation given here comes from James I. Wimsatt's seminal study *Hopkins's Poetics of Speech Sound*, which emphasises Hopkins's essays over his letters. But the letters have their own claim too, over and above his more formal writings.

For a start, when it comes to defining and characterising his innovative metrical practice, the letters clarify and correct the simplified account he offers in his best-known exposition of sprung rhythm, the *Author's Preface*. That text continues to be cited as Hopkins's definitive account, when the letters give a far fuller and more precise explanation.[5] Moreover, the genre of letter writing, the typically informal style of his correspondence, allows his literary-critical insights to emerge incidentally, irrelevantly, even irreverently. This is worth noticing because the seemingly incidental-irrelevant-irreverent observations that run through Hopkins's letters would not necessarily otherwise find a place in an essay or treatise. Or if they did, they would be muted and distorted by post hoc attempts to make them academically respectable. The informality of his criticism is exemplified by his eruptions of humour, but it extends to his desultory method of letter writing in general, notably the counter-intuitive importance of the remarks he tucks into parentheses and postscripts. Several examples of this have already been cited, and it is a habit that extends across his letters, from his earliest to his last, across diverse topics and correspondents. Incidentally, or as an afterthought, the letters are layered with meta-commentary that perpetually extends, qualifies or undercuts the main narrative.

Hopkins judged it a grievous fault in the prose of many 'modern writers', from Coventry Patmore to John Henry Newman, that they wrote prose as if 'to think aloud, to think with pen to paper' (CII 898). But that is precisely the restless strain in which Hopkins's letters are conducted. This contrasts with his essays and sermons, which are the product of much revision and rewriting: stripped-down, lean and tight. His letters, instead, tumble; they recall speech, and perhaps even the writer's voice. A paragraph in a letter to Baillie ends 'I don't know why I have said all this'; and that letter contains a number of further self-questionings, all parenthetical, that encourage an atmosphere of acknowledged spontaneity, provisionality and impressionism: '(I am assuming a great deal in saying this I fear)', '(I have been betrayed in to the whole hog of a metaphor)', 'I have been reading the twelve first (which is it? The first twelve then) books of the Odyssey', '(perhaps your cautions in criticism are here useful)' (CI 67–8). The letter looks to end with a single-sentence paragraph that explains why he cannot offer all the news he had planned to share: 'The vasty length this has oozed to forbids my telling you about the swells at Gurney's.' But the letter does not in fact end there; and even when it does eventually end, Hopkins appends a postscript of over a hundred words of ad hoc 'antiquarianism' (CI 72–3).

'Reading over what I have written above I find it very hurried and confused' (CI 346), he interjects in a letter to Dixon on sprung rhythm begun on 27 February 1879 but taken up again on 10 March; and he then attempts a clearer exposition of his metre that runs for longer than the original letter. Another postscript after a long letter to Bridges demands that his friend pray more, become a Catholic, or at least give more alms. Four days later he takes up his pen once again, and adds: 'I feel it is very bold, as it is uncalled for, of me to have written the above. Still, if we care for fine verses how much more for a noble life!' (CI 325) And then a further postscript of news and reflections; until, in the very last sentence, another day after that, he explains his delay in replying: 'I have been holding back this letter as if it wd. mellow with keeping, but it is no good' (CI 326).

While Hopkins's letters differ from his poems in their tone, therefore, notably in their habits of humour, the letters are also intriguingly different in their style of address. Highly stressed and highly wrought, his poems implicitly valorise the quality of communication he calls 'bidding' ('I mean the art or virtue of saying everything right to or at the hearer . . . discarding everything that does not bid, does not tell' (CII 547)) – where his letters delay and dally, overspill and reconstrue. It is true that the poems also exhibit their own kind of mazy and self-interrupting strain, as epitomised by the circumlocutory first line of 'The Leaden Echo and the Golden Echo' (155), or the eloquent aposiopesis of 'The Windhover' ('the achieve of; the mastery of the thing!' (132)). But the organic and inchoate quality in the letters is not, as it is in the poems, a calculated aesthetic effect performing and authenticating powerful feelings recollected in tranquillity. The letters are, of course, in some sense literary productions too. But they are also significantly shaped by two further pressures, pressures of etiquette and exigency specific to Hopkins's situation as a letter writer, and to the letter form.

Hopkins's understanding that he was not primarily writing letters for himself, but to someone else – his acute sense of his other correspondent – paradoxically expresses itself through a heightened self-awareness, as seen in his restless meta-commentary, especially marked in his use of parentheses and postscripts. Epistolary etiquette bears on exigency here in that this awareness of his correspondent provokes reflections on how much his time for correspondence is squeezed; and that this limits his opportunity not only to write, but also to revise and edit. It is a constant complaint. Many of his letters are also, of necessity, written in snatches, left off and begun again later – sometimes as much as a month later, or more.

Writing in the confessional, for instance, when 'the faithful are fewer than usual', he has to break off suddenly: 'Here comes someone' (CI 395). That letter, begun on 22 May 1880, later resumes without comment, but it must be broken off once more and is not taken back up again until 9 June: 'I had written a great deal more, about his place (to which I came on Dec. 30), but have suppressed it all after keeping it by me and reading it with my head first on one side, then on the other, at various distances and in various lights, many times over' (CI 396). He then breaks off one final time, announcing in mild despair on 18 June: 'This is a dull letter, but you can answer it by a livelier one' (CI 396).

Hopkins's poems were only completed when he was finished with them. There was rarely the same opportunity to work over his letters. Although they are typically fluent and indeed lustrously lucid in their parts, they also often feel loose in terms of their structure as a whole. He admits to Patmore, 'it often happens to me to cancel letters and it would be better if it happened oftener still' (CII 834); and there is evidence that he did in the end tear up a number of missives to different correspondents where he ultimately felt unhappy with his efforts.[6] But for those letters never sent, there are a number he sends while disclaiming them as 'dull', or as otherwise not worth sending. We may be grateful that he sent them anyway, for even those communications he most richly dispraises are invariably winning in their phrase-making, vivid in their descriptions (especially of nature), and studded with inventive ideas and observations. More than this: Hopkins's letters are typically so readable and illuminating precisely because he did not have the time to work over them, and had therefore to write out as he thought, with pen to paper.

The point is well illustrated by a fast-paced, free-flowing dispatch to Dixon begun on 27 February 1879. Although too full to paraphrase, a sense of its rolling richness may be taken by citing only the literary connections he makes: from an opening reference to Dixon's own verse, to Bridges's, to Coleridge, to general prosodical habits of the eighteenth and nineteenth centuries on the 'easily felt principle of *equal strengths*', to sprung rhythm, to Arnold on Campbell, to Marvell, to Thomas Vaughan, to Herbert, to Tennyson, to Goethe, to Burns, to Latin elegiacs in Ovid, to Horace's Sapphic and Alcaic stanzas, to Propertius's habits of metrical counterpoint, to the English rendering of Latin rhythms (CI 343–8).

There is much to be taken as well from how one topic prompts the next. And when it comes to his individual comments, there is interest not only in those subjects to which he devotes extended commentary, but even to those given a passing, colloquial gloss. Stray, subjective adjectives – such as where he warms to Marvell as 'a most rich and nervous poet' (CI 346), or where he recoils from the 'odious goodiness and neckcloth' about Wordsworth's sonnets 'which half throttles their beauty' (CI 267) – are informative about Hopkins's taste. In this mode, his comments are often sufficiently surprising that they may send us back to the writers he mentions with fresh eyes (and ears). It is, after all, Marvell's contemporary, Milton, who is

Hopkins's hero of English prosody, the poet whose verse style he most obviously emulates; and Milton was Marvell's great poetic inspiration too. But Marvell differs starkly from both Milton and Hopkins in his conspicuously symmetrical and unmimetic prosody – which is what makes Hopkins's admiration so provoking, especially his enigmatic use of the word 'nervous'.[7] As for Wordsworth, Hopkins's comment here connects suggestively with a number of other remarks scattered through the letters, notably his claim that Wordsworth, 'great sonneteer as he was', 'wrote in "Parnassian"' (CI 476).

Hopkins's literary-critical impressionism is consistent with his associative style already noted, where the main or most important subject is addressed indirectly, on the move. Here is another example:

> I think I have seen nothing of Lang's but in some magazine; also a sonnet prefixed to his translation of the Odyssey. I liked what I read, but not so that it left a deep impression. It is in the Swinburnian kind, is it not? (I do not think that kind goes far: it expresses passion but not feeling, much less character. This I say in general or of Swinburne in particular. Swinburne's genius is astonishing, but it will, I think, do only one thing.) (CI 354)

In the previously quoted passage on Swinburne's 'blethery bathos', the most salient remark is buried in parenthesis: his aspersion that Swinburne 'has no real understanding of rhythm'. Why Hopkins might make such a claim against one of the most celebrated prosodists of the nineteenth century, and what distinction is implied between understanding and *really* understanding rhythm, is of potentially great import for Hopkins's own poetics.[8] The passage just quoted similarly consigns the weightiest observations to brackets. The opening claim about Lang, a minor poet, is of little value compared with his clarifying comparison with Swinburne's poetics, which touches the distinction between 'passion' and 'feeling'. That distinction extends beyond Lang and even Swinburne, to the 'Swinburnian' model of versifying – and therefore to a fundamental preoccupation in Hopkins's poetics, as the struggle for sincere expression of emotion as against pure thought.[9]

It is, in short, when Hopkins is most incidental and unclenched that many of his most suggestive observations appear. Parenthesis, it has been noticed, is used repeatedly and effectively to create that space. As he uses it to insinuate humour, he also employs it to liberate his literary-critical impressions. In a postcard to Bridges of 9 June 1878, he writes: 'I forgot to answer about my metres (rhythms rather, I suppose)' (CI 304).[10] The key qualification – turning this time not on 'real', or 'passion' versus 'feeling', but on the word 'suppose' – is coyly tucked away from the main proposition. Where elsewhere Hopkins is more expansive on the rhythmical rather than metrical character of his prosodical experiments, he once again stages a conspicuously causal segue:

> And thereby hangs so considerable a tale, in fact the very thing I was going to write about Sprung Rhy[th]m (by the bye rhythm, not metre: metre is a matter of arranging lines, rhythm is one of arranging feet; anapaests are a rhythm,

the sonnet is a metre; and so you can write any metre in any rhythm and any rhythm to any metre supposing of course that usage has not tied the rhythm to the metre, as often or mostly it has), that I must for the present leave off, give o'er as they say in Lancashire. (CII 747)

Hopkins's 'considerable tale' cannot be told, he says, because time does not permit – as the space of the postcard would not permit extended digression. But that he nonetheless finds room for his rider within a two-line postcard, and that, here, the parenthesis so entirely overwhelms the sentence into which it is embedded, belies the breeziness of his by-the-bye-ing. Both comments are presented as adventitious, but the question of whether sprung rhythm is to be defined as a metre or character-ised as a form of rhythmical recitation is of urgent and central concern to Hopkins; and it has, with good reason, been the subject of strenuous debate by Hopkins schol-ars for almost a century.

No doubt because it is scattered piecemeal across different correspondences, and delivered, as described, indirectly and on the hoof, the literary criticism and theory that appears in Hopkins's letters has not received much scholarly attention. Where his remarks on literature are studied at all, the emphasis tends to be (as in Wimsatt's book) on the essays rather than the letters. But for the reasons suggested, the criti-cism that appears in his letters has a value to rival as well as supplement his formal theorising. It is a vital resource for helping us to better understand his achievement as a poet. Likewise, when on the topic of his own life and experiences, Hopkins's letters reward our attention on their own terms, for their felicity of phrasing and quirky set pieces – but they also confound Hopkins's self-representation in his poems, and the 'always serious' poetic persona cultivated by his literary executor. They provide a uniquely intimate portrait, in the round: poet and critic, but also friend and priest, sibling and son. From his schoolboy brag at being whipped and almost expelled for 'wildly' cheeking his teacher (CI 7), to his 'buck up' admoni-tion to Bridges sent less than two months before he died; from his insistence on the essential spring and strictness of sprung rhythm, to his avowed preference 'for glowing colours' and 'violent action' in art (CII 746); from his transports of joy at the natural world, to his self-lacerating humour at his own pitiful condition: Hopkins's letters give radiant expression to a disposition not only passionate but also playful, and to a personality that is capable – most revealingly – of being both at the same time.

NOTES

1. *Hopkins: The Major Works*, ed. Phillips, p. 132. All subsequent in-text references to poems from this edition.
2. *The Collected Works of Gerard Manley Hopkins*, ed. Thornton and Phillips, vol. 1, pp. 346, 414. Hereafter 'C', followed by volume and page number.
3. See Feeney, who takes Hopkins's 'play' to include 'fun', 'creativity', 'contest' and 'style'; also see Sonstroem. On Edward Lear as a nonsense poet who is most serious when least solemn, see Bevis.

4. See Muller, p. 43. A third Jesuit, Francis Bacon, did apparently give sincere support to the poem.
5. See Hurley, 'Darkening the Subject of Hopkins' Prosody' and 'What Sprung Rhythm Really Is NOT'.
6. To Patmore (CII 930): 'I have greatly to beg your pardon for leaving you so long unanswered. This however is the second letter begun, and the other ran some length, but is cancelled.' To Bridges (CI 455): 'I began a letter to you a short while ago, but tore it up. Meant to write I have every day for long . . . To him [Dixon] I am every day meaning to write and last night it was I began, but it would not do; however today I shall.'
7. On Milton's verse style versus Marvell's, see Creaser.
8. See Hurley, 'Rhythm', in *The Oxford Handbook of Victorian Poetry*, Chapter 1.
9. Ibid.
10. It would take another chapter to consider Hopkins's use of the postcard (a relatively new form of communication in 1878), and its equivocal status as both visual and verbal, private and public; and such a chapter would have to weigh the fact that, as a Jesuit, Hopkins's private letters were also potentially public, in that they could be opened and read by his superiors – something he had occasion to advise his correspondents, as well as to reassure them about (see, notably, CI 260).

WORKS CITED

Bevis, Matthew, 'Edward Lear's lines of flight', Chatterton Lecture on Poetry, 1 November 2012, *Journal of the British Academy* 1 (July 2013): 31–69.

Bridges, Robert (ed.), *Poems of Gerard Manley Hopkins* (London: H. Milford, 1918).

Creaser, John W., 'Prosodic Style and Conceptions of Liberty in Milton and Marvell', *Milton Quarterly* 34.1 (2000): 1–13.

Davie, Donald, *Purity of Diction in English Verse* (London: Routledge & Kegan Paul, 1969 [1952]).

Empson, William, *Seven Types of Ambiguity* (London: Random House, 2004 [1930]).

Feeney, Joseph J., *The Playfulness of Gerard Manley Hopkins* (Aldershot: Ashgate, 2008).

House, Humphry, and Graham Storey (eds), *The Journals and Papers of Gerard Manley Hopkins* (London: Oxford University Press, 1959).

Hurley, Michael D., 'Darkening the Subject of Hopkins' Prosody', *Victorian Poetry* 43.4 (2005): 485–96.

—— 'Rhythm', in Matthew Bevis (ed.), *The Oxford Handbook of Victorian Poetry* (Oxford: Oxford University Press, 2013), pp. 19–35.

—— 'What Sprung Rhythm Really Is NOT', *Hopkins Quarterly* 33.3 (2006): 71–94.

Muller, Jill, *Gerard Manley Hopkins and Victorian Catholicism* (London and New York: Routledge, 2003).

Phillips, Catherine (ed.), *Gerard Manley Hopkins: The Major Works* (Oxford: Oxford University Press, 2002).

—— and R. K. R. Thornton (eds), *The Collected Works of Gerard Manley Hopkins, Vols I–II: Correspondence* (Oxford: Oxford University Press, 2013).

Sonstroem, David, 'Making Earnest of Game: G. M. Hopkins and Nonsense Poetry', *Modern Language Quarterly* 28 (1967): 192–206.

Wimsatt, James I., *Hopkins's Poetics of Speech Sound: Sprung Rhythm, Lettering, Inscape* (Toronto: University of Toronto Press, 2006).

Part III: Twentieth-Century Letter Writing

10 The Gift of George Yeats

Matthew Campbell

In the 1925 edition of *A Vision*, William Butler Yeats printed a blank verse poem with the title 'Desert Geometry or The Gift of Harun Al-Rashid'. It had been published in the magazine *English Life* in January 1924 as 'The Gift of Harun Al-Rashid', and by the time the poem reappeared in *The Tower* in 1928, the 'Desert Geometry' title had disappeared and the original shorter title had been restored. The poem was left out entirely of the second edition of *A Vision* in 1937 (Yeats, *Variorum*, 460n). It is a monologue set in Baghdad in the eighth century, and contains within it a conversation between Kusta Ben Luka, the doctor-philosopher who is also the narrator, and the fearsome Caliph Harun Al-Rashid, who has just put his vizier to death for no reason that the poem can tell us (*Variorum* 828). Kusta sends a letter to a friend, Abd Al-Rabban, a 'fellow-roysterer once'. He asks that the letter be hidden, although he also envisages its rediscovery after long years in an obscure place. The letter contains within it a story about the ageing philosopher receiving the gift of a young wife from Harun, whose recent marriage resulted in a happiness which he offers to Kusta as an example which will 'show how violent hearts can lose / Their bitterness and find the honeycomb'.

Honeycomb is just one of a number of mysterious shapes which reappear throughout this letter-poem about the desert geometry of a secret knowledge. Another of those shapes is that of words on a page. The girl who is offered to Kusta is unnamed and, it would appear, unlettered, or at least monolingual:

> And often in those first days I saw her stare
> On old dry writing in a learned tongue,
> On old dry faggots that could never please
> The extravagance of spring; or move a hand
> As if that writing or the figured page
> Were some dear cheek.

Not so much reading as page-stroking, the girl still goes on to interrupt the aged philosopher's night-time writing, speaking like 'some great Djinn'. 'Truths without father came,' Kusta tells us, appearing as the geometry of letters on paper itself:

Truths without father came, truths that no book
Of all the uncounted books that I have read,
Nor thought out of her mind or mine begot,
Self-born, high-born, and solitary truths,
Those terrible implacable straight lines
Drawn through the wandering vegetative dream,
Even those truths that when my bones are dust
Must drive the Arabian host.

If these truths do not belong to any book that Kusta has read, they emerge as if they were writing 'terrible implacable straight lines' on a page. The *OED* tells us that to be implacable means 'cannot be appeased; irreconcilable; inexorable'. But if straight lines are unappeasable mathematical certainty, opposition without reconciliation, they are nevertheless 'Drawn through the wandering vegetative dream'. Is this the dream of an unselfconscious eternal existence, a place without action or desire in which our organs are responsive only to water and light, as in the sensitive plant of Shelley?[1] Or is it the vegetative basis of paper itself and drawn on it the inerasable ideal which is writing in ink? One result is 'truths', an ideology that 'Must drive the Arabian host'. The truths are both inexorable and rooted in a physiology which is both abstract and bodily. They can be communicated in speech, writing or even on the desert sand: the girl later marks out 'emblems on the sand' which the philosopher studies, 'day by day'.

The effect of the girl and what she tells him is utterly transformative, but Kusta introduces a great quandary into his new creative relationship. He wavers over whether he loves her for her visions or her own self, and he fears that if she loses her 'ignorance', she will 'Dream that I love her only for the voice'. He offers a solution where the girl and her 'quality of wisdom' become a unity of geometrical pattern and expression, an abstraction embodied in 'love's / Particular quality'. It is a hard argument to make:

The signs and shapes;
All those abstractions that you fancied were
From the great Treatise of Parmenides;
All, all those gyres and cubes and midnight things
Are but a new expression of her body
Drunk with the bitter sweetness of her youth.
And now my utmost mystery is out.
A woman's beauty is a storm-tossed banner;
Under it wisdom stands, and I alone –
Of all Arabia's lovers I alone –
Nor dazzled by the embroidery, nor lost
In the confusion of its night-dark folds,
Can hear the armed man speak.

There is much obscurity about the 'utmost mystery' of the desert geometry which is never explained in the poem, although it makes a kind of sense when placed in the midst of the pages of the 1925 A Vision (Vision 1925 97–102, 226–68). But there is also something moving about this uncertainty of the aged lover puzzling through the quandary over the mixed motives of his love. Does Kusta love the girl herself or is her value to him only in the mystery she has told him? Is his love for the medium or the message? The answer is that if the 'gyres and cubes and midnight things' of the utmost mystery do not have their origin in the agency or creativity of the girl, such abstractions could not have been found without the self-delighting form she gave to them, 'of her body / Drunk with the bitter sweetness of her youth'. Just as the line's play with trochaic and triple feet is allowed to work little intoxications on Kusta's speech, so youth itself intoxicates the body, and leads to the vocal or written 'new expression' which is 'of her body'. Abstraction can only find form under the banner of 'A woman's beauty'. The desert geometry of the poem, as well as the desert geometry of what the girl has given to the philosopher, along with the very gift of the girl from the despotic Harun Al-Rashid, all come together in an erotic play of power and understanding – or understanding as power – where wisdom is gained through, and is indistinguishable from, love. Quandary dealt with, power reasserted, it is ultimately the speech of 'the armed man' that is heard by Kusta at the end of the poem.

To readers of the poetry and biography of Yeats, all of this is easily recognisable as a not-so-veiled account of the relationship between Yeats and his wife Georgie Hyde Lees, twenty-seven years his younger, and a noted medium, who turned to automatic writing in the early days of what might have been a risky mismatch of a marriage. George swore Willie to secrecy, but he eventually spilt the beans about the source of the 'Self-born, high-born, and solitary truths' that had been given to him, not just in this poem but also in the second edition of A Vision.[2] And the message that came to Yeats through this medium was not at first in speech or the night-time exposition of the nameless girl in 'The Gift of Harun Al-Rashid', though that came later. Rather, Yeats's wife wrote to him in those first days of their marriage, while he sat in the same room. The writing did not come in implacable straight lines: as the voluminous manuscripts that Yeats kept show us, it was often jagged across the page, frequently in mirror writing, and interspersed with 'gyres and cubes and midnight things'.[3] The writing came in answer to questions asked of George by Yeats and through her the spirits dictating a system to describe human subjectivity and culture in a world history driven by the implacable.

Yeats revealed the source and the moment thus, in 'A Packet for Ezra Pound', added to the 1937 A Vision:

On the afternoon of October 24th 1917, four days after my marriage, my wife surprised me by attempting automatic writing. What came in disjointed sentences, in almost illegible writing, was so exciting, sometimes so profound, that I persuaded her to give an hour or two day after day to the unknown writer, and after some half-dozen such hours offered to spend what remained of life explaining and piecing together those scattered sentences. 'No,' was the answer, 'we have come to give you metaphors for poetry.' (Vision 1937 9)

There is some doubt about the veracity of the date that Yeats gives. And nobody has found this famous statement attributed to 'the unknown writer' in the many manuscripts made by George, and that Yeats kept and catalogued, usually with meticulous care. Margaret Mills Harper plausibly suggests that a document misfiled with papers relating to the 'Packet for Ezra Pound' chapter which was added to the 1937 *Vision* contains what the writer said in answer to Yeats's question: 'I give you philosophy to give you new images you ought not to use it as philosophy and it is not only given for you –' ('Reflected Voices' 270).[4] Whatever the conflicting statements about the conditions attached to the gift – 'not only given for you' or 'to give you metaphors for poetry' – there was an offer of collaboration here, one that was made in writing. The young wife entered into her married life by writing to the husband with whom she already shared a bed. And whether communications from an unknown writer, a desperate play for her husband's sexual attention, or just plain fraud,[5] the writing emerged as a correspondence initiated by George in response to her husband's queries about the course of history.

It is my contention that this celebrated collaboration between artist husband and mystic wife in the early years of their marriage was one that was carried out primarily as a correspondence, a correspondence that stretched to include more than just William and George Yeats. The many biographers and critics who have been drawn to this material agree that George's automatic script put an end to a very difficult period in the personal life of Yeats, a period which lasted through the aftermath of the Easter Rising of 1916 (and the writing of Yeats's poems about that event) and against the background of the global conflict of the Great War. As Yeats and George entered into their mystical collaboration, the 'October Revolution' in Petrograd (actually 7 November) suggested a significant ideological tilt to world events. And in January 1918, the death in the war of his friend Augusta Gregory's son, Robert, added personal loss. Yeats made much use of this matter for poetry, yes, but his family matters are not unrelated to the activities of 'violent hearts', the 'Arabian host' or 'the armed man', no matter how mysterious the connection might seem. It is a period in which he acted in ways that were not much to his credit, though his remorse is palpable in his letters and throughout the poems that he wrote during and after this period and was to publish gradually over the next decade or so. If the wife was writing to, or even for, the husband as he developed his view of history, he was engaged in other writing, both letters and poems, addressed to other women in his life, former lovers, unrequited lovers and old female friends.

The gift of George's writing was ultimately to serve as material for Yeats's poetry, as was the personal situation from which it came, one alluded to in Kusta's questioning after the motives for his attraction to the unnamed girl who reveals 'truths without father' to him. If George was the mother of the truths which purportedly came to Yeats from an unknown writer, her writing was midwife. She was, of course, far from ignorant or even monolingual. Before she married Yeats, Georgie Hyde Lees was versed not just in spiritualism and horology but also in idealist philosophy, as well as having acquired an intimate acquaintance with Yeats's *Per Amica Silentia Lunae*. That book was published earlier in 1917, and in it Yeats at first assayed his own ideas about the course of history, what the 1937 *A Vision* would later formulate as the desire 'to hold in a single thought reality and justice' while still aware that the widening gyres of world events told of implacable division (*Vision* 1937 25).

This correspondence which is so caught up in the complicated lives of the older poet and his young wife managed to achieve not so much a resolution or reconciliation as an artistic respite such as that envisaged in 'The Gift of Harun Al-Rashid'. The consequences of the gift were 'unforeseen', such as those described by Yeats a few years later when writing about his friend Aubrey Beardsley and the flawed subjectivity of the 'Tragic Generation' which had so obsessed him in *Per Amica*, as well as in the poems of this period and later in *A Vision*:

> Does not all art come when a nature, that never ceases to judge itself, exhausts personal emotion in action or desire so completely that something impersonal, something that has nothing to do with action or desire, suddenly starts into its place, something which is as unforeseen, as completely organized, even as unique, as the images that pass before the mind between sleeping and waking? (*Autobiographies* 332)

For all that Yeats viewed the lives led by his friends from the 1890s as wasted, he did allow that some of them achieved brief moments of revelation, of something 'completely organized', a something he here calls 'art'. The experience with George, between sleeping and waking, was to allow him to move beyond the personal, beyond action or desire in order to create his art. And given that movement was founded not in one subjectivity but in two and more – indeed not in one gender but in two – Yeats, like his persona Kusta Ben Luka, had to find a place to acknowledge that the 'gyres and cubes and midnight things' were after all 'but a new expression of her body / Drunk with the bitter sweetness of her youth'. The medium must be granted presence in the message.

That message was dramatised as an opposition not just between action and desire but also between Choice and Chance, and then ultimately the consummation that suggests the possible unity of such irreconcilables. The resulting poetry offers one model of such unity in the new expression of the body and, in what was for the poet, in 1917, recast as a new conception of an old experience, the sharing of sexual love. Previously in Yeats's writing that could emerge merely as a brief respite, particularly when set against action. Grappling with chance, to choose love seemed impossible. In an earlier work, *On Baile's Strand*, a heroic play from 1904, such moments were simply a distraction to the armed man. Cuchulainn says,

> I never have known love but as a kiss
> In the mid-battle, and a difficult truce
> Of oil and water, candles and dark night,
> Hillside and hollow, the hot-footed sun
> And the cold, sliding, slippery-footed moon –
> A brief forgiveness between opposites
> That have been hatreds for three times the age
> Of this long-'stablished ground. (*Collected Plays* 259)

Yeats was not quite looking for 'brief forgiveness' in his eventual account of married love, but he was to find a way in which the briefness of forgiveness might still sustain the opposites which maintained its account of creativity, drawn against the background of a new conception of heroism achieved through the gift of love as much as war.

After his marriage, the woman can appear in the poems as a temptress or witch, but also as the unasked giver of repeated moments of unity, such as those in the 1918 'Solomon and the Witch':

> For though love has a spider's eye
> To find out some appropriate pain –
> Aye, though all passion's in the glance –
> For every nerve, and tests a lover
> With cruelties of Choice and Chance;
> And when at last that murder's over
> Maybe the bride-bed brings despair,
> For each an imagined image brings
> And finds a real image there;
> Yet the world ends when these two things,
> Though several, are a single light,
> When oil and wick are burned in one;

If Solomon has been seduced by a Sheba who is taking her chance, then a choice, no matter how cruel, has still been made. These are matters which remain in the moral murk of later poems about conception and world history which raise the matter of congress and consent between the demon and the beast, or between the human and the divine. In 'Leda and the Swan' and 'The Mother of God', the choice of the women in the poems encountering winged creatures, swan and angel, can be hard to discern. To take the latter example, Yeats's Mary does not represent the God she bears within her as a gift. On the contrary, she has bought it: 'What is this flesh I purchased with my pains?' In the King James Bible, Luke 1: 38 has Mary give Gabriel her assent – 'Be it unto me according to thy word' – and in Christian doctrine such assent leads to redemption from the original sin. 'That murder' referred to in the 'Solomon and the Witch' passage above followed the Fall, and the 'appropriate pain' and 'murder' of human love and sexuality remain fallen: 'the bride-bed brings despair'. If sexual union allows 'a single light' for the repetition of the Fall at the end of the world, it does not last long. Solomon suggests this moment will be ephemeral, orgasm as prophetic of a second Fall and the destruction of the world. Sheba answers from the bed, with one brief sentence: 'Yet the world stays.' In the final lines of the poem she is pictured as insatiable, desirous to prolong the ecstatic pain: 'O! Solomon! Let us try again.'

Yeats gets away with this, insofar as it adds both assent and appetite to his new conception of the creativity which might ensue from a conception of love as oppositional. It is also funny, and the joke is on the man. In her classic account of Yeats's love poetry, Elizabeth Butler Cullingford concludes her discussion of the poem thus:

The sexual comedy that in classical fescennine verses took the form of the ribald male joking at the expense of the bride is appropriated by Yeats's Sheba. The wedding night frozen into the hieratic structure of the epithalamium is, through her provocative and teasing initiative, here opened up and prolonged into a succession of nights dedicated to sexual and occult exploration. Desire satisfied is not desire quenched, but desire continually reborn. (120)

For George and Yeats, as many biographical accounts of the early days of their marriage have speculated, the pleasure of a successful sexual union intimately accompanied a mystical one; love and the writing of letters dictated from the otherworld were as one. It was not one union, rather a series, union as iteration, either sexual – as with Sheba's request to 'try again' – or occult – as in the exhausting process of automatic writing that George carried out on a daily basis. There are also many instances in the writing where the supernatural communicators counselled sex and the procreation of children.[6] As Cullingford suggests, one conclusion from 'Solomon and the Witch' might be that the younger woman was fairly successful in managing the older husband. But Yeats was also involved in an iterative process of writing at the time, and not just the creation of art. To make way for the unforeseen there was still the process of clearing up a personal mess which resulted in some startlingly direct love poems about the consequences of the actions of a lover who felt he had behaved less than honourably. In the midst of such creativity based around the repeated encounter between man and woman – indeed a creativity with much happiness attached to it – Yeats was also writing letters and poems about the remorse attached to at least two recently failed relationships.[7] While George was writing to him, his correspondence and the poems were in illuminating relation, and her writing followed a series of unfortunate letters from him to the young woman he had spent much of the previous year before his eventual marriage to George unsuccessfully persuading to marry him. His last proposal was only five weeks before his wedding on 20 October 1917. The letter writing continued into the first days of marriage.

That woman was Iseult Gonne, daughter of Yeats's more famous lover Maud Gonne McBride. As throughout these relationships and the poems that arose from them, an armed man was lurking in the background. Maud's husband John McBride had been executed by the British for his part in the Easter Rising in May 1916. Perhaps more out of a sense of duty than any lasting sense of love, Yeats had proposed to the widowed Maud, but was rebuffed. His obsession with her daughter, younger even than George at twenty-one, and whom he had known since she was a small child, provided an extraordinary accompaniment to the greatest period of his writing of public poetry, the responses to those events of Easter Week which (among other things) seemed to have liberated from 'bitter wrong . . . some who are near my heart' ('Easter 1916', *Variorum* 393). The liberation was not followed by the choice of Yeats as husband by either of those who had previously been caught up in his rival's drunken vainglorious loutishness (Iseult had been the victim of sexual abuse by her stepfather McBride in her girlhood, evidence brought to bear in Maud's unsuccessful suit for divorce). So if Yeats was taking his chance in one way, the choice was refused.

Chosen as wife, George was to take her chance, and she succeeded. By 29 October 1917, just over a week into their marriage, Yeats wrote to his friend Augusta Gregory (who had previously counselled he marry Iseult):

Two days ago I was in great gloom (of which I hope, & believe George knew nothing). I was saying to myself 'I have betrayed three people' when I thought 'I have lived through all this before'. Then George spoke of the sensation of having lived through something before (she knew nothing of my thought). Then she said she felt that something was to be written through her. She got a piece of paper, & talking to me all the while so that her thoughts would not effect what she wrote, wrote these words (which she did not understand) 'with the bird' (Iseult) 'all is well at heart. Your action was right for both but in London you mistook its meaning'. I had begun to believe just before my marriage that I had acted, not as I thought more for Iseults sake than my own, but because my mind was unhinged by strain. The strange thing was that within half an hour after the writing of this message my rheumatic pains & my neuralgia & my fatigue had gone and I was very happy. From being more miserable than I ever remember being since Maud Gonne's marriage I became extremely happy. That sense of happiness has lasted ever since. The misery produced two poems which I will send you presently to hide away for me – they are among the best I have done. (Foster 105)

Yeats went on to assuage his friend's doubts about his marriage by flattery: 'I think Georgie has your own moral genius.'

This letter speaks back from the front line of immense emotional and psychological stress, indeed explicitly psychosomatic stress. The misery has been lifted and rheumatic pains and neuralgia and fatigue all replaced by happiness. But in Yeats's terms, the misery was lifted by matters outside the body. The neurosis of remorse – '"I have betrayed three people"' – has been replaced by a communication from the dead – '"I have lived through all this before"'. For psychosis read metempsychosis. The three people he believed he had betrayed included George and Iseult. The third might have been either Maud Gonne or indeed Yeats himself. But the sense of betrayal was then turned aside by George's communication of a past life: 'Then . . . she felt that something was to be written through her.' Yeats's letter to Gregory relays the letters from past lives in order to illuminate a breakthrough in a present one, and the writing explicitly soothes the fears of having made a choice of the wrong woman. Through George's apparently ignorant hand, the communicators counsel that all is well with the symbolic bird (Iseult, as Yeats helpfully glosses this for Gregory) and that he has made the right choice.

It is easy to see George managing Yeats with less than the ingenuousness that he ascribes to her, just as it is easy to picture the credulousness of Yeats. But by the time such matters of experience and interpretation might be brought out in the fullness of their given artistic and moral complexity in dialogue poems like 'The Gift of Harun Al-Rashid' or 'Solomon and the Witch', we can see an extraordinary dramatic achievement based in Yeats's ability to believe all this. The sudden understanding of the potential of the gifts that George was offering him meant that he could find a freedom which would enable art to be the product of all of this painful personal matter played through his correspondence. This would be formulated in the words used to describe Beardsley, the retention of self-judgement and also the exhaustion of the personal and the reconciliation of the unforeseen while in a state between sleeping and waking. George enacted all this for him, writing to him about it. Consequently, 'The misery produced two poems which I will send you presently to hide away for me – they are among the best I have done.' Lady Gregory was an unlikely first version of the 'fellow-roysterer' whom Kusta Ben Luka asked to hide the letter that carried the great secret that the simple girl has revealed to him.

These two poems were to be first published seven years after their composition, in *The Dial* in 1924, with the titles 'The Lover Speaks' and 'The Heart Replies' (see *Variorum* 449). Placed initially in dialogue with each other, they joined 'The Gift of Harun Al-Rashid' in *The Tower* four years later as 'Owen Aherne and his Dancers', brought closer together in a title which closely echoes that of the 1921 volume *Michael Robartes and the Dancer*, in which 'Solomon and the Witch' had appeared. Owen Aherne was a thinly veiled persona for Yeats, a figure he considered to have known in a past life: '"I have lived through all this before"'. In 1922 he added: 'I consider that Aherne and Robartes, men to whose namesakes I had attributed a turbulent life or death, have quarrelled with me. They take their place in a phantasmagoria in which I endeavour to explain my philosophy of life and death' (*Variorum* 821). In various forms and with various titles, these poems about Iseult retain dialogue form as their speaker suffers turbulence and quarrel. The poem initially published as 'The Lover Speaks' reads thus:

A strange thing surely that my Heart, when love had come unsought
Upon the Norman upland or in that poplar shade,
Should find no burden but itself and yet should be worn out.
It could not bear that burden and therefore it went mad.

The south wind brought it longing, and the east wind despair,
The west wind made it pitiful, and the north wind afraid.
It feared to give its love a hurt with all the tempest there;
It feared the hurt that she could give and therefore it went mad.

I can exchange opinion with any neighbouring mind,
I have as healthy flesh and blood as any rhymer's had,
But O! my Heart could bear no more when the upland caught the wind;
I ran, I ran, from my love's side because my Heart went mad.

Unlike the erratic lines and designs of George's automatic script, these are implacable straight lines indeed. If they were written from the honeymoon hotel, they were not lines written for his new wife. The first extant version held by the National Library of Ireland is reproduced in Richard Finneran's edition of the manuscript materials of *The Tower*, and is remarkably clean. The hexameters and even heptameter lines are laid out in landscape down the pages of Yeats's unlined notebook. To the date given by Yeats after the poem, 'Oct 25–26', 'GY' has added '1917' (*Tower: Manuscript Materials* 420). The letter to Lady Gregory suggests George was unaware of the poem, or at least the feelings in Yeats that gave rise to it, on 25 and 26 October 1917.

The dangers of the hexameter or alexandrine line in English were famously enumerated by Alexander Pope in *An Essay on Criticism*: 'A needless alexandrine ends the song, / That, like a wounded snake, drags its slow length along' (10). Earlier in his career Yeats was not averse to it when imported into ballad-like stanzas. Here, his implacable lines of six and seven beats and more are fully aware of the wounded snake, lingering among the monosyllables which seem so unwilling to end. 'My Heart', Yeats tells us, 'Should find no burden but itself and yet should be worn out', where a burden is both the weight of the depression under which he has been suffering and the refrain to the song he is writing out of that state. The refrain phrase, or burden, is 'went mad' but the poem is no song and the line courts the unmusicality of the monotone. As does the next, setting up the first iteration of the refrain and pushing mental dissolution out of dazed syllables: 'It could not bear that burden and therefore it went mad.' We can scan the line thus: x / x / x / x x / x / x /, where the little unstressed stretch of the line here – 'burden and' – adds to the monotony of the rhythm. Internal rhyme, too, sounds in repetitions of the word 'burden' across both lines: 'burden, bear, burden, therefore'. In the last stanza the rhymer poet claims healthy flesh and blood, but the lines lengthen even more. 'But O! my Heart could bear no more when the upland caught the wind' packs in fifteen syllables, an anapaest, an extrametrical foot, as well as the breathing pause after the exclamation. If anything, this is Thomas Hardy territory, albeit 'Norman upland' rather than Wessex hillside, a memory of failed love in which remorse is carried in a fraught metrical irregularity, albeit in recognisable stanzaic form.[8] Unlike Hardy, grimly living out his unhappy love, Yeats's repetitions tell of escape: 'I ran, I ran, from my love's side because my Heart went mad.' The palpitations there are physiological as well as metaphorical, where 'my Heart' is beating with the rhythm of his running as breathless repetition ('I ran, I ran,') into the iambic resolution of the burden which resolves nothing: 'because my heart went mad'.

Whatever happened on a 'Norman upland' as eventually ascribed to Owen Aherne here, we do know that Iseult Gonne was sharing her mother's political exile in Colleville in Calvados and that Yeats visited her there while paying suit. The family were permitted to return to London (but not Ireland) in 1917, and from there Iseult wrote to Yeats on 26 October 1917, six days after his marriage. Immediately before the communicators were writing letters to Yeats, he was writing letters to someone else. In the midst of a letter received either the day before or on the very day George started her automatic writing, and thus exactly contemporaneous with the appended dates of composition on the 'A strange thing surely' manuscript, Iseult responded to a letter written by Yeats with this piece of information:

> I burnt your first letter; it made a very ghostly little flame in the chimney.
> All our thoughts about the immediate moment were then such rubbish after
> all, since memories are so much more important. I felt your trouble as if it was

mine, and it is just as well that I did not write to you at once, for it mends no ill, if someone says: 'life is wicked', for someone else to answer: 'it is.'

I happened this afternoon to enter into a little protestant church quite bare but welcoming. I spoke to God there (for it was in the spirit of the place) as if he was a simple old friend, a kind of outlaw like ourselves yet with some influence on the authorities. 'Why should Willy of all people, not be happy; why should I who have always loved him in all affection have had any share in causing him sorrow; and how could it all be arranged?'

And the same rush of emotion came back to me as in Havre: I could almost read and hear the answer: 'Go back to Christ.' And Alas is it true? Hermas and Cypris lead to knowledge, but is peace only in Christ? I have not thought this out further, I am very sad and tired.

If only as one more kindness to me, try to be happy. It is too late and too early now to look into yourself. An abruptly new condition is bound to have a little of the fearfulness of a birth, though it may be for the better. Though it may be dreary to you, would it not be better to renounce for a time the life of emotion, and live on a few maxims of the early Patricians.

But here am I speaking as if I knew when really all I know is that I share your sadness and will share your joy when you will tell me: 'All is well.'

Give my love to Georgie; she has a sweet nature, and her kindness is no doubt the best wisdom.

Yours most helplessly

Maurice. (Gonne 91)

Iseult had addressed Yeats as 'Dear Willie' in this letter. 'Maurice' was an alter ego assumed by her in girlhood, the 'Maurice' to whom the Prologue to *Per Amica Silentia Lunae* is addressed (*Later Essays* 1). In a letter of 27 December 1916, she signed herself 'old Maurice, Knight of the great Order of Nothingness known to the ordinary world as / Iseult Gonne'. Norman Jeffares et al. connect Iseult's persona of Maurice with Saint Maurice from the third century (Gonne 74). Clearly more than one member of Yeats's amatory circle could populate their letters with past lives.

The contents of Yeats's burnt letter we can only guess at. For all of her indirect attempts at a mix of spiritual firmness and consolatory life lessons, Iseult shows that she had the good sense to burn it. Of course, that may have been Yeats's instruction. As we have seen, the poetry surrounding these love affairs is most careful about secrecy and hiding letters for posterity, even if a burnt letter has no posterity. We need not guess too much at the influence this letter had on a lover already complaining of extreme abjection. Iseult also seems to offer to take on her share of the guilt, swerving as she does between concern for the unrequited lover and an extraordinary identification of both herself and Yeats with the Catholic God she officially followed. The small matter of praying in 'a little protestant church' is one thing; characterising the God she has prayed to as 'a kind of outlaw like ourselves yet with some influence on the authorities' is a stunning idea, mixing the sacrifice of Christ with that of Iseult and Yeats's doomed love.

If we do not know what Yeats wrote in the letter, much criticism and biography has constructed the story of what happened next, under the influence of the 'sweet nature' and 'kindness' of George. But Yeats himself was already preparing the answer, in the second of the poems later attributed to 'Owen Aherne'. *The Tower* manuscript is dated 30 October, but it must be one of the two poems mentioned in the letter to Gregory on 27 October. Whether it is a poem written in the midst of the secret correspondence with Iseult (after receiving this letter from Iseult, did he give her love to Georgie?), or one that emerged after George decided to take control of the marriage, might be revealed in its quite different handling of its alexandrines, and the return of the dialogues which run all the way through these letters and poems. Certainly Iseult's final concern that Yeats tells her that 'All is well' is repeated in Yeats's letter to Lady Gregory in which he quotes George's writing telling him that 'with the bird' (Iseult) 'all is well at heart. Your action was right for both but in London you mistook its meaning.' Yeats may have grasped the offer of absolution, not Cuchulainn's 'brief forgiveness between opposites' but a gift of a more lasting forgiveness. The condition attached to the offer was marriage and it was accepted.

Before that acceptance, a struggle still needed resolution. The second part of the 'Owen Aherne' dialogue carries within it further dialogue, with another of his dancers. 'The Heart Replies' begins with laughter, perhaps the same as that of Sheba, but also that of the poet's own heart.

> The Heart behind its rib laughed out. 'You have called me mad,' it said.
> 'Because I made you turn away and run from that young child;
> How could she mate with fifty years that was so wildly bred?
> Let the cage bird and the cage bird mate and the wild bird mate in the wild.'
>
> 'You but imagine lies all day, O murderer,' I replied.
> 'And all those lies have but one end, poor wretches to betray;
> I did not find in any cage the woman at my side.
> O but her heart would break to learn my thoughts are far away.'
>
> 'Speak all your mind,' my Heart sang out, 'speak all your mind; who cares,
> Now that your tongue cannot persuade the child till she mistake
> Her childish gratitude for love and match your fifty years?
> O let her choose a young man now and all for his wild sake.'

The poem moves from the determinations of chance to the choice that is lying beside the speaker: 'I did not find in any cage the woman at my side.' Its preoccupations with the wildness that is set implacably against the caged lead the speaker only to irresolution and the half-answering in the future of the question about the ultimate importance of his inability to persuade 'the child' to marry him for the wrong reasons, where 'childish gratitude' can be mistaken for love. Gratitude, as we have seen, runs all the way through this writing of poems and letters, along with the unforeseen and the importance of making a choice after receiving the chance of the gift. 'Owen Aherne and his Dancers' speaks from the midst of this chance-taking/ choice-making dilemma, desiring both the wild and the caged, while all the time aware that the woman at his side was not found in a cage. The speaker appears to hold back from the giving of pain in these circumstances ('O but her heart would break to learn my thoughts are far away'), but the murderous power of the heart, a murderousness explicitly connected by Solomon with the fallen state of human love, is to insist on the truth: 'You but imagine lies all day, O murderer.' Whether such lies mean imprisoning the wild bird in a mere poem is also at issue. There is a simplicity of diction here which mounts to extreme artistic bareness. Four of the poem's lines are monosyllabic and line four has seventeen syllables with multiple repetitions and a near-unscannable rhythm: 'Let the cage bird and the cage bird mate and the wild bird mate in the wild.' Unlike its companion poem, 'The Heart Replies' does not seek monotone in lines that are hexameters, fourteeners or beyond. The wildness of rhythm is a violence of remorse and ludicrousness, wondering, 'How could she mate with fifty years that was so wildly bred?'

Thus the automatic writing, and thus George might say that all would be well with Iseult. For Iseult's wildness Yeats found symbolic form to follow this brief experiment with the moral dangers of the dionysiac and its attendant aesthetic dangers of the formless. A manuscript dated 'Jan 31 1926' is collected with *The Tower* manuscripts and was later to be placed in the 'A Man Young and Old' sequence which followed 'Owen Aherne' in the 1928 volume (*Tower: Manuscript Materials* 508–9). It is titled 'The Death of the Hare' and its second stanza imagines wildness relegated merely to memory.

> Then suddenly my heart is wrung
> By her distracted air
> And I remember wildness lost
> And after, swept from there,
> Am set down standing in the wood
> At the death of the hare.

The hare is both Iseult and Yeats's now-dead love for her. The love ends with wildness lost, but lost in other ways, transported without will or desire and then set down in a wood.

Yeats was to allow his other love into such places of the lost, or at least the unforeseen into which she had led him. In 1931 he published two 'Fragments' in *The Dublin Magazine*. In 1933 they were inserted into *The Tower* section of his newly published *Collected Poems*, to join 'Owen Aherne' or 'A Man Young and Old' in their preoccupation with the provenance and outcome of a tortuous personal life and eventual mystical marriage. The second fragment reads thus:

> Where got I that truth?
> Out of a medium's mouth,
> Out of nothing it came,
> Out of the forest loam,
> Out of dark night where lay
> The crowns of Nineveh.

From 'nothing' to 'forest' to 'dark night' to 'The crowns of Nineveh'. Of Nineveh nothing remains, but Yeats imagines the rediscovery of treasures and ideas long thought destroyed, like the letter Kusta Ben Luka had conveyed to his fellow-roysterer. Yeats said he got the truth out of a medium's mouth. We know that, initially at least, she wrote it to him. The rediscovery and interpretation of this truth in letters and in poetry and in mystical texts was a process with which Yeats was to spend the rest of his working life. It was a making sense of the correspondence by facing the dilemma of having 'to choose / Perfection of the life or of the work', as he puts it in another poem of 1931, 'The Choice'. Typically, Yeats leaves the dilemma unresolved. But if it were to be for the work, then the artist contemplates damnation and an implacably divided self. The poem's final couplet offers a comic half-rhyme for the poverty and guilt which follows the choice of art over life: 'That old perplexity an empty purse, / Or the day's vanity, the night's remorse.'

NOTES

1. In 'The Philosophy of Shelley's Poetry' (1900), Yeats introduced the last four stanzas of 'The Sensitive Plant' thus: 'Not merely happy souls, but all beautiful places and movements and gestures and events, when we think they have ceased to be, have become portions of the Eternal' (*Essays and Introductions* 73–4). Shelley's poem ends: 'For love and beauty and delight, / There is no death nor change; their might / Exceeds our organs, which endure / No light, being themselves obscure' (*The Major Works* 460).
2. See Maddox 76, Saddlemyer 103.
3. See George and William Butler Yeats, *Yeats's Vision Papers*, passim.
4. See also Harper, *Wisdom of Two: The Spiritual and Literary Collaboration of George and W. B. Yeats*, passim.
5. See George Yeats's letter to Olivia Shakespeare, cited in and discussed by Brown 252, Foster 106, and Saddlemyer 102.
6. See Maddox 101–4 and her account of the communicators counselling parenthood through George against Yeats's will. Their first child Anne was named after one of the communicators, Anne Hyde, seventeenth-century Duchess of Ormonde. The Ormondes were also Butlers, from whom Yeats claimed he was descended.
7. See Maddox 32 on Yeats's relationship with Mabel Dickinson which ended in 1913; on briefer love affairs see Maddox 35.
8. Hardy's *Satires of Circumstance*, containing 'Poems of 1912–13', elegies written after the death of his wife Emma, had appeared in 1914. *Moments of Vision*, published in November 1917, contained further poems of remorse arising from this unhappy marriage.

WORKS CITED

Brown, Terence, *The Life of W. B. Yeats: A Critical Biography* (Oxford: Blackwell, 1999).
Cullingford, Elizabeth Butler, *Gender and History in Yeats's Love Poetry* (Cambridge: Cambridge University Press, 1993).
Foster, R. F., *W. B. Yeats: A Life, II: The Arch-Poet* (Oxford: Oxford University Press, 2003).
Gonne, Iseult, *Letters to W. B. Yeats and Ezra Pound from Iseult Gonne*, ed. A. Norman Jeffares, Anna McBride White and Christina Bridgewater (London: Palgrave, 2004).

Harper, Margaret Mills, 'Reflected Voices, Double Visions', in Neil Mann, Matthew Gibson and Claire Nally (eds), *Yeats's 'A Vision': Explications and Contexts* (Clemson: Clemson University Press, 2012), pp. 269–90.

—— *Wisdom of Two: The Spiritual and Literary Collaboration of George and W. B. Yeats* (Oxford: Oxford University Press, 2006).

Maddox, Brenda, *George's Ghosts: A New Life of W. B. Yeats* (London: Picador, 2000).

Pope, Alexander, *An Essay on Criticism*, in *Alexander Pope: Oxford Poetry Library*, ed. Pat Rogers (Oxford: Oxford University Press, 1994).

Saddlemyer, Ann, *Becoming George: The Life of Mrs. W. B. Yeats* (Oxford: Oxford University Press, 2002).

Shelley, Percy Bysshe, *The Major Works*, ed. Zachary Leader and Michael O'Neill (Oxford: Oxford University Press, 2003).

Yeats, George and William Butler, *Yeats's Vision Papers*, ed. George Mills Harper et al., 4 vols (London: Palgrave, 1992–2001).

Yeats, William Butler, *Autobiographies* (London: Macmillan, 1956).

—— *Essays and Introductions* (London: Macmillan, 1961).

—— *Later Essays: The Collected Works of W. B. Yeats*, vol. 5, ed. William H. O'Donnell (London: Palgrave, 1994).

—— *On Baile's Strand, Collected Plays*, 2nd edn (London: Macmillan, 1954).

—— *The Tower (1928): Manuscript Materials*, ed. Richard J. Finneran, Jared R. Curtis and Ann Saddlemyer (Ithaca, NY: Cornell University Press, 2007).

—— *The Variorum Edition of the Poems of W. B. Yeats*, ed. Peter Allt and Russell K. Alspach (New York: Macmillan, 1957).

—— *A Vision* (London: Macmillan, 1937).

—— *A Vision: The Original 1925 Version*, in *The Collected Works of W. B. Yeats*, vol. 13, ed. Catherine E. Paul and Margaret Mills Harper (London: Palgrave, 2008).

11 Epistolary Psychotherapy: The Letters of Edward Thomas and Philip Larkin

Edna Longley

In 1970 Philip Larkin reviewed *Edward Thomas: A Critical Biography* by William Cooke. For Larkin, Thomas's 'miserable' life is his own worst nightmare come true. Among Thomas's miseries, in the early twentieth century, were a fraught marriage and his treadmill as a reviewer and freelance writer. Larkin comments: 'the two sides of his life were intertwined, like swimmers dragging each other down: marriage meant children, children meant more hack work, hack work meant more domesticity.' The simile betrays Larkin's habitual fear of entanglement with another person, his sense of marriage as an assault on autonomy. His inverse identification with Thomas also betrays familiarity with psycho-literary impasse. This leads him to see Thomas's poetry, written between December 1914 and his death at Arras, as a therapeutic release: 'from his mistaken and unlucky life, there arose suddenly a serene and unquestionable climax' (*RW* 188–90). Indeed, by his own account, Larkin's antithetical lifestyle was hardly misery-free. His letters, like his poems, suggest that *not* marrying and 'the toad *work*' in its salaried guise can also drag a poet down (*CPL* 89). To quote 'Dockery and Son': 'For Dockery a son, for me nothing, / Nothing with all a son's harsh patronage' (153).

This chapter compares the letters of Thomas and Larkin from a psychological angle: chiefly Thomas's letters to the poet Gordon Bottomley and Larkin's letters to his on-off girlfriend, university lecturer Monica Jones. Aside from any likeness, inverse or otherwise, between the poets (as we see, Larkin had absorbed Thomas's poems), one ground for comparison is that both are *lyric* poets, whose letters can be read as rehearsals for poetic psychodrama. The word psychotherapy implies that Thomas and Larkin write letters that seek relief from inner distress or that may themselves relieve it. The distress is sometimes explicit, sometimes unconscious. I want to consider how this distress shapes epistolary relationships; how it gives them a psychoanalytical character; whether any therapy actually occurs; whether poems, in the end, do the job better.

Nearly half a century separates Thomas (1878–1917) from Larkin (1922–85); but the latter belongs in spirit, as the former more directly, to the posterity of the 1890s: a decade that witnessed an intensification of the lyric poem. That applies not only to lyrical subjectivity but also to the lyric as form, and it was bound up with Aestheticism, the so-called 'religion of art'. Yeats, whose impact on both poets would require further chapters, always traces his own lyric 'intensity' back to *fin de siècle* sources. The 1890s also witnessed a high degree of literary neurosis, exemplified by Ernest Dowson, whom both Thomas and Larkin admired. Thomas is partly writing about himself when he calls Dowson's poetry 'an unbodied melancholy', 'the comic, terrible cry of the superfluous man' (*LNB* 61). In 'The Tragic Generation', his memoir of the 1890s, Yeats briefly entertains the idea that 'perhaps our form of lyric, our insistence upon emotion that has no relation to any public interest, gathered together overwrought, unstable men', but then posits that the matter may be more complex. As he rather briskly puts it: 'the first to go out of his mind had no lyrical gift' (Yeats 300). And indeed Yeats's letters and journals, despite one or two psychological wobbles (which made him fear madness), and despite the intensity of his lyric psychodrama, do not constitute the kind of case history that Thomas and Larkin have left behind.

All we can say, perhaps, is that these case histories locate 'instability' and abnormality somewhere in the neighbourhood of poetic vocation. Larkin tells Monica in 1966: 'Our lives are so different from other people's, or have been. I feel I am landed on my 45th year as if washed up on a rock ... Of course my external surroundings have changed, but inside I've been the same, trying to hold everything off in order to "write". Anyone wd think I was Tolstoy, the value I put on it' (*LM* 368). Larkin resisted marriage because it threatened the monastic solitude he thought crucial to creativity. Yet 'washed up on a rock' implies that resistance had psychological side effects. Thomas, in contrast, had to fight for creative solitude. In 1905, overwhelmed by reviewing, by 'days and nights full of writing and reading', he tells Bottomley that he yet persists in nursing 'my silly little deformed unpromising bantling of originality ... the one thing in my life that resembles a hope – a desire, I mean' (*LGB* 84–5). Yet he sometimes saw 'depression' and anxiety as inseparable from his creativity. One medical regime led him to wonder 'whether for a person like myself whose most profound moments were those of depression a cure that destroys the depression may not destroy the intensity – a *desperate* remedy?' (163). Thomas was more disturbed than Larkin in the sense that it took him so long to find his literary bearings, to realise what his own vocation was. In 1904 he told Bottomley: 'There is no form that suits me, & I doubt if I can make a new form' (57). For a decade more, his most 'original' writing would occur in prose books that centred on the English and Welsh countryside. Meanwhile he also produced literary-critical works, biographies, editions, anthologies. Despite being an influential critic of contemporary poetry, he always ruled out poetry as a possibility.

We associate Edward Thomas's poetry with Nature, but we should not associate it with naturalism. His early prose was influenced not only by the country books of Richard Jefferies but also by Walter Pater, who wrote the English gospel for the religion of art. Although Thomas subsequently published a book on Pater (1913), which reacted against his influence and attacked his style as remote from speech, he never lost what Pater calls 'the desire of beauty'. 'Desire' and 'beauty' are words that survive in Thomas's poetry. In *Feminine Influence on the Poets* (1910), a critical book with a terrible title, Thomas explores the psychology of the lyric poet. He proposes, for instance, that: 'It is a desire of impossible things which the poet alternately assuages and rouses again by poetry' (*LNB* 23). In 1945 Larkin is talking about himself when he seeks a friend who 'consciously accepts mystery at the bottom of things, a person who devotes themself to listening for this mystery – an artist – the kind of artist who is perpetually *kneeling* in his heart – who gives no fuck for anything except this mystery, and for that gives every fuck there is' (*SLL* 106). The distress-signals in both poets' letters often issue from the gulf between aesthetic desire and its fulfilment. Thomas goes on to say that a poet cannot 'sate' his desire by other means than poetry, and 'may turn his attempt inward upon himself' (*LNB* 23). All this raises chicken-and-egg questions. Does the original impulse to write lyric poetry betoken psychological complications that can be 'assuaged' by no other means? Do those complications verge on instability? Or is it the impulse itself, together with its frustration, that complicates or destabilises the psyche? Or, as Thomas's assuage/rouse (self-heal, self-harm) cycle implies, are both the case?

Larkin's review of *Edward Thomas: A Critical Biography* repeats the story of how a writer 'had an appointment in a London teashop with Edward Thomas, whom he did not know. On arrival he saw from the door the healthy, open-air Thomas sitting with an obvious and discontented-looking poet. Advancing to greet them, he discovered that the out-of-doors man was Ralph Hodgson: Edward Thomas was the other' (*RW* 188). Why does Larkin single out this episode? Perhaps it takes one – a poet with his own misleading image – to know one. Anthony Thwaite, Andrew Motion and others have now supplied a mass of materials that testify to Larkin's dark side, although perhaps we should just have read his poetry more closely. Larkin's letters (more than Thomas's) can make one feel a voyeur: their self-veilings as much as their apparent self-exposure. Yet, as with Thomas's out-doorsy image, Larkin the shy, witty librarian still obscures the neurotic who warns in 'If, My Darling' that the inside of his head contains 'a string of infected circles' and 'Delusions' that 'sicken inconclusively outwards' (*CPL* 41). In effect, opinion has unduly polarised between 'good' Larkin and 'bad', instead of engaging with the full psychological landscape symbolised by 'If, My Darling'. There was a surprising feelgood factor in some reviews of *Letters to Monica* (2010). Jonathan Bate thought that, had these letters then been available, the *Selected Letters* (1992) would have done less damage to Larkin's reputation: 'a much softer and more rounded picture . . . would have emerged' (*The Telegraph*, 17 October 2010). John Carey wrote: 'As always with Larkin there is an undertow of gloom . . . yet the total effect is exhilarating' (*The Sunday Times*, 17 October 2010). Nicholas Lezard later highlighted the letters' 'humanity, concern, tenderness' (*The Guardian*, 4 August 2011). Even Christopher Hitchens, while alert to pornographic subtexts and to Monica's 'possibly Aspergerish manners', approved 'a certain integrity and consistency' in the correspondence (*The Atlantic*, 2 April 2011). Certainly the letters are often tender, as well as perceptive and witty. But relief at the comparative absence of racist, fascist or misogynistic remarks (or remarks that seem so) may have distracted reviewers from symptoms of illness. For me, *Letters to Monica* is what Ted Hughes's *Birthday Letters* is not: the painful real deal. Larkin's lines about being 'fucked up' or 'One of those old-type *natural* fouled-up guys' are not only jokes (*CPL* 180, 170).

Letters to Monica and Thomas's letters to Gordon Bottomley are shaped by very different contexts. An obvious difference is that Monica belongs to the context, whereas Bottomley remains outside the situation that leads Thomas to confide in him about his mental state. Gordon Bottomley wrote verse drama as well as poems, and was later linked with Georgian poetry. In part, this friendship was just a literary friendship. They swapped views about books and writers. They gave each other creative and career advice. Bottomley corrected proofs of Thomas's works. Again, Bottomley was not Thomas's only confidant. He also shared his troubles with other friends like Walter de la Mare. Thomas begins a letter to de la Mare: 'I am glad to hear from you though it is all about me' (Kendall 133). In December 1912 he explained to Bottomley that he had been sparing him: 'I should have written except that my letters have been getting worse & worse. In fact, for 3 months I have been advertising my sorrows & decimating my friends . . . My habit of introspection & self contempt has at last broken my spirit' (*LGB* 226). Yet the fact that Thomas and Bottomley rarely met made their relationship at once special and epistolary. An invalid, living in what is now Cumbria, Bottomley suffered from lung haemorrhages, and his physical illness complemented Thomas's psychological problems. Thomas told Bottomley's wife Emily: 'It is a pity [Gordon] is not better fitted for the world & the world not better fitted for me' (218). Invalidism apart, Bottomley had the ideal writer's life: the peace and quiet that Thomas lacked. One way he helps is by keeping the possibility of such a life in view. Thomas signs off a letter: 'Oh Comforter, goodbye. It is in my mind today that you are alive & quite real & that – well, very few others are with whom I exchange talk & letters' (123).

In Thomas's letters to Bottomley, epistolary distance opens up space beyond day-to-day relationships. Their interchange does resemble that between patient and psychiatrist or counsellor or even priest: if Thomas calls Bottomley 'Comforter', Bottomley calls him 'Edward the Confessor'. Yet Thomas warns Bottomley that letters can prove slippery as diagnostic evidence: 'tho I am the Confessor, I can never confess everything to one man, even to you – I find I have unconsciously arranged my confessions according to the person & so each one of three or four . . . is frequently surprised and put on a wrong scent' (91). Larkin's letters to Monica Jones, however, are a worse minefield. In her own footnoted letters – perhaps they should be more than footnoted – Monica gives comfort but also needs it. And, while both poets may don epistolary veils or masks, Larkin is often a *consciously* dishonest confessor, as Monica's discovery of various flirtations and affairs proves. In this correspondence, distance is more ambiguous. On Larkin's side, it is, first, defensive or self-protective, allied with delay and denial. In place of the lover's usual belief that a letter is a bridge to the other's presence, but a poor substitute for it, Larkin sometimes represents the letter as a superior medium of communication – no doubt because he can control it. He says: 'I do to some extent seize up, automatically, when we meet' (*LM* 154). Monica herself says, perhaps having learned her lesson: 'I'd *like* to be able to talk more. I think I could have, when we began, perhaps' (305). Larkin does admit that his elaborate analyses of their relationship, in person and in letters, 'this almost-Russian verbiage', 'conceals I don't know what, probably nothing but funk' (155).

If verbiage also conceals infidelities, Larkin's 'Talking in Bed' exposes a deeper problem with 'talk'. In a poem set 'At this unique distance from isolation', at the opposite pole to epistolary distance, the speaker dwells on the difficulty of finding 'Words at once true and kind, / Or not untrue and not unkind' (*CPL* 129). 'This unique distance from isolation' is an extraordinary periphrasis. It's as if an infinite gap can never finally close. And if 'isolation' maximises the 'true' and 'kind' words at Larkin's disposal, 'talking in letters' logically becomes preferable. Perhaps he would have loved Facebook, precisely because it's not face-to-face. Viewed in this light, epistolary distance also protects Monica from mutual misery, from the 'unrest' figured by the poem's imagery of wind and cloud. At the same time, *Letters to Monica* hints that she may have received unkinder letters than those printed there. She writes: '[if] you don't like me enough to marry me; then it seems rather unkind for you to want to *tell* me so, & perhaps tell me the things that are wrong with me' (*LM* 306). Later, Larkin responds to an accusatory letter by insisting: 'I'm not so confident about telling the truth as you: not so sure I can, not so sure I want to. I cling to pretence like the bathing steps at the deep end. You . . . interpret [this] as deliberate and hostile deceit. It doesn't seem like that to me, more like making life livable . . . at least I claim credit for trying to be nice' (389).

Besides being mutually protective, distance paradoxically closes some of the gap. That is, letters often seem to be Larkin's best approximation to married intimacy and domesticity. Long letters – Monica wrote some very long ones – circumvent, if they do not resolve, the impasse that 'Talking in Bed' presents. For instance, when Larkin is sub-librarian at Queen's University Belfast in the early 1950s, he goes into great detail about a change of lodgings. This is at a time when Monica herself is moving house in Leicester, but there is no suggestion that their 'rooms' might ever merge – except as shared epistolary detail. Larkin writes: 'I do think of you and sympathise through every day. A new place is always disastrous. I've come to accept that as almost axiomatic . . . Such things strike at the very root of life, of daily living & peace of mind.' He involves her in his own new domestic arrangements, or lack of them. Thus he asks: 'what can I do with a Pyrex dish and top? Can I cook meat in it. It seems to get dry when I grill it. Why do my potatoes come to pieces? No, what I think you should do is send me a simple recipe every week suitable for an evening meal' (*LM* 63–4). Larkin sometimes provides almost minute-by-minute accounts of his 'daily living', as when he writes from Hull: 'Here am I, with nowhere to go & nothing to do. Outside the sun shines, the children shout . . . I'm lying on my bed. The room is airless. Oh my dear! My life is all wrong. I have to go out to awful people tonight . . . It would be such a beautiful day to be with you, and we're miles and miles apart' (168). Larkin's needs, not hers, call Monica up as a virtual presence in a shadowy vicarious epistolary marriage. He is significantly interested in another relationship which largely depended on, or resided in, letters: that between Katherine Mansfield and John Middleton Murry. By a curious and tactless transference, he sides with Mansfield (whose writing he admired) against Murry's 'playing up to her all-for-love two-children-holding-hands line of talk', while remaining 'quite content to live apart from her & indeed [finding] actual cohabitation with her a bit of a strain' (62). Eleven years later, however, he admits: 'I feel like Murry, always my *bête noire*, without your being KM.' This self-analysis occurs in a confessedly 'guilty' letter, where Larkin explains that what seems 'a brutal & gratuitous attack on you' derives from 'miserable self accusation' (305).

The *Selected Letters* made it clear that letters were more generally so important to Larkin as to be a surrogate mode of living: a way of living in writing. The speaker of 'At thirty-one, when some are rich' reflects that his 'letters to women' may be 'Stand-ins in each case simply for an act' (*CPL* 69). Larkin's letters are not just letters. Nor is getting letters just getting letters. In his introduction to the *Selected Letters*, Anthony Thwaite calls the reference to 'postmen' at the end of Larkin's poem 'Aubade' 'an image . . . of healing, of renewal, of . . . diurnal comfort' (*SLL* xi): 'Postmen like doctors go from house to house' – epistolary psychotherapy indeed (*CPL* 209). In Larkin's juvenilia letters are already a motif and metaphor. 'Letters unposted' mark the end of love (*EPJ* 58); 'memories' of love are compared to 'letters that arrive addressed to someone / Who left the house so many years ago' (54); 'the flicker of a letter' prompts an entire poem (134). Another poem aligns 'the broken edge of letters' with 'young unfinished days' as what cannot be joined 'to this Now' (191). For the young Larkin, epistolary distance is evidently Romantic distance – nostalgic, desirous – although, for Larkin, there will never be romance without distance: 'my Trouble is that I never like what I've got' (*SLL* 165). Unposted, unread or torn letters also figure a fragmented psyche. Hence 'The eyelessness of days without a letter' (*CPL* 69): 'eyelessness' disturbingly evokes someone lost in the dark. In an earlier poem the Larkin-speaker says: 'I await a letter's flop / To plait my ragged ends to formal shape' (*EPJ* 74). The idea that receiving a letter can turn neurosis into an artwork points to complications that only poetic formalising might truly assuage.

Thomas too needs epistolary comfort. Like Larkin, he complains about friends who don't write, and his correspondence with Bottomley constitutes a vicarious literary, as opposed to domestic, life. But, for Thomas, letters themselves hold less mystique. Indeed, given his constant exchanges with editors and publishers, their absence can be a relief. Yet the single allusion to letters in his poetry seems loaded with meaning. Written in June 1916, 'Early one morning' is an adapted folk song, which symbolises Thomas's likely departure to the Front:

Early one morning in May I set out,
And nobody I knew was about.
    I'm bound away for ever,
    Away somewhere, away for ever.

There was no wind to trouble the weathercocks.
I had burnt my letters and darned my socks . . . (*CPT* 126)

Thomas had indeed 'burnt his letters' – which is why we lack Bottomley's side of their correspondence. The trajectory of 'Early one morning' is ambiguous in that 'bound away' might signify bondage (to the war) as much as freedom, yet the poem is spoken in the folk-voice of a lover leaving an unhappy situation behind: 'I could not return from my liberty, / To my youth and my love and my misery.' Burning letters, which evokes burning boats or bridges, is linked with moving on from 'misery'. This suggests that, however uncertain the future, one kind of pain is now in the past, along with the need for epistolary psychotherapy.

A relevant parallel between Thomas and Larkin is that both had contact with psychoanalysis. Thomas was touched by the first wave of Freud's impact on England because, besides writing letters, he went from doctor to doctor; and because his problems were so serious that he came near to committing suicide on at least two occasions. In 1912 he received treatment from a doctor who was also a pioneering psychiatrist: the charismatic Godwin Baynes, who would later be Jung's most prominent English disciple. Baynes did help; Thomas tells Bottomley: '[He] is working magic with my disordered intellects' (*LGB* 221). He gave Thomas some perspective on his condition, and may have prompted autobiographical prose writings such as *The Childhood of Edward Thomas* (published posthumously in 1938), which, in a seeming psychic release, prepared the way for poetry. Thomas became disillusioned with Baynes, but their encounter lingers in his poetry. For instance, his narrative fable 'The Other' may be the first poetic outing for a modern version of the split self and the unconscious. Set between road and forest, the poem's inner landscape anticipates elements in Freud's essay on 'The Uncanny'. The protagonist pursues a rumoured double, with whom he also changes places 'To prove the likeness, and if true, / To watch until myself I knew' (*CPT* 40).

Larkin's interest in psychoanalysis, as a means to self-knowledge, appears in his letters to J. B. (Jim) Sutton during the 1940s. These letters amount to a consciously self-analytical portrait of the emergent artist. At Oxford, Larkin attended seminars given by the Jungian psychologist John Layard, and he told Sutton: 'I am psycho-analysing myself by means of dreams' (*SLL* 52). Despite writing a quatrain that rhymes Jung with 'dung' (*EPJ* 202), he talks of 'fuddling my head with psychology books' (*SLL* 144). These are also the years when Larkin was reading D. H. Lawrence 'like a bible' (19), and engaging with Lawrentian psychology. The self-analysis in his poems and letters is alert to psychoanalytical concepts such as denial, arrested development and primary narcissism: 'the frosted artificially sealed bivalve behaviour of my life ... psychic cripplehood'; '[a] monstrous infantile shell of egotism, inside which I quietly asphyxiate' (*LM* 23, 58). Larkin even suspects his own devotion to the poetic mystery: 'if I am not going to produce anything in the literary line, the justification for my selfish life is removed – but since I go on living it, the suspicion arises that the writing existed to produce the life, & not *vice versa*' (107). 'On Being Twenty-Six' ends:

I kiss, I clutch,

Like a daft mother putrid
    Infancy,
That can and will forbid
All grist to me

Except devaluing dichotomies:
  Nothing, and paradise. (*CPL* 25)

There are striking parallels between Thomas's and Larkin's epistolary self-analysis. Thomas asks: 'Why have I no energies like other men? I long for some hatred or indignation or even sharp despair, since love is impossible . . . Till then I must grind everything out, conscious at every moment what the result is & so always dissatisfied' (*LGB* 148). Larkin complains: 'My great trouble, as usual, is that I lack desires . . . In fact, I feel that the growing shoots of my character – though they must be more than shoots by now – had turned in on each other & were mutually neutralising each other' (*SLL* 152). Thomas writes of having 'attained a degree of self-consciousness beyond the dreams of avarice (which makes me spend the hours when I ought to be reading or enjoying the interlacing flight of 3 kestrels, in thinking out my motives for this or that act or word in the past until I long for sleep)' (*LGB* 129). Larkin writes: 'Lawrence wd describe me as all tangled up in the web of my self consciousness . . . & really if I could bring about some alteration in my mental state I think it would be for my self consciousness to be switched off. I don't mean any kind of shyness, but an inability to forget myself that quite inhibits any mental activity of the unconscious sort' (*SLL* 159). Inter alia such quotations (which could be multiplied) evince a similar sense that something is blocking the creative channel between the conscious mind and the unconscious. Larkin says: 'One might as soon expect rabbits to come out & play in some glade lit by the glare of headlights' (159). Larkin, of course, is writing, or trying to write, poetry; whereas Thomas doesn't even know he isn't. But this undiagnosed source of Thomas's trouble connects with Larkin's laments when not writing, or unable to complete, a poem. On one occasion he tells Monica, who has attempted to console him: 'I don't think you quite catch my meaning about what-is-the-matter. I agree I can keep out of jug & earn a living & enjoy myself – it's only writing, or not writing, that irritates me' (*LM* 109). He attributes his lack of creative impulse to 'something cold & heavy sitting on me somewhere' (his inner toad), adding: 'Will power can do nothing unless the impulse is there first' (107).

That again raises the chicken-and-egg riddle: does a psychological block cause writer's block or vice versa? Or are they interdependent? Certainly, Larkin and Thomas's case histories, as documented by their letters, strengthen the view that poetry has something to do with 'mystery' or at least the unconscious. Hence the disproportion between the volume of their 'writing' and the concentration of their lyric art: a mismatch which also strengthens the view that a poet is not quite the same thing as a 'writer'. There can be half-good novels or adequate prose, but if a poem falls short, it falls. Even one line may mar, if not fatally injure, as when Larkin's cheap shot at classical music spoils the ending of 'For Sidney Bechet': 'Scattering long-haired grief and scored pity' (*CPL* 83). Keith Douglas pointed out in 1940: 'The expression "bad poetry" is meaningless: critics still use it, forgetting that bad poetry is not poetry at all' (Douglas 123). Larkin's and Thomas's struggles with poet's – rather than writer's – block suggest that some peculiarly complex psycho-literary chemistry is required for a poem to come into its unpredictable being. If, as Larkin says, 'writing a poem is not an act of the will' (*RW* 84), 'intentionality' becomes an unfathomable (rather than theoretically irrelevant) concept. For Thomas: 'Anything, however small, may make a poem; nothing, however great, is certain to' (*LNB* 55). In the light of his poetry, Thomas's creative prose generally appears 'an act of the will': missing its true mark. It disguises the fact that he began with poet's block. By the same token, a problem with the publication of Larkin's letters, poetic juvenilia and poetic misfires, however fascinating, is that they might clutter the lyric core of his achievement. Mark Lawson once observed on BBC Radio 4's *Front Row* that Larkin was no longer just the author of a few slim volumes. But actually he is just that, and that's what matters. I should be the last person to object since I have extensively annotated Thomas's poetry, but the periphery can sometimes blur rather than clarify the core.

Did epistolary psychotherapy work for Thomas? It probably contributed to the fact that, by 1913, he had the analysis if not the cure. He told a new epistolary friend, Eleanor Farjeon:

> You see the central evil is self-consciousness carried as far beyond selfishness as selfishness is beyond self denial . . . and now amounting to a disease, and all I have to fight it with is the knowledge that in truth I am not the isolated selfconsidering brain which I have come to seem – the *knowledge* that I am something more, but not the belief that I can reopen the connection between the brain and the rest. (Farjeon 13)

Yet eighteen months later, Thomas wrote his first poem: the connection had been reopened or opened in a different way. Clearly, two external factors were crucial: the Great War (including the way in which it mobilised his devotion to the English countryside and English literature), and meeting – and reading – Robert Frost. The literary-historical moment coincided with the historical moment. Thomas's alertness to contemporary poetry meant that he was ready for Frost. His poem 'There was a time' dwells on the paradox that his enlistment has somehow been curative, but implies that poetry, 'melody', has come to the rescue too:

> There was a time when this poor frame was whole
> And I had youth and never another care,
> Or none that should have troubled a strong soul.
> Yet, except sometimes in a frosty air
> When my heels hammered out a melody
> From pavements of a city left behind,
> I never would acknowledge my own glee
> Because it was less mighty than my mind
> Had dreamed of . . . (*CPT* 128)

Part of the paradox is that Thomas does not invoke the war as fulfilling a patriotic urge (other poems manifest his unique version of patriotism). He has volunteered on behalf of an impersonal force that 'would neither ask nor heed his death'. 'There was a time' includes a retrospect on epistolary psychotherapy: 'weakness was all my boast. / I sought yet hated pity till at length / I earned it.' In having seen 'weakness' as the only alternative to being 'a strong soul', Thomas parallels Larkin's binary sense of entrapment between 'devaluing dichotomies: / Nothing, and paradise'. The source of the parallel may again be aesthetic desire: reluctance to settle for less than full intensity.

Internal factors shaped Thomas's soul-change too. The direction of his criticism and the nature and quality of his autobiographical prose suggest that some inner evolution began before 1914, also the key year of his friendship with Frost. He wrote to Bottomley, two months after the bad period signalled in his letter to Farjeon: 'I will not be such a nuisance again just yet, as I am at last realising I had better fight my battles instead of sending out lists of the opposing forces' (LGB 230). Here again, recovery figures as becoming less dependent on letters, written or received. Yet Larkin is inaccurate in calling Thomas's poetry 'a serene and unquestionable climax' – 'unquestionable', perhaps, but scarcely 'serene'. In many ways his poems retread the psychological ground covered by his letters, while war remains an ambiguous Muse. Yet writing poetry (as Larkin does perceive) was his conclusive therapy or concluded the need for therapy. Thomas's most important letters, from 1914 to his death, are his letters to Frost. There are one or two depressive relapses and some neediness when Frost fails to write. But their interchange, if shadowed by war, pivots on poetry.

In Larkin's case, poetry could not come to the rescue since it had been there, or should have been there, all along. Indeed, his letters register its diminishing returns in a double sense. In 1975 he tells the novelist Barbara Pym that 'the notion of expressing sentiments in short lines having similar sounds at their ends seems as remote as mangoes on the moon' (SLL 521). Two epistolary poems from the early 1980s, which address fellow-poets on public occasions, allude to the difficulty of writing a poem as you get older. Larkin represents himself to Gavin Ewart as 'attic'd with all-too-familiar / Teachers of truth-sodden grief' and as scrapping bad (or non) poems (CPL 216). He hails Charles Causley: 'Dear CHARLES, My Muse, asleep or dead, / Offers this doggerel instead' (217). This implies that a verse letter is no lyric: the worst of both worlds, perhaps. Meanwhile correspondence with Monica had dwindled by 1972, partly because they seem to have discovered the telephone, partly because Larkin was visiting Leicester more often since his mother was in a nursing home there. Monica herself became ill and, during the last few years before Larkin's death (1985), they settled into something like married life in Hull. This cannot really be called a choice. Monica then barely left the house until her own death in 2001. Such an ending, which also involved much alcohol, was the disastrous outcome that Larkin's letters forebode: 'I fear we are to turn slowly into living reproaches of the way I have dallied and lingered with you, neither one thing or the other' (LM 303).

A difference between Thomas and Larkin is that Thomas's psychic health fluctuates, whereas Larkin's letters record some irrevocable stalemate, rigidity, paralysis, trap, fate: 'You can look out of your life like a train & see what you're heading for, but you can't stop the train' (379). He tells Monica: 'My nature, perhaps, is rather like a spring – it can be stretched out straight, but when released leaps back into a coil' (41). It seems predetermined that there should be no middle way, no 'grist', between 'Nothing, and paradise'. He says: 'Every now & then I open the little trap door in my head & look in to see if the hideous roaring panic & misery has died down. It hasn't, and I don't see why it should' (317). Larkin's letters never speak of 'fighting battles'. Therapy seems to stop at 'verbiage' or diagnosis: 'Ends in themselves my letters plot no change' (CPL 69). Perhaps that distinguishes them from poems: the ending of 'The Trees' plots change as rhythm, not just as exhortation: 'Begin afresh, afresh, afresh' (166). Since Larkin lets no doctor invade the shell of his ego, self-diagnosis morphs into addictive self-medication, letter writing being one of the habits that 'make life livable' rather than lived. Thomas's analytical self-images are usually less deterministic. Perhaps contingency played a larger part in his illness, whereas Larkin refers to 'violence / A long way back' (215). Similarly, while Thomas's letters repeat themselves, they are not the loop-tape that Letters to Monica becomes – sometimes consciously so: 'I suppose one shouldn't be writing letters like this at 44' (LM 365). Perhaps Larkin needed a war.

Larkin also, of course, wrote diaries, burnt, at his request, after his death. He panics when he is ill in hospital and thinks that Monica may find in his flat material written 'partly to relieve my feelings'. He fears 'exposing [her] to the embarrassment & no doubt even pain' of reading it (279). The burnt diaries provide a vista in which Larkin's textual self-expressions become a murky receding palimpsest. Logically, diaries, letters and poems (as Dickinsonian 'letters to the world') should fall into some kind of sequence as regards implied audience: oneself, self and other, whatever readers are out there – although a poem might have all three audiences in mind. Yet some writers' diaries and letters wink at posterity, especially in this archive- and reputation-conscious age. John Crace's Guardian 'Digested Read' satirised Here and Now (2013), literary letters between Paul Auster and J. M. Coetzee: 'Dear Paul, I have been thinking about the way in which so many novelists have been cashing in by writing letters to one another which are then later published in book form' (The Guardian, 26 May 2013). As Crace indicates, self-consciousness is the giveaway, the absence of warts and all. Admittedly, even the most private diary or letter may be more performative, less transparent, than it appears: witness Thomas's recognition that he has 'unconsciously arranged [his] confessions according to the person'. But arranging confessions for posterity – as a pre-emption of posterity – is a different matter. Larkin's diaries certainly seem to have been for his eyes only, although he is less worried about his letters when a Larkin archive is mooted for Hull. Yet he would hardly have expected intimate letters to be made available, and he tells Anthony Thwaite (the editor who would make them so): 'if you want to flog your letters, name yr price. There will then be an inexplicable fire . . . I don't reckon I will let them have much' (SLL 497). Contrariwise, some poems are destined for drawers, and Thomas conceived all lyric poetry as not written 'for the public' but 'in a sense unintentionally overheard' (LNB 22). We may be on firmer ground if we assume a progressive sequence as regards complexity of 'talk', the degree of 'formal shape'. Larkin gives the impression that his diaries are abusive rants, that they involve pornography and rawly violent emotion. But if he and Thomas turn the matter of their letters into poetic psychodrama, what makes it poetry? Why should we wish to 'overhear'?

Thomas's poem 'Beauty' contains motifs that recur in his letters: exhaustion, irritability, depression; bad behaviour towards his wife and children; suicidal thoughts. In one letter he tells Bottomley: 'An east wind or a wind from underground has swept over everything. Friends, Nature, books are like London pavements when an east wind has made them dry & harsh & pitiless. There is no joy in them . . . I have no idea what it means, but I crawl along on the very edge of life, wondering why I don't get over the edge' (*LGB* 180). In another letter he regrets that he cannot respond to 'a beautiful still evening', and says: 'So I am writing to you, which . . . simply clarifies my introspection a little but will not – I know well – lead it anywhere' (130). The poem does more than 'clarify . . . introspection'. It leads somewhere. It represents something leading somewhere. In fact, it may comment on the difference between epistolary psychotherapy and poetry:

> What does it mean? Tired, angry, and ill at ease,
> No man, woman, or child alive could please
> Me now. And yet I almost dare to laugh
> Because I sit and frame an epitaph –
> 'Here lies all that no-one loved of him
> And that loved no one.' Then in a trice that whim
> Has wearied. But, though I am like a river
> At fall of evening while it seems that never
> Has the sun lighted it or warmed it, while
> Cross breezes cut the surface to a file,
> This heart, some fraction of me, happily
> Floats through the window even now to a tree
> Down in the misting, dim-lit, quiet vale,
> Not like a pewit that returns to wail
> For something it has lost, but like a dove
> That slants unswerving to its home and love.
> There I find my rest, and through the dusk air
> Flies what yet lives in me. Beauty is there. (*CPT* 58)

'Beauty' does not so much repeat as concentrate epistolary motifs. The difference between Thomas's letters and his poem is that between the 'wailing' pewit and the dove that 'slants unswerving'. As a definition of poetry, this recalls Dickinson's 'tell it slant'. The first part of the poem, where exaggerated speech rhythms dramatise a series of moods, is a composite, epitomised by the 'epitaph', of how Thomas has previously 'framed' his alienation from self and world. Then this portrait is further concentrated into imagery: the cold river, the file. In Thomas's poetry, the analysis conveyed by such images goes deeper as they take on a richer sensory life. Here analysis also seems to yield results. Self-division continues, but in more positive form: 'This heart, some fraction of me', 'what yet lives in me'. And what survives is, crucially, indexed to the aesthetic impulse: 'Beauty is there.' Or poetry has come to the rescue. It's ambiguous as to whether 'beauty' is interior or exterior: tree or poem. In any case, 'Beauty is there' reflexively coincides with the poem ending. And perhaps we can feel the therapeutic force of 'beauty', of reading as well as writing poetry, if we attend to the rhythm and imagery of recovery that build in the last eight lines.

The speaker of a lyric poem, the lyric 'I', can be at once patient and therapist in ways that implicate the reader. In 'Beauty', drama, imagery and rhythm objectify the 'self' until it connects with our selves. The poem activates psychic bio-rhythms which are not just particular to Thomas. That also applies to Larkin's 'Wants'. It might be said that, as Larkin's Muse recedes, a reverse development occurs: psycho-analytical language, epistolary language, prosaic language, resurfaces and weakens the poetry. This is true of a late poem with an unsubtle title: 'The Life with a Hole in it'. Here Larkin defines 'life' as immobilised, 'locked' and 'Blocked' by a 'Three-handed struggle between / Your wants, the world's for you' and predetermination as death (CPL 202). The 'wants' of the earlier poem, less narrowly Larkin's own, sym-bolise possible dark truths about human nature in existential rather than abstract terms. The refrain lines that enclose each of the two five-line stanzas are 'Beyond all this, the wish to be alone' and 'Beneath it all, desire of oblivion runs'. 'Wants' again concentrates (or anticipates) motifs from letters: 'the wish to be alone', sex and marriage, death-fear, death-wish. Larkin figures society's demands as text and image: 'invitation-cards', the family 'photographed under the flagstaff', 'the artful tensions of the calendar' (42). This may imply that poetry, with its own more 'artful' tensions, can see 'beyond' and 'beneath' such inscriptions or prescriptions – including letters. And rhythm, as well as use of the first-person plural, once again draws the reader in. The refrain lines, with their key-change, are powerfully and disturbingly seductive. They prove, as prose cannot do, the psychological point and give it universal weight.

Writing to Jim Sutton, Larkin calls a poem 'the crossroads of my feelings, my imaginings, my wishes, & my verbal sense' (SLL 173). This is an image for the lyric's complex chemistry. Perhaps comparing letters and poems as psychological events, as psychoanalysis or psychotherapy, tells us something about the difference between the poetic crossroads and the two-way – sometimes one-way – epistolary street.

ABBREVIATIONS OF MAIN WORKS CITED

CPL: Anthony Thwaite (ed.), *Philip Larkin: Collected Poems* (London: The Marvell Press/Faber and Faber, 1988).

CPT: Edna Longley (ed.), *Edward Thomas: The Annotated Collected Poems* (Tarset: Bloodaxe, 2008).

EPJ: A. T. Tolley (ed.), *Philip Larkin: Early Poems and Juvenilia* (London: Faber and Faber, 2005).

LGB: R. George Thomas (ed.), *Letters from Edward Thomas to Gordon Bottomley* (London: Oxford University Press, 1968).

LM: Anthony Thwaite (ed.), *Philip Larkin: Letters to Monica* (London: Faber and Faber, 2010).

LNB: Edna Longley (ed.), *A Language Not to be Betrayed: Selected Prose of Edward Thomas* (Manchester: Carcanet, 1981).

RW: Philip Larkin, *Required Writing: Miscellaneous Pieces 1955–1982* (London: Faber and Faber, 1983).

SLL: Anthony Thwaite (ed.), *Selected Letters of Philip Larkin* (London: Faber and Faber, 1992).

SLT: R. George Thomas (ed.), *Edward Thomas: Selected Letters* (Oxford: Oxford University Press, 1995).

OTHER WORKS

Bate, Jonathan, 'Review', *The Telegraph*, 17 October 2010.

Carey, John, '*Letters to Monica* by Philip Larkin', *The Sunday Times*, 17 October 2010.

Crace, John, '*Here and Now: Letters by Paul Auster & JM Coetzee* – digested read', *The Guardian*, 26 May 2013.

Douglas, Keith, *Collected Poems* (Oxford: Oxford University Press, 1978).

Farjeon, Eleanor, *Edward Thomas: The Last Four Years* (Oxford: Oxford University Press, 1958).

Hitchens, Christopher, 'Philip Larkin, the Impossible Man', *The Atlantic*, 2 April 2011.

Kendall, Judy (ed.), *Poet to Poet: Edward Thomas's Letters to Walter de la Mare* (Bridgend: Seren, 2012).

Lezard, Nicholas, 'Love, in other words', *The Guardian*, 4 August 2011.

Yeats, W. B., *Autobiographies* (London: Macmillan, 1955).

12   Lorine Niedecker's Republic of Letters

Siobhan Phillips

I

'As a Gray wrote Increase Lapham: / pay particular attention / to my pets, the grasses' (Niedecker 105). The three-line poem from *New Goose*, Lorine Niedecker's 1946 volume, is characteristic of its author because of its source as well as its style. From first to last, Niedecker's work takes material and inspiration from correspondence. This small poem quoting letter writers, published early in her career, looks ahead to multi-paged poems quoting letter writers collected in her last book. Her work moves from letter-indebted poems like 'Asa Gray . . .' or 'van Gogh' in the 1940s through the letter-indebted poems of *For Paul* in the 1950s to the letter-indebted poems like 'His Carpets Flowered' or 'Thomas Jefferson' in the 1960s. Indeed, the last lines in her final manuscript, *Harpsichord & Salt Fish*, quote a letter from Charles Darwin to the same Asa Gray of her earlier poem (299). Her own letters, meanwhile, prove her interest in these writings – she records her love for 'calm, timid-looking Darwin', for example, and her worry that her poem about him is 'good but not as deft as the Jefferson' (Niedecker and Corman 227, 231). To Niedecker, letters were a vital form to both read and write.

   This form promotes philosophical paradoxes that Niedecker recognised. Letters manifest a kind of interaction that may be as important as – or even more important than – the information transmitted. A letter's necessary recognition of an audience makes this interaction public, in contrast to other kinds of writing – like diary or lyric – traditionally taken to indite an internal conversation. Yet a letter's necessary recognition of particular others keeps this interaction private, in contrast to other kinds of writing – like essay or novel – often presuming a general readership.[1] Letters thus show the symbiosis of the private and the public roles, proving them neither distinct nor synonymous. Over the course of her career, Niedecker wrestled with the difficulties of this combination. They were especially pressing for a writer of her era, beginning her work in the shadow of a modernist movement which emphasised the public/private divide, and for a writer of her gender, developing her work on the borders of patriarchal family structures which emphasised the same division. Through her work with these challenges, Niedecker's work mines a feminist promise inherent to epistolary culture. Her late work, then, is hardly as historical as it seems. When her last poems take up the letters of eighteenth-century politicians, Niedecker finds a culmination to the questions that guided her own life as a twentieth-century writer.

Criticism has not yet described adequately the epistolary theory latent in Niedecker's work. More often, citations from her letters contribute to a biographical narrative proving the difficult circumstances that her writing overcame. These circumstances were legion.[2] She lived on the flood-threatened spit of land called Blackhawk Island, a finger pointing into Lake Koshkonog, Wisconsin, where family property seemed to augment rather than diminish her insecurity. Finances forced her to leave Beloit College before graduating and may have prompted a brief, bewildering marriage to a nearby farmer in the 1930s. Niedecker worked on the Federal Writers' Project in Madison, found odd jobs typing and editing, and scrubbed floors at a hospital – to which she walked, daily, starting at five in the morning. Her correspondence narrates efforts to install plumbing, attempts to patch holes in the walls, difficulties with failing eyesight, anxiety about taxes. She describes mixing buckwheat pancakes on a winter night and setting 'the yeasty batter to rise over night on top shelf of my bookshelves', since 'on the floor it would turn to ice' (Penberthy 175). Or pulling up her waterlogged carpet, 'soaked and gooey and weighing a ton', after a bout of high water (251).

Emotional struggles compounded these practical ones. It would be difficult to overestimate how alone Niedecker was – mentally as well as physically. She had little immediate company on Blackhawk Island, littler still that provided intellectual sustenance, and few readers in any location. Letters provided what collegiality she could find. When she writes, in one, that she was 'thinking of living' in her large mailbox, the joke has metaphorical resonance (Peters 92). Her house was most important as a space to send and receive mail, and her real 'living' lay in the exchanges with far-away others. Most important was her exchange with Louis Zukofsky, who provided Niedecker with a trusted, admired champion of her work. Zukofsky's epistolary company could be as difficult as it was sustaining, however. The two met after Niedecker wrote a letter in response to the 1931 issue of *Poetry* that Zukofsky edited, and their correspondence soon led to her visiting him in New York. While Niedecker hoped for a romantic relationship, and may have became pregnant with Zukofsky's child, Zukofsky insisted that she return to Wisconsin and may have directed her to abort the baby.[3] Their correspondence continued for more than thirty years after, through Zukofsky's marriage to another woman and through the early life of his only son. Niedecker's acceptance of these conditions shows how much the letters meant to her. Her admiration of Zukofsky as a writer, and her affection for Zukofsky as a person, compounded her sheer need for another writer to read her work and another person to share her experience.

These biographical details contribute to a sense of rescue in the steadily growing discussion of Niedecker in general and Niedecker's letters in particular. Her exchange with Zukofsky, replete with deference to his thwarted egoism, makes any belated recognition of Niedecker feel like righting an injustice. Compounding this sense is the fact that Niedecker tried and failed to turn her correspondence with Zukofsky into two books: a collection of letter excerpts, culled from his writing to her and designed to honour his greatness, as well as a series of poems, based on details from letters to her and dedicated to his son. Zukofsky's suspicion of both projects doomed them to remain unpublished – a scenario all too typical to scholars like Jenny Penberthy, who regrets how this more famous male author overshadows his less famous female peer, or to Marjorie Perloff, who writes of the 'profound pathos' in *For Paul* (Penberthy 3; Perloff 160). Penberthy's invaluable editing efforts, which have provided an authoritative *Collected Works* and a record of the Niedecker-Zukofsky correspondence, aim to restore Niedecker's voice, exposing to a wider audience work that was for too long confined to just a few.

To credit these letters adequately, however, requires a reading of their contribution to Niedecker's style and philosophy as well. If letters helped Niedecker turn poems into a 'communicative, intersubjective art' (Penberthy 59), they also made such art into an original social vision. Explorations of Niedecker's letter-indebted work can revise descriptions of that vision, countering the suspicion that Niedecker turned away from politics in the 1960s, after her more pointed 1930s activism (Peters 187), or the assumption that her attention to the letters of great men in history could have no bearing on her contributions to progressive feminism.[4] Niedecker's final volume not only emphasises her steady investigation of the letter form, but clarifies the stakes of that investigation: a confrontation, ultimately a feminist confrontation, with the question of public and private.

II

That question was often manifest in the division of artist and person. To read the personal letters of noteworthy men and women is to blur the boundary between a professional figure and a human individual, and Niedecker seems to have relished this fact in her avid reading of collected letters – her library included correspondence of Byron, Jane Carlyle, Dickinson, Flaubert, Freud, James, Kafka, Lawrence, Millay, Pound, Santayana, Stevens and Woolf, as well as a collection of *The World's Greatest Letters*; her poetry uses correspondence from van Gogh, Henry James, Mary Shelley, Darwin and Audubon, as well as Gray, Lapham, Adams and Jefferson.[5] In a 1969 letter to Cid Corman, she clarifies one reason she prized these materials; while she 'can't read' Morris's poems, she values him 'as a man, as a poet speaking to his daughters and his wife – o lovely' (Niedecker and Corman 187). Niedecker can overlook the 'flowery designs' that are anathema to her own spare writing when she discovers an author 'speaking' to members of his family. Niedecker values letters for the connection they dramatise more than the content they cover or even the style they support.

It makes sense, then, that she wished to present the same 'loveliness' when she collected Zukofsky's letters to her, which she began to do in the 1960s. This proposed book could show her favourite writer, like Morris, 'as a man, as a poet'. While the project capitalised on Niedecker's epistolary interests, however, it also focused opposition to them. Zukofsky's response suspects the conflation (man, poet) in Niedecker's comma. Whereas Niedecker believes that Zukofsky's letters to her are 'something he wrote not just for me but the world', Zukofsky distrusts the elision of specific and universal audiences (Niedecker and Corman 73). As Niedecker's misgivings indicate, the only collection of letters Zukofsky might countenance would be one that treated only public material, however that was defined. Niedecker tries to adhere to his principles, destroying 'the parts of the letters that [Zukofsky] wouldn't want the public to see' (Niedecker and Corman 59). But Niedecker was rueful about such cuts, since they excised what she valued. She is 'not above a word or two that brings in the *human*'; to her, these words are not 'gossip' or 'biography' – equally suspect to Zukofsky – but 'chunks of beautiful literature' (73).

Literature versus gossip, art versus personality: this debate, of course, touches on a key tenet of modernist aesthetics. It shows, therefore, the reliance of such aesthetics on a public/private split. Often, modernism would keep art safely public: new-critical description, after all, sees art as 'an object of public knowledge' – dividing the timelessly available product from the situated details of its production (Wimsatt and Beardsley 470). When Wimsatt and Beardsley made such descriptions normative, in a 1946 essay, they hardened into critical dogma Eliot's 1919 questions about 'escape from personality' and Yeats's 1937 distinction between the artistic speaker and 'someone at the breakfast table' (Eliot 73; Yeats 509). Lyric was the exemplum, since a poem was defined precisely in its detachment from contextual specificities (Keats's well-wrought urn, self-sufficiently atemporal). And letters were a stumbling block, since correspondence could not be so detached (Keats's theory of beauty, written to a friend).[6] Zukofsky, a good modernist in this respect, worked to overcome that epistolary condition when reading others' correspondence, forgetting 'all but the impersonal detail', as he made sure to stipulate in a 1971 talk (*Prepositions* 28). Zukofsky used the same standard when editing his own letters or Niedecker's letters to him.

Zukofsky's editing of Niedecker's words demonstrates an arrogation of single-person authority as well as an assumption of impersonal standards. This is the second way in which modernist aesthetics relies on public/private divisions. In this, however, modernist theory makes art private – private property. Indeed, endorsement of impersonality, in modernist theory, co-existed with a concern for ownership.[7] This was marked in Ezra Pound, for example, who drew up a detailed proposal for perpetual copyright in 1918.[8] Zukofsky, again, was a good modernist on this issue, not to mention a good follower of his mentor Pound, since he was steadily concerned with control of his work. He would produce just enough copies, for example, to secure copyright for a limited printing, and refuse other publishing opportunities because of copyright concerns (Scroggins 174, 320, 352). Letters elude such control, since the dynamics of correspondent dialogue make it difficult to separate one party's contribution from another's, and the facts of correspondent material also make it difficult to separate one party's holdings from another's. Zukofsky took care to overcome this obstacle, however, demanding that Niedecker return to him even the paper record of her work on his correspondence. 'LZ writes I must send him my carbon of letters, insists on it,' she reports to Corman (Niedecker and Corman 74).

Archives now reify such insistence, since records of Niedecker's and Zukofsky's exchange, including manuscripts of Niedecker's poetry she sent to Zukofsky, are currently housed at the Zukofsky Archive of the Harry Ransom Center. Labelled and preserved under a single name, the repository promotes what Libbie Rifkin calls the '(self) objectification' of a modernist artist during the institution-building of postmodernism (103). Rifkin's phrase nicely indicates both impersonality and ownership, proprietorship of personal identity and estrangement from personal details.[9] But in this sense the archive, like the larger project of academic institutionalisation of which it is part, does not preserve so much as create the ideals of modernist aesthetics. Materials *in* the archive, by contrast, challenge an account of the artist as an impersonal or an individual creator, and do so through letters in particular – not just the correspondence of Zukofsky with Niedecker, but also his exchanges with Pound, Robert Creeley, Robert Duncan, Cid Corman and William Carlos Williams. The last could have been talking about the effect of letters when he wrote to Zukofsky that '[y]ou are best when you talk to the small circle' rather than 'a vaguer public' (Zukofsky and Williams 442). Niedecker would agree. The question of epistolary public troubles the course of Niedecker's career specifically as well as the legacy of modernism generally.

III

Niedecker worked consistently to make the 'small circle' of correspondence coincide with the 'vaguer public' of poetry. For her, such coincidence was a political as much as an aesthetic preference. So much is clear in her poems of the 1930s and 1940s – the era of Niedecker's Writers' Project work and of her most explicit involvement with the Communist Party. Letters help her to practise art as a noncommercial exchange among specific, connected persons. 'Audubon', for example, begins with the speaker unable to sell his work and troubled by debts (Niedecker 107–8). '[M]ust I migrate back / to the woods unknown,' he asks, 'strange / to all but the birds / I paint?' A final stanza implicitly answers the question in the negative by making it clear to whom he is writing:

> Dear Lucy, the servants here
> move quiet
> as killdeer.

Here is another nineteenth-century artist and man speaking, like Morris, to a woman in his family. Audubon turns to his wife, after inability to find buyers, as if to remind himself of his standing with a more intimate and less commercial public. A proof of endearment as well as a protocol of epistolary address, 'Dear Lucy' assuages his anxieties as a failed professional in a foreign country. The answer does not retreat from professionalism, however, so much as shift its grounds, since Audubon's comparison to killdeer proves his authority as a naturalist *through* his affections as a husband – much as Asa Gray and Increase Lapham, in the Niedecker poem already quoted, proved a similar authority through their friendship for each other. 'Audubon' goes further than 'Gray', moreover, in that final verse, where the speaker's call to Lucy implies mutual solidarity with overlooked servants. Audubon's acceptance of familiar relationship, in response to the frustrations of market exchange, also empathises with unfamiliar others disempowered by the same economics.

Poems of *New Goose* follow the epistolary lessons of work like 'Asa Gray', judging large-scale abstractions of laws and markets by the small-scale particularities they produce or magnify – while demonstrating how small-scale interactions could revise the inadequacies of large-scale processes. The opening of a *New Goose* manuscript, for example, presents a letter-poem '[t]o a Maryland editor' that describes how '[t]he enclosed poems are sepa / rated by stars to save paper' – stars that '"we couldn't get away / with . . . down here . . . on the brow / of Washington"' (Niedecker 110). Ad hoc economising takes on deeper import when it suggests the humbly sized works that follow constitute a national identity. These poems are 'rated' not by commercial viability but by their patriotic 'stars' – American stars, meant for the capital. Niedecker can venture that suggestion, however, only through epistolary mutuality. The 'we' in her phrase about Washington, presumably a quotation from her addressee, means that her own *Goose* poems become '*your* night's / folk-tongue' (emphasis added). Niedecker sidesteps the traditional relationships of publishing, in which an editor serves as a buyer and conduit to a general audience, for the more intimate relationships of correspondence, in which an editor serves as a co-creator and participant in a particular conversation. But she shows that very intimacy, paradoxically, to affirm the poem's potential as a national document. In this modernist writing, letters turn private messages into public practices – and vice versa.

The result tumbles together different voices in a mosaic of familiarities: not just the Niedecker-like speaker accosting the reader, as if an old friend, with 'Remember my little granite pail?', but also a 'sharecropper' making his meagre living, the wife speaking of '[m]y man', the worker with a debilitating illness and a cold stove (Niedecker 96, 98, 97, 96). In Niedecker's poetics, voices from her reading mingle with voices from her experience, all speaking in the first person directly to the reader: General Rodimstev's story of endurance, van Gogh's report of creativity and hunger, Black Hawk's argument against land ownership (104, 108, 99). If Niedecker's epistolary poetics works to prove that '[p]oems are for one person to another', as she wrote later in a summary of her beliefs, her poems also work to multiply the instances and varieties of that one-on-one conversation (Niedecker and Corman 121). A letter's privacy-in-public means a public of many privacies. The result not only expands the reach of the 'folk' setting in Niedecker's *New Goose* but also levels the hierarchies among the folk included – a great painter finding inspiration at the beach, say, and an anonymous speaker in an old coat on 'Capital Hill'. *New Goose* promotes the socialism of Niedecker's politics through poetic style as well as poetic content.

When Niedecker's late work ventriloquises the correspondent voices of Jefferson and Adams, she remembers the goals of this earlier work, emphasising the egalitarian intimacy in a specifically American polity. Indeed, Niedecker would already have connected Jefferson to letters through her perusal of Zukofsky's poetry: the

1930s sections of 'A' use Jefferson's and Adams's writings in Zukofsky's own medita-
tion on Marxist politics and American history.[10] The import of Zukofsky's 1930s
letter-quotation, however, differs from that of Niedecker's, prompted more by
anxiety about democratic mass culture than by appreciation for democratic mass
intimacy. In this, Zukofsky follows not only Pound, who took up Jefferson and
Adams as models of political and economic policy in the *Cantos*, but also Henry
Adams, who wrote a history of Jefferson's administration as well as a bitter novel
called *Democracy* and a late account of *The Degradation of the Democratic Dogma*.
Zukofsky worries about the 'levelling' inherent to that degradation ('A' 73). This
is a personal problem, for a neglected artist like Zukofsky or Adams, as much as a
political one. '[V]ain / To expect proper appreciation in this world,' Zukofsky quotes
elsewhere from a letter of Adams ('A' 78).

The constriction of smaller audiences, then, could be a retreat from the indifference of the public sphere rather than a reformation or reimagination of its workings.
By the end of 'A'-12, Zukofsky cites Jefferson's 1793 letter to Madison that despises
'the tumult of the world' and prefers 'happiness in the lap and love of my family
. . . owing account to myself alone of my hours & actions' ('A' 247; Jefferson and
Madison 781). Such 'accounts' constrict economics to the household at its root,
subsuming that happy household into a self-sufficient, withdrawn 'myself'. In the
latter half of 'A', Zukofsky's own household underwent a similar subsuming in order
to serve as a similar refuge.[11] In her own poems, Niedecker tried to follow.

IV

She did so through the particular focus of Zukofsky's familial poetry: his son. Indeed,
the Jefferson quotation above comes in 'A' after a reference to 'Paul's first cursive'.
Beginning in the 1940s, Niedecker strove to use the same material, crafting details
from Zukofsky's letters about his child into poems that she sent back to the father.
The result, a manuscript titled *For Paul* that went unpublished in its intended form
during her lifetime, makes Niedecker a figure within Zukofsky family life by asserting
her rights as an artist of that existence. She versifies a description of evening rituals
in the Zukofsky household, for example, with a poem beginning 'Ten o'clock /
and Paul's not in bed!', envisioning what Zukofsky's letter had told her about 'the
family / around the bathroom tap' (Niedecker 151). When Zukofsky applies for a
Guggenheim, Niedecker even proposes to him that she should perhaps 'apply for
Gugg. too – we three could repair (with that little main spring of our lives, Paul)
to a Guggenheimer island in the Pacific for awhile' (Penberthy 167). The dream's
comparison of parental roles and poetic ambition repeats the underlying impetus of
For Paul. This book brings Niedecker's epistolary engagements closest to her poetic
investments by conflating a private relationship with a professional ambition.

But the failure of *For Paul* reveals problems in such conflation. As Niedecker's
dream account might already know, with its wistful note of impossibility, Louis and
Celia Zukofsky are a couple, not a trio. Their offspring literalises the creativity that
they have undertaken as a pair. By the end of her *For Paul* sequence, Niedecker

seems to recognise as much: 'Violin Debut' recognises what 'two who sent the flow thru him have done' (Niedecker 161). The 'twoness' of parental production, in this 'flow' of artistry, does not include the 'three' of friendly collegiality. The 'twoness' of procreation may not even acknowledge its *offspring* as a distinct party: a dash, in Niedecker's final stanza, conflates 'what he's done with his life' with what 'the two . . . have done'. For Paul to be 'true to himself', in this poem, is for Paul to be 'a knife / behaved' – the last word, alone on a final line, conflating artistic discipline with obedience to parental prescriptions. And parental prescriptions seem to be fatherly prescriptions above all. In the book's penultimate poem, Niedecker describes how 'my cutting friends' concise art . . . exacts their violinist son / to make it come clean-sung' (160). Here, Zukofsky's standards direct the wife's and son's achievement, his 'cutting' concision Paul's well-behaved 'knife'. The creativity of the couple, then, is ultimately patriarchal; the boundaries of the heteronormative family forbid any outsider who would challenge the creative rule of the father.

Indeed, Niedecker recognises, in *For Paul*, how family life and family creativity are subject to Zukofsky's strict definitions of private life and private property. 'They live a cool distance,' Niedecker begins her poem, noting their remove from the world beyond. While Zukofsky did use facets of his family life in his writing – Niedecker's poem beginning 'Oh ivy green', for example, remembers a poem from Paul that also appears in 'A'-20 (Niedecker 159; Zukofsky 'A' 436) – these published details, like the public debut that ends *For Paul*, appear under Zukofsky's control. Indeed, the 'cutting friend' to whom Niedecker sent this poem asked her to cut portions of the *Paul* manuscript (Penberthy 69). These requests prefigure the exchanges over Niedecker's editing work, in which Niedecker hoped to 'bring in the *human*' by publishing her friend's letters as literature. 'A tough game, art,' she writes in a couplet of *For Paul*, 'humanity's other part' (Niedecker 161): the terse rhyme leaves unclear whether the human and the artistic are complementary or opposed. But it suggests the 'toughness' of the question for one writing to or about Zukofsky.

The manuscript as a whole accepts the privacy of Zukofsky's control as a condition of its very existence. This privacy links source and audience in the closed circuit of Zukofsky's authority.[12] '*Should* the title be FOR PAUL??' Niedecker writes to her friend about her book (Penberthy 230). 'Yes, I guess so. Nice if whenever it's printed, Paul's handwriting: AND I ACCEPT – PAUL. Suzz? If he does accept! !' The ambiguous, affectionate 'Suzz' is part of Niedecker and Zukofsky's private language in their correspondence; in this instance, the word helps Niedecker to venture the idea that Zukofsky's endorsement, through his son's, could replace that of a wider audience. The premise of *For Paul* resists that wider audience (Penberthy 70); when she and Zukofsky both submitted work to a 1949 poetry award, Niedecker's only befuddled the judges. 'Who is Paul?' asked one in a note, regretting that her 'lovely' verse was ineligible because it fell 'outside the called for "social significance" category' (Penberthy 168). In *For Paul*, unlike *New Goose*, the specificities of correspondence could refuse rather than invite a reader's engagement – and could block rather than constitute a poem's significance.[13] The dichotomy of public and private seems a limiting choice rather than an animating interdependence.

Indeed, the 'social significance' of *For Paul* may lie in its limits, in its demonstration of the difficulty of an epistolary poetics. If letters are to manifest their feminist potential, they must manage what Carole Pateman has summarised as the principal goal of feminism, to dismantle 'the separation and opposition between the public and private spheres' (118). For Niedecker, that meant moving beyond the influence of a man who would reinforce their boundaries and the frustrations of a relationship that left her precisely nowhere among them. After *For Paul*, Niedecker began to do just that.

V

Events of the 1950s and early 1960s helped to encourage this development. Niedecker's mother passed away in 1951 and her father followed in 1954. These deaths encouraged Niedecker's rumination on the linked detriments of matrimony and ownership, evident in those poems of the *For Paul* era that were not about the younger Zukofsky. In 'I rose from marsh mud', for example, she describes the wedding of a 'little white slave-girl / in her diamond fronds' who is joined 'for life to serve / silver. Possessed' (Niedecker 170). Focusing on the 'possession' of property or wedlock, Niedecker's account of the conventional family indicts its complementary links to masculinity and capitalism – a combination she continues to suspect even after her 'Depression years'. She includes her poem of that title, in fact, as part of the *For Paul* manuscript; it describes a daughter driven to debt by caring for her father (165).

Niedecker still hoped for a marriage of her own – directing her hopes, after 1960, to a widowed dentist from Milwaukee named Harold Hein, who began to visit her regularly. Hein read literature, helped her with odd jobs, and took her to see his family; yet when Niedecker made her expectations plain, Hein wanted no more than friendship. A few years after this disappointment, Niedecker agreed to marry Al Millen, a painter with a drinking problem who did not appreciate art (Niedecker remembers in a poem how Millen 'wades the muddy water fishing, / falls in, dries his last pay-check / in the sun, smooths it out / in *Leaves of Grass*' (208)). Her approach to their nuptials was noticeably, even brutally, practical: 'for warmth / if not repose' she writes in her poem beginning 'I married' (228). Yet the marriage offered some emotional repose, it seems, as well as some practical warmth. Niedecker could at last draw up a will that did not leave everything to the Zukofskys, for example. By the mid-1960s, letters between Niedecker and Zukofsky had slowed in frequency; her decision to collect his letters, in fact, could be an acknowledgement of conclusion, a concession to endings that were prompted by more than age. As her editing project clarifies their different approaches to correspondence, it also allows her to see that correspondence more objectively, perhaps, to assess their two-person exchange with the eye of a third.

A real third party helped in this effort. Beginning in 1960, Niedecker corresponded regularly with Cid Corman, a poet and publisher who valued both Objectivist poetry and poetic epistolarity as much as Niedecker did. Corman recognised in correspondence, moreover, the genre's particular gifts. If Niedecker worries, for example, that she 'probably shouldn't write so often' even if she 'always seem[s] to have something to say', Corman knows that letters can be a force of sheer companionship between people, quite apart from the content of their communication (Niedecker and Corman 193; Corman, 10 July 1961).[14] (That fact, of course, has been a signal feature of the letter genre from Charles Lamb's description of the 'solecism of two presents' in 'Distant Correspondents' to Derrida's suspicion of 'presence' in *The Post Card* (Lamb 105; Derrida 463–88).) Likewise, Corman fostered the correspondent paradox of a public intimacy: he wrote his letters to specific people but knew that literary letters would likely be read by others (Corman, 17 September 1959, 6 October 1959). And he demonstrated a correspondent suspicion of private property: he refused to sell the second series of his journal *Origin* and did not share Zukofsky's obsession with copyright (Corman, *Gist* xxxii; Corman, 4 May 1961). Their sympathetic views made Corman a useful ally during Niedecker's editing frustrations – so much so that Niedecker worries whether Zukofsky might be hurt. 'I wdn't want him to feel a conspiracy between you and me against him!' she tells Corman (Niedecker and Corman 73).

Corman not only shares Niedecker's ideas about letters but also serves as an audience of letters; he published excerpts from poets' correspondence, including Niedecker's, along with verse in his journal *Origin*. This choice assumed the value of letters as part of a poet's production, allowing Niedecker to see that her work in both correspondence and verse could be generally relevant *and* specifically addressed. Writing for Corman – at once a friend, a fellow poet, an editor – allowed her to move past the frustrations of *For Paul* without abandoning her commitment to epistolary models of writing and reading. *Homemade Poems* is one result: Niedecker sent this self-produced volume to Corman in 1964,[15] followed by nearly identical books, now called *Handmade Poems*, to Zukofsky and Jonathan Williams. Work within the collections uses epistolary material ('Santayana's' transcribes a passage from that writer's correspondence; 'LZ's' and 'Letter from Ian' use material from correspondence Niedecker received; 'Some float off on chocolate bars' uses a phrase from her correspondence to Corman), but the collection itself seems most indicative of Niedecker's poetic epistolarity. Blurring the line between gift and product, these volumes expand the letter-like premise of her poem 'To a Maryland editor' and revise the letter-like construction of *For Paul*. Niedecker resists the calibration of literary prestige by yardsticks of impersonality and profitability when she stakes her value as a writer on her production of 'homemade' and 'handmade' offerings. Yet her three-fold contribution also refuses to peg her writing to any one (man's) acceptance. Thus while the contents cover Niedecker's newly marital domestication (she notes that 'many things are better / flavored with bacon'), the volume presents a poet who is a woman writer in her own right (Niedecker 200). Fittingly, the penultimate poem asks '[w]ho was Mary Shelley': 'What was her name / before she married?' (212).

Subsequent work found Niedecker ready to plumb both the historical roots and the political implications of an epistolary publicity. She did both through her deep 1960s reading in works of Jefferson and Adams – and through the poems she wrote from this research. As Penberthy writes, the long poems of the 1960s 'summarize and culminate her career' while showing what 'she turned to after her plans for the Zukofsky letters were frustrated' (95) – along with, perhaps, her plans for her own life. Niedecker began her longest poem about the founding fathers in 1969, just after depositing her Zukofsky correspondence manuscripts at the Ransom Center, and she wrote her first after Hein's response of 'no marriage / friend' (Niedecker 190). This begins a redress of Niedecker's frustrations by focusing precisely on Abigail Adams's name 'before she married'. John's love letters to 'Miss Abigail Smith', Niedecker's poem narrates, record her 'faults . . . you read, you write, you think / but I drink Madeira // to you . . .' (191). The ironic catalogue predicts a relationship of two 'writers' and 'thinkers', in which letters set husband and wife on the equal plane that was their lifelong, literary, correspondence with each other. The record of that collegiality, moreover, is part of the history of a country as well as a marriage. Niedecker's poem begins with 'the wild and wavy event / now chintz at the window' that was 'revolution', and she wrote to Corman that she might title it 'She Watched the Battle of Bunker's Hill' (Niedecker and Corman 31). Abigail's correspondence shows how a woman might achieve public importance through seemingly private observations – and suggests that public events are incomplete without the same.

VI

Those findings are even clearer in 'Three Americans', from *Harpsichord & Salt Fish*, probably the last of the Jefferson/Adams group to be written (Niedecker 285–6). John Adams 'is our man', Niedecker begins,

> but delicate beauty
> touched the other one –
>
> an architect
> and a woman artist
> walked beside Jefferson
>
> Abigail
> (Long face horse-name)
> cheesemaker
>
> chicken raiser
> wrote letters that John
> and TJ could savour

Abigail can walk with 'John' and 'TJ', rather than behind or apart, because of the letters that pass among them. Epistolary sociality admits a 'woman artist' whose artistry appears not only in writing but also in architecture, cooking and animal husbandry – and whose letters are 'savoured', like a meal, by her male letter-writing colleagues. The threesome of 'Three Americans' imagines something other than the 'three' of Niedecker's Guggenheim dream. Here, friendship is less like the awkward emendation of a closed coupling and more like the liberating mark of a fluid intimacy. Niedecker's title emphasises the exemplary nature of this intimacy: for these three Americans, local friendship is national politics. Their association demonstrates the potential in their young country, where 'founding fathers' walk with mothers and talk of architecture and cheese; it serves as an effect and model of democratic principles which TJ and John fought to establish. Niedecker's poem, then, resists the more pessimistic ramifications of 'A', or even *For Paul*, in which private relationship could seem like a withdrawal from – rather than the fruition of – public ideals.

This transposition makes women like Abigail more central to the political narrative of America and men like Jefferson more connected to the seemingly apolitical world of family life. It was Abigail's letters, in fact, that broke the silence between Jefferson and Adams after the two men's disagreement. When Jefferson's daughter died in 1804, Abigail wrote to her former friend to express her sorrow – avoiding conflict, she hoped, by directing her message to 'no other than the private inhabitant of Monticello' (Adams, Adams and Jefferson 268). Despite this stipulation, the letters that followed quickly move toward public matters. Yet Jefferson makes sure to add that he feels 'political events . . . most strongly' in their 'unfortunate bearings on my private friendships' (271). The Adams/Jefferson friendship, that is, confuses political and personal productively and ineluctably. Niedecker's poems of Thomas Jefferson, in *Harpsichord & Salt Fish*, follow this epistolary admission on the part of her subject: the Jefferson poems are not the *For Paul* poems in part because Jefferson did not – as Zukofsky did – endorse a patriarchal family structure dependent on a public/private divide. 'Thomas Jefferson Inside', for example, sets the work done by Congress next to the work done by 'Daughter Polly of the strawberry / letter' – the same daughter whom Abigail writes to mourn (Niedecker 291). The long poem 'Thomas Jefferson', which opens Niedecker's collection, returns to the same 'strawberry letter' for a similar suggestion: 'the strawberries / were safe // I'd have heard – I'm in that kind / of correspondence // with a young daughter – if they were not' (278). Jefferson reports on the doings of his household as if these are vital to the security of the state, and as if a daughter's letters contribute to shared stewardship of an American land.

'Thomas Jefferson' does recognise a possible tension between nation and family, political duties and intimate cares; Niedecker's poem opens, for example, with Jefferson exclaiming that his 'wife is ill! / And I sit / waiting / for a quorum' (275). This lament seems to deprecate the importance of democratic process in the face of personal tragedy. Like Zukofsky, Niedecker quotes the Jefferson who wanted to turn away from his state responsibilities; one section, using Jefferson's description of political honours as 'splendid torments', longs for grandchildren and 'chestnut trees' at Monticello (279). Another hopes for 'the last of labors // among conflicting parties' so that he might return to 'my family'. In Niedecker's poem, however, this longing manifests Jefferson's proto-socialist political ideas, which resist 'French frills and lace' and would bow 'to everyone he met' (278). When Jefferson rejects 'Hamilton and the bankers' to tell his relatives that 'we shall sow our cabbages /

together', he makes his household labours the proof of, rather than the alternative to, civic work and a civic vision. His household planting tends the fruits of democracy – the same, perhaps, apparent in the animal husbandry among 'three Americans'. Jefferson's letters are the fitting genre for the good that Niedecker recognises in his and his country's philosophy. Intimate specificities are the origin and the end of general abstractions.

This makes Niedecker's poem about 'Thomas Jefferson' a facet of her feminist potential, even if it seems odd to argue as much about a poem that treats a famous statesman writing to and about his daughters. When she cites the activities of a household, however, as a part of the activities of a state, she anticipates a central concern of the still-incipient second-wave feminism. The activists of women's liberation questioned the modern and liberal division of personal and political just as surely as Niedecker and other post-modern writers questioned the modernist and liberal division of private and public. Critics have outlined dangers in this line of questioning: on the one hand, as Lauren Berlant has argued, it could mean an enervation of the public, which rewrites the mixed legacy of nineteenth-century sentimentalism (2–26). On the other hand, as Theresa Man Ling Lee has argued, it could mean a standardisation of the private, which risks the terrifying results of twentieth-century totalitarianism (166–7). Niedecker's return to eighteenth-century examples challenges us to look behind these later dangers, finding in earlier eras a model for post-modern revivification of the public sphere. Jefferson and Adams were part of a country small and young enough that they could see concerns for the growing nation as analogous to concerns for their intimate circle and the ideals of their growing nation as applicable to the same. (Hannah Arendt, writing about the American revolution just a few years before Niedecker's poems, extols an early American version of democracy in which Jefferson could look at Congress as a 'circle of his friends' (*On Revolution* 128).) The intimate publicity of correspondence as a genre in Niedecker's work mimics the friendly politics of these writers.

Niedecker's pursuit of a certain potential in correspondence, then, marks her pursuit of a certain potential in Enlightenment. 'Suddenly got the urge to read all I could about the French Enlightenment,' she writes to Corman while working on 'Thomas Jefferson'. 'Did so want Diderot's Letters to Sophia Volland. . . . Only thing I mourn is that Tom Jefferson didn't get to Diderot in time before his (D's) death' (Niedecker and Corman 226–7). In Niedecker's poetry, the letter-saturated era of Jefferson and Diderot demonstrates the potential of egalitarian sociality as a progressive tool. Niedecker recognises the promise of what Michael Frazer has recently described the 'sentimentalist Enlightenment', posed against the 'rationalist' version so often promoted as monolithic (Frazer 3–11 ff.). And though Jefferson's racism shadows his role in that promise, just as Niedecker's racism shadows her use of it,[16] the American heritage of this enlightened epistolarity remains a potential in her writing. It links Niedecker's work not only to postwar feminists but also to postwar political philosophers, beginning to re-examine the grounds of American governance.[17]

These connections help to redescribe Niedecker's own correspondences even as they illuminate her use of others'. A sly comment to Zukofsky, in a late letter, provides one opportunity: as he waits for a copy of a volume of her poems, she tells him to '[b]e patient, as John Adams wrote to Abigail when she was in a hurry for him to get the Declaration of Independence set up and signed (and to include in it the Ladies) but this lady will timidly ask' (Penberthy 296). In comparing the realisation of her poetry collection to the ratification of her country's charter, Niedecker playfully reinforces the implications of her correspondent poetics. The undeclared principles of her work aspire to a liberating interdependence of public and private for the citizen-writers in any nation.

NOTES

1. Many theorists of letters have described the intermediacy of letters as a form; see especially Hammer 167, Jolly and Stanley 79, Treseler 24, 74–7.
2. For biographical details, I am indebted to Margot Peters's biography.
3. Biographers differ on the reliability of reports about Niedecker's pregnancy and abortion. Scroggins disputes the idea as unverified 'gossip', but Peters offers several corroborating sources (Scroggins 473–4; Peters 274–5).
4. The best recent criticism of Niedecker's work, for example, contrasts a focus on the feminist socialism of her surrealist poetry with a focus on the 'psychobiography' of her 'epistolary exchanges' (Jennison 138), while I hope to show that Niedecker's use of epistolarity is an important part of her writing's ideological force. This ideology provides a positive alternative to the negative vision that Rachel Blau DuPlessis describes as Niedecker's 'critical discomfort with gender norms, class assumptions, and Americanist ideology' (114).
5. I am indebted to the list of Niedecker's books provided at the Friends of Lorine Niedecker website: <http://www.lorineniedecker.org/documents/Niedeckerlibrary.pdf> (last accessed 26 June 2014).
6. Virginia Jackson's study of 'lyric reading' uses letters to counteract the idea of an acontextual lyric in the case of Dickinson (118–65).
7. For the confluence of modernism and copyright, see Saint-Amour (12).
8. For a description of Pound's copyright work in context, see Spoo (48–64).
9. See Rifkin's complete discussion for a complementary account of Zukofsky's archival institutionalism 'at an intersection of public and private' (106).
10. Jennison describes Zukofsky's use of epistolarity in order to connect 'the complex dynamics of nation-formation with the transnational migrations of labor' (21).
11. The latter half of the poem moves away from the historical and political themes to focus on personal and familial events; see Ahearn's *Introduction* for a description of this development (134).
12. Even Marjorie Perloff, who argues that '*Paul* becomes [Niedecker's] own poetic child', describes how the collection includes a deferential homage to Zukofsky (170).
13. Jenny Penberthy's excellent account describes the 'awkwardness about many of the "For Paul" poems . . . the poems are often opaque and the uninitiated reader is rebuffed by the private inscriptions' (70).
14. The sentiment bears comparison to Corman's poem 'It isn't for want', a connection for which I am indebted to Julia Bloch.
15. *Lost and Found: The CUNY Poetics Document Initiative* published in 2012 a facsimile copy of this volume, edited by John Harkey, which provides an essential service to Niedecker scholarship.
16. Letters confirm that Niedecker, in Peters's words, 'dreaded selling to blacks because they put

off other buyers, lowering value', even as Niedecker hated 'the hypocrisy of paying lip service to racial equality' while engaging in real housing discrimination (127).

17. Of particular note here is Arendt, whose analysis of American revolutionary politics connects to an early fascination with the politics of the salon and an increasing emphasis on the politics of intimate relationships – as evident in her discussion of Karl Jaspers (*Men* 73). See Benhabib for a discussion of Arendt's salon as an alternative, more gender-egalitarian, public sphere (15–23).

WORKS CITED

Adams, John, Abigail Adams and Thomas Jefferson, *The Adams-Jefferson Letters: The Complete Correspondence Between Thomas Jefferson and Abigail and John Adams*, ed. Lester J. Cappon, vol. 1 (Chapel Hill: University of North Carolina Press, 1959).
Ahearn, Barry, *Zukofsky's 'A': An Introduction* (Berkeley: University of California Press, 1983).
Arendt, Hannah, *Men in Dark Times* (New York: Harcourt, 1968).
—— *On Revolution* (New York: Viking Press, 1963).
Benhabib, Seyla, *The Reluctant Modernism of Hannah Arendt*, new edn (Oxford: Rowan & Littlefield, 2003).
Berlant, Lauren, *The Female Complaint: The Unfinished Business of Sentimentality in American Culture* (Durham, NC: Duke University Press, 2008).
Corman, Cid, *The Gist of Origin, 1951–1971* (New York: Grossman, 1975).
—— letter to Louis Zukofsky, 17 September 1959, Louis Zukofsky Collection, Harry Ransom Center, University of Texas at Austin.
—— letter to Louis Zukofsky, 6 October 1959, Louis Zukofsky Collection, Harry Ransom Center University of Texas at Austin.
—— letter to Louis Zukofsky, 4 May 1961, Louis Zukofsky Collection, Harry Ransom Center, University of Texas at Austin.
—— letter to Louis Zukofsky, 10 July 1961, Louis Zukofsky Collection, Harry Ransom Center, University of Texas at Austin.
Derrida, Jacques, *The Post Card: From Socrates to Freud and Beyond*, trans. Alan Bass (Chicago: University of Chicago Press, 1987).
DuPlessis, Rachel Blau, 'Lorine Niedecker, the Anonymous: Gender, Class, Genre and Resistances', in Jenny Penberthy (ed.), *Lorine Niedecker: Woman and Poet* (Orono, ME: National Poetry Foundation, 1996), pp. 113–37.
Eliot, T. S., 'Tradition and the Individual Talent', *The Egoist* 6.5 (1919): 72–3.
Frazer, Michael L., *The Enlightenment of Sympathy: Justice and the Moral Sentiments in the Eighteenth Century and Today* (Oxford: Oxford University Press, 2010).
Hammer, Langdon, 'Useless Concentration: Life and Work in Elizabeth Bishop's Letters and Poems', *American Literary History* 9.1 (1997): 162–80.
Jackson, Virginia, *Dickinson's Misery: A Theory of Lyric Reading* (Princeton: Princeton University Press, 2005).
Jefferson, Thomas, and James Madison, *The Republic of Letters: The Correspondence Between Thomas Jefferson and James Madison, 1776–1826, Volume Two: 1790–1804*, ed. James Morton Smith (New York: Norton, 1995).
Jennison, Ruth, *The Zukofsky Era: Modernity, Margins, and the Avant-Garde* (Baltimore: Johns Hopkins University Press, 2012).
Jolly, Margaretta, and Liz Stanley, 'Letters as/not a genre', *Life Writing* 2.2 (2005): 75–101.
Lamb, Charles, 'Distant Correspondents', *The Works of Charles and Mary Lamb, Volume II: Elia and the Last Essays of Elia*, ed. E. V. Lucas (London: Methuen, 1903), pp. 104–8.

Lee, Theresa Man Ling, 'Rethinking the Personal and the Political: Feminist Activism and Civic Engagement', *Hypatia* 22.4 (2007): 163–79.

Niedecker, Lorine, *Collected Works*, ed. Jenny Penberthy (Berkeley: University of California Press, 2002).

—— and Cid Corman, *'Between Your House and Mine': The Letters of Lorine Niedecker to Cid Corman, 1960 to 1970*, ed. Lisa Pater Faranda (Durham, NC: Duke University Press, 1986).

Pateman, Carole, 'Feminist Critiques of the Public/Private Dichotomy', *The Disorder of Women: Democracy, Feminism, and Political Theory* (Stanford: Stanford University Press, 1989), pp. 118–40.

Penberthy, Jenny, *Niedecker and the Correspondence with Zukofsky, 1931–1970* (Cambridge: Cambridge University Press, 1993).

Perloff, Marjorie, '"L. Before P.": Writing "For Paul" for Louis', in Jenny Penberthy (ed.), *Lorine Niedecker: Woman and Poet* (Orono, ME: National Poetry Foundation, 1996), pp. 157–70.

Peters, Margot, *Lorine Niedecker: A Poet's Life* (Madison: Terrace Books, 2011).

Rifkin, Libbie, *Career Moves: Olson, Creeley, Zukofsky, Berrigan, and the American Avant-Garde* (Madison: University of Wisconsin Press, 2000).

Saint-Amour, Paul K., 'Introduction', in Paul K. Saint-Amour (ed.), *Modernism and Copyright* (Oxford: Oxford University Press, 2011), pp. 1–36.

Scroggins, Mark, *The Poem of a Life: A Biography of Louis Zukofsky* (Emeryville, CA: Shoemaker & Hoard, 2007).

Spoo, Robert, 'Ezra Pound, Legislator: Perpetual Copyright and Unfair Competition with the Dead', in Paul K. Saint-Amour (ed.), *Modernism and Copyright* (Oxford: Oxford University Press, 2011), pp. 39–64.

Treseler, Heather, 'Lyric Letters: Elizabeth Bishop's Epistolary Poems', dissertation, University of Notre Dame, 2010.

Wimsatt, W. K. Jr, and M. C. Beardsley, 'The Intentional Fallacy', *Sewanee Review* 54.3 (1946): 468–88.

Yeats, W. B., *Essays and Introductions* (New York: Macmillan, 1961).

Zukofsky, Louis, *'A'* (Berkeley: University of California Press, 1978).

—— *Prepositions: The Collected Critical Essays* (Hanover, NH: Wesleyan University Press, 2000).

—— and William Carlos Williams, *The Correspondence of William Carlos Williams and Louis Zukofsky*, ed. Barry Ahearn (Middletown, CT: Wesleyan University Press, 2003).

13 'Wherever you listen from': W. S. Graham and the Art of the Letter[1]

Angela Leighton

W. S. Graham's poem 'The Constructed Space' – a poem which has often been read as a manifesto for his poetics – opens with the line 'Meanwhile surely there must be something to say'. This typical worry about 'something to say' is then quickly subsumed into an 'abstract scene' between two figures: 'us two whoever / We are. Anyway here we are,' Graham lightly riddles. Seeking a message quickly gives way to the poem as public statement, at odds both with the poet's subjective presence and with his intentions of meaning: 'Achieved against subjective odds', it is 'Mainly an obstacle to what I mean'. Having 'something to say' or 'mean', then, is quickly blocked by the poem's own obstacle course, where the poet acknowledges the presence of another 'between us two'. It is the sense of two which helps to construct this 'Constructed Space' – a 'here' conceived as nowhere, a communication conceived as 'obstacle' to communication, and a speaking, not by the dominant lyrical pronoun, the poet's 'I', but as a space for language 'between us two whoever / We are'. Questions of personal experience or identity are casually shrugged off by 'whoever / We are'. Thus the poem, 'this abstract scene', is a 'public place' where intelligences meet, and where the poet reaches to the sense of another. We don't know much about this space except that, at least for a time, we're in it: 'Anyway here we are,' Graham abruptly announces. Meaning, whatever that may be, proceeds from 'here' (P 161–2), from this precise configuration of words, which is both a visual space and an aural line between poet and reader. Certainly, the urgent sense of an addressee is never far from Graham's poetic consciousness.

The art of the letter has always lurked in the shadows of literature proper. For critics, a rich source of biographical information, giver of names, places, dates, the letter also offers an insight into unguarded communication, bound by an assumption of privacy. The letters of writers may also, of course, be treasure troves of first thoughts, trial runs, experiments in thinking and writing which have not yet found their 'public place'. Yet already in our culture the letter as intimate object, addressed to you, signed by me, sealed and sent on a journey, may seem to have become a dying art. Perhaps it has been dying for some time. Two decades ago Frank and Anita Kermode, in the *Oxford Book of Letters*, observed that the form was under threat, from the telephone, fax and email (Kermode and Kermode xix); today we might add Facebook, Twitter and Skype. Although some might still write emails to look like letters, addressing, spacing and signing them with the old formalities, the product is essentially different. It's not just the absence of an enclosed, handled object; it's also the difference in time. The letter must travel to reach its reader, its message dependent on delivery. This sense of time taken and space overcome defined the letter long before even the telephone threw it into relief. In her own, open 'Letter to a Young Poet', Virginia Woolf recalled the opinion of 'the old gentleman [who] used to say' that the 'penny post . . . has killed the art of letter-writing' (182). Started in 1840, the penny post already appeared to some too speedy and cheap a method of delivery for the gravitas of the letter. Something about the weighty substance of the form is defined by its laborious delivery: not only the time it takes to write, but also the time it takes to send. Between missive and response there is a lag.

That element of delay may sometimes be terribly resonant. For instance, all Elizabeth Barrett Browning's letters to her father after her elopement were returned to her at his death, unopened, even the one edged in black to signify a death. Those sealed letters express, more harshly than anything, how the letter's mute appeal might be refused – a refusal strengthened and renewed, year after year, in the fact that they were kept, unopened. Another Elizabeth, Elizabeth Bishop, knew the emotional trauma of letters arrived too late. She once received a postcard from a repudiated lover who had, meantime, committed suicide. The card just read: 'Go to hell, Elizabeth' (Millier 112). In her poem 'The Bight', the double meaning of 'old correspondences' haunts the poem, creating an uncanny connection between the epigraph, 'On my birthday', the storm-wrecked white boats in the harbour, and the 'torn-open, unanswered letters' with which they are compared. After the eagerness of 'torn-open', the sudden temporising of 'unanswered' – what has happened between opening and not answering? – hints that other things, as well as boats, are 'not yet salvaged, if they ever will be, from the last bad storm' (Bishop 47). That letters are like boats only works if that 'last bad storm' provides the connection: a wrecking which leaves both unusable. The poem's date, 'On my birthday', is thus strangely darkened by letters (or are they cards?) 'torn-open, unanswered' – reactions hardly suited to the object – and, between the two, by a pause the length of a comma, or a lifetime.

Letters, then, are creatures of time: the time it takes for them to be written, delivered, opened, read, pondered, replied to, or just left unnervingly pending. As a result, there is a potential dead letter at the heart of every missive: 'cries like dead letters sent / To dearest him that lives, alas! Away', as Hopkins puts it (Poems 101). That 'dearest him', whether friend, father, fellow-artist, muse, lover or God, makes the letter difficult and precious, hopeful and risky, precisely by being 'away'. That a literal 'Dead Letter Office' existed at this time, for mail incorrectly addressed, highlights the oddness of Hopkins's phrasing: 'like dead letters sent' suggests almost an intention and foresight of misdelivery, as if the address were too open to be known and the letter already 'dead' before 'sent'. As John Durham Peters puts it, in *Speaking into the Air*, in acts of communication 'such elliptical sending is as important as circular reciprocity' (152). Certainly, as a form of communication, the letter is always to some extent thrown to chance, to the delays of time and to the vagaries of a destination, topographical or personal, that cannot be guaranteed. Its intimate direct speech may thus remain unanswered, unreceived, even by a 'dearest him', and its route, like this very poem's, may only lead to another Dead Letter Office.

In trying to define the art of the letter, then, critics and poets have always struggled with a form as elusive as it is specific. Tom Paulin, in 'Writing to the Moment', asks if there is 'a poetics of the familiar letter?' and answers in the negative, that letters 'construct themselves on an anti-aesthetic, a refusal of the literary' (216). His 'to the moment' identifies letter writing as largely improvisatory, immediate, personal, spurning the labour of finish which marks the aesthetic work. 'The gifted correspondent has to appear negligent of effect' (228), he explains. The phrasing, however, might betray the very opposite, since 'to *appear* negligent of effect' already sounds like a worked-for *effect* of negligence, as onerous, perhaps, as writing a poem. Langdon Hammer, in an article on Bishop's letters and poems, argues that the 'personal letter exists on the threshold of literature, where ordinary and literary discourses interact' (163), though quite what divides 'ordinary' and 'literary' is not made clear. This 'generic indeterminacy' (164), he claims, characterises a poem like Bishop's 'The End of March', which uses the language 'of a letter to one's self, really a kind of muttering' (176). But 'muttering' does not necessarily signify the absence of an addressee. Rilke once used a similar image in a letter, when he wrote to his close confidant Lou Andreas-Salomé: 'this might be, between us, the right moment after all to push a few half-words, murmurish as they are, out onto the old accustomed leaves' (Rilke 234). His correspondent then duly acknowledged the communicable power of mere murmuring: 'Your "murmurish" words murmured *so many things* to me – thank you for them!' (235). No sooner are distinctions made, between aesthetic and non-aesthetic, between poems and letters, between murmurish murmurs and purposeful communication, than their dividing lines start to wobble.

Certainly, examples of this thin line might be found anywhere among the great duos of epistolary writing: Robert and Elizabeth Barrett Browning, Hopkins and Bridges, Frost and Untermeyer, Bishop and Lowell, Rilke and Andreas-Salomé. The letter may be the place where a poem takes shape, where lines of poetry emerge from the prose, where talking to another becomes talking to oneself, and therefore where distinctions break down. The fact that both the lyric and the letter tend to depend on an addressee, named or implicit, human or non-human, also suggests their closeness of form. Jonathan Culler, in a seminal statement, has proposed that the apostrophe or address can be identified 'with lyric itself' (137). William Waters, in *Poetry's Touch*, then extends Culler's thesis, arguing that lyrical poetry is 'not so much a stable communicative situation as a chronic hesitation, a faltering, between monologue and dialogue, between "talking about" and "talking to", third and second person, indifference to interlocutors and the yearning to have one' (8). It would not be hard to extend this to the letter's addressed 'you', who may be a real person or merely a pretext for talking to oneself; who may elicit a language of heartfelt directness or of composed literariness. In particular, Waters's sense of the 'chronic hesitation' of lyric 'between monologue and dialogue', between its need for and indifference to 'interlocutors', might also describe the shifting purposes of the letter. Jacques Derrida, in his own epistolary exploration in *La Carte Postale* (1980), acknowledges at the start the switch-back tactics of the epistolary address: 'The word – apostrophizes – speaks of the words addressed to the singular one, a live interpellation (the man of discourse or writing interrupts the continuous development of the sequence, abruptly turns toward someone, that is, something, addresses himself to you), but the word also speaks of the address to be detoured' (4). So, the 'singular one', perhaps the individually named addressee, becomes in the course of the sentence 'someone', then merely 'something', then a generalised 'you' from which the address itself is finally 'to be detoured'. Refusing to be caught on the hooks of I and you, Derrida characteristically lets the writing both invoke and negate them. If address is the mainspring of the letter, its defining rationale and purpose, it may also be the source of its continually re-addressing detours.

A general poetics of the letter, then, is probably impossible, quite apart from the fact that letters are as varied as their reasons for being written: at one end of the literary spectrum, Tennyson or Eliot, brisk businessmen of the letter, anti-aesthetic and utilitarian in the extreme; and at the other end, Keats, Hopkins or Rilke, who use the letter to think into poetry, indeed, to savour the distance between writer and addressee in order to find in it the space, the 'constructed space' perhaps, for those murmurs or mutterings which are the beginning of poetry. That the letter involves an address to a named reader, and that it is characterised by time and delay in the writing and sending, are two probably ubiquitous features, but features loosely shared with the lyric poem.

To turn at this point to one of the great letter writers among poets, W. S. Graham, is to find all these conflicts at play. The publication of his *Selected Letters* in 1999 has only increased the standing of this once neglected but increasingly admired poet. A Scot, born in Greenock, who lived most of his life in Cornwall, Graham was cut off from many of the literary movements of his time. He took his artistic bearings, instead, from painters and sculptors, particularly those of the St Ives school: Roger Hilton, Terry Frost, John Minton, Ben Nicholson, Peter Lanyon and Bryan Wynter. Although Graham was often living within walking or cycling distance of them, he would nevertheless write to them: letters of apology, anguish, argument, concern or sheer delicious bravura. At the start, it seems, he was driven by loneliness. Living in a friend's ramshackle caravan in 1943, he wrote rather forlornly to Ben Nicholson: 'I've been here three months and I would like to talk to someone. I'm quite alone here. Could I please visit you' (L 16). That theme of loneliness then becomes a recurring motif: 'I haven't seen a soul over Christmas and new year' (L 78), he grumbles in 1949. A year later he muses to the Scottish poet Edwin Morgan: 'What do I write to say? I don't know. I haven't spoken to anyone for five days' (L 118). In 1958 he apologises: 'Forgive me how I go on for company', adding 'I'm terribly desperate for a pair of shoes or boots' (L 156). His practical needs were sometimes as exigent as his need for company. In 1975, he is still harping on loneliness: 'Of course, maybe I'm just lonely and I must write something' (L 297). By 1979 he can sum up: 'I am an expert of aloneness' (L 356). Unfortunately, Graham was not a conserver of paper – he burned swathes of letters and manuscripts, and when he moved house, tended just to walk out, leaving the door wide open – so little remains of the return correspondence. Yet for all his pleading, these letters do not immediately elicit an answer, and the loneliness they bewail is never assuaged. Indeed, it comes to seem the condition for writing at all, as if the yearning to find a listener, a reader, were the mainspring of such epistolary outpourings. That 'chronic hesitation . . . between monologue and dialogue' becomes, in these letters, an almost flirtatious game of need and rejection, asking and refusing, a playing fast-and-loose with the imagined addressee. 'In this letter do not expect anything direct,' Graham explains. 'I am only practising how to speak to speak myself out of myself' (L 297). There is a sense in which he was courting the long-distance communication of the letter in order to learn how 'to speak to speak'. And such speech was not to get 'out of myself', in the familiar phrase, but 'to speak myself out of myself'. This strange kind of self out of the self is less an escape from 'myself' than a rediscovery or reinvention of it – a way of speaking about, as well as from, it. Graham's curious epipsychidion depends on practising epistolary evasions from which his correspondent must learn not to 'expect anything direct'.

In spite of these cries of loneliness, Michael Snow, the editor of the letters, has confessed his surprise at discovering how many artists Graham knew. He gives a vivid account of his first visit to the poet, in the late 1950s, when, trying to conduct an interview, he found his questions increasingly ignored and rerouted. Instead of answering, Graham would slip into a bizarre monologue, a game of self-invention in which he became, 'in quick succession, a Red Indian chief, an explorer trudging through the snow, or Livingstone lost in the jungle . . . At intervals he would burst into song, Scottish ballads or snatches of operatic arias, sung with great voice and considerable feeling' (Snow 11). Anything so straightforward as an interview had to be parried by voices, voices intent on imagining rather than disclosing identity. Some idea of what this might have been like is found in a letter to Anthony Astbury of 1978. Without warning or apology, Graham launches into one of his explorer's fantasies:

> Why did I set out anyhow on this white hell of a journey? Who to find? . . . The dogs have very good been. Remember them. I had to eat Jessie. It was necessary. She was unusually tough (I've eaten dogs in China, on the banks of Yangtze in a barge-haulers' village . . . where I was summoned by Ezra Pound to help him translate but I fell into the midnight water of the moon and was not a great help.) but a certain part which shall not be mentioned went down alright.
>
> Please don't think I am unhappy. The dogs have been very good. I almost ate you the night before last but I realised there wouldn't be anybody to write to.
> (L 343)

This weird farrago of hunger, heroism and arctic loneliness – themes which recur in much of the poetry – suggests that being 'myself out of myself' was both second nature and a rich source of invention. The hapless correspondent can only be a passive onlooker or, worse, more meat to the story – though not yet eaten, for the good reason that 'there wouldn't be anybody to write to'. For the tale needs a listener, the letter an addressee. Somebody out there alleviates and justifies the loneliness of the traveller-writer – or rather not somebody but, once again, 'anybody': 'there wouldn't be anybody to write to'. Just 'anybody' might do, so long as there is some leash out into the world of ordinary facts. In this game of epistolary derring-do, hilarious in the sanity of its madness, the recipient of the letter is only another inter- changeable game-player, whose role is to be 'anybody' to the poet's own, perpetually recast 'myself'. From this place, where the only rescue from the demands of Ezra Pound's translations might indeed be the madman's 'midnight water of the moon', the poet casts himself doubly as letter writer, while also making mincemeat of the epistolary conventions of address: 'I almost ate you the night before last'. As Michael Snow hints – his own surname more grist to Graham's imaginative mill – it was not the most grateful form of communication for the poet's friends.

Indeed, friends who received missives like this might be forgiven for assuming Graham was drunk. Certainly, drink took its toll of inspiration and energy among the artistic community in Cornwall. Anthony Frost has recalled the yearly cricket match, 'artists against farmers', which the farmers always contrived to win by ensuring a mid-time break in the pub (9). The poet Arthur Caddick recalled being disturbed one night by a noise outside, and finding 'Sydney [Graham], with Ruth Hilton, and a bottle of Scotch' in 'a clump of artichokes' at the bottom of the garden. Invited in, 'Sydney, in full voice, harangued me on prosody till half-past three' (148). Roger Hilton's second wife, Rose, has blamed Graham for enticing the painter into drink-fuelled, wasted days: 'in St Ives, [the] routine disappeared. Sydney would come over and stay all day – and that was three times a week!' (Frost 10). Certainly, a drinking binge three times a week does not sound too much like loneliness. 'I am such a shy man,' Graham once admitted, 'I have to take to the drink to meet somebody' (L 278). The relationship with Hilton, fond, inspiring, abusive, quarrelsome, became increasingly violent till, for the last three years of Hilton's life, they ceased to meet altogether. 'All this virile anger and destruction,' Graham once accused his friend. 'Why not somehow say it through your paintings' (L 235). One painting by Hilton which might be saying it is called 'Elephants Fighting'. With a wonderfully absurd ferocity, it shows a couple of circus elephants, tusk to tusk in battle, in front of some minimally drawn tents. It is now owned by another artist, Maggi Hambling, who explains: 'I'd had it on the wall for at least three months before I realized that there was a line of writing in it – across the painting just above the centre. It reads "women and children last", which made me laugh' (in Lambirth 254). Those half-visible words behind the paint might be quietly answering Graham's accusation, noting the cost to 'women and children' of their friendship's bull aggression.

For all her regrets about their drunken quarrels, however, Rose Hilton also admit-ted that 'Roger loved Sydney' (in Lambirth 211). There was a deep, tormenting bond between them, which is evident in the tussles of the letters. Graham begins one of them: 'My dear (are you my dear?) Roger, across the moors and roads like lines . . .' (L 234), and signs off, increasingly without punctuation: 'Are you a man or a dog? But I like you fine as you are do I maybe don't ask me I think you're spif-fing' (L 235). So the double-talk goes on, love/hate, endearment/abuse, man/dog. Meanwhile that key word, 'lines', not only makes a connection between painting and poetry, arts of the visible line, but reminds us that 'roads like lines' lead out, and must take time to travel along. Such lines will be taken by the letter itself, which goes in time 'across the moors and roads' towards the dear enemy living 'alas! Away'. So the love letter recalls its saving distance, the time taken in lines of writing, and then in lines of delivery, before it reaches the beloved, difficult addressee. From the safety of that epistolary distance it may be possible to say such things as 'My dear (are you my dear?)' without locking horns or taking to drink.

In another letter to Hilton, Graham follows up the declaration 'I do not know whether I love you or not' with an aside which shows him typically ducking into indirections. He wonders: 'How can anything be said from one man to another? The sent-out meaning always goes somewhere astray in the saying.' Then, as if to show how that straying goes, he adds: 'The man on the radio has just given the synopsis of the next act . . . He says something like "and really under the guise of the female castrato she falls in love with Belovio who is really her aunt in the guise of a painter"' (L 221). Quite who falls in love with whom in these letters is no easier to decode. Shape-shifting, sex-changing, game-playing, the daft plot of a romantic opera suits Graham's games of verbal disguise. So 'the sent-out meaning', the direct address of 'whether I love you or not', goes happily astray, taking that Derridaean detour of the apostrophe into the mad pantomime of '"really her aunt in the guise of a painter"'. Who is 'really' who is not a question to be ascertained by the conventions of address: I and you. Instead, the private twosomes of the letter are exploded by Graham into the imagination's multiplying word-games and identity-shifts. Nor is this merely a matter of emotionally self-protective, male jousting – jousting which, in the absence of Hilton's replies, seems like tilting at shadows. It is also a deep-seated resource of Graham's writing. The letter form gives him scope to act out a drama, premised on the necessary loneliness of writing, in which everything is up for invention, including the real-life players. As Graham puts it, a little more demotically: 'Who the fucking hell am I anyhow? Do not answer. Ever' (L 221). It might also be a command to that other reader of letters, peeping over the shoulder of the addressee: the literary critic.

Graham's early essay 'Notes on a Poetry of Release' (1946), in which he first defines his poetics, contains two words which are central to his later practice: 'line' and 'obstacle'. 'I try to remember those adventures along those lines of words' (L 382), he declares, characteristically turning straight lines into 'adventures'. He also points out that 'All the poet's knowledge and experience . . . is contained in the language which is obstacle and vehicle at the same time' (L 380). Like that 'obstacle' in 'The Constructed Space' – 'mainly an obstacle to what I mean' – here too it offers a stumbling-block in the ride to meaning. Poetry's language is vehicular access and road-block at once. A favourite 'line' of Graham's, which recurs in letters and poems, seems to encapsulate this ambiguity: 'I fall down darkness in a line of words' (L 222), he writes to Hilton, quoting from a poem written many years before, 'No, Listen, for this I Tell' (1942). To fall down a line is, of course, both to follow the linear way of words, and to meet the obstacle in a 'fall'. If all writing is a line on the page, to 'fall down' it is to know that poetry's directions, although still a line in time, have nothing to do with consequentiality or progress. Instead, they may become precipices into 'darkness', plunging out of their level ways.

However, there is another reason why the line should signify for Graham. It is a word which brings together the literal act of writing, the visual arts of the drawn line, and also the line of sound which carries through poetry (Leighton 210–19). This becomes clear in a poem which, like so many, takes its title from the form of a letter: 'Dear Who I Mean'. This poem sends out a missive to some unnamed 'Dear' – '(are you my dear?)' – both known and meant, yet anonymous. Graham then figures the letter as a kite which goes towards its 'Dear', but fails suddenly:

> Dear who I mean but more
> Than because of the lonely stumble
> In the spiked bramble after
> The wrecked dragon caught
> In the five high singing wires
> Its tail twisting the wind
> Into visibility, I turn
> To where is it you lodge
> Now at the other end
> Of this letter let out
> On the end of its fine string . . . (P 160)

Made in part of 'printed paper' (P 161), this poem-letter-kite first goes out and up into the wind. Graham may at some level be recalling Dickens's poetic alter ego, Mr Dick in *David Copperfield*, who also lets his manuscripts fly. But Graham's kite flyer seems less adept, speaking already after 'the lonely stumble / In the spiked bramble'. The speaker has met an obstacle which trips him up, and the kite has snagged. Yet 'language . . . is obstacle and vehicle at the same time'. This is not necessarily a misdirected poem, wrecked and lost in its delivery, but one which needs 'the lonely stumble' of its author in order to hold its distant reader lodged, somewhere, 'at the other end'. The poem-as-letter works by keeping its reader at bay, at the stumbling-block. After all, 'Dear who I mean' is 'more / Than *because* of the lonely stumble' – more dear, it seems, because held at the place where language, though 'let out / On the end of its fine string', stalls. From that place 'at the other end', the dear reader does not receive a very clear message, or even a very bright dragon, but rather something else, rather like a flat-packed toy, to 'Reassemble': 'You might even / Reassemble for your own sake / A dragon' (P 161), he concludes.

If this is about poetic language, it is specifically also about language *sounded*. The displaced message is caught, waylaid by wires overhead, which might be a telegraph or might be a stave: '*five* high singing wires,' Graham writes, as if the kite's twisting tail gets transposed into music on the way. On the one hand, the tail twists 'the wind / Into visibility', as if into a picture; on the other, it catches on those 'singing wires' and adds its own queer notation. The 'fine string' of the kite, which sends a letter out to some 'Dear who', does not simply reach its object and ask to be read, but meets the obstacle which reroutes its meaning and snags into music. It is precisely the wrecked kite that the reader must reassemble.

So although Graham often draws on a painterly vocabulary, his sense of the

musical lines of poetry is even stronger. He himself had a good singing voice –
Andrew Lanyon recalls that Caddick and Graham had 'deep resonant voices like
two great wirelesses' (in Frost 7). He once considered training as a professional
singer, and was an enthusiastic singer of part-songs down at the pub. Certainly,
musical imagery fills his letters. 'My long poem . . . becomes like the work of a com-
poser,' he writes to John Minton in 1945, '. . . a kind of counterpointing idea going
all through' (L 45). 'Larks mount the invisible elevators of May coloraturawise' (L
126), he writes elsewhere, letting the visual image of 'elevators' be cancelled in order
to make way for that brilliant figure of sound: 'coloraturawise' – the very word see-
hears the twisting line of it. When Graham writes about lines he is as often hearing
as seeing something: 'good real verse . . . should always have its almost hesitation for
a moment between one line and the next. That is why we make our "say" in lines' (L
169), he tells Norman Macleod. Often in his letters, he pauses to comment on the
music he hears on the radio. For instance, of a Mozart violin concerto, he explains:
'The violinist in this is so very exact and "clean" in his playing. He makes almost a
visual line in the air – I think of Klee's phrase – "taking a line for a walk"' (L 78).
Like a dog, Klee's line is partly on a lead, partly going its own way. For Graham, it is
a line of sound 'in the air', heard 'almost' visually, as if one could see it in 'the mind's
ear' (L 162) and so make the shape of a tune. Everywhere in these letters visual
metaphors mix with aural ones, painters tussle with musicians, as Graham seeks an
explanation of poetry in which lines might configure synaesthetically. 'THE EAR
SPEAKS MORE THAN THE TONGUE LISTEN –' (L 37), he expostulates to
John Minton, defining poetry as a kind of listening in to listening, till what speaks is
the silent sound of it. That 'THE EAR SPEAKS' tunes us in to the speaking effect
of silence – not passive silence but a listening silence, a great hall of silence, open
to all the singing wires and wirelesses of the poem. Like Hopkins's famous remark to
Bridges, 'but take breath and read it with ears' (Letters 79), as if ear-reading required
the singer's deep breath, Graham's ear-speaking taps into the auditory pressure of a
great silence. For this poet, to take '"a line for a walk"' is to parade it, not only on
paper, visibly, and not only along the ways of grammar and signification, but also in
the open vestibules of the inner ear.

In 1970 Graham addressed Robin Skelton in a letter with: 'Are you there? Can
you hear me tapping along the invisible lines?' (L 246). Graham often wrote on
his typewriter, thus tapping out another kind of acoustic-visible line. The fierce
injunction 'Can you hear . . .?' not only collars its correspondent, urgently, accus-
ingly, but also opens up the spaces and times of the letter's as yet unlistened-to art.
Of course there's nobody there. The letter goes out on the off-chance that there will
be a listener, eventually, at the other end, but meanwhile there is only the delay,
the longer or shorter time it takes for words to be delivered along all their many
lines. Perhaps letters have this in common with poems: that they constantly look
for, perhaps listen for, good listeners, while knowing that those will be not yet. The
lines of Graham's letter, like those of his poems, lead to a kind of listening which
rarely finds an easy or satisfying message in his communications. The dividing line
between the two genres seems very thin, perhaps non-existent. Certainly, for this
poet, letters are poems in the making, and poems are very often letters. Their titles

acknowledge it: 'Three Letters', 'Seven Letters', 'The Eighth Letter', 'Letter X', 'A Note to the Difficult One', 'Dear Makar Norman', 'Dear Bryan Wynter', 'To My Wife at Midnight', 'How are the Children Robin', 'Yours Truly', 'Dear Who I Mean', 'A Letter more likely to Myself'. The idea of a poem as an address to someone who cannot (yet) answer for themselves involves a knotty contradiction which Graham loves to exploit. These ought to be epistolary lyrics, directed to a known and named someone. Their playful, loving, ragging tone invokes a reader who ought to be an intimate, answerable to a message. But although constructed as direct addresses – 'How are the Children Robin' – very often the address gets lost (like the question mark here), the sent-out meaning goes astray, and communication turns into poetic obstacle to communication. Long before Derrida theorised the apostrophic detour of the letter, Graham was already sending out these extraordinarily inventive, identity-deregulating, address-reassessing constructions. That such poems, with their indirections, their 'chronic hesitation' between monologue and dialogue, come close to the methods of his letters might suggest that the distinctions between epistle and lyric, personal and impersonal, private and public, are very far from watertight.

In one late letter to Robin Skelton, which begs Skelton not to stop his regular payments for Graham's manuscript worksheets, the signing off runs into a bizarre short story, thus trenching on yet another genre divide: 'I will say cheerio farewell love to both now and begin a Graham's Fury Tale and go till the paper O is all stopped' (*L* 290). Thus the poet vents his fury at needing and begging for money, while producing another object, a manuscript story, which might help turn charity to payment. The 'Fury Tale' is yet another free-wheeling account of the lucky inconsequentialities of writing. It is the story of a Word, who cannot read and does not know who he is, who wanders from place to place, mouth to mouth and mouth to ear, in search of his beloved Princess. Word's travels take in all Graham's favourite images: going into the 'whorl' of an ear, till 'in the inner dark the anvil was struck', or travelling along telegraph wires 'in cahoots with the electric', or curled in a book in a library: 'Page 955, para five, two lines down, he in print slept dreaming of his name' (*L* 291). In a sense, this is about language in search of its reader, in search of the addressee who will give name and meaning (and perhaps payment) for its words. All the lines Word follows are attempts to reach the beloved royal reader, who awaits somewhere at the other end of the journey. If letters depend on their addressees, so too, Graham seems to suggest, do stories and poems. All the 'obstacles of communication' on the way to that destination, traversed in the time it takes to read, are part of the strange, and strangely delayed, message that goes from writer to reader. William Waters, writing about the lyric, proposes that 'since the messenger can never arrive . . . your dreamed-up substitute for it is itself the only message worthy of the name' (77). Graham's improvised story seems to enact just such a hiatus in Word's purposeful-purposeless journey. Finally, with the help of 'a boy with a clear musical voice' (*L* 291) – a poet-figure presumably – Word finds his way to the Princess. It is not, however, the boy-poet who discovers Word's real name, but the Princess who greets him with brisk and delighted recognition: 'Your name is Fuck said the Princess and they lived happily ever after' (*L* 292). The story ends with an address which perhaps combines Graham's own furious feelings – fuck to Skelton? – and a satisfying act of love which ensures the fairy-tale ending, 'ever after'. As an allegory of the reading process this repeats, in another form, an old obsession: that literary communication is an epistolary gesture of faith in the destination; that writing goes out in time along its lines – story lines or print lines, lines of time or lines of place – in the hope of finding the beloved reader who will recognise something to reassemble from its words, or Word: 'Your name is Fuck.'

It might be possible, then, to plot a latent poetics of the letter in Graham's writing – a poetics which crosses the genre boundary between letters and poems. Two final poems suggest the extent to which writing, for Graham, is a call to an addressee, in time and out of it. 'I leave this at your ear for when you wake' (P 166) is the title of his lovely gift-poem to his wife, Nessie Dunsmuir. It is a poem full of sounds: the calling owl, the silent house, 'the speaking sea', footsteps on stone, a 'listening' at the door, a 'ticking' clock, the sleeper's 'breath', the gulls' cry. All these are gathered up and contained in that pointed deixis 'this', as if Graham, staggering home late from the pub, were saving all the noises of the night to give to Nessie, who is asleep. But 'this' also makes a little noise of its own, a tiny rustle of paper 'at your ear'. It is not left at your bedside or your pillow, note, but 'your ear', as if the poet-postman were delivering his work to an addressed listener, not for instant reading but for 'when you wake'. The poem must take time to reach the 'ear', maybe a long time – at least till morning. So Graham enacts, once again, the epistolary distance in time that underlies all his writing. To write *to* someone is to have to wait, not knowing if the message will be found or read as intended – in fact, knowing that there will be a necessary rerouting, an 'obstacle' in the means, and that the only message to be received at the other end might be the receiver's own 'dreamed-up substitute'. Meanwhile, 'when you wake' measures out the time before 'this' thing, whether letter or poem, is read, understood, made sense of, made more sense of, and thus generally justifies the poet's intention. For 'this' is not a mere monologue, written for the self, but a dialogue – 'maybe I'm just lonely and I must write something' (L 297) – even if a dialogue broken by the crucial hiatus of a delay.[2]

In some cases the delay may be even longer than a night. 'Are you there are you there listening?' (L 264) Graham once wrote in a letter to the painter Bryan Wynter. A similar question crops up in the poem titled 'Dear Bryan Wynter'. 'Are you there at all?' the poet asks, then adds:

Speaking to you and not
Knowing if you are there
Is not too difficult.
My words are used to that. (P 258)

Indeed, all Graham's letters and poems 'are used to that', playing as they do on the paradoxical, near-and-far-ness of the addressee. 'Not / Knowing if you are there' is the condition of the letter – that word to the ear, private and familiar, which is also a word thrown upon the happy chances of the airwaves and the post. 'Dear Bryan Wynter' addresses its object like any of Graham's letters, with a mix of cajoling raillery, tomfoolery and sheer verbal fun. 'Do you want anything? / Where shall I send something?' (P 259) he asks, as if seeking an address. And indeed an address might be what he is after, but in a wider sense. For Bryan Wynter is dead and the poem is an elegy. 'The Bryan Wynter poem shatters me still' (L 331), Graham wrote three years later. His elegies are some of his best poems, but their range is still that of the casual letter. 'This is only a note / To say how sorry I am / You died,' it begins, as if still expecting an answer 'when you wake'. The extra distance of death is only an extension of the letter's time-lines. Perhaps the letter was always, at some level, elegiac, its urgent invocations only a desperate measure of speech against the odds of silence and space, against the odds that the lines might go awry, be tangled in another, different wiring, and never reach the beloved ear. That the letter is always in some sense a dead letter is a knowledge that pervades all Graham's work. The greatness of his writing lies in letting us *hear* that elsewhere – the absence that lies round all poems and letters, making them lonely things, but things which also reach out along their lines to the sleeping listeners who might, when they wake, make sense of them.

'The Thermal Stair' was written for another painter friend, Peter Lanyon, who died in 1964 in a gliding accident. Lanyon had become a keen glider, and many of his later paintings look at the Cornish landscape from above, through an abstractingly airy distance. Graham's title recalls one painting in particular, called *Thermal*, which seems to be all sky, except for an indistinct stairway below on the left. Graham picks up that hint of a Jacob's Ladder and writes 'The Thermal Stair', as if to suggest a slower way up to the thermals in his own lines. The poem begins with 'I called today, Peter, and you were away' (P 163). It's a heart-stopping first line, which casts the poem as a note left in the man's absence – the kind of note you might slip through a door, finding that a friend is out. But the sense of 'called' must be readjusted, as must the word 'away', for this is closer to Hopkins's 'alas! Away'. Poems, even poems to the dead, are letters always implicitly listening for a reply, casting for the soundwaves that will take their dogged imperatives – 'Find me', 'Sit here', 'Give me', 'Climb here', 'listen' – to the desired listener. This poem, like so many others, opens up into the sound of listening – that imaginary space, or perhaps 'constructed space', any poem makes. In that space, emphasised by the words which pause to hear themselves at each line end, the voice of the listener is cast. It is as if writing spoke to listening, and thus created an ear at the heart of its own noises – an ear into which the thermal stair (of the cochlea perhaps?) might still reach.

'The Thermal Stair', then, is not only a memorial and an elegy to the dead; it is also an audition of the dead, a checking out of the dead as listener at the end of the line(s):

> Uneasy, lovable man, give me your painting
> Hand to steady me taking the word-road home.
> Lanyon, why is it you're earlier away?
> Remember me wherever you listen from.
> Lanyon, dingdong, dingdong from carn to carn.
> It seems tonight all Closing bells are tolling
> Across the Duchy shire wherever I turn. (P 166)

Graham's 'word-road' is not the painter's road, though it may benefit from a painter's helping 'Hand'. If the poet's lines need steadying (particularly when the 'word-road' is a drunken route back from the pub after closing time), those lines are also time-lines, sent out to all the many addressed listeners of the poem. None of those reply in any conventional sense. But they might attend, audibly, at the imagined other end of the poem's time, turning the poet's lonely monologue into a kind of alternating, recipient dialogue: 'dingdong, dingdong'. The address, whether epistolary or poetic, measures the distances 'away' that must be travelled in speech – distances even as unpredictable and unlikely as to the dead – and meanwhile opens a path or road to the other listeners, ourselves, who, somewhere behind all the named 'yous' of a poem, might try to listen back: 'Remember me wherever you listen from.' If not instantly, at least 'when you wake'.

NOTES

1. An early version of this chapter appeared as 'Only practising how to speak: W. S. Graham's Art of Letter Writing', *PN Review* 200 (2012): 54–8.
2. Natalie Pollard, in her book *Speaking to You: Contemporary Poetry and Public Address*, argues that the lyric 'participates in a world of overlapping social relations' (2) and that Graham 'uses his interlocutors to explore the issues of class, patronage, national allegiance, and identity' (20). She thus gives a much more political and social slant to the 'changeable identities' in Graham's letters. Another much more feminist reading is Rebecca Anne Barr's 'W. S. Graham and Epistolarity'.

ABBREVIATIONS OF MAIN WORKS CITED

L: W. S. Graham, *The Nightfisherman: Selected Letters of W. S. Graham*, ed. Michael and Margaret Snow (Manchester: Carcanet, 1999).
P: W. S. Graham, *New Collected Poems*, ed. Matthew Francis (London: Faber, 2004).

OTHER WORKS

Barr, Rebecca Anne, 'W. S. Graham and Epistolarity', *Journal of British and Irish Innovative Poetry* 4 (2012): 51–63.
Bishop, Elizabeth, *Elizabeth Bishop: Poems, Prose, and Letters*, ed. Robert Giroux and Lloyd Schwartz (New York: The Library of America, 2008).
Caddick, Arthur, *Laughter from Land's End*, ed. Rod Humphries (St Ives: St Ives Publishing Company, 2004).
Culler, Jonathan, *Pursuit of Signs: Semiotics, Literature, Deconstruction* (Ithaca, NY: Cornell University Press, 1981).
Derrida, Jacques, *The Post Card: From Socrates to Freud and Beyond*, trans. Alan Bass (Chicago: University of Chicago Press, 1987).
Frost, Anthony, 'The Real St Ives Story', *Tate Online*, 1 September 2006, <http://www.tate.org.uk/context-comment/articles/real-st-ives-story> (last accessed 7 July 2014).

Hammer, Langdon, 'Useless Concentration: Life and Work in Elizabeth Bishop's Letters and Poems', *American Literary History* 9 (1997): 162–80.

Hopkins, Gerard Manley, *The Letters of Gerard Manley Hopkins to Robert Bridges*, ed. Claude Colleer Abbott (London: Oxford University Press, 1955 [1935]).

—— *The Poems of Gerard Manley Hopkins*, ed. W. H. Gardner and N. H. MacKenzie (Oxford: Oxford University Press, 1970).

Kermode, Frank, and Anita Kermode (eds), *The Oxford Book of Letters* (Oxford: Oxford University Press, 1995).

Lambirth, Andrew, *Roger Hilton: The Figured Language of Thought* (London: Thames & Hudson, 2007).

Leighton, Angela, *On Form: Poetry, Aestheticism, and the Legacy of a Word* (Oxford: Oxford University Press, 2007).

Maber, Peter, '"The poet or painter steers his life to maim": W. S. Graham and the St Ives modernist school', *Word & Image* 25 (2009): 258–71.

Millier, Brett C., *Elizabeth Bishop: Life and the Memory of It* (Berkeley: University of California Press, 1993).

Paulin, Tom, 'Writing to the Moment: Elizabeth Bishop', *Writing to the Moment: Selected Critical Essays 1980–1996* (London: Faber and Faber, 1996), pp. 215–39.

Peters, John Durham, *Speaking into the Air: A History of the Idea of Communication* (Chicago: Chicago University Press, 1999).

Pollard, Natalie, *Speaking to You: Contemporary Poetry and Public Address* (Oxford: Oxford University Press, 2012).

Rilke, Rainer Maria, *Rainer Maria Rilke and Lou Andreas-Salomé: The Correspondence*, trans. Edward Snow and Michael Winkler (New York: W. W. Norton, 2006).

Snow, Michael, 'When We Who We Think We Are: Encountering W. S. Graham', *Aquarius* 25 (2002): 11–14.

Waters, William, *Poetry's Touch: On Lyric Address* (Ithaca, NY: Cornell University Press, 2003).

Woolf, Virginia, 'A Letter to a Young Poet', *Collected Essays*, ed. Leonard Woolf (London: Chatto & Windus, 1966), pp. 182–95.

14   Fire Balloons:
The Letters of Robert Lowell
and Elizabeth Bishop

Paul Muldoon

I

Let me begin at the end, as one so often does with a letter as a poem, and read the last few lines of Elizabeth Bishop's 'The Armadillo':

> *Too pretty, dreamlike mimicry!*
> *O falling fire and piercing cry*
> *and panic, and a weak mailed fist*
> *clenched ignorant against the sky!* (P 84)

I want to spend the next while thinking about the extent to which letters may provide a system for allowing us to better understand a work of art, in this case several works of art by Robert Lowell and Elizabeth Bishop. I'll be thinking about the extent to which it is appropriate for either the reader or the writer to draw on material from 'private' letters in making literature, an issue on which Lowell and Bishop disagreed. I'll be looking at a poem by Lowell, 'Skunk Hour', in the light of letters between himself and Bishop, and, in the first instance, a poem by Bishop, 'The Armadillo', in the light of letters between herself and Lowell. The Lowell-Bishop correspondence extends to 800 pages and, as edited by Thomas Travisano and Saskia Hamilton, was published in 2008 under the title *Words in Air*. I'll be suggesting that the correspondence between Lowell and Bishop was more often than not guarded rather than unbuttoned, more often than not representing an iron fist in a velvet glove but, sometimes, a velvet fist in an iron glove. I take as my cue the description by Bishop of a fist being 'mailed' both in the sense of being covered in protective armour 'composed of interlaced rings' and also as 'a bag or packet of letters or dispatches for conveyance by post' (*OED*). I'll be focusing on the letters in *Words in Air*, but I'll also draw on other sources, including *Elizabeth Bishop and The New Yorker*, edited by Joelle Biele, in which we're given access to some of the behind-the-scenes dealings between Bishop and the poetry editor of *The New Yorker*, Howard Moss.

On 15 August 1956 Bishop had sent 'The Armadillo' to Moss with a typically self-effacing cover letter that allowed him to pass on it with no harm done:

Dear Howard:
    Here is a Nature Note. Since I realize you really don't want to run a Brazilian column, I won't be surprised if you feel you can't use it. Send it back and I'll save it for a Brazilian group I'm working on. (NYR 180)

Bishop's winning tendency to downplay herself is not lost on Howard Moss, however. On 24 August 1956 he responds:

Dear Elizabeth:
    We love THE ARMADILLO, which is charming and much more. We would like, if you don't mind, to put 'Brazil' in parentheses under the title to place the poem, and a word from you about what 'time of year' these fire-balloons are used would help us run it at the right time to go with the suggested sub-title. (NYR 180)

Had Howard Moss been privy to the correspondence of Bishop and her doctor, Anny Baumann, he would have been only too aware of the 'time of year':

Fire balloons are supposed to be illegal but everyone sends them up anyway and we usually spend St. John's Day and the nights before and after watching the balloons drift right up the mountain towards the house – there seems to be a special draught; Lota has a sprinkling system on the roof because of them. & They are so pretty – one's of two minds about them. (Millier 275–6)

St John's Day is a Christianised version of the midsummer solstice, a so-called pagan festival in which the bonfire played a significant role given its mirroring and mimicry of the sun. That the prophet St John the Baptist is described as 'not only a burning but a shining light', a distinction remarked upon by Jonathan Edwards in his discussion of John 5: 35, provides the perfect connection between worshippers of the sun and worshippers of the Son of God.
    Bishop's own sense of the precise date of St John's Day turns out to be a little hazy, at least from the evidence of her 3 September 1956 letter to Howard Moss, in which she unconsciously refers to the prophet John in her use of the word 'prophetic':

Dear Howard:
    I'm glad you liked The Armadillo. I wish I wrote prophetic poems sometimes instead of the recollected kind – the fire balloons start appearing in June. They are used mostly to celebrate St. John's day – that's either June 14th or 15th – the biggest holiday here. I think they are also used for another saint sometime in August – anyway, one sees them frequently in the month of June, and occasionally in July and August. (NYR 181)

As it happens, the feast of St John falls on 24 June, which is why the publication of the poem in *The New Yorker* would be held for almost a year, until 22 June 1957.

By that time a few changes will have taken place. In that letter of 3 September 1956, Bishop had suggested a typographical shift:

> I think that perhaps the last stanza would look better italicized; what do you think? If it is, perhaps I could leave off the final exclamation point. I also think that 'escaping' in the fifth stanza would be better exchanged for 'forsaking'. I trust that's my final tinkering. (*NYR* 181)

The shift from 'and steadily escaping us' to 'and steadily forsaking us' is a significant one since it underscores the Christian iconography already underscored by 'the kite sticks of the Southern *Cross*'. We might remember that the phrase *Eli, Eli, lama sabachtani* attributed to Christ on the cross is generally rendered as 'My God, my God, why hast thou *forsaken* me?' Moss's reply of 21 September 1956 had been both punctual and punctilious:

> Dear Elizabeth:
> Here's the proof of THE ARMADILLO and your check. We've had a change of mind about the title. We think it looks better if Brazil is put into the title after a dash – rather than the sub-title I first suggested. We also think putting the last stanza into italics is a good idea, and if you still think so, we'll have it set up that way when it comes out. (*NYR* 182)

Neither Bishop nor Moss expands on why the use of italics for the last stanza is such a great idea. We know that italicisation may denote any of a range of ideas including emphasis, foreign phrases, the introduction or definition of terms, an indication of a character's thought process or, in this case, an amalgam of all of these. It's not inconceivable, indeed, that the last stanza of 'The Armadillo' may be read as the musing of a Christ figure on the state of the world. The final exclamation mark isn't dropped, in the end, as if to emphasise that emphasis isn't the main business of the italicisation, though the line ('*clenched ignorant against the sky!*') looks a little like a visual representation of a fire balloon itself. The idea that the last stanza is somehow 'other', though, is a relevant one. It's as if it's an organ that has somehow been harvested and transplanted into the body of this text in the manner of Miss Marianne Moore.

The name of Marianne Moore was certainly one that would come to the mind of Robert Lowell, writing to Bishop on 10 June 1957, just before 'The Armadillo' appeared in *The New Yorker*:

> I've read your poems many times. I think I read you with more interest than anyone now writing. I know I do, but I think I would even if it weren't for personal reasons. 'The Armadillo' is surely one of your three or four very best. I thought the title mistaken at first, a Moore name – though I suppose the armadillo is much too popular and common garden animal for her – for an out-

of-doors, personally seen and utterly un-Moore poem. However, 'Armadillo' is right, for the little creature, given only five lines, runs off with the whole poem. Weak and armored, I suppose he is those people carrying balloons-illegal-to their local saint. (*WIA* 204)

Unconsciously, perhaps, Lowell has hit upon a connection between that 'local saint' and the armadillo in that he's tapped into the system of imagery that links armour and light. 'Let us therefore cast aside the deeds of darkness and let us put on the armour of light,' as St Paul exhorts the Romans (13. 12). In addition to the light symbolism associated with St John the Baptist, there is a corresponding symbolism, of dark associated with the 'ancient owls' and their nest. The owl that is associated with Athena and darkness flies in the face of Christ and his role as 'light of the world'. In medieval Christian iconography the owl is associated with sin, with the Jews who preferred darkness to light, and, in Saint Jerome, it seems, as a symbol of a false deity. One false deity for Lowell, by the sound of it, might have been Moore herself.

It's fascinating to see the very first mention of Miss Moore, as he calls her, in a breathless, bristling letter from Lowell to Bishop written on 14 January 1948. The subject is outwardly his negotiations on behalf of the Library of Congress, for which he worked as poetry consultant:

In the middle of this letter my one real Library thorn has begun to prick me: the buying from Harvard at some expense and absolutely endless and incomprehensible technicalities, letters, copyright forms, discussions with the interminable Dr. Spivack of the Music Division, correspondence with Professor Packard and the President of Harvard: of – John Brinnin, Paul Engle, Eberhart, Ted Spencer, JG Fletcher (something not even a poem but polyphonic prose), Jeffers (almost impossible to follow) and Miss Moore (which you've heard) Judas-Jesus!!! (*WIA* 21)

It's almost as impossible to follow Lowell as Jeffers but I'd like to propose here that the odd formulation of 'Judas-Jesus!!!' is an indicator of Lowell's deep-seated but unspoken antipathy towards Moore and his feeling that he has betrayed Bishop's long friendship with her. When he refers, in his letter of 10 June 1957, to 'The Armadillo' being 'an out-of-doors, personally seen and utterly un-Moore' poem, it's hard not to read this as a critique of Moore being academic, abstract and, in some profound sense, unsuccessful.

He's thinking, perhaps, of an owl that appears in an early Moore poem, 'The Hero', published in *Selected Poems* (1935):

Where there is personal liking we go
    where the ground is sour; where there are
    weeds of beanstalk height,
    snakes' hypodermic teeth, or
    the wind brings the 'scarebabe voice'

from the neglected yew set with
   the semi-precious cat's eyes of the owl –
awake, asleep, 'raised ears extended to fine points,' and so
on – love won't grow. (*Complete Poems* 8)

This 'owl' is a progenitor of the 'ancient owl' that appears in 'The Armadillo', while both an owl and, of all things, an 'armadillo' have shown up in, of all places, a letter from Bishop to Moore herself, written on 5 June 1956:

> After all this time, I've just found out we have armadillos here – I see one crossing the road in the headlights at night, with his head and tail down – very lonely and glisteny. There's also a kind of small owl that sits in the road at night – I had to go out and shoo one away from the front of the car last night. They have large eyes; when they fly off look exactly like pin-wheels – black and white. (Millier 275)

Some of these details carry over into the poem, almost word for word, as in 'with his head and tail down' appearing as 'head down, tail down'. In general, we see how a 'nature note' in the context of a letter is either transferred wholesale like the 'head down, tail down' example or, more often, improved upon when it becomes literature with a capital L.

A case in point would be the 'pin-wheels – black and white' which becomes a hyphenated 'black-and-white'. The 'pin-wheel' description has been dropped, probably because it's less striking than the general system of imagery, including the fire balloons themselves, that has now been foregrounded in the poem. In other words, the 'pin-wheels' would now seem fussy and excessive, causing a reader to engage in unnecessary work of the kind William Empson describes:

> An example of the second type of ambiguity, in word or syntax, occurs when two or more meanings are resolved into one. There are alternatives, even in the mind of the author, not only different emphases as in the first type; but an ordinary good reading can extract one resultant from them. (48)

An awareness of Bishop's description of the 'pin-wheels' in her letter allows us to see how she came to some decisions when the poem was being constructed. One may deduce, for example, that the 'wheel' component may have been thought to be too close to the '*whirling* black-and-white' to be allowed houseroom, while the hyphenated 'black-and-white' might force readers to individuate it as a concept and have us visualise something akin to a 'pin-wheel'. The 'pin' component has been at once included in and cancelled out by the phrase 'stained bright *pink* underneath'. As well as providing evidence of the kind William Empson would rule out of court about improvement to, or refinements of, a 'nature note', letters also provide evidence that descriptions may sometimes lose something of their first gleam and glow. I'm thinking here of Bishop's use in her letter to Moore of the word 'glisteny' which, when standardised to 'glistening', loses rather a lot of its effect. The counter argument is that 'glisteny' draws too much attention to itself and would lend further support to the final stanza's setting down the case against the non-italicised body of the poem as being '*too pretty, dreamlike mimicry*'.

II

On the subject of mimicry, let me appeal now to a letter Lowell writes to Bishop on 11 September 1957, a letter marked by his usual penchant for self-dramatisation:

> I've been furiously writing at poems and have spent whole blue and golden Maine days in my bedroom with a ghastly utility bedside lamp on, my pajamas turning oily with sweat, and I have six poems started. They beat the big drum too much. There's one in a small voice that's fairly charmingly written I hope (called 'Skunk Hour,' not in your style yet indebted a little to your 'Armadillo.') (WIA 230)

The subtext here, though it's hardly too *sub*, is that Elizabeth Bishop writes 'in a small voice that's fairly charming'. The word 'charming' has a distinctly pejorative tinge. We remember Howard Moss used it of the poem when he described it as being 'charming and much more' with the accent firmly on the 'and much more'. It's hard to know if Lowell is even aware of how condescending he is, any more than Bishop is cognisant of the near version of Lowell's name she has introduced into the description of 'the pair / of owls' followed up by the 'armadillo' itself. Substantial components of the name Lowell are to be rather bold-facedly found there, and it's no accident, I suspect, that there's a break after the word 'pair', a comment on the circumstance in which Lowell and herself would, or could, never be a 'pair'.

By the time Lowell was writing to Bishop about 'Skunk Hour', on 11 September 1957, they'd been friends for almost exactly ten years. Just a month before, in August 1957, Lowell had indeed written to Bishop about their relationship. I'll quote at length from this long letter since it strikes me as the most heartfelt, and is certainly the most heartbreaking, of their long correspondence:

> I want you to know that you need never again fear my overstepping myself and stirring up confusion with you. My frenzied behaviour during your visit has a history and there is one fact that I want to disengage from all its harsh frenzy. There's one bit of the past that I would like to get off my chest and then I think all will be easy with us.
>
> Do you remember how at the end of that long swimming and sunning Stonington day after Carley's removal by Tommy, we went up to, I think, the relatively removed upper Gross house and had one of those real fried New England dinners, probably awful. And we were talking about this and that about ourselves and I was feeling the infected hollowness of the Carley business draining out of my heart, and you said rather humorously yet it was truly meant, 'When you write my epitaph, you must say I was the loneliest person who ever lived.' (WIA 225)

If we may take a moment to break away for a little intertextual commentary on the letters of Bishop, Lowell and, in this case, Moore, we might cast our minds back to Bishop's description to Moore of the armadillo 'with his head and tail down – very *lonely* and glisteny'. This was the lonely Bishop whom Lowell addressed in an unpublished poem entitled 'The Two Weeks' Vacation' and which is quoted by Ian Hamilton in *Robert Lowell: A Biography* (1983):

'You and I, I and you,'
The old stuck ballad record repeated –
My Darling Elizabeth, we were alone
And together – at last
More or less hand in hand
On the rocks at Stonington;
For thirteen days we had been three . . .
My old flame, Mrs. X – never left us,
Each morning she met us with another
Crashing ensemble,
Her British voice, her Madame du Barry
Black and gold eyebrows.
She survived a whole day of handline
Deep sea fishing for polock [*sic*], skate and skulpin [*sic*],
Making me bait her hooks. (134)

This portrait of Carley Dawson is less flattering of her than its author, who loves to present himself as 'callous', a word he finds himself using as he continues his August 1957 letter to 'the loneliest person who ever lived':

Probably you forget, and anyway all that is mercifully changed and all has come right since you found Lota. But at the time everything, I guess (I don't want to overdramatize) our relations seemed to have reached a new place. I assumed that [it] would be just a matter of time before I proposed and I half believed that you would accept. Yet I wanted it all to have the right build-up. Well, I didn't say anything then. And of course the Eberharts in-laws wasn't the right stage-setting, and then there was that poetry conference at Bard and I remember one evening presided over by Mary McCarthy and my Elizabeth was there, and going home to the Bard poets' dormitory, I was so drunk that my hands turned cold and I felt half-dying and held your hand. And nothing was said, and like a loon that needs sixty feet, I believe, to take off from the water, I wanted time and space, and went on assuming, and when I was to have joined you at Key West I was determined to ask you. Really for so callous (I fear) a man, I was fearfully shy and scared of spoiling things and distrustful of being steady enough to be the least good. (*WIA* 225–6)

One needs at least sixty feet of this letter to get a sense of just how looney, in the loonatic sense, Lowell is as he takes off.

'Callous' is not a term he uses in his letter of 21 August 1947, only the second he wrote to Bishop:

Dear Elizabeth:
  (You must be called that; I'm called Cal, but I won't explain why. None of the prototypes are flattering: Calvin, Caligula, Caliban, Calvin Coolidge, Calligraphy – with merciless irony.) (WIA 7)

In just the way Lowell insists that he doesn't 'want to overdramatize' and proceeds to use terms such as 'stage-setting', so he insists that he 'won't explain why' he's nicknamed Cal and then proceeds to give a roll-call of possibilities. Lowell continues:

I'm glad you wrote me, because it gives me an excuse to tell you how much I liked your New Yorker fish poem. Perhaps, it's your best. Anyway I felt very envious in reading it – I'm a fisherman myself, but all my fish become symbols, alas! The description has great splendor, and the human part, tone, etc., is just right. I question a little the word breast in the last four or five lines – a little too much in its context perhaps; but I'm probably wrong. (WIA 7)

This seems an odd note to strike in a second letter to a poet one barely knows about a poem that has already been published. The word with which Lowell is having a problem is not 'breast', as it happens, but 'breasts', and it occurs in the third to last line of 'At the Fishhouses', a title Lowell should surely be able to manage rather than describe it as 'your New Yorker fish poem'. The litany of praise should include something beyond the term 'etc.', I propose, if it's to strike a chord within the breast of the recipient of the praise.

  The one sentiment that rings true in all of this is 'I felt very envious in reading it', an indicator of Lowell's notorious desire to be king of the cats. It's interesting, too, that the image at which he balks has to do with suckling and sustenance and, in the general sense, the idea of forebears. This in the context of a second letter by Lowell which is by way of response to a second letter from Bishop in which she was thanking Lowell for his enthusiastic Sewanee Review notice of her work in which he commented on Marianne Moore as forebear:

It is obvious that her most important model is Marianne Moore. Her dependence should not be defined as imitation, but as one of development and transformation. . . . Compared with Moore, she is softer, dreamier, more human and more personal; she is less idiosyncratic, and less magnificent. ('Thomas, Bishop, and Williams' 187–8)

Let me skip forward to January 1973, to another letter from Lowell to Bishop in which he takes a sideswipe at Moore:

The Pelican must be Marianne, but aren't all her animals her? Their carefully noted anatomies given Moorish virtue? Oh thanks thanks for your lovely magnifying paperweight. Will I someday stare thru the white flower or coral, half-blind, to read letters. (*WIA* 739)

The pelican to which Lowell refers is 'The Frigate Pelican', the subject of a 108-line poem printed in Moore's *Selected Poems* of 1935 so drastically revised to forty-seven lines that one will look in vain for the reference to an animal to which Moore appends this note in her 1951 *Collected Poems* and the 1967 *Complete Poems of Marianne Moore*: 'Giant tame armadillo. Photograph and description by W. Stephen Thomas of New York' (265). That 'giant tame armadillo' has, one might say, resurfaced and been restored in Bishop's poem, as have a couple of images that have survived into the last version of 'The Frigate Pelican':

> The others with similar ease,
> slowly rising once more,
> move out to the top
> of the circle and stop

> and blow back, allowing the wind to reverse their direction. (25)

That might be a description of the fire balloons in 'The Armadillo', as indeed might this:

> He glides
> a hundred feet or quivers about
> as *charred paper* behaves – full
> of feints. (26)

These carryings over from Moore to Bishop may be unconscious on Bishop's part. Not so Lowell's appropriation of Bishop in 'Skunk Hour', right down to the assumption of her name in line 4:

> Nautilus Island's hermit
> heiress still lives through winter in her Spartan cottage;
> her sheep still graze above the sea.
> Her son's a *bishop*. (191; my emphasis)

This is a kind of double whammy for Lowell, since 'Nautilus Island's hermit / heiress' is a version of Moore, author of 'The Paper *Nautilus*' (my emphasis), while it was Moore, in an introduction to Bishop as long previously as 1935, who wrote of her:

> One notices the deferences and vigilances in Miss Bishop's writing, and the debt to Donne and to Gerard Hopkins. We look at imitation askance; but like the shell which the *hermit*-crab selects for itself, it has value – the avowed humility, and the protection. ('Archaically New' 175–6)

We can be fairly confident that 'avowed humility' is not a charge Moore would ever have laid at Lowell's door, a fact that may have wounded him even as he welcomed it.

As for 'imitation', here's Lowell's own self-assessment in a letter of April 1958 as he describes a teaching stint in Chicago: 'I used your "Armadillo" in class as a parallel to my "Skunks" and ended up feeling a petty plagiarist' (WIA 258). The shift from 'imitation' to 'plagiar[ism]' is one that Lowell may have anticipated as early on as 3 December 1957 when he announced: 'I'm dedicating "Skunk Hour" to you. A skunk isn't much of a present for a Lady Poet, but I'm a skunk in the poem' (WIA 239). So much for Lowell's later musings on Moore and all her animals being 'her'.

Lowell's depiction of himself to Bishop as a 'skunk' may be influenced partly by a regret for the behaviour to which he'd alluded in his letter of a mere four months earlier (August 1957), in which he described himself as being 'callous':

> Let me [say] this though and then leave the matter forever; I do think free will is sewn into everything we do; you can't cross a street, light a cigarette, drop saccharine in your coffee without really doing it. Yet the possible alternatives that life allows us are very few, often there must be none. I've never thought there was any choice for me about writing poetry. No doubt if I used my head better, ordered my life better, worked harder etc., the poetry would be improved, and there must be many lost poems, innumerable accidents and ill-done actions. But asking you is *the* might have been for me, the one towering change, the other life that might have been had. (WIA 226)

III

I'm going to move towards a conclusion here by thinking about letters as 'the other life that [a poem] might have had' and a poem as 'the other life that [letters] might have had'. I begin with Bishop's response to Cal on his dedication to her of 'Skunk Hour', a response no less calibrated than any of his missives to her: 'I still like the skunk one enormously, although I suppose it's exercises compared to the other ones' (WIA 246). This is brilliantly judged. On the one hand it takes into account the debt the poem pays to her own work and plays it down. On the other it's no less incendiary in its description of 'Skunk Hour' as 'the skunk one' than had been Lowell in describing 'At the Fishhouses' as 'the *New Yorker* fish poem'. The non-agreement of the singular 'it's' and the plural 'exercises' is every bit as sly. The suggestion is that several, perhaps quite a number, of Lowell's poems are *mere* exercises. I know that some readers will think I'm exaggerating the nasty subtext here, but I do want to suggest that, despite their outward bombast, these letters have their inward tendency to quietly bombard. Let's not forget Lowell's strategically placed comma in his description of 'The Armadillo' as 'Perhaps, it's your best'. Let's not forget that these writers are interested in commas, willing to engage in discussions over them.

Here's Howard Moss again, on the subject of commas in 'The Armadillo':

I think all the other suggestions are clear, except I'm not sure about the commas in the last line of stanza 3. It depends, I think, on whether you mean Mars to be going down, as well as Venus, or whether you're simply qualifying Venus, then refer to Mars with no qualification, and then go on to the pale green one. I hope that makes sense, but please do what you want with the punctuation. I think the line is clearer with the commas if you're referring to three separate things, each with or without its own qualifiers. (NYR 182)

The comma is an outward expression of the kind of hesitancy that lies behind a phrase like 'I still like the skunk one enormously'. Let's face it, the burden of this is 'I haven't stopped liking the skunk one, just as in other cases, I've initially liked your poems but then gone off them'.

My own reading of this goes back to the intertextuality of the Bishop-Lowell letters to which I referred earlier. I believe that even the most careless of these letters are written not only with care but with a career-sense that includes the distinct possibility – no, the absolute certainty – that they would one day be published and pored over with the kind of scrutiny we're bringing to them even today. My theory, which is probably going to sound a bit far-fetched, is that the 'I still like' from Bishop's letter of 14 December 1957 refers directly to a line Lowell had used in his letter of June 1957, the one in which he had described 'The Armadillo' as 'surely one of your three or four very best': 'I'm awfully relieved that Lota has my number and *still likes* me best of your poets' (WIA 204; my emphasis). The number that Lowell hopes Maria Carlota Constellat de Macedo Soares has is Number 1. A Brazilian architect who was also Bishop's lover, Lota is always some sort of persistent if not very present threat to his vision of Bishop being his Number 1.

This was the vision of 'the other life that might have been had' which he'd described in his letter of 15 August 1957, the letter in which he'd also mused on 'free will': 'I do think free will is sewn into everything we do; you can't cross a street, light a cigarette, drop saccharine in your coffee without really doing it.' Again, I think Bishop has this litany in mind when she comes to write to Lowell, in August 1965, in response to his letter of 16 July in which he had written a blurb for her new book. The blurb had read:

> I am sure no living poet is as curious and observant as Miss Bishop. What cuts so deep is that each poem is inspired by her own tone, a tone of large, grave tenderness and sorrowing amusement. She is too sure of herself for empty mastery and breezy plagiarism, too interested for confession and musical monotony, too powerful for mismanaged fire, and too civilized for idiosyncratic incoherence. She has a humorous, commanding genius for picking up the unnoticed, now making something sprightly and right, and now a great monument. Once her poems, each shining, were too few. Now they are many. When we read her, we enter the classical serenity of a new country. (WIA 580)

Bishop writes back to Lowell: 'I like especially of course, being "curious" and "sprightly" – both words I hope I really live up to' (WIA 582). Bishop is all too aware, surely, that the word 'curious' cuts two ways, meaning both 'careful attention to detail' and, more often in the popular imagination, 'somewhat surprising, strange, singular, odd, queer' (*OED*). The same is true of the word 'observant', which means both 'quick to notice and perceive' and, less attractively, 'dutiful'.

When one examines the entirety of the Lowell blurb, as she must have, one sees that its resonant lines have an underbelly of resentment. He writes that 'she is too sure of herself', generally a form of put-down. He cannot help but acknowledge that something 'cuts so deep', oblivious to its description of his own being wounded. He writes that her poems are 'many' with a suggestion that they might somehow be '*too many*', the phrase that would balance 'too few'. The entire blurb is shot through with the imagery associated with the 'fire balloons' – the poems are 'shining' and 'too powerful for *mismanaged fire*'. It's no wonder then that it should be in this same letter of 2 August 1965 that Bishop announces: 'I don't think I told you – but I finally decided to put your name under the Armadillo poem, since you have liked it' (*WIA* 582–3). Again, the tone of this is perfectly judged. It's even, and it's in some sense *getting even*. Bishop has taken on Lowell's disaffected air and mimics it perfectly. Are we really to believe that Bishop would have forgotten that she had planned to dedicate 'The Armadillo' to Lowell? And that's the title of the poem, not 'the Armadillo poem'. It's under the title, moreover, that she's 'finally decided to put your name', not under the poem itself. That would suggest that the poem was written by Lowell, rather than merely *rewritten* by him in 'Skunk Hour'. The phrase 'since you have liked it' is charged also, proposing as it does that Lowell may once have liked the poem but no longer does. Bishop continues in this vein:

> And well – we may be a terrible pair of log-rollers, I don't know – however – I do know that I meant every word I said and I think you do too, in the kindness of your heart. I've just read through a huge anthology – *A Controversy of Poets* – and your familiar three poems in that are the ONLY ones I'd – well, cross the street for. Possibly one or two others are good, but not even comparable, really. (*WIA* 583)

This is hot air, and Bishop knows it. As I suggested earlier, the phrase 'well, cross the street for' is prompted by a memory of Lowell's 15 August letter from 1957, almost ten years earlier, in his musings on 'free will'.

She acknowledges, in dedicating 'The Armadillo' to Lowell, something she hadn't quite acknowledged in those almost ten years – just how central Lowell's own role is in the poem. The occasion of the poem, as we've seen, is the Feast of St John the Baptist, also known as St John the Forerunner, who anticipates Christ in the way that Bishop might be seen, particularly by Lowell, to have anticipated him. 'The Armadillo' may have been a poem Lowell would 'carry in [his] billfold and occasionally amaze people with' (*WIA* 324), but it also made straight the path for 'Skunk Hour'. In October 1965, Lowell would again write to praise the poems in *Questions of Travel*, for which he'd already written the blurb:

> My favorites are 'Brazil' – how I envy the historical stretch at the end, so beautifully coming out of the vegetation – 'Manuelzinho's' a dazzling masterpiece

– 'Armadillo' – how proud and swell-headed I am about your dedication, one of your absolutely top poems, your greatest quatrain poem, I mean it has a wonderful formal-informal grandeur – I see the bomb in it in a delicate way. (WIA 591)

'The bomb' is indeed *the* bomb, of the kind that had been tested over Bikini Atoll on 20 May 1956, almost three months to the day before Bishop sent her 'Nature Note' to Howard Moss at *The New Yorker*:

Last night another big one fell.
It splattered like an egg of fire
against the cliff behind the house.
The flame ran down. (P 84)

'The Armadillo' also enacts a kind of baptism by fire familiar to Lowell from more conventional armaments, such as the firebombing of Hamburg in 1943 which had prompted him to become a Conscientious Objector, refuse military service and serve a prison sentence in New York. As she made her dedication to Lowell in 1965, Bishop was formalising the vision of him that is informally abundant in the poem.

Let me close by making a couple of points about the version of Lowell who appears there and who may come to influence Lowell's version of himself. For example, in a letter written in March 1959, Lowell would describe himself as having in him 'the Puritanical iron hand of constraint and the gushes of pure wildness' (WIA 295), almost a version of the love and war (Venus and Mars) vying for supremacy in 'The Armadillo'. 'The Puritanical iron hand' is a reworking, surely, of the italicised '*weak mailed fist*'. That italicisation is itself a device that Lowell would appeal to in a letter written as late as 1972 and responding to Bishop's famous 'big one' she dropped on him for quoting, or misquoting, letters from Elizabeth Hardwick that he'd incorporated into poems in *The Dolphin*. Bishop had complained that:

One can use one's life as material – one does, anyway – but these letters – aren't you violating a trust? IF you were given permission – IF you hadn't changed them . . . etc. But *art just isn't worth that much*. (WIA 708)

The italicisation of the sentence may be read as a restatement of the argument, if we may term it such, of the last stanza of 'The Armadillo' in which the 'pretty' response is inadequate to either the fate of the animals before fire or the fate of the citizenry of Hamburg or the Bikini Atoll or Rio de Janeiro in the face of their predicaments.

It was an argument that had been rather succinctly put by Marianne Moore in 'The Frigate Pelican': 'Be gay / civilly? How so?' (26). The moral responsibilities raised by Bishop in the case of Lowell's treatment of Elizabeth Hardwick and her letters are dealt with by Lowell as follows:

I take your moral objections are confined to the letters, and not to all of them. Several can be handled and perhaps improved by using some of the lines in italics, and giving the rest, somewhat changed, to me. (WIA 715)

This idea must have struck an odd chord in Bishop's breast, particularly if she'd remembered the extent to which she herself had taken a couple of key phrases in the last stanzas of 'The Armadillo', only 'somewhat changed', from Lowell's notice of her in the *Sewanee Review*: 'Compared with Moore, she is softer, dreamier, more human and more personal; she is less idiosyncratic, and less magnificent.' Again, there's a sense that Lowell can't help but allow himself to 'wobble and toss' even as he seems set to praise Bishop. It's hard not to read the phrase 'less magnificent' as another put-down. 'Softer' and 'dreamier' are hardly qualities we normally associate with first-rate poetry, yet Lowell seems entirely oblivious to their less than ameliorative associations.

Bishop's far from oblivious, though, which is why she folds the pejorative vocabulary of Lowell's notice into these final stanzas:

So soft! – a handful of intangible ash
With fixed, ignited eyes.

Too pretty, dreamlike mimicry!
O falling fire and piercing cry
and panic, and the weak mailed fist
clenched ignorant against the sky! (P 84)

When Lowell praises the armadillo because he (and it is a *he*) 'run[s] off with the whole poem', it's yet another projection of himself that Bishop, his forebear, with all her customary forbearance, has already figured in.

ABBREVIATIONS OF MAIN WORKS CITED

NYR: Elizabeth Bishop, Howard Moss, Katherine White et al., *Elizabeth Bishop and The New Yorker: The Complete Correspondence*, ed. Joelle Biele (New York: Farrar, Straus and Giroux, 2011).

P: Elizabeth Bishop, *Poems, Prose, and Letters*, ed. Robert Giroux and Lloyd Schwartz (New York: Library of America, 2008).

WIA: Elizabeth Bishop and Robert Lowell, *Words in Air: The Complete Correspondence Between Elizabeth Bishop and Robert Lowell*, ed. Thomas Travisano with Saskia Hamilton (New York: Farrar, Straus and Giroux, 2008).

OTHER WORKS

Bishop, Elizabeth, *One Art: Letters*, ed. Robert Giroux (New York: Farrar, Straus and Giroux, 1994).

Empson, William, *Seven Types of Ambiguity* (London: Hogarth Press, 1984 [1930]).

Hamilton, Ian, *Robert Lowell: A Biography* (London: Faber and Faber, 1983).

Lowell, Robert, *Collected Poems*, ed. Frank Bidart and David Gewanter (London: Faber and Faber, 2003).

—— 'Thomas, Bishop, and Williams', in Lloyd Schwartz and Sybil P. Estess (eds), *Elizabeth Bishop and Her Art* (Ann Arbor: University of Michigan Press, 1983), pp. 186–9.

Millier, Brett C., *Elizabeth Bishop: Life and the Memory of It* (Berkeley: University of California Press, 1993).

Moore, Marianne, 'Archaically New', in Lloyd Schwartz and Sybil P. Estess (eds), *Elizabeth Bishop and Her Art* (Ann Arbor: University of Michigan Press, 1983), pp. 175–6.

—— *The Complete Poems of Marianne Moore* (London: Faber and Faber, 1967).

15 Last Letters:
Keats, Bishop and Hughes

Jonathan Ellis

I

What is a last letter? Perhaps the unfinished and unsent letter that Vincent van Gogh had with him when he fatally wounded himself on 27 July 1890, a fact poignantly revealed by his brother Theo's handwritten note (you can still see it in pencil at the very top of the manuscript page): 'the letter he had on him on 27 July, that horrible day'.[1] Or is it the letter that van Gogh actually finished and sent, dated 23 July 1890, four days before he actually shot himself? The letter that arrived certainly looks finished, illustrated with sketches of paintings that still astonish with their energy and life. These are not just copies of paintings, but companion pieces that are an integral part of van Gogh's conception of what a letter might be. Put simply, letters were not simply about communicating information for van Gogh, what we might call nowadays gossip or news; letters were also a form of sketchbook, a visual poetry. In his last letter, or at least in his last sent letter, van Gogh is both talking to his brother and sketching for us, living in the present but also writing for posterity. Lost to time *and* somehow immortal.

One might argue that all literature does this, or rather all great literature. Shakespeare is both a Renaissance man and (in Jan Kott's famous words) 'our contemporary'. He belongs to history but still speaks to us today. And yet the character, the very tense of a letter, is not quite the same as in other literary genres. Letter writers address themselves to the future even when they are talking about and in the present. Van Gogh's last letter to Theo is also meant for us. Perhaps this explains why there are at least two versions? He wanted to make sure that at least one of these last letters survived.

I would like to turn to another series of last letters, this time from John Keats, arguably the greatest poet letter writer. Keats, like van Gogh, always kept two audiences in mind when writing a letter: the person or people he was writing to and, hovering after and beyond their reading of his words, our reading too. Keats's letters to his never-to-be-future wife, Fanny Brawne, are some of the most touching letters ever written. Keats is famous as a poet of touch, or rather, one might say, as a poet of almost-touch. His frozen lovers on the Grecian Urn may look 'happy', but can a love that is 'still to be enjoyed' forever really be that enviable? In one of Keats's last ever letters, written from Naples to his friend Charles Brown the day after being released from quarantine, the poet speaks as if he were one of these urn-bound lovers come briefly back to life, still hoping against hope to catch up with Fanny:

> Naples. Wednesday first in November [1820].
>
> My dear Brown,
>   Yesterday we were let out of Quarantine, during which my health suffered more from bad air and a stifled cabin than it had done the whole voyage. The fresh air revived me a little, and I hope I am well enough this morning to write you a short calm letter; – if that can be called one, in which I am afraid to speak of what I would the fainest dwell upon. As I have gone thus far into it, I must go on a little; – perhaps it may relieve the load of WRETCHEDNESS which presses upon me. The persuasion that I shall see her no more will kill me. I cannot q— My dear Brown, I should have had her when I was in health, and I should have remained well. I can bear to die – I cannot bear to leave her. Oh, God! God! God! Every thing I have in my trunks that reminds me of her goes through me like a spear. The silk lining she put in my travelling cap scalds my head. My imagination is horribly vivid about her – I see her – I hear her. There is nothing in the world of sufficient interest to divert me from her a moment. This was the case when I was in England; I cannot recollect, without shuddering, the time that I was prisoner at Hunt's, and used to keep my eyes fixed on Hampstead all day. Then there was a good hope of seeing her again – Now! – O that I could be buried near where she lives! I am afraid to write to her – to see her hand writing would break my heart – even to hear of her any how, to see her name written would be more than I can bear. My dear Brown, what am I to do? Where can I look for consolation or ease? If I had any chance of recovery, this passion would kill me. Indeed through the whole of my illness, both at your house and at Kentish Town, this fever has never ceased wearing me out. When you write to me, which you will do immediately, write to Rome (poste restante) – if she is well and happy, put a mark thus +, – if – Remember me to all. I will endeavour to bear my miseries patiently. A person in my state of health should not have such miseries to bear. Write a short note to my sister, saying you have heard from me. Severn is very well. If I were in better health I should urge your coming to Rome. I fear there is no one can give me any comfort. Is there any news of George? O, that something fortunate had ever happened to me or my brothers! – then I might hope, – but despair is forced upon me as a habit. My dear Brown, for my sake, be her advocate for ever. I cannot say a word about Naples; I do not feel at all concerned in the thousand novelties around me. I am afraid to write to her. I should like her to know that I do not forget her. Oh, Brown, I have coals of fire in my breast. It surprised me that the human heart is capable of containing and bearing so much misery. Was I born for this end? God bless

her, and her mother, and my sister, and George, and his wife, and you, and all!

Your ever affectionate friend,

John Keats. (396–7)

We know, as Keats almost knows but cannot say, that 'better health' will not come and that there is no 'chance of recovery'. The knowledge of Keats's death, a little under four months after writing this letter, cannot help but affect our reading of it.

Epistolary critics rarely comment on this very singular aspect of reading published letters: the close relationship between the end of the book in our hands and the end of another person's life signalled by their last written farewell. Philip Larkin's anxious-sounding comments on the day of death itself, what one might term a person's 'deathday' – 'One of the quainter quirks of life is that we shall never know who dies on the same day as we do ourselves' (218) – is only true from the perspective of the letter writer. The letter reader always has this knowledge before them. Indeed, it is difficult approaching the conclusion of a collection of letters ever to forget it. Many collections of correspondence are subtitled 'A Life in Letters' as if they told the author's life-story directly to the reader, as if, as is often wrongly assumed, letters were autobiography by another name. Such ideas ignore the fictive nature of epistolary writing, not to mention the fact that there are always several authors involved in such life-writing exercises, not least the recipients of the letters who are of course authors themselves. Editions of letters do mark the end of a person's life, however. There are thankfully few letters that arrive after we are gone.

Keats's awareness of the closeness of death sounds in almost everything he says. Writing to Fanny's mother on 24 October 1820, he confessed to not feeling 'in the world' any more (395). Leaving England on 30 September, he felt as if every letter was his last, every moment potentially significant. 'The thought of leaving Miss Brawne', he writes, 'is beyond every thing horrible – the sense of darkness coming over me – I eternally see her figure eternally vanishing' (394). Keats, typically selfless, fears not death itself or even the act of dying (far worse, rationally speaking, than to be dead), but the thought of Fanny living on without him. The repetition of 'eternally', like the repetition of 'happy love' in 'Ode on a Grecian Urn', is a sound of frustration. Keats, like Orpheus, seems doomed to watch his Eurydice continually disappearing. Such letters feel like they are written on the very threshold between life and death, as if their termination might be timed with the actual termination of the person writing them. As Keats himself put it: 'A sudden stop to my life in the middle of one of these Letters would be no bad thing for it keeps one in a sort of fever awhile' (394).

The thrill of reading letters like these is in part the thrill of living other people's lives vicariously. We live through them as if they concerned our existence as well. The consequence of such a close identification with letter writers like Keats is that we are trapped by their epistolary stories as well. As Keats 'eternally' sees Fanny 'eternally vanishing', so we are forced to reimagine him being haunted by this sight forever. Letters keep epistolary selves speaking even when the 'real' person has gone. They give us the illusion of listening to that person again, as if, as is sometimes the case with Keats's letters to Fanny, they are writing from the next room. In loving letter writing, then, one is perhaps admitting to living in the past, or not living in the past so much as living eternally in a present of the letter writer's choosing.

I have not discussed Keats's letter to Charles Brown in detail yet. One of the first things to note is Keats's very real sexual frustration. It is not just the thought of not seeing her that will 'kill' him. Equally, if not more, frustrating is the thought of not having had sex with her. 'My dear Brown,' he says confidingly – and this does seem like something worth sharing in confidence – 'I should have had her when I was in health, and I should have remained well.' How do we read such statements now? The comma separating the two clauses creates ambiguity. Is Keats regretting two distinct things here? A failure to make love to Fanny and a failure to get well? Or are these two matters connected in Keats's mind? Perhaps he believes sleeping with Fanny might have cured him? It is at moments like these that we become more than simply a second reader of the letters (the first, Charles Brown, is long since gone and has no answers to share any more). In trying to make sense of Keats's words, to untangle the significance of nineteenth-century punctuation, we turn ourselves into sympathetic listeners, attuned to an unseen person's confessions but fated never to be able to reply. Published letters are like letters without return of address. We want to continue the conversation further, to receive answers to questions such as those posed by Keats's awkwardly placed comma. But while we do have a name and an address, nobody lives there any more. At best we are talking to our self, at worst to a book full of ghosts.

Keats managed one more letter to Brown on 30 November 1820, though in his imagination he was already dead: 'I have an habitual feeling of my real life having past, and that I am leading a posthumous existence' (398). Keats had given up reading letters and writing poetry by this stage, the former because he could not bear 'the sight of any hand writing of a friend I love', the latter because everything 'necessary for a poem' he felt to be 'great enemies to the recovery of the stomach' (398). Writing was Keats's life. When it was no longer possible, he felt already dead. In writing we can still find him, as we can still find those he loved. This belief in epistolary presence is why Keats fears the very sight of another person's 'hand writing'. In both letters to Brown, he is anxious not to hear news of anyone he loves, particularly Fanny: 'To see her name written would be more than I can bear.' It is significant that Keats separates the words 'hand' and 'writing'. In reading a letter he sees two things simultaneously, a person's handwriting on the page and, through this sight, a literal hand, writing. Keats cannot touch Fanny when he reads her letters or sees her name, but he is merely an imaginative leap from doing so. The ink becomes not just a courier of language, a marker of words, but something live that bridges the distance between two people.

Keats's faith in letters not so much as a mind thinking or a person speaking but as a 'hand writing' is one of the most intimate and moving descriptions of the power of literary correspondence. It encourages us to imagine the act of letter writers writing and, related to this, the art of letter writing *as* writing. In drawing attention to the hand, we are forced to reconsider that which is mentioned but rarely revealed in most editions of published letters: the paper, the ink, the handwriting. Frank and

Anita Kermode, in their introduction to *The Oxford Book of Letters*, state that it is 'a curious fact that until quite recently [they are writing in 1995] . . . it was thought rather disgraceful to type a personal letter, as if an idiosyncratic and possibly half-legible script were an important part of the message' (xx). One is tempted to reply that handwriting, however legible, *is* 'part of the message'. Indeed, in many letters it is the most important element of the message. This is particularly apparent in Craig Oldham's edited collection of handwritten letters from designers in which he actively encouraged correspondents for their thoughts on letter writing 'in hand-written form and onto their stationery':

> There is always something nice about receiving a letter, especially today as email, text, status updates and tweets dominate our communication, leaving many to lose sight of the things that have been around for a while – like ink and paper. However, I believe it is important they don't. The handwritten work is rapidly fading from our everyday, and when a medium begins to erode which embodies so much of our personality and individuality, our emotions, and our ability to communicate, one has to wonder what will be the consequence.

Oldham is articulating as new what Keats knew almost two centuries ago: that we ignore handwriting at our peril.

Keats's sense of himself as leading 'a posthumous existence', never entirely 'present in the world', is visible long before his last illness and certainly long before these last letters. On 8 July 1819, for instance, he speaks of his love for Fanny and her love for him as if they were both already dead. 'I love you the more in that I believe you have liked me for my own sake and for nothing else – I have met with women whom I really think would like to be married to a Poem and to be given away by a Novel' (267). On 27 February 1820, after reading 'two volumes of Letters written between Rousseau and two ladies', he wondered what Rousseau would have said 'at seeing our little correspondence! What would his Ladies have said? I don't care much – I would sooner have Shakespeare's opinion about the matter' (362). 'Thank God', Keats writes, 'that you are fair and can love me without being Letter-written and sentimentaliz'd into it' (363). Keats does not explain what 'being Letter-written' might entail, though he leaves us in no doubt about it being rather unpleasant. He loves Fanny, just as he loves her letters, for existing on a human rather than on a hubristic stage. Keats is not a 'Poem' or 'Novel' for Fanny, but a person. For all his modesty, of course, Keats does think his love for Fanny an appropriate subject for poetry and letter writing. Letters that ask for 'Shakespeare's opinion' are surely written not just for Fanny but to readers who live after them. He appears to have little doubt we will be reading them afterwards.

Keats's unique mix of modesty and self-confidence in regard to the value of his correspondence is present in another letter to Fanny, this time from March 1820. Keats had been confined at home for several weeks after suffering a severe haemorrhage in February. Yet he cannot break off the habit of corresponding with her at least several times a week, even when he can see her from his window and talk to her every night. What he imagines during the day is almost as important to him as anything that has actually happened. The following letter is a good example of this. Keats has nothing much to say, but he makes saying nothing a matter of some significance:

My dearest Girl,

In consequence of our company I suppose I shall not see you before tomorrow. I am much better to day – indeed all I have to complain of is want of strength and a little tightness in the Chest. I envied Sam's walk with you to day; which I will not do again as I may get very tired of envying. I imagine you are now sitting in your new black dress which I like so much and if I were a little less selfish and more enthousiastic [sic] I should run round and surprise you with a knock at the door. I fear I am too prudent for a dying kind of Lover. Yet, there is a great difference between going off in warm blood like Romeo, and making one's exit like a frog in a frost – I had nothing particular to say to day, but not intending that there shall be any interruption to our correspondence (which at some future time I propose offering to Murray) I write something! God bless you my sweet Love! Illness is a long lane, but I see you at the end of it, and shall mend my pace as well as possible

J – K (370)

In terms of content, this letter has little to recommend it to historians of the age or indeed historians of poetry. Keats's attempts to reassure Fanny about his health make it difficult if not impossible to tell exactly how he is feeling. He admits to being 'much better to day' but still wanting 'strength' and suffering 'a little tightness in the Chest'. The reference to illness at the close of the letter as a 'long lane' at the end of which the poet hopes to meet Fanny is too poetic to be reliable. How far along the 'long lane' to death (not recovery) was Keats at this point? Historians of nineteenth-century England would be just as nonplussed. Apart from the eccentric capitalisation and spelling, there is not a single reference to place the letter in a particular year, decade or even century. Readers curious to know about the history or politics of England in 1820, for example, would find nothing of note here.

Yet arguably the lack of news, poetry or politics is actually beside the point, both of this letter and of letter writing in general. While we can and frequently do find these things in letters, in Keats's correspondence just as much as in the correspondence of other writers, I doubt whether this is really why some letters last more than others, both in terms of being published and remaining in print and also in terms of being read and reread by future generations of readers. What moves us in these letters is the idea of the mind's to-ing and fro-ing in exquisite words and phrases, the time spent not in doing something well but in saying something memorably.

In a famous letter to his friend John Taylor on 27 February 1818, Keats shared with him a 'few Axioms' on poetry, the first of which he describes as poetry's need to 'surprise by a fine excess and not by Singularity' (69). His letter to Fanny is a prose-poem version of this axiom. It is characterised not by commonplace expressions and phrasing but by extremity, an 'excess' to use Keats's words of gesture and thought. The letter's humdrum beginning, its talk of health and when he will see her again, is quickly replaced by a fantasy of walking with her and surprising her 'with a knock at the door'. Keats exposes and makes fun of the sort of romantic clichés that one might expect to find in another person's love letters. He envies her walk without him but promises not to do so again lest he 'get tired of envying'. He admits to prefer imagining her in a 'new black dress' to actually running round to see her wear it. If he were 'a little less selfish and more enthousiastic [sic]', he points out, he might prefer the reality to the dream: 'I fear I am too prudent for a dying kind of Lover.' Such questions – about the relative value of dreams and poems over the reality of experience – are asked again and again in Keats's poetry. Here they are given letter form. Who knows if Fanny was amused or annoyed at such honesty? Is it better to be imagined a muse or loved as a real person? Keats doesn't seem to know the answer either. He presents himself as playing a part somewhere between Romeo and the Frog Prince. There is a great difference, he observes, 'between going off in warm blood like Romeo, and making one's exit like a frog in a frost'. Such descriptions movingly and wittingly evoke Keats's dilemma as a warm-blooded young man who can seduce others through words but is rendered cold and neglected by bodily illness. To 'make one's exit like a frog' is not just to be ignored, of course, but to be trampled underfoot. Keats is talking about his fear of death and, in addition to this, his fear of being forgotten. The invocation of Shakespeare's *Romeo and Juliet* and its star-crossed lovers is an appropriate one for Keats and Fanny, who must both have believed their chances of happiness similarly cursed.

Is Keats also alluding to his recently composed sonnet for Fanny, 'Bright star! Would I were steadfast as thou art'? The poem, probably composed between October and December 1819, was a Shakespearean sonnet. I cannot help but think Keats is doubly preoccupied about his posthumous life at this point. On the one hand, he mourns, as Romeo does, the loss of his true love. On the other hand, he is worried what posterity will make of the words he has left behind. Will he be spoken of in the same way as Shakespeare? From having 'nothing in particular to say to day', therefore, Keats manages, as he himself acknowledges, to 'write something'. We learn as much about Keats as a writer here as anywhere else. For it is here that his competing feelings about himself as a writer leak out in analogies and questions. The parenthetical promise to Fanny – that he will 'at some future time' propose offering their correspondence to (John) Murray, a prominent bookseller and publisher in London – is a continuation of the theme. Keats hopes that he will be famous enough to merit the publication of his letters. While the evidence of previous letters demonstrates his belief in the artistic value of this correspondence, he does not at this stage know whether the reputation of his poetry will foster or hinder its eventual appearance. He is not just imagining Fanny in her 'new black dress' next door, therefore, but also imagining a new copy of their letters. The bringing to life of both images depends on his becoming a quite literal 'dying kind of Lover'. One can't become Romeo or indeed Shakespeare without 'making one's exit', whether one does it in the shape of a romantic hero or a frog. Keats may be speaking of 'to day' but his thoughts are continually on 'tomorrow', the 'end of it' where he hopes to 'mend my pace as well as possible'.

As readers of the letters almost two centuries later, mending our pace is just as difficult. We want to stay with Keats in his 'to day', still dreaming of Fanny 'with a knock at the door', yet we know that the door to that time is permanently closed, that the 'future time' of both correspondents' death has been and gone. In order to read 'something' we depend on illness having an end. 'Murray', the bookseller-publisher-reader, is the parenthetical future that comes after if not between Keats and Fanny and the parenthetical reader we, too, inevitably become. At the same time, the figure of Murray is always there in Keats's mind, interrupting their correspondence. He is the figure of death Keats cannot evade and the possibility of fame he can dream of but never really see.

II

The history of letter writing is always a story about time. Most letters, particularly most modern letters, are dated and postmarked. We can time their conception and delivery to at least a date, sometimes an hour, much as we time and announce the arrival of a new child. The very form of a letter is also subject to time, or rather to three distinct but overlapping time zones: the time it takes to write a letter, the time it takes for the letter to be delivered, and the time in which the letter is finally read. This is what most differentiates what is now called snail mail from e-mail or Twitter in which, while there is delay between composition, delivery and arrival, it doesn't feel like it. Immediacy has its advantages, of course, but also its drawbacks. You can do business by e-mail but what about courtship? The letter's famous protean qualities, its ability to be all things to all people, make defining letters in terms of genre difficult, if not impossible. How do you define a genre that encompasses the extreme formality of business correspondence with the extreme intimacy of a love letter?

Epistolary critics have spent at least the last three decades answering this question. For Mikhail Bakhtin, a letter, like any other linguistic utterance, is always 'half someone else's' (in Vice 50). One can interpret this quite literally, I think. A letter once sent is the physical if not the intellectual property of its recipient. This explains why so many letters are destroyed, lost or go missing. Their survival depends on the care of their recipient. For Hélène Cixous, a letter gives us access to human touch: 'there is no material that so faithfulstrangely [sic] keeps the trace of breathless emotions in the limbs of the words' (73). Letters are the next best thing to human touch. Perhaps, for some correspondents, they are better than touch. There are countless examples of epistolary friendships spoiled by the authors actually meeting. For Jacques Derrida, letters upset the idea that our identities are singular. 'Doubtless we are several,' he admits, 'and I am not as alone as I sometimes say I am' (6). Letters cite and respond to other people and are nearly always written with somebody else in mind, both the person we are writing to and often a future audience afterwards. If all language is intertextual, letter writing is explicitly so, in both its composition and eventual fate. For Jacques Lacan, the question of who owns a letter is as important as its actual subject matter. Why, he asks, do authors frequently request their letters be returned? 'Might a letter on which the sender retains certain rights then not quite belong to the person to whom it is addressed? Or might it be that the latter was never the real receiver?' (41). For all their differing emphases and writing styles, a consensus of sorts does emerge from reading these four critics together. Letters, they suggest, are never written by a singular 'I' to a singular 'you'. The 'I' that authors the letter is nearly always citing somebody else, even if he/she is not aware of it, and/or performing an identity that may change depending on the receiver. Equally, the 'you' that receives the letter is often in danger of being forgotten or erased, by the author wanting the letter back, or an editor ignoring the fact that the recipient ever existed. This dilemma can be summed up in a simple question still relevant today. Who do (or did) we write letters for? Ourselves or other people?

The history of letter writing is a story about time and what time does to people. As Franz Kafka once said in a famous letter to Milena Jesenská in 1923: 'The easy possibility of letter-writing must . . . have brought into the world a terrible disintegration of souls' (182). In her chapter in this book, Angela Leighton describes letters as 'creatures of time: the time it takes for them to be written, delivered, opened, read, pondered, replied to, or just left unnervingly pending. As a result, there is a potential dead letter at the heart of every missive.' Might anxiety about time be the letter's defining characteristic: a fear, more or less always articulated, not about the composition of the letter, but about the letter actually getting there in one piece, the letter literally making it through? In this sense, to paraphrase Marshall McLuhan, the medium of letter writing, in particular its time-dependence, *is* the message. Letters are always late, never on time. Every letter is potentially a last letter, both the last letter we send and the last letter we receive.

This brings up the question of whether we are already talking about a dead art form? Has letter writing had its time? Have we already read its last days? Given the number of elegiac books on the subject in the last couple of years – Simon Garfield's *To the Letter: A Journey Through a Vanishing World* (2013), Philip Hensher's *The Missing Ink: The Lost Art of Handwriting* (2012), John O'Connell's *For the Love of Letters: The Joy of Slow Communication* (2012), Ian Sansom's *Paper: An Elegy* (2012), and Liz Williams's *Kind Regards: The Lost Art of Letter-Writing* (2012) – it is tempting to say yes, letter writing is dead. The last letters have been written. As an *Observer* editorial put it in October 2010:

> Cultural treasures will be lost if we no longer put pen to paper . . . Will booklovers in years to come be able to read *The Collected Emails of Zadie Smith* in the same way that we can enjoy [Saul] Bellow's letters? Inky manuscripts contain insights that can be lost forever to the backspace key. It is a curious paradox. We live in an age saturated with commentary, obsessed with recording the moment. And yet we could end up understanding less about people living today than about those who came before.

Such laments are not as new as one might think. The death of letter writing has long been forecast. Early nineteenth-century writers thought the arrival of the penny post in 1840 signalled the death of letter writing. Later on in the century, the telegram become the main threat. Twentieth-century writers feared the telephone. In the twenty-first century, it sometimes feels as if a new epistolary rival is invented every year. John Freeman's *The Tyranny of E-mail*, for example, was only published in 2009, but already feels somewhat dated. Twitter is mentioned just three times. Facetime had not even been invented at the time of its publication. Who knows what new technology or app will be introduced between the writing of this statement and its publication? Perhaps every generation of letter writers thinks it will be the last. In other words, might the discourse of last letters not just be older than we imagine but also connected, as Leighton suspects, to one of the defining characteristics of letter writing: its preoccupation with time? As an aside, it is worth noting the number of new books, journals and websites devoted to handwritten letters in the last few years, handwritten letters not just from the past but also being composed now. Letter writing does not feel like an art form about to pass into extinction any time soon.

III

The remainder of this chapter looks at the discourse of last letters in the writing of twentieth-century poets Elizabeth Bishop and Ted Hughes. In particular, it scrutinises the close relationship of the last letter to aesthetic and theoretical debates about the permanence of art over life, mind over matter, and writing over speech. Last letters are on the side of life against death even as they edge perilously close to silence. An art form that has spent a long time dying but is not quite dead yet, the letter tests what it means to live in time and how we reawaken that time when the letter writer is dead.

Elizabeth Bishop was born in 1911 and died in 1979. As a child growing up in a small village in Nova Scotia in the 1910s, daily visits to the post office were part of everyday life. How many of us even visit the post office once a week nowadays? In Bishop's autobiographical story 'In the Village' (1953), she recalls being sent to post a package to her mother every week. Bishop's mother committed herself to a psychiatric hospital in 1916, when her young daughter was just five years old. Bishop's maternal grandparents hoped the situation was temporary and that she would return home quickly. She never did, dying there seventeen years later, the same month as Bishop's graduation from Vassar College. Bishop was not to know this at the time, but when she came to write the story in the 1950s, almost forty years afterwards, she knew how her mother's life had ended. And yet the story is written in the present tense as if the events were still happening, as if, in some way, she were writing her mother a letter (might this story be the prose equivalent of a verse epistle?):

> Every week my grandmother sends off a package. In it she puts cake and fruit, a jar of preserves. Moirs chocolates.
> Monday afternoon every week.
> Fruit, cake, Jordan almonds, a handkerchief with a tatted edge.
> Fruit. Cake. Wild-strawberry jam. A New Testament.
> A little bottle of scent from Hills' store, with a purple silk tassel fastened to the stopper.

Fruit. Cake. 'Selections from Tennyson.'

A calendar, with a quotation from Longfellow for every day.

Fruit. Cake. Moirs chocolates.

I watch her pack them in the pantry. Sometimes she sends me to the store to get things at the last minute.

The address of the sanitarium is in my grandmother's handwriting, in purple indelible pencil, on smoothed-out wrapping paper. It will never come off.

I take the package to the post office. Going by Nate's, I walk far out in the road and hold the package on the side away from him. (115–16)

Bishop's story is about a particular time in her own life, the tragic exile of her mother from what she felt to be the paradise of her early childhood in turn-of-the-century Canada, but above and beyond the particular details of this narrative lies another narrative, the letter or parcel as something still magically alive, still waiting to be opened. We never learn if any of the packages arrived safely. We certainly never hear anything about the mother's reaction. This is a package that might as well have been dropped in the ocean. Yet for all the correspondence's frustrations, its one-way traffic, there is something touching about the grandmother's attempts to keep speaking to her daughter, and, by implication, Bishop's own attempt to keep this line of communication open. A reply may come one day. The most significant detail for me is the grandmother's handwriting. Written 'in purple indelible pencil', 'it will never come off'. This is a dead letter that seems strangely alive, strangely timeless.

Here is another Bishop letter, this time a real one, to her fellow poet Robert Lowell. In the final three paragraphs Bishop takes Lowell to task for talking about old age too much, for writing what I would like to term a too self-conscious 'last letter':

I am now going to be very impertinent and aggressive. Please, *please* don't talk about age so much, my dear old friend! You are giving me the creeps . . . The thing Lota admired so much about us North Americans was our determined youthfulness and energy, our 'never-say-die'ness – and I think she was right! In Florida my hostess's sister had recently remarried again at the age of 76, for the 3rd time – her 2nd marriage had been at 67 – and she and her husband, also 76, went walking miles on the beach every day, hand in hand, as happy as clams, apparently, and I loved it. (A very plump, pretty, sweet lady – as naïve as a very small child.) Of course – it's different for a writer, I know – of course I know – nevertheless, in spite of aches & pains I really don't feel much different than I did at 35 – and I certainly am a great deal happier, most of the time. (This in spite of the giant oil tankers parading across my view every day . . .) I just *won't* feel ancient – I wish Auden hadn't gone about it so his last years, and I hope you won't.

However, Cal dear, maybe your memory *is* failing! – Never, never was I 'tall' – as you wrote remembering me. I was always 5 ft 4 and ¼ inches – now shrunk to 5 ft 4 inches – The only time I've ever felt tall was in Brazil. And I never had 'long brown hair' either! It started turning gray when I was 23 or 24 – and probably was already somewhat grizzled when I first met you. . . . Well, I think I'll have to write *my* memoirs, just to set things straight.

It will be nice to see you – Caroline and I had a 'real nice visit' as they say in Florida and I'm looking forward to seeing her again. Alice is at BU Business School, poor dear – and will soon be coming for dinner after her class on 'Taxes' – which she insists she *loves*. So I must stop and slice some green beans – See you later, alligator, as they also do say in Florida –
  With love,
    Elizabeth (778–9)

Bishop's letter-writing self lives very much in the present tense. We not only hear her voice – 'my dear old friend! You are giving me the creeps' – but even share her view: 'This in spite of the giant oil tankers parading across my view'. We even know what she is about to prepare for dinner: some green beans. Of course, the letter is about remembering too, or rather it is about Bishop correcting Lowell on *his* remembering. After providing her own version of events, she even promises 'to write *my* memoirs, just to set things straight'. One could read more into this statement if one liked. The two poets were still negotiating the aftershocks of a spectacular epistolary semi-falling-out over Lowell's decision to publish versifications of his wife Elizabeth Hardwick's letters in the 1973 collection *The Dolphin*, something Bishop urged him not to do by citing three of her various authors on writerly ethics, including Thomas Hardy, Gerald Manley Hopkins and Henry James. Yet in this letter, nearly three years later, there is a sense of letting things go, of living and writing in the present moment. Indeed, we can almost kid ourselves she is still alive. This letter feels as if it were just written, as if we, just as much as Lowell, might hear from her soon.

IV

The attraction of letters lies in such moments: the illusion of presence. Perhaps this is what John Donne is referring to in his verse epistle 'To Sir Henry Wotton', which begins: 'Sir, more than kisses, letters mingle souls; / For, thus friends absent speak' (47). This is one of the main reasons why we read letters in the first place, to make 'friends absent speak'. I would like to turn my attention now to the English poet Ted Hughes, whose last collection of poems was called *Birthday Letters* (1998), a collection in which he addressed, as if she were alive, as if she could be contacted in a letter, his first wife, Sylvia Plath. Plath was no stranger to letter writing as a form of talking to the dead. Her most iconic poem, 'Daddy', can be read as a variation on the dead letter, addressed to a father figure who can never reply to his daughter's accusations and taunts. 'I never could talk to you,' the poem's speaker states at one point, while at the same time doing what she states is impossible, talking to you (223). Hughes borrows this trope in the *Birthday Letters* poems. Although Plath is dead and cannot in any real sense reply to these poems, her voice is continually present throughout the collection, not just as a memory but as if he were actually talking to her. Writing poems as if they were letters brings Plath back to life. It restores her to time again.

Hughes talks about this process explicitly in a letter to Seamus Heaney on 1 January 1998: 'I hit on the direct letter as an illegal private transaction between her & me – then simply followed the clues, and they piled up' (703–4). Why might a letter to a wife, even a dead wife, be 'illegal'? What law has Hughes broken? The first time I read this letter I thought Hughes was simply being metaphorical. Now, I wonder if he is actually describing an aspect of grief that is rarely spoken about: the belief that the dead person is not gone but remains here. Remains not as object, as ashes or body, but as active subject, living, speaking, writing. Talking to the dead as if they were alive feels 'illegal' because of the contemporary taboo that forbids prolonged mourning and certainly forbids prolonged talking to the dead as if they were still with us. To remain behind obviously gives Hughes the last word, of course. Plath literally cannot reply. Her response has to be imagined by Hughes, or by the reader. Julian Barnes writes eloquently about this in his book, *Levels of Life*:

> Ford Madox Ford said, 'You marry to continue the conversation.' Why allow death to interrupt it? . . . So I talk to her constantly. This feels as normal as it is necessary. I comment on what I am doing (or have done in the course of the day); I point out things to her while driving; I articulate her responses. I keep alive our lost private language. I tease her and she teases me back; we know the lines by heart. Her voice calms me and gives me courage. I look across at a small photograph on my desk in which she wears a slightly quizzical expression, and answer her quizzing, whatever it might be about. Banal domestic issues are lightened by a brief discussion: she confirms that the bath mat is a disgrace and should be thrown away. Outsiders might find this an eccentric, or 'morbid', or self-deceiving habit; but outsiders are by definition those who have not known grief. I externalise her easily and naturally because by now I have internalised her. The paradox of grief: if I have survived what is now four years of her absence, it is because I have had four years of her presence. And her active continuance disproves what I earlier pessimistically asserted. Grief can, after all, in some ways, turn out to be a moral space. (102–3)

If one marries 'to continue the conversation', might writing about that marriage after the death of one of the partners be a way of continuing the conversation too? Perhaps this is what a letter might be as well, a conversation continued between two people who can no longer be together. Barnes literally talks to his wife constantly. Hughes wrote his wife over sixty poems, at least two for every year of her absence.

By way of conclusion, I would like to cite briefly from one of the letter-poems not included in *Birthday Letters*, a poem from the Ted Hughes archive at the British Library. The poem, called 'Last letter', was sensationally published in the *New Statesman* in October 2010. Introducing the poem, guest editor Melvyn Bragg called it Hughes's 'final poem' (42), as if it were his last piece of poetic writing. As far as I can tell, there is no evidence that this was Hughes's final poem. The most we can say is that it is perhaps his last poem on the subject of Sylvia Plath. Plath's body was found on the morning of Monday, 11 February 1963. The second stanza of the poem describes Hughes's memories of the Friday before this, Friday, 8 February 1963, the last time he saw Plath alive:

> Your note reached me too soon – that same day,
> Friday afternoon, posted in the morning.
> The prevalent details expedited it.
> That was one more straw of ill-luck
> Drawn against you by the Post-Office
> And added to your load. I moved fast,
> Through the snow-blue, February, London twilight.
> Wept with relief when you opened the door.
> A huddle of riddles in solution. Precocious tears
> That failed to interpret to me, failed to divulge
> Their real import. But what did you say
> Over the smoking shards of that letter
> So carefully annihilated, so calmly,
> That let me release you, and leave you
> To blow its ashes off your plan – off the ashtray
> Against which you would lean for me to read
> The Doctor's phone-number. (43)

The biographical details of the poem, in which Hughes talks of receiving a note from Plath the Friday before her suicide, cannot be verified. Did Plath, as Hughes describes, then burn the note in front of Hughes when he ran round to her London flat to check she was safe? Whose 'last letter' does the poem's title even reference: Plath's last letter to Hughes, or this, his last letter to her? If the last letter is Plath's, it became a lost letter on the same day it was sent, though it did reach its destination, paradoxically arriving too soon to prevent Plath's suicide rather than too late. If the last letter is Hughes's, it too is a form of dead letter, addressed to a person no longer living, arriving too late to prevent either of their deaths. It is important to remember that Hughes chose not to publish the poem in his lifetime. An archive is a form of Dead Letter Office for literature, a place where poems, letters and other writings are preserved rather than published, though many do see the light of day eventually. In other words, both last letters go missing in the poem, Plath's by arriving too early and then being destroyed, Hughes's by being written too late and then being placed in an archive. They are further letters about time, in particular about our perception of time as untimely. Why did *it* rather than you or I come between us? Yet for all the despair that reading such a poem provokes, it is, like most letters, defiantly on the side of life against time. Plath and Hughes may both be dead, but they never seem so in letters.

A last letter, whatever its destination, always has a posthumous existence that in a curious feature of epistolary writing reverses time and miraculously brings the dead back to life. After 'Daddy', Plath's most famous poem is probably 'Lady Lazarus', a poem in which the speaker promises to come back from the dead: 'A sort of walking miracle' (244). Most authors keep this promise alive in their letters. They reach out a hand, a hand writing that we almost feel we can touch. 'See here it is,' Keats tells us in his fragmentary poem that also resembles a letter. 'I hold it towards you' (701).

NOTES

1. Both letters can be found at *Vincent van Gogh: The Letters*, an online edition of van Gogh's correspondence, edited by Leo Jansen, Hans Luijten and Nienke Bakker, available at <http://www.vangoghletters.org/vg/> (last accessed 7 July 2014). The unfinished, unsent letter is catalogued as Letter RM25 in the archive. The letter that arrived, and that is normally seen as van Gogh's last letter, is Letter 902.

WORKS CITED

Barnes, Julian, *Levels of Life* (London: Jonathan Cape, 2013).

Bishop, Elizabeth, *Poems, Prose, and Letters*, ed. Lloyd Schwartz and Robert Giroux (New York: Library of America, 2008).

—— and Robert Lowell, *Words in Air: The Complete Correspondence Between Elizabeth Bishop and Robert Lowell*, ed. Thomas Travisano with Saskia Hamilton (New York: Farrar, Straus and Giroux, 2008).

Cixous, Hélène, *Love Itself in the Letterbox*, trans. Peggy Kamuf (Cambridge: Polity Press, 2008 [2005]).

'Cultural treasures will be lost if we no longer put pen to paper', Editorial, *The Observer*, 10 October 2010.

Derrida, Jacques, *The Post Card: From Socrates to Freud and Beyond*, trans. Alan Bass (Chicago: University of Chicago Press, 1987).

Donne, John, *John Donne*, ed. John Carey (Oxford: Oxford University Press, 1990).

Hughes, Ted, 'Last letter', *New Statesman*, 11 October 2010: 42–4.

—— *Letters of Ted Hughes*, ed. Christopher Reid (London: Faber and Faber, 2007).

Kafka, Franz, *Letters to Milena*, ed. Willy Haas, trans. Tania and James Stern (London: Vintage, 1999).

Keats, John, *The Complete Poems*, ed. Miriam Allott (London: Longman, 1970).

—— *Letters of John Keats*, ed. Robert Gittings (Oxford: Oxford University Press, 1970).

Kermode, Frank, and Anita Kermode (eds), *The Oxford Book of Letters* (Oxford: Oxford University Press, 1995).

Lacan, Jacques, 'Seminar on "The Purloined Letter"', trans. Jeffrey Mehlman, in John P. Muller and William J. Richardson (eds), *The Purloined Poe: Lacan, Derrida and Psychoanalytic Reading* (Baltimore: Johns Hopkins University Press, 1988), pp. 28–54.

Larkin, Philip, *Letters to Monica*, ed. Anthony Thwaite (London: Faber and Faber, 2010).

Oldham, Craig (ed.), *The Hand.Written.Letter.Project* (Manchester: United Theory of Everything, 2011).

Plath, Sylvia, *Collected Poems*, ed. Ted Hughes (London: Faber and Faber, 1981).

Vice, Sue, *Introducing Bakhtin* (Manchester: Manchester University Press, 1998).

Index

[Index entry in **bold** indicates an author's essay in this volume]